IN TRIUMPH'S WAKE

ALSO BY JULIA P. GELARDI

Born to Rule

Julia P. Gelardi

IN TRIUMPH'S WAKE

Royal Mothers, Tragic Daughters,

AND THE PRICE THEY PAID

FOR GLORY

 ST. MARTIN'S GRIFFIN ❧ NEW YORK

IN TRIUMPH'S WAKE. Copyright © 2008 by Julia P. Gelardi. All rights
reserved. Printed in the United States of America. For information,
address St. Martin's Press, 175 Fifth Avenue, New York, N.Y. 10010.

www.stmartins.com

The Library of Congress has catalogued the hardcover edition as follows:

Gelardi, Julia P.
    In triumph's wake : royal mothers, tragic daughters, and the price they paid for
glory / Julia P. Gelardi. — 1st ed.
        p. cm.
    Includes bibliographical references.
    ISBN 978-0-312-37105-0
    1. Queens—Europe—Biography. 2. Empresses—Europe—Biography.
3. Europe—Kings and rulers—Biography. 4. Europe—History. 5. Mothers and
daughters. I. Title.
    D107.3.G35 2008
    940.09'9—dc22

2008025777

ISBN 978-0-312-58603-4 (trade paperback)

First St. Martin's Griffin Edition: December 2009

10 9 8 7 6 5 4 3 2 1

To my parents

Contents

PART I
Queen Isabella and Catherine of Aragon

PART II
Empress Maria Theresa and Queen Marie Antoinette

CONTENTS

PART III

Queen Victoria and the Empress Frederick

Simplified Genealogy

CASTILE-ARAGON (SPAIN) AND ENGLAND

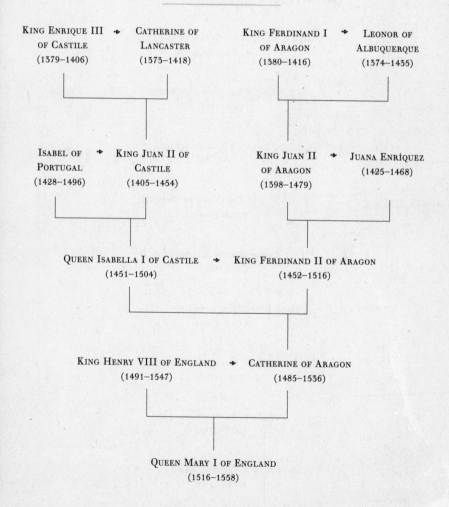

CASTILE, HABSBURG, FRANCE

QUEEN ISABELLA I OF CASTILE
(1451–1504)

|

JUANA "LA LOCA," QUEEN OF CASTILE
(1479–1555)

|

HOLY ROMAN EMPEROR FERDINAND I
(1503–1564)

|

CHARLES II OF AUSTRIA
(1540–1590)

|

HOLY ROMAN EMPEROR FERDINAND II
(1578–1637)

|

HOLY ROMAN EMPEROR FERDINAND III
(1608–1657)

|

HOLY ROMAN EMPEROR LEOPOLD I
(1640–1705)

|

HOLY ROMAN EMPEROR CHARLES VI
(1685–1740)

|

EMPRESS MARIA THERESA
(1717–1780)

|

QUEEN MARIE ANTOINETTE OF FRANCE
(1755–1793)

GREAT BRITAIN AND GERMANY

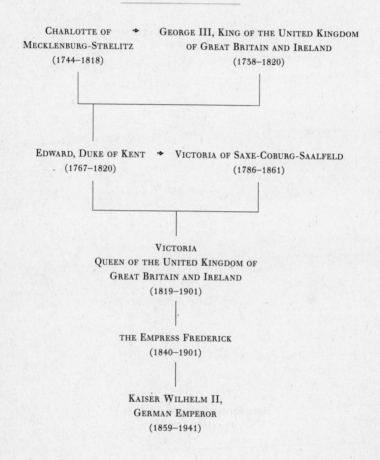

CHARLOTTE OF   ❖   GEORGE III, KING OF THE UNITED KINGDOM
MECKLENBURG-STRELITZ   OF GREAT BRITAIN AND IRELAND
(1744–1818)   (1738–1820)

EDWARD, DUKE OF KENT   ❖   VICTORIA OF SAXE-COBURG-SAALFELD
(1767–1820)   (1786–1861)

VICTORIA
QUEEN OF THE UNITED KINGDOM OF
GREAT BRITAIN AND IRELAND
(1819–1901)

THE EMPRESS FREDERICK
(1840–1901)

KAISER WILHELM II,
GERMAN EMPEROR
(1859–1941)

Main Personalities

Castile/Spain

Isabella (1451–1504)—Queen of Castile and León. Known also as Isabella la Católica. Daughter of King Juan II of Castile and Isabel of Portugal. Married Ferdinand II of Aragon in 1469. Mother of Catherine of Aragon. See *Ferdinand*.

Children:

1. Isabel (1470–1498) (Queen of Portugal)
2. Juan (1478–1497)
3. Juana I (1479–1555) (Queen of Castile)
4. Maria (1482–1517) (Queen of Portugal)
5. Catherine (1485–1536) of Aragon—See Catherine

Ferdinand II (1452–1516)—King of Aragon and of Castile as Ferdinand V. Also known as Fernando el Católico. Son of King Juan II of Aragon and Juana Enríquez. Married Isabella of Castile in 1469. Father of Catherine of Aragon. See *Isabella*.

England

Catherine (1485–1536)—Queen Consort of England, known as Catherine of Aragon. The youngest child of Queen Isabella of Castile and King Ferdinand II of Aragon. Married first to Arthur, Prince of Wales, in 1501 and second, from 1509 until 1533, to King Henry VIII of England. Mother of Mary I. See *Henry VIII*.

Henry VIII (1491–1547)—King of England. Son of King Henry VII and Elizabeth of York. First wife, Catherine of Aragon, was the daughter of Ferdinand of Aragon and Isabella of Castile. Henry VIII's other wives were: Anne Boleyn, Jane Seymour, Anne of Cleves, Catherine Howard, and Catherine Parr. See *Catherine*.

Children:

1. Mary I (1516–1558) (mother: Catherine of Aragon)
2. Elizabeth I (1533–1603) (mother: Anne Boleyn)
3. Edward VI (1537–1553) (mother: Jane Seymour)

Habsburg/Austria

Maria Theresa (1717–1780)—Archduchess of Austria, Holy Roman Empress, Queen of Hungary and Bohemia. Daughter of Holy Roman Emperor Charles VI and Elisabeth-Christina of Brunswick-Wolfenbüttel. Married Francis Stephen of Lorraine, who became Holy Roman Emperor Francis I, in 1736. Mother of Marie Antoinette of France. See *Francis I*.

Children:

1. Maria Elisabeth (1737–1740)
2. Maria Anna (1738–1789)
3. Maria Caroline (1740–1741)
4. Joseph II (1741–1790) (Holy Roman Emperor)
5. Maria Christina (1742–1798)
6. Maria Elisabeth (1743–1808)
7. Charles Joseph (1745–1761)
8. Maria Amalia (1746–1804)
9. Leopold II (1747–1792) (Holy Roman Emperor)
10. Maria Caroline (stillborn 1748)
11. Maria Johanna (1750–1762)
12. Maria Josepha (1751–1767)
13. Maria Carolina (1752–1814) (Queen of Naples and Sicily)
14. Ferdinand (1754–1806)
15. Maria Antonia (1755–1793)—See Marie Antoinette
16. Maximilian (1756–1801)

Francis I (1708–1765)—Born Francis Stephen of Lorraine, son of Duke Leopold Joseph, Duke of Lorraine and Elisabeth-Charlotte of Orléans. Elected

Holy Roman Emperor in 1745. Married Maria Theresa of Austria in 1736. Father of Marie Antoinette. See *Maria Theresa*.

Joseph II (1741–1790)—Eldest son of Empress Maria Theresa and Holy Roman Emperor Francis I. Reigned as Holy Roman Emperor, from 1765 to 1790 and as King of Hungary and Bohemia from 1780 to 1790. Married first Isabella of Parma (d. 1763), second Maria-Josephe of Bavaria (d. 1767).

France

Louis XVI (1754–1793)—King of France. Son of Louis, Dauphin of France, and Marie-Josèphe of Saxony. Married Archduchess Maria Antonia (Marie Antoinette) of Austria in 1770. Executed in Paris January 1793. See *Marie Antoinette*.

Marie Antoinette (1755–1793)—Born Archduchess Maria Antonia of Austria, youngest daughter of Empress Maria Theresa and Holy Roman Emperor Francis I. Married future King Louis XVI of France in 1770. Executed in Paris October 1793.
Children:
1. Marie-Thérèse-Charlotte (1778–1851)
2. Louis-Joseph (1781–1789)
3. Louis-Charles (1785–1795)
4. Sophie Hélène Béatrice (1786–1787)

United Kingdom

Victoria (1819–1901)—Queen of the United Kingdom of Great Britain and Ireland, Empress of India. Only child of Edward, Duke of Kent, and Victoria of Saxe-Coburg-Saalfeld. Married in 1840, Prince Albert of Saxe-Coburg-Gotha. Mother of Vicky, the Empress Frederick. See *Albert*.
Children:
1. Victoria (1840–1901) (the Empress Frederick)
2. Edward VII (1841–1910)
3. Alice (1843–1878)
4. Alfred (1844–1900)
5. Helena (1846–1923)
6. Louise (1848–1939)

7. Arthur (1850–1942)
8. Leopold (1853–1884)
9. Beatrice (1857–1944)

Albert (1819–1861)—Prince Consort of the United Kingdom. Born Prince Albert of Saxe-Coburg-Gotha, son of Ernst I, Duke of Saxe-Coburg-Gotha, and his first wife, Louise of Saxe-Gotha-Altenburg. Married Queen Victoria in 1840. See *Victoria*.

Prussia/Germany

Frederick III (1831–1888)—German Emperor or Kaiser and King of Prussia from March 9, 1888, until June 15, 1888. Son of German Emperor Wilhelm I and Augusta of Saxe-Weimar. Married in 1858, Victoria, the Princess Royal, eldest child of Queen Victoria. See *Victoria*.

Victoria (1840–1901)—German Empress, Queen of Prussia, and Princess Royal of the United Kingdom. Eldest child of Queen Victoria and Prince Albert. Married in 1858, Prince Frederick Wilhelm of Prussia. Known within her family as Vicky, after her husband's death, she took the title Empress Frederick. Mother of Kaiser Wilhelm II.
Children:
1. Wilhelm II (1859–1941) (German Emperor)
2. Charlotte (1860–1919)
3. Henry (1862–1929)
4. Sigismund (1864–1866)
5. Viktoria (1866–1929)
6. Waldemar (1868–1879)
7. Sophie (1870–1932) (Queen of Greece)
8. Margarethe (1872–1954)

Wilhelm II (1859–1941)—German Emperor or Kaiser and King of Prussia. Son of German Emperor Frederick III and Victoria of the United Kingdom. Eldest grandchild of Queen Victoria. Married first, in 1881, Augusta Viktoria of Schleswig-Holstein-Sonderburg-Augustenburg, and second, in 1922, Princess Hermine Reuss.

Chronology

Part II

Empress Maria Theresa and Queen Marie Antoinette

Part III
Queen Victoria and the Empress Frederick

Introduction

We can credit three of history's most influential monarchs—Queen Isabella of Castile, Empress Maria Theresa of Austria, and Queen Victoria of the United Kingdom—for helping to shape today's world. These extraordinary women also gave birth to three prominent women: Catherine of Aragon, Queen of England; Marie Antoinette, Queen of France; and Vicky, Germany's Empress Frederick, respectively. The daughters' lives dramatically changed the course of European events too, albeit with much less auspicious outcomes. Though the pages of history resonate with these six women's legacies, no written work has yet grouped them together, or examined the very special bond that united them and unites so many—that of mother and daughter.

With this in mind, I set out to illuminate the relationships between Isabella and Catherine, between Maria Theresa and Marie Antoinette, and between Victoria and Vicky. What makes their familial bonds most poignant, and places the pairings uniquely in the annals of history, is that the mothers were successful, even remarkable rulers, while their daughters, all consorts of reigning European monarchs, suffered the opposite fate. For none of the three daughters—Catherine, Marie Antoinette, and Vicky—came to match the reputations of Queen Isabella, Empress Maria Theresa, and Queen Victoria. The daughters, with their bittersweet fates, were in essence left in the triumphant wakes of their unsurpassable mothers, whose legacies continue to be felt today.

Most interesting is the fact that these three pairs lived through different eras. Isabella and Catherine were medieval and Renaissance queens, whereas Maria Theresa and Marie Antoinette lived in the Age of Enlightenment. Victoria and Vicky, meanwhile, lived when the Industrial Revolution quickened the pace of life. Moreover, they witnessed the huge expansion of the British Empire—the mother giving her name to the age known as the Victorian era.

Equally fascinating is charting the Habsburg fortunes from Isabella of Castile's time down through the centuries, especially in the lives of Maria Theresa and Marie Antoinette. As we read about Maria Theresa, we encounter an emboldened Prussia, which will have an impact on the next set of royals, Queen Victoria and her daughter, the Empress Frederick. During the Victorian era, Prussia and its dynastic family, the Hohenzollerns, dominated the European political scene at the Habsburgs' expense.

Rarely does one encounter such a unique set of women in history. Theirs is a tale of colossal achievement and monumental failure. The daughters' misfortunes are made more poignant by the fact that they were married off strategically to achieve specific political goals. The potential good that the future reigning consorts could bring to their adopted countries and, by extension, to Europe was incalculable. The failure of that potential to be fulfilled constitutes the tales of tragedy in the following pages.

Far from being mere footnotes in history, the daughters' unfulfilled destinies had far-reaching effects, the repercussions of which can still be felt today. Because of his doomed marriage to Catherine of Aragon, King Henry VIII broke away from the Roman Catholic Church, triggering the English Reformation and the violent religious conflicts that accompanied it. Marie Antoinette's legacy is inextricably linked to the French Revolution and the ensuing modern revolutions that emulated it, setting the world aflame. Vicky envisioned a liberal Germany that would take its place on the world stage, but this aspiration for a vibrant democracy vanished with the untimely death of her husband, Emperor Frederick III. Frederick's brief reign proved insufficient to get Germany to rise to political maturity. Under the reign of Vicky's son the infamous Kaiser Wilhelm II, Germany plunged, along with other European powers, into the conflagration that became World War I.

Each of the royal mothers left an indelible mark. Some six hundred years later, it is easy to forget the extent of Queen Isabella's mark on history. Yet such was the power she possessed and such were her achievements that contemporaries and historians of a later age have ascribed astounding superlatives to her. One of the queen's contemporaries, the Italian historian of Spain, Peter Martyr, gave one such glowing opinion. Here, he said, was "among the Queens and the powerful . . . one who does not lack either the valor to undertake great endeavors, or the constancy to carry them through." Isabella of Castile was "stronger than a strong man, more constant than any human soul, a marvelous example of honesty and virtue; Nature has made no other woman like her."[1] Hundreds of years later, the noted historian Antonia Fraser described Queen Isabella in a similar vein, writing of her as "the wonder of Europe,"[2] one who "showed herself from the first a remarkable character as well as a redoubtable one."[3]

Empress Maria Theresa was no less accomplished a monarch. In his biography of her, Edward Crankshaw summarized Maria Theresa's achievements: "She had loosened the prison bars of feudal Austria and made it possible for all her peoples to move into the nineteenth century without revolutionary violence. In her remarkable person, empirical, practical, and kind, she had achieved the most that can be expected anywhere of any sort of government at any time—and more than is achieved by most. She had held her society together, encouraged its individual talents, and left it better than it was before."[4]

Queen Victoria has been portrayed in equally glowing terms. The queen's eminent biographer Elizabeth Longford rightly described Victoria as "a legend" who left "the impression of greatness" among her subjects and "the world."[5] The historian Sir Sidney Lee has noted of the queen: "She had become an institution, an enduring symbol of the majesty of her people, and an emblem of the unity of an empire which comprised more than one-fifth . . . of the habitable globe."[6]

Whereas the mothers' prestige remains largely untarnished today, history has been unkind to their daughters—these ill-fated women who were unable to live up to their early promise. Catherine of Aragon is pitied, Marie Antoinette maligned, and Vicky largely forgotten. Their reputations continue to be completely overshadowed by their mothers'. The time has come to bring to light the stories of these daughters alongside those of their mothers. Even though the mothers' accomplishments dwarf those of their daughters, readers will find vestiges of greatness in the daughters as well. When tormenting struggles in foreign lands came the daughters' way, their reactions illustrated that they were indeed the worthy offspring of such notable women.

This book by no means offers a full biography of each woman. Instead, it paints three comparative portraits, highlighting the similarities and differences between these royal mothers and daughters. By placing these women together and viewing them through the prism of the distinct times in which their dramas played out, we can more fully appreciate their contrasting and often moving fates. It is my hope that this book will whet the reader's appetite to delve more deeply into the fascinating lives of these royal women.

PART I

QUEEN ISABELLA

and

CATHERINE OF ARAGON

I

CALLED TO RULE

The dramatic stories of three unparalleled sets of royal mothers and daughters—stories that span half a millennium—begin with the birth of Queen Isabella of Castile, "an extraordinary woman who was also an extraordinary monarch, one of the most powerful the world had ever known."[1] The saga unfolds in the far southwest corner of Europe, some six centuries ago, on the Iberian Peninsula. There, on a melancholy, austere expanse of land known as Castile—a wide plateau in hues of bronze, gray, and green—Isabel of Portugal, queen consort of King Juan II of Castile, gave birth to baby girl. It was April 22, 1451, Holy Thursday. The birth occurred in the small summer palace of the baby's father at Madrigal de las Altas Torres. A multitowered agricultural town of a few thousand inhabitants located inland on the plains of Castile in the province of Ávila, Madrigal was named for its many towers, built to help fend off attackers. Inside Madrigal's arched and gold-flecked, domed church of San Nicholas, the baby infanta of Castile was baptized and welcomed into the Roman Catholic Church.

Isabella's birthplace exhibited Muslim and Christian influences, most visibly through the palace and town walls, constructed in the Mudejar style. The Mudejar style, which pervaded Madrigal and many parts of Spain, is characterized by a unique interpretation of Western themes dominated by Muslim influences. The Muslim factor was to loom large in the future Queen Isabella's life. For centuries, Muslims from North Africa, often referred to as the Moors, had dominated swaths of the Iberian Peninsula. By the time of Isabella's birth, other Muslims, the Ottoman Turks, were on the march from present-day

Turkey into eastern Europe, bent on conquering peoples and territories by the sword. Their progress stoked fear among many Europeans.

Little fanfare accompanied Isabella's birth, for no one viewed the baby as having a great role in the future. Enrique, her elder half brother, was already married and destined to succeed their father, King Juan. In that day, brothers superseded daughters in the line of succession. When, in 1453, Queen Isabel gave birth to Isabella's brother, Alfonso, young Isabella slipped a step further away from the Castilian throne and that much more removed from a position of power.

Yet if the throne itself seemed elusive, there was always the possibility that the infanta from Castile, like many princesses before and after, would be a useful commodity in the royal marriage market. Even though princesses were not first choices as rulers, they were valuable as brides to cement alliances between dynasties. Consequently, royal daughters were potentially significant players in the complicated, high-stakes game of international diplomacy.

In order to survive, let alone flourish, in times marked by peril and political machinations, the infanta Isabella had to navigate her way through the treacherous waters of medieval Castilian court life. Turbulence clouded the girl's early years. One of the young Isabella's biggest challenges was her mother's increasingly unstable disposition. Queen Isabel had arrived in Castile at age nineteen, attractive and innocent. Unfortunately, however, her position was thwarted by the king's scheming favorite, Álvaro de Luna. Luna had hoped that Queen Isabel would be a malleable ally. However, not only was she intractable but she saw through Luna's ruse. Queen Isabel obstructed Luna's plans to dominate the monarch. The queen's opposition to Luna's pernicious influence on her husband marked her as Luna's enemy, and the corrupt, arrogant, and power-hungry courtier therefore eyed her warily. Hostility grew between them. Soon, suspicions of Luna and his ill treatment of the queen were on everyone's lips. Isabel's unstable behavior during her pregnancy with Isabella fed the rumors. A melancholy descended that was soon to overwhelm the queen. Some in Isabel's entourage surmised that the cause of the queen's depression was poison ordered by Luna.

Eventually, Luna's manipulations caught up with him. His use of imprisonment and execution as tools to maintain power, plus his unpopular hold over the king, combined to make Luna a hated figure. Queen Isabel's utter contempt for the man sealed his fate. By gaining so many enemies, Luna paved the way for his own downfall. Charged with treason, he was executed in 1453.

Under King Juan's weak reign, which saw much fighting among his nobles,

Castile's international prestige plummeted. Aware of his failure, toward the end of his life, Juan II wryly observed that he should have been the son of a mechanic instead of becoming Castile's king. Isabella's feckless father died after an ineffectual forty-nine-year reign. There was much truth in the harsh observation. "King Juan did one thing and one thing only for posterity, and that was to leave behind him a daughter who in no way resembled her father."[2] But first, the unlamented Juan II was succeeded by King Enrique IV, son of Juan's first wife, Maria of Aragon. Enrique, nicknamed the Impotent, proved to be even more disastrous a monarch than his father.

King Juan's death left Isabella and her younger brother, Alfonso, in their mother's care. The family of three lived in the small castle in the Castilian town of Arévalo. Arévalo, with its stretches of greenery and cornfields, offered Isabella and Alfonso plenty of opportunity to enjoy life outside. The energetic Isabella spent her early childhood there indulging in outdoor pursuits, often accompanied by her best friend, Beatriz de Bobadilla, the daughter of the governor of Arévalo castle. The friends were a study in contrasts: Beatriz was dark-haired and effusive, while Isabella, the fair-haired one, was restrained and mature. Beatriz and Isabella became like sisters. Among their favorite forms of exercise was riding. Fearless with horses, Isabella became an accomplished horsewoman and indulged in hunting all manner of game, both docile and dangerous. She even hunted down a bear, felling it with a javelin from her own hands. Riding and hunting were time well spent, for they taught the infanta patience, endurance, and an ability to ward off exhaustion.

Central to Isabella's life during these formative years was her mother. The widowed Queen Isabel saw to it that her daughter and son were imbued with the same veneration for the Roman Catholic Church that she herself possessed, a rigorous faith steeped in asceticism. Isabella's first tutor at Arévalo was a Franciscan priest, the provincial head of Castile, Fray Juan de Tolosa. He and the numerous other Franciscans there made a profound impact, and in time Isabella became devoted to the order. These clerics instilled a piety and love of the Church that were to remain with her all her life.

Two others contributed to Isabella's spiritual education: Fray Gonzalo de Illescas, Prior of Guadalupe, and Fray Lope Barrientos, Bishop of Cuenca. So important were these two men of the cloth that it is not far-fetched to conclude that they, "more than the mother, greatly influenced the religious orientation which was given to her [Isabella's] studies: Franciscans of Arévalo, well chosen pious ladies of the court . . . [and] the Mendicant Fray Martín de Córdoba." De Córdoba was so enthusiastic about his pupil that he wrote a book dedicated to the education of young noblewomen. He gave the book to Isabella on her sixteenth birthday with the recommendation that she "brilliantly reflect chastity and purity in all this kingdom."[3]

Isabella's piety was more than automatic, based purely on obedience and external practices. Instead, Isabella linked her faith to reason. "She herself accepted no faith merely because as a reward she was promised understanding at some later time. She was one of the creators, and yet also a creature of the new modern age, and she therefore accepted human reason and bowed before a single truth. This 'unchangeable' truth was based on the existence of God and praised by Saint Augustine as the 'source of all happiness.' "[4]

For those imbued with devotion like Isabella, a life centered on God became a raison d'être. Living in service to God, one's soul would journey toward the ultimate goal: eternal salvation. A faith-filled life could also bring solace to those on earth, particularly in times of great troubles—and Isabella grew up in such times. Hers was a world fraught with uncertainty and danger. No matter one's station, it was a harsh life peppered by plagues and other diseases, along with constant warfare.

Queen Isabel raised her children as well as she could; however, the melancholy that first manifested during the queen's pregnancy with Isabella escalated into insanity at Arévalo. Incessantly mourning her dead husband, the dowager Queen Isabel descended into *"profunda tristeza"* (a profound sadness).[5] As she fell deeper into madness, the queen shut herself off from the world and stared blankly. Or she might have been found, as legend has it, "fleeing up and down the dark stairs of the castle pursued by the ghostly voices cawing Luna's name."[6]

Her mother's madness, her father's death, and life under the watchful eye of her half brother, Enrique, shadowed the early years of the future Queen Isabella's life. It was a far more unhappy and unstable youth than that enjoyed by her daughter Catherine. Yet in spite of the challenges that came Isabella's way from the earliest days, she was intent on not letting life's vicissitudes divert her. As a child, Isabella had shown determination, bravery, and an unswerving devotion to God—characteristics that she was to call upon in the future and qualities that her daughter Catherine of Aragon was to share fully.

As a female with little prospect of succeeding to the throne, Isabella received an education that was circumscribed at best. Though her mother had ensured Isabella's spiritual formation, her study of academic subjects was limited. The child learned to read and write Castilian well, but her knowledge of foreign tongues, particularly Latin, the language of the educated, was negligible.

Her tutors were able men, usually priests who were educated at the University of Salamanca, founded in 1218. Isabella studied music, grammar, and rhetoric. She was exposed to the philosophy of St. Thomas Aquinas and Aristotle. Poetry was a favorite with Isabella, who most likely read Dante in Spanish. Her tutor drummed in histories of her royal forebears, so that Isabella was well aware not only of their long, distinguished lineage but also of their lengthy crusade against the Moors. Not forgotten in her training were valued female accomplishments, such as sewing, painting, embroidery, and dance. The nexus for nearly all Isabella's education, however, was religion. Even her artistic endeavors had the glorification of God as their impetus; she labored over items such as decorations and standards created for altars. As a product of the Middle Ages, Isabella's life was steeped in faith. As predictable as the seasons of the year, life revolved around the liturgical calendar. Days and momentous events were punctuated by the chiming, tolling, or pealing of church bells. Central to the Church's teachings were the sacramental aspects of the faith, which imbued life with a profound sense of the presence of God.

Besides her deep-seated attachment to Roman Catholicism, Isabella came to understand her future role instinctively. Even as a child, she seemed filled with a presentiment that she would be called to rule. The infanta Isabella, in her Arévalo years, "gained a self-possession, a pride in her royal lineage, a sense of both entitlement and responsibility, a regal bearing and a high morality inseparable from religion and ruling well. . . . In her veins, she had learned, ran the blood of warriors, of heroic Goths and Moorfighters, of monarchs and saints, of powerful men and women. Hers was a heritage for a queen."[7]

For nearly eight centuries, a long, drawn-out battle for the soul of the peninsula unfolded, pitting the region's Muslims and Christians against each other. Though the two warring groups, along with the Jews, had at times coexisted, the overarching theme of Muslim-Christian relations from the 700s into Isabella's lifetime was of war. Ever since the Arabs invaded Spain in 711 via the Strait of Gibraltar and established their faith and culture in the region, Christians had sought to regain their lands. Thus was born the struggle that came to be known as the *Reconquista* or the Reconquest of Christian lands on the Iberian Peninsula. The legendary Castilian hero and conqueror of the Moors in Valencia in the late eleventh century, El Cid, added luster to the lengthy battle for the land that was to become Spain.

The march toward the re-Christianization of the Iberian Peninsula was cemented by a decisive Christian victory in 1212 at Las Navas de Tolosa. This, along with the gains made by the King of Castile and León, St. Ferdinand, of

Córdoba in 1236 and Seville in 1248, pointed to the inevitable total defeat of the Moors.

At the time of the future Queen Isabella's birth, the Iberian Peninsula consisted of the following main kingdoms: Aragon on the east, bounded by the Mediterranean Sea; its large neighbor, Castile, comprising Andalusia, Extremadura, Murcia, Old and New Castile, León, Asturias, and Galicia; Navarre on the Pyrenees near France; and Granada in the south. The elusive territory of Granada, the Moors' last stronghold, was the still-painful reminder that the Christians' work was incomplete. Granada represented the last trophy in the struggle to liberate Iberia and bring it back into the Christian fold.

In spite of the steady gains of the past, during Isabella's youth, the final chapter of the Reconquista seemed more in the realm of dreams than reality. Islam had gained new traction in the ongoing war with Christendom. Only two years after Isabella's birth, Constantinople, the seat of the Christian Byzantine Empire, fell to the Muslim Turks after a dramatic siege. This event shook Europe to the core and reinforced fears of an Islam in the ascendant. The crescent was again making its mark against the cross. The Ottoman Turks' victory over the Christians at Constantinople in 1453 reinvigorated the Islamic world and created new impetus for them to proceed farther into Europe, this time westward from Asia Minor. The Muslim juggernaut battered its way through the Continent, devastating most of the Balkans, and reaching as far as the Danube.

That a woman would one day reverse this seemingly unstoppable tide of Muslim gains from the eastern end of the Continent, then emerge the victor against the Moors in the final chapter of the Reconquista, was unthinkable. But before achieving that historic triumph, the girl from Madrigal de las Altas Torres and Arévalo had to fight her way through the maze of courtly intrigues, for "Isabella's path to the throne" was not "straightforward, let alone inevitable."[8]

Isabella later recalled how she and her younger brother were ultimately "inhumanely and forcibly uprooted" from the arms of "my mother the queen."[9] They were ordered to live at King Enrique IV's court, away from Queen Isabel. Isabella thus became the ward of the king and his consort, Queen Juana. The weak and vacillating king and his immoral and scheming queen were indisputably unsavory characters. The court—with its distracting gossip and political posturing—proved an uncomfortable atmosphere for the circumspect Isabella and her brother.

Bearded and redheaded, Enrique IV was large in stature but ungainly. He could cast a fierce gaze upon anyone, yet he failed to accomplish anything that might have gained his people's respect. Unsuccessful as a war leader and highly susceptible to the influence of court favorites, Enrique managed through incompetence to earn the enmity of his subjects. Aside from being an ineffectual ruler, he was widely believed to be impotent and a cuckolded husband. The flirtatious Queen Juana, who reveled in displaying her femininity, did not hide her admiration for the ostentatious and good-looking courtier Beltrán de la Cueva. When, in 1462, several years after she married King Enrique, the queen gave birth to a daughter, also named Juana, many were convinced that de la Cueva, and not Enrique, was the real father. The unfortunate baby took on the moniker La Beltraneja from birth because of her supposed illegitimacy. The queen's scandalous behavior was highly distasteful to the straitlaced infanta Isabella.

Not all the individuals Isabella dealt with in her youth were as unsavory to her as King Enrique or Queen Juana, to whom the king had entrusted his half sister for her education. Alfonso de Carrillo, Archbishop of Toledo, who could muster countless soldiers to defend a cause he espoused, became a champion of the infantes Isabella and Alfonso. The prelate took a paternal and political interest in the rudderless children and became an influential friend on whom Isabella could lean for counsel.

Though she was half sister to the king, the infanta Isabella's rights to the crown remained tenuous. When she was thirteen, her chances of becoming sovereign of Castile was not really altered when Enrique was compelled formally to name Alfonso as his heir, since La Beltraneja's dubious parentage was too much for the king's rebellious nobles to stomach.

In 1466, with civil war brewing, pitting the king against his nobles, Enrique ordered Isabella, Queen Juana, and La Beltraneja to Segovia, where they could be carefully watched. King Enrique saw the teenage Isabella as a useful political pawn. Marrying her off to a suitor of his choice—preferably the King of Portugal, Afonso V, his own brother-in-law—might strengthen Enrique's position. However, Enrique must have been exasperated to find his half sister unmalleable. It was already evident that he had to contend with a young woman determined to chart her own destiny. The contours of Isabella's life and her role in creating it were already taking shape.

As King Enrique's armies and his enemies clashed and important towns fell to the rebel nobles of Castile, the aristocracy became emboldened. The nobles promoted Isabella's brother, Alfonso, to be the new King of Castile. People were forced to take sides. The Castilians suffered throughout this crisis, with near anarchy prevailing in town and countryside. Amid the fighting, the rebel nobles did not ignore Isabella. They were intent, above all, on preventing King Enrique from marrying her off to Afonso V. Instead, the rebellious nobles insisted that she marry Pedro Girón, brother to Juan Pacheco, a powerful courtier of Enrique IV. Enrique consented. Isabella was mortified. The much older Girón, coarse and debauched, was her very antithesis. There was nothing Isabella could do but pray fervently for deliverance from what to her was a fate worse than death. In April 1466, her prayers were answered when Girón died from an infection.

Another death, this time of one closer to Isabella's heart, took place on July 5, 1468. Her brother succumbed to what appeared to be the plague; others thought it was poisoning. Taking stock of the growing chaos in her country, and realizing that she would forever be a pawn unless she herself assumed power, Isabella immediately made her move for the throne. When announcing Alfonso's imminent death, the seventeen-year-old Isabella declared: "The succession of the reign and the dominions of Castile and León belonged to me as the legitimate heir and successor."[10] She was supported by Pacheco and Archbishop Carrillo. Alfonso's death radically changed Isabella's fortunes. By reminding others of her right as heir (La Beltraneja having been shunted aside by Enrique IV), Isabella marked herself as the next legitimate sovereign of Castile. But that was as far as she was willing to go.

At seventeen, Isabella already showed evidence of self-possession, fortitude, and farsightedness. Unwilling to become a tool of an ambitious clique of nobles, she risked a split with Archbishop Carrillo, her surrogate father, who with other rebellious gentry urged her to usurp the crown. Carrillo saw this moment as a golden opportunity for his protégée, and a perfect opportunity to rid Castile of the highly inept Enrique IV, a cause for which the archbishop and his supporters had long fought.

Tempting though the offer was, the coolheaded and quick-witted teenager concluded that she must bide her time and resisted all pressure to mount a coup. Isabella emerged from a convent in Ávila, where she had been cosseted for her protection after Alfonso's death, refused to overthrow her half brother, and declared, "I am content with the title of Princess."[11]

Her loyalty to Enrique paid off. The king and his rebellious nobles reached a compromise, of which Isabella was the beneficiary. At Toros de Guisando in Ávila, before a crowd of hundreds, Enrique IV declared Isabella his heir in 1468 and gave her authority over her marriage.

Now that she was the official heir, Isabella's fortunes brightened. Not only did she receive holdings from which she derived income and prestige but the future queen's stature as a bride correspondingly rose. Suitors for Isabella's hand included King Enrique's long-favored candidate, King Afonso V of Portugal; as well as the Duke of Guienne, heir to King Louis XI of France; and a brother of England's King Edward IV.

However, the one Isabella herself favored was Ferdinand, son of King Juan II of Aragon. Ferdinand of Aragon, born on March 10, 1452, to King Juan and his second wife, was a year younger than Isabella. King Enrique had already offered Isabella as a bride to King Juan's eldest son and heir, Carlos, Prince of Viana, but that match fell through with Viana's death. His stepmother (Ferdinand's mother) was an ambitious Aragonese noblewoman who would brook no opposition to her son becoming king. She was thought to have poisoned Viana. The wily King Juan, who highly favored Ferdinand over Carlos anyway, lost no time in negotiating a marriage between Ferdinand and Isabella. By May 1469, King Juan was promoting a marriage between Ferdinand and Isabella keenly.

Juan calculated that, by having Isabella marry Ferdinand, Aragon would fare much better against the rebellious Catalans within the kingdom. Moreover, a united Castile and Aragon would pose a formidable threat to Juan's enemy, King Louis XI of France. In 1468, as a token of his favor and to make his son a more attractive candidate for Isabella, Juan II made Ferdinand King of Sicily, which then belonged to the Aragonese crown.

Though she had not yet met him, in Isabella's eyes Ferdinand was the most suitable candidate for a future husband. He was her second cousin; they both descended from the royal house of Trastámara. A marriage between them naturally offered the tantalizing dynastic opportunity of uniting Castile and Aragon and would fortify Isabella's claim to Castile's crown. From a personal viewpoint, Ferdinand also appeared to be the most tantalizing suitor, for unlike the other candidates, he was young and vigorous, reputed to be handsome with a winning personality. Full-lipped with a prominent forehead, good strong physique, and of medium height, the prince also cut a fine figure on a horse. It was said that "he carried himself boldly both on horse and foot."[12] Ferdinand's eyes were "bright with a certain joyful dignity," while "his head [was] well set on his shoulders, his voice clear and restful."[13] A fine sportsman who excelled at jousting, Ferdinand was able to keep his composure in the most stressful moments, an ability that would serve him in good stead. Seasoned from a tender age by uprisings, war, and intrigues to rival those of the Castilian court, Ferdinand was more than ready to face military and political challenges. In short, here was a husband worthy of the headstrong, candid, and independent Isabella.

And what of Isabella herself? What kind of a young woman had she become? By the late 1460s, Isabella had the makings of a leader. Intelligent with keen powers of observation, she refused to be subsumed by the endless machinations of those around her. As an outsider and a pawn in Enrique IV's court, immersed in the Castilian civil wars, Isabella had learned to weigh the options, determining which would serve her interests as a sovereign and those of Castile. Physically, she was of medium height with a tendency to plumpness. Of a very fair complexion, her pleasing face was flush with the glow of youth. Her greenish blue eyes and masses of reddish gold hair were her most prominent features. She was known for being dignified and courteous. One contemporary described Isabella as "most gracious in her manners."[14] Better educated than Ferdinand, Isabella was also an uncompromisingly upright character with firm convictions, characteristics that would not abate. She had a gravity that would later manifest in an aura of majesty that she flaunted when needed.

The main obstacle to the couple's union was King Enrique IV, who still insisted that Isabella marry the Portuguese king. This the princess refused, and she was within her rights to say no. Enrique had agreed, at Toros de Guisando, that Isabella had the right to refuse any suitor he proposed. Isabella said as much to a courtier who urged her to marry King Afonso, stating defiantly: "My marriage is not supposed to be arranged against my will."[15] With Enrique ready to renege on his agreement and threatening to imprison his half sister, Isabella felt no compunction about marrying the man she chose for a husband without his approval.

And so Isabella made a bold move, fleeing north to Valladolid in the hope of uniting herself in marriage to Ferdinand of Aragon. At one point during the daring flight, in order to elude capture by forces led by Archbishop Fonseca, who were loyal to King Enrique, Isabella sought refuge in a convent near her birthplace, Madrigal de las Altas Torres. Also hurrying to her, this time in answer to her pleas for help, were five hundred soldiers commanded by Isabella's friend and mentor Archbishop Carrillo. Her fate hinged on which of these two forces arrived first. Isabella's "faith must have been tested to the uttermost as she peered out from the wooden windows of the convent across the silent summer plain and wondered to which of the two archbishops the first troops to break the shimmering horizon would belong."[16] In the end, the first troops to reach Isabella belonged to Carrillo.

Isabella prevailed in her efforts to escape King Enrique. Ferdinand made his way to her disguised as a mule driver. When he arrived, the eager bride recognized her previously unseen groom, picking him from his companions and excitedly exclaiming, *"Ese es, ese es!"* (This is he!)[17] Upon finally meeting, the seventeen-year-old Ferdinand and eighteen-year-old Isabella were pleased with each other, a fact that boded well for the future.

On October 19, 1469, at Valladolid, Archbishop Carrillo married Isabella of Castile and Ferdinand of Aragon in a nuptial Mass, the requisite Papal Bull granting dispensation to the impediment of consanguinity being read. Though unbeknownst at the time to Isabella, this bull turned out to have been forged by Carrillo and King Juan II of Aragon in a desperate bid to ensure that Ferdinand and Isabella marry. Upon discovering the ruse, the couple petitioned Rome for the necessary bull (which Pope Sixtus IV granted in 1471).

Valladolid erupted in revelry over the wedding, with several days of feasts and processions. As part of the marriage arrangement, Ferdinand agreed to respect Castilian laws, and, most important, the nature of their joint rule emerged, for Ferdinand and Isabella would share titles and affix their names jointly to everything that needed their imprimatur. Also of great significance was the promise that "when she and he had in their joint power those kingdoms [of Castile and Aragon] they were obliged to war against the Moors, enemies of the holy Catholic faith, as other Catholic kings, their predecessors, had done."[18]

Thus began the famous marriage and exceptional political partnership of Spain's Ferdinand and Isabella. A dynamic and significant historical force, they became the parents of Catherine of Aragon, as recognizable a figure in her own right as her father and mother.

2

CONSOLIDATION OF POWER

Isabella's vigilance had paid off. She had steered her way through King Enrique IV's court and outmaneuvered her oppressive half brother by marrying Ferdinand of Aragon without Enrique's consent. Now there was no stopping her. Marriage to Aragon's next king all but assured Isabella's role as Castile's next sovereign. It was a trajectory that would lead to the birth of their daughter Catherine, whose historical role contrasts so radically with that of her mother. What Catherine's parents would achieve was to lay the basis for the creation of Spain.* The union of the kingdoms through their marriage catalyzed "a new national state that would grow by war, policy and accident throughout Catherine's girlhood to a great dynastic power, enriched by fabulous new-found lands, and struggling for first place in Europe."[1]

From the beginning, the bride and groom found, to their delight, that they had many values and interests in common, particularly when it came to their faith. Their personalities complemented each other. "Isabel was decisive, indeed resolute to the point of intransigence, and very serious, if with a gift for irony. She gave her trust sparingly but when she did, wholeheartedly." Ferdinand, by contrast, "was deft of mind, affable, and cocksure; his gallantry softened her edges and won her. . . . Her earnestness reinforced an intensity latent in him. Both of them were quick to take a stand; and both had the gift of self-

---

*Though Ferdinand and Isabella did not include the word "Spain" in the string of regions of which they were sovereigns, it is generally accepted that they laid the foundations for the nation that was to become Spain. In this book, the word "Spain" will periodically be used when referring to Castile during and after the monarchs' reign, as well as Castile and Aragon under Ferdinand and Isabella's reign.

monitory, curbing impetuosity, and especially they both had the ability to re-assess whatever the other thought insurmountable."[2]

This is not to say that the couple were completely of the same mind. Ferdinand enjoyed drinking and playing cards. Isabella, who did not drink wine, preferred reading above all and having discussions on theology, literature, or poetry. She also loathed gambling, and according to a courtier, "she did not wish to see nor to hear liars, coxcombs, rascals, clairvoyants, magicians, swindlers, fortune-tellers, palm-readers, acrobats, climbers and other vulgar tricksters."[3] In their views on marital vows, Ferdinand and Isabella also differed. Much to his wife's horror, Ferdinand conducted discreet liaisons with a number of women, fathering several illegitimate children, whereas Isabella remained faithful. So scrupulous was she in maintaining her marital vows that years later, whenever Ferdinand was absent, Isabella "slept in a dormitory, with her daughters or with other ladies or maidens of the court, so as not to give rise even to the suspicion of scandal."[4]

Despite Ferdinand's infidelity, Isabella remained devoted to him until the end. Near the time of her death, Isabella asked that, upon Ferdinand's death, her body be buried with his in order that "our bodies may symbolize and enjoy beneath the ground the close relationship that was ours when we were alive."[5] Ferdinand, even though he strayed from his marital vows, was nearly as devoted to his wife, valuing her judgment keenly. In later years, he was to write to Isabella of his devotion, telling her when they were apart of how he looked forward to their meeting and being together "as we were in our first love."[6]

The couple's personal union was equally evident in their political aspirations for the unity of Castile and Aragon. Isabella and Ferdinand's shared goal of seeing their kingdoms united can be seen in their motto, *"Tanto monta, monta tanto"* (As much as the one is worth so much is the other). Symbols the couple adopted also reinforced this unity. Ferdinand's became the yoke, which stood for the *Y* or *I* in his wife's name, while Isabella embraced as her symbol *flechas,* or arrows, the *F* standing for her husband's first initial. On coins of the realm, both their heads appeared, while in documents, Ferdinand's and Isabella's signatures were affixed together.

Within a year of their wedding, Isabella gave birth to the couple's first child, a girl named Isabel, like her mother. The only request Isabella made during the grueling delivery was that her face be covered by a veil in order to hide her pained expressions. Though she was cherished by both parents, little Isabel's arrival was tinged with disappointment. Castile may have allowed females to succeed to the throne, but the same could not be said of Aragon. Consequently, the desire for a male heir remained high for Isabel's parents.

Since her marriage had infuriated Enrique IV, Isabella's path toward the Castilian throne took a turn for the worse. In 1470, Enrique disinherited her in an ostentatious ceremony in which he promoted La Beltraneja as his heir. Isabella actively promoted her cause in the hope that her appeals would garner support. Ferdinand was of little help to his wife at the time, for his attention was focused on France, which he and his father fought to win back the Aragonese possessions of Roussillon and Cerdagne in the Pyrenees.

Despite Enrique's public repudiation of Isabella as his heir, doubts concerning the succession continued. Things came to a head as the king lay dying. One account has Enrique declaring La Beltraneja as his successor, whereas another has him leaving the question of the succession to six counselors, four of whom were known supporters of Isabella. Yet another account has Enrique remaining mute when asked who was to be his successor.

The moment of truth came on the night of December 11, 1474, when the forty-nine-year-old Enrique IV died. The important question of who was to succeed him went unanswered. For Isabella, however, no doubt lingered. When she heard of her half brother's death, the twenty-three-year-old Isabella donned white for mourning and attended the rituals to honor the dead. Two days later, to take possession of Castile as a monarch in her own right, she mounted a ceremony highly charged with symbolism. Isabella insisted on coronationlike ceremonials in Segovia before a crowd of townsfolk and dignitaries including prelates, nobles, knights, counselors, and the papal emissary.

To the fanfare of trumpets, a dazzlingly arrayed Isabella made her appearance, "a beautiful and stately figure, clad from head to foot in white brocade and ermine. Gems sparkled at her throat, at her bridle, at the arch of her foot; and her mount was caparisoned with cloth of gold."[7] At Segovia's majestic turreted *alcázar* (castle) jutting forth from the top of a prominent rock, Isabella was received "under a canopy of rich brocade" by the city's notables, who "escorted her in solemn procession to the principal square . . . where a broad platform . . . had been erected for the performance of the ceremony."[8]

On a raised platform before the Church of San Miguel in the castle's main square, Isabella received oaths of allegiance from important individuals. The traditional monarch's symbol in Castile was a golden orb topped with a cross, but Isabella chose the sheathed sword of state, "with the point downward, resembling a cross." She made a profound statement, for "the sword recalled not only the royal conquerors who had wrested Spain from the Moors, but also the feats of the warrior maid Joan of Arc, earlier in the century."[9] In unsheathing the sword of state at her accession ceremony, Isabella declared her intention to follow in these illustrious footsteps.

The unsheathing of the sword of state marked a significant moment in Isabella's accession ceremony, for "it demonstrated in dramatic fashion, the new queen's intention to act like a king and rule with power and justice, of which the unsheathed sword was a recognized symbol."[10] In recording the momentous event, Alonso de Palencia, the royal chronicler, noted that the sword of state was carried "after the use of Spain, so that it could be seen by everyone, even the most distant, and so that they should know that she who had the power to punish the guilty with royal authority was approaching."[11] The unsheathed sword was carried before her as she made her way to the church to attend a thanksgiving Mass. The queen "humbly prostrated herself before the high altar, giving thanks to God for bringing her safely through so many perils, and asking the grace to rule according to His will."[12]

"The fact that Isabella's accession took place at all was [also] remarkable. She succeeded to the throne of what had become, by the Middle Ages, the largest and most powerful kingdom in the Iberian Peninsula, possessing about two-thirds of the region's population and natural resources, as well as the bulk of its territory."[13] During Isabella's ceremonial proclamation as queen, Ferdinand was nowhere in sight, preoccupied as he was with Aragonese problems. At the news of his wife's accession to the Castilian throne, Ferdinand rushed to her side. Their formal reunion emphasized Isabella's ascendance to the crown and her legitimate hold over Castile, with Ferdinand respectfully approaching his wife inside the gates of Segovia's *alcázar*. Support for Isabella's rights as Queen of Castile and the peninsula's provident future was evident in Segovia. Prominent men of the city acclaimed the new sovereign with the words *"Castilla, Castilla por el Rey Don Fernando è por la Reyna Doña Isabel, su muger, proprietaria destos Reynos* (Castile, Castile for the King Don Ferdinand and for the Queen Doña Isabel, his wife, queen proprietor of these kingdoms)."[14] It was the first time in hundreds of years that a queen reigned in Castile in her own right. The word *proprietaria* signified Isabella's proprietorship of Castile. She was Castile's queen regnant, with Ferdinand as king consort.

Friction between husband and wife inevitably occurred over Isabella's summary assumption of power. In an era when males were accustomed to dominant roles in the private and public spheres, Queen Isabella's sudden elevation to a position of power was bound to rankle a man of pride and virility such as Ferdinand. Moreover, though any children born to them were in line to inherit the Castilian crown, he could not succeed Isabella as King of Castile in the event of her death. Ferdinand's manly pride nearly made him return to Aragon. It took the concerted efforts of Archbishop Carrillo and Pedro Cardinal González de Mendoza, Primate of Spain, to ease the tension between the royal partners.

Ultimately, though, Isabella pleaded her case before Ferdinand herself. During a meeting that prelates and aristocrats attended, Isabella's husband listened to his wife's reasoning. "This subject, Señor, need never have been discussed, because where there is such union as by the grace of God exists between us, there can be no difference. Already, as my husband, you are King of Castile, and your commands have to be obeyed here; and these realms, please God, will remain after our days for your sons and mine."[15] Isabella went on to convince Ferdinand that her claim to the throne was imperative by cleverly reminding him that, since their only child thus far, the princess Isabel, was a female, her rights to the throne had to be maintained. Failure to do so could mean that any future husband of Isabel's, most likely a foreigner, "might allege that these realms belonged to him even by the collateral line, and not to your daughter the Princess, on account of her being a woman . . . whence it may follow that the kingdom may pass into the hands of a foreign race."[16] Thus through her "arguments [did] the queen . . . [succeed] in soothing her offended husband, without compromising the prerogatives of her crown."[17] Thanks to Isabella's cogent arguments and Ferdinand's willingness to listen, their acrimony dissipated. Their mutual love had also won the day. From then on, Ferdinand and Isabella worked together tirelessly for what they perceived to be the best for Spain.

No sooner had Queen Isabella and King Ferdinand sorted out their differences and emerged with plans for Spain's future than war erupted. The Portuguese King Afonso V proposed to marry La Beltraneja himself and attacked Castile in the hope of dethroning Isabella and securing the throne for La Beltraneja. The stakes were high on both sides. If King Afonso succeeded, Castile would be united with Portugal. If he failed, Castile would unquestionably belong to Isabella.

Besides the war with Portugal, the Castilian coffers were nearly empty, numerous towns still dithered over their allegiance to Isabella and Ferdinand, and to rub salt in the wound, in a fit of pique, the fickle Archbishop Carrillo abruptly changed allegiance to La Beltraneja. On many fronts, the struggle with Portugal over control of Castile seemed almost a lost cause for Queen Isabella. Yet however hopeless the war appeared to be, the queen knew that she had no choice but to fight. To have appeased the Portuguese would have meant certain defeat for Castile. Not only would Isabella have lost her crown but Castile would likely have been subordinated to Portugal's designs indefinitely. There was, therefore, no alternative but to go on with the struggle.

In the spring of 1475, Afonso V invaded Castile, but support for him was not widespread. He was willing to withdraw his troops, but at a high price. Isabella would have to yield Galicia or León to him. Even Ferdinand recommended that his wife accept Afonso's terms, but "Isabella rejected these proposals. She wrote to her husband that she would not give up one inch of Castilian territory and that she would soon be joining him at the front. She herself was Castile, she said, and she loved her country. She loved each district of Castile, the mountainous regions and the peasants and fanatical priests who inhabited them; she loved bright and fertile Andalusia with its bold merchants and daring mariners; she loved poor Galicia and the Galician fishermen. She resolved to defend the entire country with all the means at her disposal."[18]

Ferdinand and Isabella set about defending her inheritance. Throughout the War of the Castilian Succession, as the struggle came to be called, Queen Isabella immersed herself in all aspects of the conflict. Far from letting others run the war, the queen organized numerous tasks and influenced the direction of the conflict. Unwilling to countenance defeat, she tirelessly led and inspired. At one point, while Ferdinand rushed to Burgos to help the crown's cause there, Isabella "galloped to Toledo, 130 miles south, to bring back reinforcements of new levies. She then made a wide and rapid swing to León, more than two hundred miles north, to rescue the province from a treacherous governor."[19]

With Ferdinand providing strategic knowledge and skilled leadership to over fifty thousand soldiers, Isabella feverishly campaigned to gain as much support for her cause as possible. Pregnant with her second child, the queen braved exhausting, primitive conditions. She rode from one Castilian town to another, urging her subjects to fight. The queen paid a heavy price for her efforts—she suffered an excruciating miscarriage, losing the male heir she and Ferdinand had so coveted.

Though Portuguese troops outnumbered the Castilians, who were suffering from exhaustion, Queen Isabella's faith in her cause paid off. By March 1476, the tide turned. Ferdinand took advantage of a Portuguese military blunder and defeated the enemy on an open plain near Toro in the province of Zamora. Holding Toro was key, as the town offered good access into Castile. Spurred by cries invoking the saints "Santiago y San Lázaro!" the Castilians emerged victorious in battle.[20]

Though Ferdinand personally led the Castilian troops into battle at Toro, Isabella played a significant role. Her leadership prevailed when twenty thousand Portuguese soldiers surrounded King Ferdinand and his troops. The queen, "threatened with defeat, was spurred on to almost superhuman activity. Like all great soldiers, she saw the advantage of attack. If the enemy's force outnumbered hers, it must be divided. She sent troops to assail [King Afonso's] base. . . . She hurled others against his right flank. Finally she discovered that a town at his rear, commanding his line of communications, was poorly guarded. She sent two thousand cavalry to seize it."[21] Thanks to Isabella's tenacity and leadership, Afonso retreated and headed for Toro, where Ferdinand's army defeated him.

At Torsedillas, from where Isabella directed other aspects of the war, the thrilling news of her husband's victory prompted a grateful queen to manifest her thanks to God, publicly and humbly. The twenty-four-year-old Isabella walked barefoot in the cold from the palace where she was staying to the monastery of St. Paul outside the city, "giving thanks to God with great devotion, for the victory that the King her husband had given his people."[22] Two years later, King Afonso of Portugal renounced his rights, as well as those of La Beltraneja, to Castile's throne, thus securing Isabella's hold on the crown. La Beltraneja's efforts to wrest power from Isabella finally ended when the former retired to a convent and took the veil.

The Portuguese defeat had significant repercussions. Instead of uniting with Portugal, Castile under Isabella united with Aragon. If Isabella had been usurped by La Beltraneja, she would have been merely Ferdinand's consort, meaning that their energies would likely have devolved largely upon the Aragonese kingdom. And "since Aragon's interests had always been directed towards the Mediterranean, it is hardly likely that its rulers would one day have listened to the proposals of a visionary sailor [by the name of Christopher Columbus] who thought he could sail westward across the Atlantic Ocean to China."[23]

The year 1479 also saw Ferdinand succeed his father as king of Aragon. With the two crowns united, a political partnership formally emerged. Ferdinand II's kingdom of Aragon and Isabella's kingdom of Castile forged a nation that eventually became Spain. Through their first decade together, husband and wife increasingly identified with each other, their union setting the tone for political unification. This spirit was essential to the creation of Spain and ultimately placed it on the path of unprecedented greatness. Evidence of their unity as a couple and as monarchs can be seen in Ferdinand and Isabella's building of a monastery in Toledo, the historic walled city on seven hills looming above the river Tagus. Toledo, together with Segovia and Granada, was one of Castile's three great cities. The monastery—with its elaborate Flemish Gothic design that came to be called Isabelline in honor of the queen—bears the name San Juan de los Reyes, the "los Reyes" referring to the kings, meaning the royal couple.

The monastery's founding was also a manifestation of the couple's religious devotion, which very much underpinned their rule. Isabella chose the name San Juan in honor of her patron saint, John the Evangelist, who is thought to have authored the biblical book of Revelation. The queen associated herself with his symbol, the eagle, which was "commonly believed [to be] emblematic of Christ and the sun. The eagle symbolized resurrection, salvation, renewal; and in medieval Europe it stood as an allegory for, among other things, legality of royal descent, rejection of intruders in lawful succession,"[24] all bound to resonate with a religious queen who had fought for her right to the throne.

Such ideals and concepts of kingship were largely expounded by Isabella's valued adviser, her confessor, Hernando de Talavera, who reinforced the queen's desire to become a wise and devoted sovereign, morally upright and always working in God's service. It therefore came as no surprise that, in erecting the monastery of San Juan de los Reyes, Isabella was not merely giving thanks but also manifesting her steadfast conviction in her present and future role as sovereign. The founding of the monastery also announced "its sponsor's commitment to the battle against evil in this world."[25]

The couple's thanksgiving at Toledo for their victory over the Portuguese demonstrates Isabella's increasing use of ceremony to reinforce the monarchy's significance, as well as that of the Catholic faith. Since a large part of her role as queen was meant to inspire and to be respected, it was only fitting that she and Ferdinand present themselves publicly in regal splendor. Privately the couple preferred a simple life, yet in moments of public scrutiny, Isabella ensured that she appeared attired in dazzling clothes, her court bathed in grandeur. In Toledo, during these heady days of celebrations, Isabella flaunted a spectacular ruby collar while dressed in a richly embroidered brocade gown emblazoned with the lions and castles of Castile. And she lost no opportunity in celebrating significant victories by publicly attending Masses to give thanks to God.

The constant fusion of religion and monarchy was not unusual for the time. To understand this, it must be remembered that "Ferdinand and Isabella and their contemporaries thought of monarchy not primarily as we do today in terms of supreme power in the state or of unlimited legislative capacity, but as a relationship to God."[26] For Castile in particular, monarchs before Isabella had already viewed themselves as anointed kings, a concept that even in the ineffective reign of King Enrique IV remained undiluted. Not surprisingly, the young queen embraced this "Christianized form of monarchical absolutism, so that its continuation was effectively the only policy in Isabella's mind, when she seized power in December 1474."[27]

Defeating Portugal in the War of the Castilian Succession did not end the king and queen's struggles; the possibility of being deposed still lingered. Ferdinand and Isabella therefore worked together to consolidate their hold on the throne and pacify Castile, the larger and more powerful of the two kingdoms. Decades of civil war and inefficient, corrupt government in the hands of Isabella's father, Juan II, and her brother Enrique IV had left Castile an unstable kingdom, allowing near anarchy to wreak havoc and instilling fear in many of the people. Criminal activity in particular was widespread. Violent assaults, marauding bandits, and widespread theft blanketed the countryside. None was immune from the terror; even churches were subjected to constant thievery. To counter this chaos, Isabella created the Hermandad, a type of national police unit based on the Holy Brotherhood or Santa Hermandad from the twelfth century. The Hermandad consisted of ordinary men, a sort of citizens' militia, who diligently patrolled areas under their jurisdiction. On guilty offenders, they dispensed justice swiftly and cruelly. Torture, amputation, and immediate execution were not uncommon. So effective did the Hermandad become in ridding the Castilian countryside of terrorizing bandits and the like that, some twenty years after its founding, the brotherhood had transformed into a less cohesive and fearsome organization, its mandate fulfilled.

Just as challenging as the brigands and criminals who frightened townspeople and country folk alike were the nobles whose allegiance to the crown had proved fickle. To counter a powerful and volatile nobility that might easily turn on her as they had on her relatives, Isabella moved to neutralize those in opposition to her by using a clever three-pronged assault on aristocratic privileges. Under her orders, financial, military, and noble prerogatives were substantially diminished. The nobility were ordered to surrender huge amounts of revenues, revenues they had arrogated to themselves, to the royal treasury. Isabella also weakened the aristocracy's ability to carry out wars against each other and the monarchy by razing their castles, the very edifices from which Castile derived its name. These numerous castles had been used as bases for protection while the nobles launched endless raids on their prey, including the crown. Thus did Isabella chip away at her potential adversaries and, in the process, consolidate the monarchy's power. In time, the royal couple was to control all the orders, along with the wealth attached to them.

Much as they would have liked to subjugate the aristocracy completely, such a policy would not have worked to their advantage and might have been politically fatal. In all their efforts to subdue Castile's nobles, Ferdinand and Isabella were careful not to alienate them and therefore cultivated a good number of their nobles, including formerly rebellious ones, by treating them mercifully. Thus, through a carefully crafted combination of keeping the nobility in check while granting them privileges did Isabella lay the groundwork for the monarchy's revival.

Geography made her quest to pacify Castile problematic. There was no proper capital. Mountains, valleys, and rivers dot the kingdom's landscape. Geographically, Castile's wide, flat, and arid plateau, the Meseta, dominates. The sunbaked Meseta can be unforgiving, with bitingly cold winters and uncomfortably hot summers. On the west, the Meseta slopes toward the Atlantic Ocean; on the east, it merges toward the Mediterranean Sea. The northern parts of the Meseta are abutted by the Pyrenees Mountains and the Galician and Asturian pastures. Meanwhile, in the south, where Andalusia is located, the geography is particularly diverse, offering a microcosm of Castile and the Iberian Peninsula. Andalusia's rugged Sierra Nevada, rivaling only the Swiss Alps in height, are not far from deserts, beaches, and valleys. The south also suffers from intense heat and lack of rain. However, the fertile Andalusian plain provides an exception, irrigated by the Guadalquivir River and its tributaries. Yet the rivers found on the peninsula were difficult to traverse. For "a river may be either a highway for those who desire to travel along its course, or a barrier for those who wish to cross it; but the Spanish rivers, with the possible exception of the Guadalquivir, are emphatically the latter rather than the former. Since they all rise on the high north central plateau, their current is for the most part so swift as to render it impossible for those journeying east and west to navigate them, while the same fact renders them the more difficult to ford for travellers going north and south."[28]

Dusty, primitive roads connecting towns and cities compounded the challenges, making travel in the era of Isabella's Castile uncomfortable and often arduous. This, however, did not stop the queen from visiting many parts of her kingdom. In fact, Ferdinand and Isabella's court was largely peripatetic. Being on the move suited Isabella, ever the horsewoman, who never hesitated to rush to a location that demanded her attention. Her very presence at a crisis made an impact, often in her favor, and so the queen was always prepared to go at a moment's notice to where she was needed. The court's mobility also allowed the monarchs to dispense justice personally. Isabella, seated regally on a throne, listened attentively to cases brought before her, weighed the evidence presented, then pronounced judgment. Some of the cases involved minor disputes; others compelled the queen to confer the death sentence. Isabella's reputation grew as she dispensed justice throughout her kingdom, for not only were her judgments deemed fair but many knew that their queen was incorruptible, refusing to accept bribes or confiscate the properties of the guilty.

As in all aspects of her life, Queen Isabella's practice of making personal appearances was intrinsically connected to her piety. She became convinced "that the righteousness of her ideas would inevitably win over her subjects because the Almighty was on her side. The phrase 'with the help of Our Lord' frequently appeared in her letters and conversations."[29] Nor was Isabella alone in linking her piety with the governing of her realm. One contemporary had observed this, noting how "many men believed that Isabel[la] was created miraculously for the Redemption of lost kingdoms."[30] So exalted had the queen become, in many people's estimation, that contemporary accounts referred to her as a "second Virgin Mary."[31] Taken in the context of the times, these highly exultant views were not far-fetched but in keeping with a widespread feeling of anticipation that greeted the royal couple's assumption of power. For "at the time of Isabella's disputed accession to the Castilian throne, and in the succeeding years, there was an extraordinary weight of expectation on her and her husband's shoulders."[32]

Queen Isabella's visits throughout Castile went a long way in cementing her hold over her kingdom. Despite dangers posed by the Portuguese and Moors in the provinces of Extremadura and Andalusia, the queen set her sights on controlling the region. Undeterred by the dangers and difficulties of such a task, Isabella journeyed through torturous paths, past the domineering Sierra Nevada, and pressed her will on the south. She pacified the region by imposing her control over two wealthy and rebellious feuding nobles, the Duke of Medina Sidonia and the Marqués of Cádiz. Isabella relied on the sheer force of her personality to bring the recalcitrant duke and marqués to heel. Both begged to be forgiven and acquiesced to their queen's demands.

In June 1478, in the midst of her struggle for the throne of Castile, the queen gave gave birth in Seville to a son, Juan. The arrival of a male heir eight years after the birth of their first child filled Isabella and Ferdinand with great satisfaction. Equally ecstatic were the people of Seville, who erupted in delight at the news, with celebrations lasting for days. When Isabella formally presented Prince Juan to God at Seville's cathedral, the occasion was lavish, rife with gestures that emphasized the dynasty's importance. As important as the prince's birth was personally and politically to Isabella, fate would later cast

Juan as a mere footnote in history. Instead, posterity would recognize another of Isabella's children, because of her marriage to England's King Henry VIII.

In the fall of 1479, the queen made a solemn entrance in Toledo without King Ferdinand. Accompanying her was the heir, Prince Juan, before whom the Cortes (parliament) swore a loyalty oath. While in Toledo, Isabella gave birth in November to her second daughter, Juana, the child who was to cause many heartaches in years to come. By this time, Isabella had largely succeeded in the unenviable task of taming her unruly kingdom. She was only twenty-eight. And though Granada continued to remain the domain of Moorish rulers, the queen would soon commit to securing that elusive territory.

Never far from Isabella's mind was the need to build Castile into an important state, and as the years passed, the queen was gratified to see her wishes come true. In her endeavors, Isabella was motivated by something greater than power. Indeed, she achieved her victory over King Afonso of Portugal and the ensuing successes in pacifying Castile not to gain power solely for power's sake but to eliminate chaos. To a woman passionate about order, chaos within her kingdom was nothing short of anathema. Thus, the queen's battles with her opponents were driven by a desire to rule effectively, to bring accord to her divided subjects. What "Isabella wanted [in essence, was] to be constructive and not destructive, to unite and not to cause disharmony."[33] Even so, the challenges were enormous. With 5 million inhabitants by 1500, the domain over which Isabella ruled was the most populous state on the Iberian Peninsula. Castile and Aragon's combined population matched that of England but was well behind the neighboring 15 million Frenchmen. Nevertheless, "the combined area of Ferdinand and Isabella's domains, 385,000 square kilometres in the crown of Castile and 110,000 square kilometres in that of the crown of Aragon, was almost equivalent to that of the mighty French kingdom, and equal to a large part of the fragmented Holy Roman Empire."[34]

At the time, Castile was largely rural, with 80 percent of the population peasants. The nobility and Church were the largest landowners. Nobles owned "97% of the territory of the Peninsula, either directly or by jurisdiction." This essentially meant that "1.5% of the population owned almost the entire Spanish territory."[35] Clearly the elite held much of the country's wealth, while the general populace had long endured being used by noble factions as "battering rams in their internecine struggles."[36]

An extreme climate, bad soil, and poor farming techniques kept the people impoverished. Plagued by internal instability and economic disunity, the region also suffered from a dearth of raw materials, necessitating the importation of many basic necessities. Moreover, a highly diverse topography cut across Castile, Aragon, and the neighboring countries. This made travel and communications difficult. It all meant that the road to great achievements for Spain was narrow and arduous.

Moreover, military threats from France in the north and al-Andalus, with its capital at Granada in the south, were of constant concern. Nevertheless Ferdinand and Isabella forged ahead. Far from viewing these and other challenges as insuperable, the monarchs faced them, always looking for ways to overcome or eliminate the problems that kept Spain from emerging as a major power. Along with pacifying the kingdom came economic reforms that included standardizing tariffs on imported and exported goods as well as eliminating taxes on traded commodities between the two kingdoms. Standardizing currency put an end to monetary disarray, particularly since only a limited number of royal mints were authorized to make the coinage of the realm.

Thanks to their determined and persistent efforts, Ferdinand and Isabella's "reign represents a key moment in the genesis of the 'modern Spanish state.' "[37] The intense cooperation between the two monarchs toward accomplishing common goals was unprecedented, for theirs "was an experiment in collaboration unequalled in its time."[38] That Spain's accomplishments can be traced to the couple's ability to work as one cannot be underestimated. And it was from their union that "a spirit of national identity"[39] grew. Thus, "the unity of their persons transcended the disunity of their dominions, and gave reality to a Spain that was something more than merely Castile and Aragon."[40]

Though "both monarchs were uncompromising supporters of strong authority . . . it is meaningless to think of them as 'absolutist'; [instead it should be remembered that] . . . their concept of sovereignty was mediaeval."[41] "Ferdinand and Isabella were [thus] in every sense the last mediaeval rulers of Spain: like mediaeval kings, they administered the realm, dispensed justice and made war, in person. In not a single decisive act of their reign did they proceed through delegated authority."[42] It is a measure of Isabella's character that "at no time did the queen ever exceed her traditional powers, and even her phrase, 'my royal absolute power,' which occurs seven times in her will, was of mediaeval origin and implied no extension of authority."[43] In other words, Isabella may have exercised her authority to the hilt, but she never overstepped the established boundaries of that authority.

Even though a small percentage of the population, the nobility, held economic sway, all classes could savor the peace they had craved for generations. The populace welcomed the relative stability that emerged with Ferdinand and

Isabella's rule. Out of the ashes of chaos emerged a society in which order was restored, where the highborn and lowly alike knew that they had a king and queen they could rely on. Here at last were sovereigns who took into account the well-being of all their subjects. Years after Ferdinand's and Isabella's deaths, a contemporary of theirs recalled admiringly how "they were rulers of our realm, of our speech, born and bred among us. They knew everybody, gave honours to those who merited them, travelled through their realms, were known by great and small alike, and could be reached by all."[44]

Castile's significance as the largest and most powerful kingdom on the Iberian Peninsula meant that King Ferdinand, who was as astute as his wife, spent the majority of his time and energy on Castile. Ferdinand also knew that Isabella's kingdom needed more attention than his. Therefore, in the course of nearly forty years in power, he spent a surprising majority of the time living in Castile while leaving the governing of Aragon to a series of trusted viceroys.

The program of internal reforms instituted by Ferdinand and Isabella contributed markedly to making Spain a reality. These reforms, plus bold adventures in the coming years, meant a significant shift for this once disorderly region of the Iberian Peninsula. A nation transformed, rejuvenated, and invigorated soon emerged. Castile and Aragon—the "Spain" that came to be under the rule of Isabella and Ferdinand—grew from strength to strength, accompanied by a newfound confidence. Recognition of this new power was evident in international relations. European monarchs came to see Spain as a valuable ally in pursuing their foreign policy aims. And Spain, under the king and queen's direction, was equally determined to leverage itself on the world stage. This was all to have a profound impact upon Queen Isabella's children, especially her youngest daughter, Catherine.

3

THE CONQUEROR OF GRANADA

he 1480s brought new struggles for Isabella. But instead of fighting for her crown as she had in the past, the queen went to war for a different cause: she fought for souls, for the Church and God. Never far from Queen Isabella's priorities was the all-important issue of heresy, against which she remained uncompromisingly resolute.

Heresy involved, as St. Thomas Aquinas pointed out, the corruption of dogmas by those who confessed the faith of Christ. By its very nature, heresy entailed intentional malice, leading to the destruction of the soul. Heresy was therefore nothing to be trifled with. Since the fourth century, with the appearance of Arianism, which denied the divinity of Christ, the Church has taken heresy very seriously. If left unchecked, beliefs deemed incorrect, inconsistent, and suspicious would likely lead to the confusion and corruption of true believers. Not only could such corrupted beliefs consign souls to eternal damnation but if left uncurbed, heresies might also lead to the Church's destruction. Heresy, therefore, was a mortal threat to the souls of men and to the Church as an institution. Here then, was a terrifying scenario for Isabella. To prevent such a double catastrophe from erupting required a severe mechanism designed for rooting out false believers: the Inquisition.

Modern Western society is so pervasively secular and far removed from its Christian roots today that it is difficult to fathom the extent to which previous generations were consumed by issues such as heresy. Yet it should be recalled how deeply embedded Christianity was in the Middle Ages. By this time, society had "evolved . . . on a Christian basis. Men had agreed, or at least had appeared to agree, on an all-enveloping theory of society which not only aligned virtue with law and practice, but allotted to everyone in it precise, Christian-oriented tasks."[1] And "because the Christian society was total it had to be compulsory; and because it was compulsory it had no alternative but to declare war on its dissentients."[2] The Church did just that with the introduction of the Inquisition.

This preoccupation with heresy did not begin with Queen Isabella, nor was it confined to Spain. Though the burning of heretics made the Spanish Inquisition infamous, the Papal Inquisition operated the same way in Germany and France. The Albigensian Crusade of 1209–1255 was launched to defeat the Cathars, a heretical sect in southern France.

Just as the Church waged a battle against the Cathars, in Castile it targeted *conversos* via the Inquisition. *Conversos,* or converts (whether forced or voluntary) to Catholicism from Judaism, had been a fixture in the Iberian Peninsula for some time. The term *converso* was not strictly limited to new converts but was passed down to the *conversos'* descendants.* *Conversos* had been generally compelled to change their religion owing to the widespread antagonism toward Jews that pervaded the peninsula (and Europe) for generations. These intolerant views became an obsession with many so that *conversos,* along with Jews and *mudéjares* (Muslims in Christian territories), lived in an atmosphere increasingly permeated with suspicion and fear. By the time of Queen Isabella's accession, the *convivencia,* or period of coexistence, that had existed for years was rapidly unraveling. The Inquisition was unleashed amid this acrimony and mistrust, first against the *conversos.*

On the European continent, anti-Jewish hostility erupted. Pogroms involving the killing of thousands of Jews took place through the Middle Ages: in the Rhineland in 1096 and 1146, in England in 1190, and in Prague in 1389. In Castile, ferocious anti-Jewish sentiment reached a peak in 1391, when massacres broke out in the major cities of Toledo, Valencia, and Seville, resulting in the deaths of thousands more Jews. Through the years animosity toward Jews never abated, forcing the beleaguered minority to endure further restraints on their liberty.

Before Isabella's reign, in 1412 and 1449, restrictive laws were put into place targeting Jews and *conversos.* This all meant that "the unbaptized, that is the Jews, were not members of the society at all; their lives were spared but otherwise they had no rights. Those who, in effect, renounced their baptism by infidelity or heresy, were killed. For the remainder, there was total agreement and total commitment."[3] Whether compelled to convert to Christianity through

---

*Moors who changed their faith to Christianity were technically *conversos* as well.

fear or for economic reasons, Jewish rabbis gave prescient warnings of the future. Rabbi Yitzhak Arama cautioned *conversos*: " 'You will find no rest among the gentiles, and your life will hang in the balance.' Of the *anusim* (forcible converts) he prophesied: 'One third burnt by fire, one third flying hitherto to hide and those who remain living in deadly fear.' "[4]

The Jews in Castile were permitted religious freedom but were excluded from society at large and lived in separate communities known as *aljamas*. They were barred from holding prominent positions in organizations such as the military, yet some Jews were able to place themselves at the forefront as doctors, scholars, and financiers—with even the king and queen relying on the financial acumen of individuals with Jewish origins. These included David Abulafia, who took charge of supplies for the troops in the upcoming Granada War; Abraham Seneor, treasurer of the Santa Hermandad, and Isaac Abravanel, who supervised the tax on sheep. So prominent were Jews in administrative roles in Castilian finances that a foreign visitor pointed out that Isabella's "subjects say publicly that the queen is a protector of Jews."[5]

Conversos fared much better than nonconverted Jews. *Conversos* constituted the artisan class, a highly motivated group who possessed a good deal of capital. Through the ages, many *conversos* assimilated and became sincere believers in Christianity. Some had reached the upper echelons of society, marrying into the nobility and holding high offices at court. King Ferdinand's financial advisers were *conversos,* as were several of the monarchs' secretaries. *Converso* doctors were also employed by the court. Even the monarchs themselves had *converso* ancestors, Isabella through her great-grandmother María de Padilla, and Ferdinand through his mother, Juana Enríquez.

The Church too had its share of prominent members with *converso* blood, among them Fray Hernando de Talavera, Queen Isabella's confessor and a member of the Hieronymite order. Unlike the worldly Cardinal Mendoza, who was acknowledged to have sired three sons, Talavera was widely admired for his moral rectitude, spartan life, and straightforward sermons. Although he composed his sermons for a simple congregation, his words were influential with the queen. With his large eyes, earnest gaze, and high forehead hinting at a keen intellect and pious countenance, Talavera appeared to be the kind of priest who could be of immense help to the queen. But what truly drew Isabella to Fray Talavera was his deeply attuned faith. Isabella had been profoundly affected by this Hieronymite priest ever since her twenties, when she knelt before him to be confessed and Talavera remained seated. When a perplexed Isabella commented that both parties usually knelt, the priest corrected her, telling Isabella that "this is God's tribunal; I act here as his minister, and it is fitting that I should keep my seat, while your Highness kneels before me.' "[6] Realizing that the priest would act not as her subject but as God's representative in the confessional, Queen Isabella was so impressed that she humbly replied: "This is the confessor that I wanted."[7]

Talavera remained an influential counselor to Isabella. In the Hieronymite monk, the queen found not only a personal confessor but also a valued adviser who placed her role as sovereign within the context of their highly pietistic era. Talavera gave Queen Isabella, who was eager for his counsel, a devotional tract that amounted to a blueprint for a reign which "built upon Spanish traditions of kingship and advice to princes. . . . Talavera urged [Isabella to] strive for perfection of character and he assumed that 'it is a calling to aspire to perfection of your estate. If you are Queen, you ought to be a model and stimulus to your subjects in the service of God.' "[8] They were lessons she never forgot and always strived to fulfill. In time, Queen Isabella passed similarly themed lessons on to her daughter Catherine of Aragon.

For Jews and *conversos* alike, the 1480s marked a distinct shift as attitudes against them hardened throughout Castile. Numerous *conversos* were rightly or falsely thought to be insincere in the practice of the faith and were suspected of being secret Judaizers, who clung to the old religion. This perception cast them as seditious threats to society.

The situation for *conversos* became more grave as denunciations against them took on a life of their own. These fresh accusations ultimately denied the *conversos* "their protective shield—i.e., their Christian identity."[9]

World events moved Ferdinand and Isabella to impose the Inquisition. Fear gripped Christians, for "in the closing years of the fifteenth century Christianity was hard-pressed on every side."[10] Muslim aggressors were on the march, and to many people, including Isabella and Ferdinand, unified and devout Catholicism was the clearest chance of resistance and victory. Divisiveness among Christians had contributed to the Fall of Constantinople in 1453 to Muslim invaders. The Great Schism of 1054 saw Christianity nearly rent asunder by its division into the Western and Eastern branches. The mutual suspicion that beset both groups continued well into the Middle Ages, playing into the hands of the Ottoman Turks in 1453. When the Byzantine Emperor Constantine XI pleaded with Western Christians to come to the aid of Eastern Christians in their desperate bid to defend Constantinople from Islamic attack under the leadership of Mehmet II, no substantial help came. This schism, then, had "cast a long shadow over Constantine's attempts to defend the city."[11] Mehmet noted this Christian disunity "with more than passing interest. Fear of Christian unity [after all] had always been one of the guiding principles of Ottoman foreign policy."[12] Christian disunity, therefore, facilitated the collapse of the Byzantine Empire. That collapse, a direct result of Constantinople's fall, not merely was a victory for Mehmet II, but also "confirmed the Ottoman Empire as the great superpower of the age."[13] The fall of that city, which saw one of the greatest churches in Christendom, the Hagia Sophia, converted into a mosque, traumatized Europe. The fall was "considered the tragic end of the classical world."[14]

Even though the historic event shook Christian Europe, Western powers continued to dither after the fall and failed to liberate the city. This emboldened Mehmet II to overrun Serbia, opening the way for Islam to penetrate farther into Europe. For Isabella, the lessons of Constantinople were plain to see. Heresy, if left unchecked in Castile, could create an equivalent of the Great Schism within the Castilian Church. In the upcoming Granada War, the Church needed to be solidly orthodox to withstand troubles. Queen Isabella could not risk disunity that might bring about a disaster like the fall of Byzantine Christianity. The stakes for Castile, for Europe, indeed for Christendom were too high. Subversive individuals within the Church, therefore, needed to be expunged immediately.

Only weeks before Isabella ordered the Inquisition instated, Muslim invaders attacked again. Without warning, in 1480 the Turks, ordered by Mehmet II, invaded Otranto, on the heel of the Italian Peninsula, compelling the Pope to call for a crusade to free the port from the Muslim invaders. Ferdinand and Isabella heeded the call, sending ships in 1481 to help drive away the Turks.

The horrors of Otranto brought the sacking of Constantinople that much closer. Christian Europe trembled at the news that another city had fallen into the hands of Muslim invaders. Some twelve thousand out of Otranto's twenty thousand inhabitants were slaughtered, including the city's bishop, who was brutally sawed in half. The cathedral was desecrated when the Muslims turned it into a stable for their horses. And eight hundred inhabitants who refused to convert to Islam were summarily decapitated. Determined to recapture Otranto, the son of the King of Naples, aided by Aragonese, Castilian, and Venetian forces, attacked the city, returning it to Christian hands in 1481.

Otranto's fall galvanized Ferdinand and Isabella into action. Otranto brought the festering problem of Granada sharply into focus. The time was fast approaching when Granada needed to be liberated. But before an attack could be launched, the more immediate problem of heresy needed to be addressed. To King Ferdinand and Queen Isabella, Granada's liberation could not succeed without a reinvigorated Church in Castile. They were, in effect, creating a Church militant.

For Isabella, cleansing the Church's membership of false converts was tantamount to curing the body of a deadly infection. In her eyes, faith did not include tolerance and compromise. To Isabella, tolerance of heretical views undermined conviction, and lack of conviction led to religious chaos. If Christianity and its central message of salvation from Christ contained immutable truth, then the Church, as the vessel that propounded that truth, could function properly and with authority only if clarity, precision, and orthodoxy prevailed within it. Accordingly, dissent and heretical views had no business corrupting the Church. "As the Queen of Castile, Isabella was obliged to dispel religious anarchy from the Castilian church just as she had checked criminal disorder in its towns."[15]

Leading the charge to curb heresy in the Castilian Church were members of the Dominican Order, a formidable and influential group of priests founded by St. Dominic in 1216. Renowned for their intensity, brilliant preaching, and defense of orthodox teaching, the Dominicans counted among their members one of the Church's greatest theologians, St. Thomas Aquinas.

Two Dominicans—Alonso de Hojeda and a stern and forbidding priest whose name was later to become synonymous with the Spanish Inquisition: Tomás de Torquemada—sealed Isabella's mind in the matter. Like Talavera, Torquemada had *converso* blood and was a valued adviser to Isabella in his capacity as another of her personal confessors. De Hojeda and Torquemada convinced Isabella that false converts existed, compelling the queen to act.

In choosing to institute the Inquisition, Isabella was motivated not by malice but by good intentions. Her objective was to save her subjects' souls from eternal damnation. Isabella wanted false or dithering Christians to turn away from erroneous beliefs and commit wholeheartedly to the faith that led to eternal salvation. In trying to root out hypocritical Christians, she hoped to prevent the faith from being undermined. Above all, the queen wanted the repentance of souls in order that they might be led to Heaven. Queen Isabella also brought the Inquisition to Castile because she was spurred by an acute conscience. For she believed that to have "deliberately avert[ed] her eyes from the crime [of heresy], was . . . spiritually irresponsible, tantamount to committing heresy herself."[16] The queen did not institute the Inquisition cursorily but gave the matter careful thought, for "Isabella, pious and God-fearing though she was, was not an easy woman to convince."[17] Moreover, the queen "appears to have been by nature pragmatic, skeptical and ironic, not personally given to religious extremes."[18] She was also "strong-minded and impossible to intimidate."[19]

Having come to a decision, Queen Isabella and King Ferdinand formally requested a Papal Bull for the establishment of an Inquisition in Castile. Pope Sixtus IV granted it in 1478. Later the Pope disagreed over the manner in which the Inquisition was being conducted and its vulnerability to abuses. Isabella and Ferdinand objected, claiming that the effectiveness of their fight against heretics and infidels relied on their free rein over the Spanish Church. Sixtus IV eventually relented. The Pope ultimately assured Isabella of his confidence in her diligence over the matter. However, because everything associated with the Spanish Inquisition now fell squarely on the crown, whatever its positive and most certainly all its negative aspects became associated with Ferdinand and Isabella.

Far from enthusiastically enforcing the Inquisition, Isabella ordered a new catechism drawn up so that *conversos* might come to understand their faith better. The queen waited for two years, hoping that she would receive favorable reports. The reports, however, were overwhelmingly negative, a sign in Isabella's eyes that many *conversos* were not true believers. Ferdinand and Isabella felt compelled to act and in 1480 authorized the appointment of Inquisitors for Seville. The zealous Torquemada eventually became Grand Inquisitor of Spain.

Once the Inquisition began in earnest, fear and intimidation grew. The Inquisitors' demeanor added to the drama and heightened tensions. In keeping with the heavy duty before them, these men of the cloth often appeared forbidding. "The judges of the Holy Office took every denunciation seriously; they could not afford to treat any accusation lightly, for the eternal repose of the accused's souls was assumed to be at stake, and, in almost every case, the Inquisitors were men of great probity on whom their responsibility weighed heavily."[20] The Spanish Inquisition, which was to last beyond Isabella's lifetime, has earned a notorious reputation, yet "in its rules of evidence it was probably a notch above most contemporary courts, clerical or civil."[21]

The Inquisition had abusers, but

> even in the period when the gruesome turnover was most rapid, [it] was never gratuitously bloodthirsty, but generally mild by the standards of the time. By the very nature of its task few accused escaped without any form of punishment; this was because the crime of heresy was so destructive in its effects on the heretics's soul, that

it was better in case of doubt to assume guilt, and relieve the accused of the effects of his supposed sin by the imposition of confession and penance, than to give the prisoner the "benefit of the doubt." On the other hand, the overwhelming majority of the Inquisition's punishments were mild, ranging from simple acts of public penance to fining and imprisonment.... It is of course true that the Inquisitorial tribunals were ruthless in the use of torture to obtain evidence; but again, the barbarities of torture must be judged against the torments that awaited in hell a heretic who did not confess his fault.[22]

Moreover, "its judgments and its treatments of prisoners were on the whole less harsh than the sentences imposed by secular courts. During the three and half centuries of the Spanish Inquisition, 25,000 people are thought to have been sent to the stake. To keep this terrible and tragic figure in perspective, however, we should not forget the witchcraft scare that raged through Europe in the sixteenth and seventeenth centuries (and was treated with remarkable sanity by the Inquisition). In Germany alone, in the space of one hundred years, *100,000* so-called witches were burned to death."[23]

Queen Isabella's quest to cleanse the Castilian Church was not to end with the Inquisition. The queen, advised and aided by two highly trusted clerics, Hernando de Talavera and Francisco Jiménez de Cisneros, radically reformed the Church itself. Corruption, poor education, immorality, and lax piety were rooted out. The queen visited convents, where she had a positive effect on the nuns. Here, the queen "anticipated the appearance of another zealous reformer, St. Teresa of Ávila [St. Teresa of Jesus], whose writings would complete the spiritual transformation of the convents ninety years later."[24] It would appear that these two significant forces in the Spanish Church, St. Teresa and Queen Isabella, shared similar devotional writings. The Venerable Juan de Palafox, Bishop of Osuma, concluded "that if the saint had been queen she would have been another Catholic doña Isabella and if this enlightened Princess Isabella had been a nun, she would have been another St. Teresa."[25]

The changes Isabella imposed on the Church were thorough and transformative, making Spain "the nation par excellence of religious reform."[26] So successful were the queen's reforms that years later Spain avoided the religious turmoil that swept Europe and shattered the Church via the Reformation.

Queen Isabella had foreseen and masterfully created Spain's future design, one step at a time. Its proportions and features were clear to her, with perspective reinforced by her devotion. "The throne, once achieved, had to be strengthened and dignified. Royal authority established, the nobles could be brought into line. With the nobility subdued and cooperating, the social and economic ills of the country could be attended to—justice established, trade secured, the currency cleansed and reorganized. After the physical cure would come the spiritual: the Faith must be purified, the clergy reformed. United physically and spiritually, the nation could then move to its age-old dream, the conquest of Granada, the final expulsion of the Moors. After that the horizons were unlimited: Europe, Africa, the sea."[27]

King Ferdinand and Queen Isabella's quest to complete the Reconquista now took center stage. Isabella's upbringing was saturated with stories of her royal ancestors who had battled the Moors in order to win back for Christ the Iberian Peninsula. In the centuries since the Muslims had invaded the region in the eighth century, "the history of medieval Spain [was], more than anything else, the struggle for supremacy in that peninsula between the Muslims and Christians."[28] The southern kingdom of Granada remained the one territory left under Muslim rule. Isabella never stirred from her goal of reconquering Granada. Wrestling that kingdom from its Moorish rulers had always been for her a crucial goal. To have failed on that score would have meant that her reign had been a disaster.

The conquest of Granada "was an initial step in a larger campaign against Mohammedanism in which Spain eventually came to see itself as responsible for the defense of a Christian Europe increasingly threatened by the resurgent power of the Crescent."[29] The Muslim sieges of Constantinople and Otranto were just two of the most recent events that had stunned Europeans. For Castilians, the possibility that Spain could be the next target was a frightening prospect, especially if the Muslims from Africa and the Ottoman Empire combined forces. The Castilians' anxiety was no overreaction. The Mediterranean Sea and proximity to North Africa made the kingdom indeed vulnerable to attacks from marauding Islamic forces.

The fact that Granada, as the last holdout of Islamic rule in the peninsula, was still unconquered made the campaign to retake the area a paramount goal. It was thus to Andalusia, and Granada in particular, that King Ferdinand and Queen Isabella turned their attention in 1480. Granada was the jewel in the crown that was the long, drawn-out struggle known as the Reconquista, which had preoccupied Castile's monarchs since the eighth century.

From the 800s, the Reconquista increasingly took on a Christian purpose as foes of the Moors embraced as their patron saint the apostle James, son of Zebedee. St. James of Compostela, or Santiago de Compostela, also came to be known as Santiago Matamoros, *Matamoros* meaning "Moor slayer." It was believed that St. James (whose body was thought to have been discovered in Galicia, in northern Spain) had led Christians to triumph over the Moors. His scallop-shell symbol was soon emblazoned on Christian banners defiantly waved in battle.

The reconquest of Iberia by Castile's Christian kings had become so successful by the mid-thirteenth century that the kingdom of Granada was all that remained in Muslim hands. Consisting of the provinces of Almería to the east, Málaga to the west (both with their busy ports), and Granada in the center, the kingdom contained some 300,000 people at the time Isabella's campaign began in earnest. This narrow strip of land—some 180 miles long and 25 miles wide, surrounded on one side by the Mediterranean Sea and on the other by the Sierra Nevada—was a wealthy enclave, a vital link in the gold trade of Saharan Africa as well as a significant trade region for silk. The capital city, Granada, on two towering hills, was the heart of this thriving region; and crowning the capital was the Alhambra. Glistening like amber, the honey-tinted palace, home to Granada's kings, was a magnificent complex perched mightily above the city. A combination fortress, palace, and city, the Alhambra (its name meaning "red castle") appeared impregnable. Inside the complex were buildings decorated in fine Moorish style, with intricately carved stonework. The surroundings fanned out into beautiful gardens with fountains delicately spouting from the ground. Invading troops would have to fight hard to claim this fortress, the undisputable gem of the kingdom.

Granada was both a necessary and an irresistible prize in Isabella's eyes. Living in heady times, when opposing sides unapologetically fought to the hilt for their causes, Isabella had a reputation equal to those of Iberia's famed warriors of the past. Like these warriors—El Cid and St. Ferdinand—Queen Isabella committed to shape the destiny of Iberia, and to create a more vigorous and unified Christian identity in the process. She took up the mantle of her crusading forebears. She prepared to make good on her vow to liberate Granada from Islamic rule.

In 1476 Mulay Hassan, Granada's belligerent king, refused to give Ferdinand and Isabella their customary tribute, disdainfully sending the message that "the kings of Granada who paid tribute are dead; our mint now coins only blades of scimetars and heads of lances."[30] Angered by this defiance, the Spanish monarchs were unable to act, because they were embroiled in the War of the Castilian Succession. Mulay Hassan, meanwhile, interpreted their inaction as impotence.

Isabella convinced Ferdinand to acquiesce to her wishes regarding Granada. Defeat of the Moors had always been a shared objective of theirs, so much so that their marriage agreement had stipulated that Ferdinand would aid Isabella in this quest. Hence, instead of pursuing his own dream of regaining from the French the Catalan counties of Roussillon and Cerdagne, Ferdinand eventually threw his support behind Isabella's cause. It was not the first time that he conceded to her, nor was it to be the last. Among their contemporaries, it was Queen Isabella more than King Ferdinand who generally made a striking impression. More careful observers also noted the queen's ability to exercise "tangible control over her husband. The chronicler, Alonso de Palencia, recalls the impressions of a German traveler, Nicolaus von Poppelau, in 1481: 'The king did nothing without the consent of the queen; he did not seal his own letters until the queen had read them, and if the queen did not approve of one of them the secretary tore it up in the presence of the king himself.' "[31]

King Ferdinand was no lackey of the queen, however. His manly pride and own deep concern over the fate of Aragon were enough to get him and Isabella into occasional marital discord. Constantly subsuming Aragon's interest to that of Castile had the understandable effect of annoying Ferdinand. Yet he frequently deferred to Isabella's views, as injurious as doing so was to his pride. Married for over a decade, King Ferdinand had come to appreciate his wife's steadfastness, judgment, commitment, and unflagging energy. Not only did the king genuinely love his wife but he also had a profound admiration for Isabella's intelligence and devotion to their faith and to Spain. As a couple, personally and politically, they continued to be an ideal match, with much of their thinking meshing in harmony. In the case of the Granada War, Ferdinand and Isabella worked in tandem, drawing support and inspiration from each other, united in their desire to see the Reconquista completed.

To Isabella, war was a fact of life that could not be avoided. In waging war, however, her goal was always peace. For Isabella had "envisioned peace in a medieval fashion as a restoration of order. . . . Peace was a kingdom under a good ruler, a kingdom in equilibrium, harmony and justice, everyone doing what they should, behaving as they should. What they should do was to live life in accord with their status, soberly and morally."[32]

Emboldened by the monarchs' earlier inability to extract the tribute from him, Mulay Hassan launched a surprise attack in 1481 on the small Christian town of Zahara. Those who resisted were slain, while the rest of the population became slaves in Granada. The breaking of the truce and attack on Zahara enraged many Castilians, including Ferdinand and Isabella, who, having beaten the Portuguese in war and instituted the Inquisition, were now in a position to launch their attack against the Moors.

Hence, in 1482 the Christian offensive in Granada commenced. In retaliation, Queen Isabella's onetime foe the Marqués of Cádiz and his forces traversed the mountain passes and captured the wealthy town of Alhama, deep within Granada. The Christian takeover of Alhama made a profound impression on the Moors, who had thought that town impregnable. Cries of "Alhama is fallen! Alhama is fallen!" reverberated, along with "The key of Granada is in the hands of the enemy!"³³

The fall of Alhama, only twenty-five miles from the city of Granada, forced Mulay Hassan to fight. Ferdinand and Isabella then went to the aid of Cádiz. The king and his troops rode quickly toward Alhama, while Isabella went more slowly toward Córdoba. The queen took a slower pace because she was heavily pregnant. Nevertheless, her condition did not stop Isabella from gathering supplies, troops, and money for the war.

Because of the difficult terrain and its position inside enemy territory, the monarchs' advisers urged them to desert Alhama. The queen refused. Reminding her timid counselors what war entailed, Isabella retorted that "it was well known that all wars extracted high costs and required labor. That had been carefully considered before the King and I entered upon the idea of the conquest against the King of Granada; this city [Alhama] is the first we have won and it was thus impossible to contemplate giving it back."³⁴ At that, Ferdinand marched to Alhama and took possession of the city; Mulay Hassan again retreated. In keeping with the religious overtone of the war, a pattern was set whereby mosques were consecrated as churches by order of the queen, their interiors adorned with opulent Christian symbols such as valuable chalices, richly textured altarcloths, and gilt crosses given by Isabella herself.

Yet garrisoning Alhama was risky and costly. Counselors to the monarchs at one point advised them to demolish the town, but Isabella indignantly dismissed this suggestion. To do so would be to have fought in vain and to dishonor the dead who paid the ultimate price to win Alhama for Christianity. "What!" cried the mortified queen, "what then, shall we destroy the first fruits of our victories, shall we abandon the first place we have wrested from the Moors? Never let us suffer such an idea to occupy our minds. It would give new courage to the enemy, arguing fear or feebleness in our councils. You talk of the toil and expense of maintaining Alhama; did we doubt, on undertaking this war that it was to be a war of infinite cost, labor, and bloodshed? And shall we shrink from the cost, the moment a victory is obtained, and the question is merely to guard or abandon its glorious trophy? Let us hear no more of the destruction of Alhama; let us maintain its walls sacred, as a strong-hold granted us by Heaven in the centre of this hostile land, and let our only consideration be, how to extend our conquest, and capture the surrounding cities."[35] Queen Isabella won her point; Alhama was not destroyed.

In the midst of preparations to extend the campaign against the Moors in June 1482, with Isabella heavily engaged in provisioning the Castilian troops through methodical requests for artillery and food, the queen went into labor in Córdoba. The delivery was particularly traumatic, the worst of her confinements, because she gave birth to twins. Only one, María, named in honor of the Virgin Mary, survived. Motherhood did not keep Queen Isabella from focusing on prosecuting the war against the Moors.

The Granada War was a decadelong series of battles and skirmishes numbering in the thousands. Moorish fortresses and towns took advantage of the kingdom's hilly terrain. They were strategically built in dominating fashion. Therefore, battles took the form of sieges, often reliant on heavy artillery, which the Castilians lacked. Unfazed by the challenge, Queen Isabella scoured her country and Europe for help. She ordered the nobility to provide leadership and men for the fight. She also requisitioned each district to furnish troops and artillery. From Italy came twelve-foot Lombard guns capable of throwing marble bullets weighing up to 165 pounds from twenty-inch muzzles. These heavy guns successfully pounded the enemy's formidable fortifications. From Flanders and Sicily came engineers. Swiss mercenaries, among the finest fighting men on the Continent, and soldiers from present-day France, Germany, Italy, England, and faraway Poland arrived. Isabella's Granada venture united Europe's peoples in a common cause. The war also united the Spanish populace like never before, despite the difficulties and sacrifices that such a prolonged engagement entailed. "For a decade the conflict harnessed the energies of the entire population of southern Spain in providing soldiers, food and supplies; the inevitable state of emergency provoked a huge rise in prices in Andalucia. It was a total effort by one civilisation to subdue another."[36]

As leaders, Ferdinand and Isabella apportioned their tasks, each taking roles that suited his or her talents. Ferdinand led and fought in the battlefield, while Isabella, as usual, excelled in multitasking. A dynamo whose ceaseless activity as quartermaster contributed greatly to the successful prosecution of the war, Isabella was able to solve problems involving everything from men-at-arms to matériel. Gathering enough men to fight, plus supplies, artillery, and animals, was a daunting and continual demand, as were the geographic challenges found throughout Granada. Transporting men, supplies, and artillery through mountainous terrain and treacherous cliffs interspersed with rocky valleys could be nightmarish. Added to all this was the fighting spirit of the Muslims. Ruthless and fearless, they were exceptionally gifted horsemen. Fighting on horseback, they were especially frightening to their enemies. A determined Isabella did not let these staggering difficulties stand in her way. Nothing and no one was going to stop her from vanquishing the Moors. Once she had acquired the men and artillery she needed, the queen tackled the problem of transporting this army numbering in the tens of thousands. She requisitioned oxen and mules. Men were sent ahead to clear the way for the people, artillery, and supplies needed to battle the enemy.

Isabella also created field hospitals, the Queen's Hospitals, the first time such an endeavor was instituted in western Europe. The hospitals were much admired and spurred other European countries to emulation. The Queen's Hospitals consisted of six large tents set up in the battlefield, designed to care for over a thousand wounded soldiers. Surgeons and nurses, paid from the queen's purse, tended to the wounded and the sick. Some four hundred covered wagons served as ambulances. Of all Isabella's endeavors in her role as quartermaster, her hospitals proved to be the most humanitarian. They were also evidence of the queen's consummate attention to details.

Isabella also saw to the war's funding. Two prominent Jews—Abraham Senor and Isaac Abravenel—lent their extensive financial expertise to the crown and helped bring in desperately needed money. The queen contributed personally to the war chest when she pawned her jewels to help pay her soldiers.

In this protracted struggle between Christians and Muslims, there were inevitable setbacks on each side, and casualties were high. In 1483, the Castilian army suffered humiliating defeats, and the best of Castile's nobility were among the many wounded, captured, or killed. The Castilians' fortune, however, turned favorable soon enough, thanks to the capture of Boabdil.

Boabdil was the son of Mulay Hassan by his concubine Zoroya, a lovely blue-eyed blonde who had been a Christian slave. Boabdil, diminutive and blond like his mother, had grown into a young man with little of his father's fiery nature and natural fighting abilities. Though he was the designated heir, Boabdil was unpopular among his countrymen. Zoroya, upon hearing of her son's capture, offered a highly tempting ransom that involved the release of many Christian prisoners in Moorish hands. Some thought there was no choice but to accept this offer. Others thought Boabdil had to remain a captive. Unable to reach a compromise, all conceded that the decision must be left to Queen Isabella. She promptly ordered that Boabdil be released after securing a guarantee from him that he had now become the Castilian monarchs' vassal. From then on, Boabdil was duty-bound to aid the Castilians in their fight for Granada. He was thus required to betray his father.

Queen Isabella's decision was a clever one, for it played off the internal rivalries that beset the Nasrid dynasty of Granada. Zoroya, it turned out, had been spurned after many years by Mulay Hassan for a Greek slave, Ayesha. Fearing the loss of her influence and power as well as of Boabdil's inheritance, Zoroya fomented a rebellion within Granada. By playing on this internecine rivalry, the astute Isabella had hoped to further weaken the dynasty.

Throughout the decadelong struggle, Queen Isabella never tired or wavered. Nothing was too arduous, nothing too demanding. "She braved hardships, long journeys on horseback; she hurried to the post of danger, regardless of weather or ill health; she cased her body in armour . . . appeared at the head of her armies, and . . . communicated to them her dauntless spirit. . . . She arrived in person, at critical moments, the harbinger of victory . . . she was the soul and spirit of the campaign."[37]

In the spring of 1485, King Ferdinand, accompanied by many of Castile's nobility, marched toward Ronda, another city perched on a rocky promontory, protected by a mighty citadel and surrounded on three sides by walls and towers. A frighteningly precipitous ravine also surrounded the city. The prospect of taking Ronda was daunting, yet if successful, the city's capture would help isolate the port of Málaga. And so Ferdinand set off to tighten the noose on Granada. Queen Isabella, meanwhile, supported her husband and troops by sending enormous amounts of supplies, including four thousand animals to haul them. All in all, it took 25,000 soldiers and 13,000 horses for the Castilians to lay siege to Ronda.

After two weeks' fighting, Ronda fell in May, the white flag of surrender clearly signaling another victory for Ferdinand and Isabella. Upon entering the city, Castilian forces raised the cross over the citadel's tower, along with the royal banner and that of Santiago. The elderly Cardinal Mendoza, who frequently accompanied King Ferdinand in his battles, made his way to the main mosque to consecrate it. Thus, following previous custom, "conquered mosques were ritually purified and rededicated as churches, to Santa María de la Encarnación, the Spíritu Sancti, Santiago, San Juan el Evangelista, and San Sebastián, the last quite possibly a barbed response to the Muslims increasing use of poisoned arrows."* True to form, Queen Isabella sent bells, crosses, vestments, and altarpieces to these newly consecrated churches.[38]

Undoubtedly one of the most moving scenes after the capture of Ronda came when the gates of the city's dungeon were flung open. Out came ragged Christian captives—men, women, and children—whose skeletal frames chained to leg irons provoked pity from their deliverers. Isabella met these people on the steps of Córdoba's cathedral. The newly freed captives, with matted hair and few clothes, fell on their knees in gratitude, weeping at her feet. Deeply moved by their plight, Queen Isabella had them fed and cared for. As a reminder to future generations of what the Granada War was about, Isabella ordered that the rusting chains that had imprisoned these captives be attached to the walls of San Juan de los Reyes in Toledo.

The fall of Ronda made a deep impression on the Moors. Some ninety-four towns in western Granada gave up to the Castilians. However, another setback demoralized the Castilians when the Count of Cabra and his troops suffered a defeat at the Moors' hands at Moclin. Ferdinand wrote to Isabella asking for her advice as he rode to Cabra's rescue. Along with Cardinal Mendoza, she agreed to the Bishop of Jaén's suggestion that Ferdinand attack the castles of Cambil and Albahar before storming Moclin. Ferdinand complied with his wife's wishes. However, once he neared the castles, the king found it impossible to move his heavy artillery through the mountainous terrain. Undeterred, Queen Isabella commanded that the impossible be done. Some six thousand men were ordered to labor day and night, carefully disassembling nature's barricades. The laborers created nine long miles of road, opening the way for the Christians to advance. Simply put, it was a stupefying feat. "Almost an entire mountain was levelled, valleys were filled up, trees hewn down, rocks broken and overturned; in short, all the obstacles which nature had heaped around, entirely and promptly vanished. In little more than twelve days, this gigantic work was effected, and the ordnance dragged to the camp, to the great triumph of the Christians and confusion of the Moors."[39] The Moors, unable to defeat the Christians' destructive fighting, surrendered the castles to King Ferdinand. As it turned out, even mountains fell to Queen Isabella's imposing will.

Such were the times during Isabella's last pregnancy. She returned to Córdoba but did not settle there for the impending birth. Instead, because of the floods in the city, which came with the incessant rains, Cardinal Mendoza sug-

---

*Saint Sebastian, an early Christian martyr, is often portrayed shot with arrows.

gested that she and the court stay at his palace at Alcalá de Henares. A grateful Isabella accepted. Alcalá de Henares, the favored city of the archbishops of Toledo, was on a riverbank on the Meseta and fortified by massive walls. In the well-appointed palace, with its courtyards and gardens, Queen Isabella gave birth on December 16, 1485, to her last child, a girl she named Catalina, who one day would come to be known in history as Catherine of Aragon.

Though Isabella was Castilian in habit and thought, the blood of English ancestors coursed in her veins. She descended from the Plantagenet and Lancastrian royal houses. John of Gaunt's daughter Catherine of Lancaster was Isabella's paternal grandmother, and it was this English great-grandmother for whom Catherine of Aragon was named. Another of Princess Catherine's ancestors was the famous Eleanor of Aquitaine, queen consort of King Henry II of England. This was a lineage that portended Catherine of Aragon's later role as the first of Henry VIII's queens.

Added to the excitement over Princess Catherine's birth, and the victories at Ronda and Moclin, a letter from the immensely wealthy and influential Andalusian noble the Duke of Medinaceli caught Queen Isabella's attention. He had written to discuss a certain seaman who intended to sail the sea to the west. The duke urged Isabella to meet with this individual and possibly sponsor his endeavor. The seaman's name was Christopher Columbus. Medinaceli believed that if Castile did not sponsor the adventurer, Columbus was sure to offer his services instead to France. Well aware of the limited funds available, Isabella could not take on this seafaring adventure. Nevertheless, she did not want the mariner approaching the French and so instructed Medinaceli to send the thirty-five-year-old Columbus to her. They finally met in April 1486 in Córdoba. The intrepid navigator from Genoa had carefully cultivated friendships and acquaintances among those who counted in Castile. He was now before the king and queen, the highest personages in the land. At last, the two extraordinary visionaries whose impact can still be felt in many parts of the world met face-to-face. Columbus cleverly appealed to the queen's two abiding passions, "the purification of the church and conversion of the infidel. Columbus raised the possibility of discovering new lands and people who could be converted to Christianity as well as the wealth that would accrue to the crown from a new route to the Orient."[40]

Still, Isabella was not ready to commit. Instead, the queen prescribed that theologians and scholars study Columbus's project and report back their findings. For the time being, a war needed to be won. Despite several reversals, Ferdinand and Isabella's victories rapidly multiplied. More than ever, the monarchs were bent on vanquishing their enemies. And vital to the war effort was the queen herself. Isabella, ever industrious, diligent, and unrelenting, was well on her way to becoming the conqueror of Granada.

4

THE WONDER OF EUROPE

fter only a decade on the throne, Isabella had reined in Castile's disparate elements—from the lowliest to the mightiest. In such a brief time, the queen had burnished the crown to a luster unthinkable at her accession. The monarchy was feared and, more important, respected, within Castile and outside. In 1484 a foreign visitor reported that "everyone trembled at the name of the queen."[1] Even incremental successes by Ferdinand and Isabella in the Granada War had raised their reputation to new heights on the Continent—so much so, in fact, that "Isabella and Ferdinand's victories over the Granada Moors were rapidly assuming legendary proportions in ducal palaces and manor houses across Western Europe."[2]

Onlookers throughout the Western world were impressed by the Castilians' progress in Granada under the leadership of their queen. The Granada War was one in a long line of bloody clashes that pitted Islam against Christianity. While the crescent triumphed in Moldavia in eastern Europe, and in areas by the Black Sea, King Ferdinand was emboldened by Ronda's fall. Isabella sent letters to her husband, sharing her insights, telling him that she prayed to God "until He gives you the city and all the kingdom. . . . The dead weigh on me heavily, but they could not have gone better employed."[3]

Now in her mid-thirties, Isabella had lost none of the vigor and confidence that she had possessed in her youth. In fact, the queen was busier than ever, ceaselessly thinking, plotting strategy, acting, and constantly on the move. She prodded her counselors for advice, pushed her secretaries to work furiously, thought always of her armies and acted on their behalf, urged on Ferdinand and his generals, and prayed endlessly for victory.

Assiduous in attaining her goals, Isabella possessed incredible energy that she used toward achieving her objectives. The queen had no patience when it came to "notions of irresistible fate. She believed that the human will, under God, was the supreme factor in existence."[4] When it came to exercising that will during the Reconquista, Isabella directed it to absolute victory. Indefatigable throughout the decadelong struggle, the queen exuded energy, hope, and confidence. King Ferdinand appreciated and treasured this quality in his wife and deployed her in times of necessity, such as her visits to the troops. In sum, Queen Isabella was indispensable to the campaign's success.

Isabella did not disappoint when she visited her soldiers. During one such visit, she appeared every inch the queen seated on a chestnut mule with a saddle of silver gilt. Dressed dazzlingly in brocade and velvet, her head adorned by a black hat embroidered on the crown and rim, Isabella inspected the thousands of men who paid her homage. Accompanying the queen was her teenage daughter, Isabel, equally bedecked in velvet and brocade, and the infant Princess Catherine. Queen Isabella told her soldiers, "You should be happy because as knights you have defended the Faith from the dangers that threaten the land that have caused us so much hardship in this life. God knows our cause and will not forget our difficulties and will remember them in the other [world]."[5]

The Christians' successes increased in part because they astutely stoked the divisions that racked the Moorish leadership. Instead of uniting, as the Castilians and Europeans had now done in the face of their common enemy, Islam, the Moorish leadership continued to fight for supremacy among themselves. Rivalries among Boabdil, his uncle, El Zagal, and Mulay Hassan did nothing to help their cause. At one point, Mulay Hassan fled Granada, as did El Zagal, allowing Boabdil to be proclaimed king. Then El Zagal and his followers forced Boabdil to flee to Castile, leaving Granada with yet another ruler. Old Mulay Hassan died in 1485, concentrating the rivalry between El Zagal and Boabdil.

In 1485, the Castilians fought hard to win Málaga, an important port on the Mediterranean. The city was ringed by mountains and the sea, as well as fortified by artillery and eager warriors for Islam. Castile's army found the fighting difficult, but fight on they did, with seventy thousand men under King Ferdinand's orders. Málaga resisted the onslaught. At one point, a stalemate ensued, prompting the Moors to circulate rumors designed to discourage the Castilians. Ferdinand then reached for one of the most reliable weapons at his disposal: He called for his wife.

Not surprisingly, the queen, now a legend among the troops, came willingly.

Isabella urged her soldiers at Málaga on, bolstered their confidence, reassured them of their just cause. Again, the queen's presence and words had an electrifying effect. Emboldened, Isabella's men fought on, supported by the timely arrival of desperately needed reinforcements. Ferdinand then invited Málaga's citizens to surrender, to which they replied with a barrage of artillery fire. But by keeping their nerve, the Castilians soon had the advantage.

Ferdinand's patience finally gave way when the city's leaders threatened to burn Málaga and hang their Christian prisoners. He answered the threat with his own ominous warning that, if a single Christian captive were harmed, he would put the whole of Málaga to the sword. This had the desired effect. Málaga surrendered unconditionally in August 1487.

Upon entering the city, Ferdinand and Isabella's troops scoured Málaga for Christian captives. All in all, some sixteen hundred men and women were freed, a number of them having been chained in dungeons from five to twenty years. The king and queen entered Málaga and inside a tent, before a makeshift altar, met with these wretched captives, many still in chains. When these former prisoners "found themselves restored to liberty, and surrounded by their countrymen, some stared wildly about as if in a dream, others gave way to frantic transports, but most of them wept for joy."[6] Upon meeting their king and queen, the grateful captives fell on their knees and tried to kiss Ferdinand's and Isabella's feet, but were prevented from doing so by the monarchs. The newly freed captives "then prostrated themselves before the altar, and all present joined them in giving thanks to God for their liberation from this cruel bondage."[7] The king and queen ordered the prisoners freed from their chains. They were then clothed, fed, and given money to return to their homes.

The royal couple chose the city of Baza for the next round of fighting. The capture of Baza, a Moorish stronghold under El Zagal, was a necessary step for the Castlians to complete their reconquest. It was a daunting task, for the approach to Baza was covered by thick groves, the city itself encircled by a formidable fortress and mountains. Yet strategically, the Christian capture of Baza made sense. It would mean that the Castilians had taken the east, leaving the capital, Granada, completely vulnerable. Two years in the making, the attack on Baza, the beginning of the eastern campaign, took many months to complete, because of fierce resistance from the Moors. Casualties on the Castilian side amounted to a staggering twenty thousand men. Retreat was on everyone's mind—except Isabella's. Instead, she faced the appalling challenges head-on. Working furiously to get help to Ferdinand and the troops, the queen dispatched six thousand men to clear the roads, then ordered supplies sent through. Even an empty treasury, the result of years of war, did not stop her. The queen begged for more funds from Jews and magnates. Isabella then unhesitatingly pawned more of her precious jewels.

Even resupplied, the soldiers remained dispirited under harsh conditions, prompting Ferdinand to call again for his wife. In early November 1489, at Baza, Queen Isabella buoyed her troops' morale so that the men felt ready to bear arms again for their queen and their faith. The army cheered wildly for their queen. " 'Her presence filled us with joy,' " noted an eyewitness, " 'and re-animated our spirits, which were sinking under the weight of such long perils, vigils and sufferings.' Even the Moors suspended hostilities and leaned from their battlements to watch."[8] Isabella's presence in Baza startled the Moors, who viewed the queen as an unbeatable enemy. Miraculously, only three days later, El Zagal surrendered Baza and his other territories unexpectedly to the Castilians. The long-held dream of capturing Granada itself could very well turn into a reality under Queen Isabella's reign.

The years had made Isabella a little stouter; nearly forty, she no longer enjoyed the flush of youth so evident when she married. But the queen still retained the personal qualities that made her such a fascinating figure. Among the qualities that served Isabella and her cause well was a tenacious spirit. To Isabella, the impossible was not some unconquerable obstacle but an opportunity to push herself to heroic proportions. Tireless, optimistic, and supremely confident, the queen became the army's indispensable patron.

As the Christians were now encamped near the fabled city of Granada, Queen Isabella had expressed a wish to see the last stronghold of the Moors. From the nearby town Zubia, the queen, King Ferdinand, and their children gazed upon the beauty of Granada, a city they had heard much of and yearned so long to bring into the Castilian fold. Princess Catherine was only five years old at the time, a special joy to her mother, as the youngest often are. Together, the royal family marveled at the Alhambra, the ultimate symbol of Islamic domination in the Iberian Peninsula.

The Christians' final conquest seemed imminent. It was as if all the pieces were falling into place. Victory was inexorably on the march for the Castilians. But an unexpected disaster nearly ruined everything. One evening after Isabella had retired, the flame from a candle brushed the silken folds of the royal pavilion. In an instant, the queen's tent was engulfed in fire and asphyxiating smoke. Soon the whole camp was up in flames. Isabella narrowly escaped with her family. By the time it was all over, nearly everything had been incinerated, but the royals were unhurt. Refusing to be bowed by this setback, Ferdinand

and Isabella ordered that a new encampment be built. What rose after three months of frenzied work was a city of stone laid out in the form of a cross, complete with towers, from the tallest of which was raised the famous massive silver cross that the Christian army always took to battle. The soldiers asked her permission to name the city Isabella. The queen, though touched by the gesture, refused. She insisted instead that the name be Santa Fe, or Holy Faith, to remind one and all of the nature of the Granada War.

The building of Santa Fe completely demoralized the people of Granada. As they lost hope, hunger set in. King Ferdinand and his troops employed their usual tactic, blocking the flow of food into the capital. Military resistance by the Moors soon crumbled. By autumn, secret negotiations were opened, ending with the signing of the articles of capitulation.

The day for the official handover was January 2, 1492. Boabdil, with his family and fifty retainers, made his way out of the city to meet the king and deliver the keys of Granada. King Ferdinand, Queen Isabella, their children, and the court, dressed festively for the momentous occasion, were not yet at Granada but "near the village of Armilla, their eyes fixed on the towers of the royal fortress, watching for the appointed signal of possession."[9] Then came the moment everyone had been waiting for. From the Torre de la Vela (the Great Watch Tower) of the Alhambra rose the glimmering silver cross, signaling that the Christians had taken possession of Granada. Next came the thrilling sight of the royal banner and that of St. James fluttering from the Alhambra. With this shouts of joy rang out from the Christian army: "Santiago! Santiago! Castile! Castile! For King Ferdinand and Queen Isabella!"

With the Reconquista now completed and their greatest triumph fulfilled, the king and queen fell on their knees in gratitude to God, followed by a multitude around them numbering in the thousands. The royal choir then sang the hymn of praise *Te Deum laudamus*. "And such was the happiness that they all began to cry. Later [that day] all the great lords, who were with the king, went to where the queen was and kissed her hand [in obeisance] as queen of Granada."[10]

His deed done, a dejected Boabdil left for his small territory in the Alpujarras region. Unable to resist one last look at his former kingdom, Boabdil turned and gazed upon the city for the last time. His indignant mother then admonished the broken son with the words "You do well to weep like a woman for what you failed to defend like a man!"[11] The place where Boabdil saw Granada for the last time thereafter was known as "the Last Sigh of the Moor."

King Ferdinand and Queen Isabella, in a procession that stood out for its magnificent pomp and ceremony, made their formal entry into Granada on

January 6, 1492, the feast day of the Epiphany. In another moving encounter with captured Christians, this time with some five hundred still in chains, the sovereigns released the group overcome with tears of joyful deliverance.

Once their entourage made its way to the main mosque, now reconsecrated as a church, the royal couple attended a Mass to give thanks, then made their way to the Alhambra. From the presence chamber that had been for so long the seat of Moorish power in Iberia, a triumphant King Ferdinand and Queen Isabella held court, receiving the homage of Granada's inhabitants.

Isabella and Ferdinand "had brought the epic to triumphant conclusion, rung down the curtain on a dazzling new act in the mounting drama of their career. Nothing had been wasted; everything had been justified, explained, crowned by God—the years of labor and privation, the long nights of numb fingers at a piled desk, the planning, the riding, the sleety passes and dark gorges, the wounds and suffering of their people, the blood . . . the dead."[12]

A jubilant King Ferdinand sent the news of the Moorish empire's end to Pope Innocent VIII, telling him that "this kingdom of Granada, which for over 780 years was occupied by infidels . . . has been secured."[13] Rome was ecstatic, with Masses said in thanksgiving, the city illuminated, and bells pealing throughout. No less rapturous was the reaction through the rest of Europe, where in many capitals bonfires were lit and church bells rang in celebration.

The bells in St. Paul's Cathedral in London also rang in thanksgiving. Inside the cathedral a solemn Mass was held, ordered by England's King Henry VII. Greatly impressed by Ferdinand and Isabella's victory over the Moors, King Henry ordered the prelates and noblemen at court to march to the cathedral. There, they heard the Lord Chancellor praising the victors of Granada and telling those present about "the prowess and devotion of Ferdinando and Isabella, kings of Spain; who have, to their immortal honor, recovered the great and rich kingdom of Granada . . . for which this assembly and all Christians are to render laud and thanks to God, and to celebrate this noble act. . . . Whereby it is to be hoped that there shall be gained not only new territory, but infinite souls to the Church of Christ."[14]

Fernando del Pulgar, Isabella's secretary and chronicler, had no doubt as to who should be credited with the success of the Granada War: "War against the Moors began at this queen's behest, and continued by her diligence until the entire realm of Granada was won."[15] The conquest of Granada was without a doubt Queen Isabella's greatest triumph. Not without reason was she considered "the Wonder of Europe."[16] And because Isabella was a woman during an era dominated by men, her accomplishments were all the more unique.

After the victory at Granada, Isabella was not content to rest on her laurels. She left herself little time to recuperate at the Alhambra, which now became her palace. There were more plans to conceive and execute, more goals to accomplish. Far from being distinguished by one significant event, the year 1492 was the *annus mirabilis,* or the miracle year, of Spanish history, which saw three momentous events: the conquest of Granada, the expulsion of the Jews, and Columbus sailing off under the patronage of Queen Isabella.

Christopher Columbus was among those who witnessed the historic surrender of Granada. Born in 1451 to a Genoese weaver, Columbus, a contemporary of Isabella's, dreamed of lands beyond the sea. Isabella had created a committee to look into this "Enterprise of the Indies."

In 1489, this committee returned their verdict. They rejected the navigator's plan, concluding that it was impossible to achieve. After the surrender of Granada, Isabella and Columbus met. When he received an answer, it was a definitive no. A dejected Columbus accepted the final verdict and prepared to go to France. However, one of the adventurer's supporters, the *converso* Luís de Santángel, Keeper of the Privy Purse, pleaded with Queen Isabella to invite Columbus back. To let him go now, argued Santángel, would be to miss a golden opportunity and allow another power to reap the benefits that might accrue from his voyage of discovery. Funds for the project, Santángel told the queen, could be found. After receiving Columbus again in audience, Ferdinand and Isabella agreed to the explorer's plans on his terms. He would become admiral and viceroy, as well as governor-general of undiscovered lands. He would also be entitled to one-tenth of the profits from the venture. A grateful Columbus wrote that "in all men there was disbelief, but to the Queen, my lady, God gave the spirit of understanding and great courage."[17] Isabella, ever the visionary, took the risk.

In August 1492, under the patronage of Queen Isabella of Castile, Christopher Columbus set sail at last with his crew on three ships, the *Niña,* the *Pinta,* and the *Santa María.* On the other side of the vast Atlantic, unexplored lands awaited him. Far from discovering a new route to the Orient, Columbus was about to discover a new world. History was set to be made.

The third significant event of 1492 took place before Columbus set sail. The Charter of the Expulsion of the Jews, which occurred in the spring, was one of Ferdinand and Isabella's most controversial acts. The expulsion was carried out in the name of "unity."

The conquest of Granada had gone a long way to achieve the unity central to Isabella's aspirations. Although physical unity was intact, the monarchs still "had not achieved religious unity, since large numbers of Jews and still larger numbers of Muslims remained in the lands under their rule."[18] It was this form of unity—religious—that Isabella believed was essential for Castile. In a modern pluralistic society, this fixation on religious unity is incomprehensible. However, Queen Isabella lived in an era saturated by faith. She believed unequivocally that Christianity was the one true religion; therefore it is unsurprising that she was determined to have as many of her subjects as possible adhere to that faith, so that their souls might not be excluded from God's promise of salvation.

For Ferdinand and Isabella, the Islamic-Jewish situation was tied to two dangers confronting Castile. These dangers were first political and military. A Muslim threat from North Africa and the Ottoman Turks pressing westward through land and sea was still a distinct possibility.

> The other danger was religious. In this respect, Islam was no longer seen as a dangerous enemy. In a theological calculation, it could, so to speak be discounted . . . [for] the attraction of Islam to converts, so powerful in the days of Muslim advance, waned with the Muslim retreat. Even the mighty victories of the Ottomans did not, as had the earlier victories of the caliphs, persuade large numbers of the conquered that Islam was indeed God's true religion.
>
> The Jews, however, were a different matter. . . . Being pre-Christian and not post-Christian, [their faith] could not be dismissed as a heresy or an aberration. . . . The Hebrew Bible, renamed the Old Testament, had been adopted by the Christians, who added a new testament to it, explaining how Christ had come to complete the revelation and to fulfill the promises that God had given to the Jews. By this logic, the Jews should have been the first to welcome and to accept the new dispensation and to merge their identity in the Christian church as the new beneficiary of God's choice.
>
> Many Jews did indeed accept this view and were the nucleus of what later became Christendom. But the persistent refusal of others and the survival of Judaism as a separate religion were seen by many Christians as impugning the central tenets of their faith. Jews, unlike Muslims, could not be accused of not knowing the Old Testament or of being unaware of the Choice and the Promise. Their unwillingness to accept the Christian interpretation of these books and of these doctrines thus challenged Christianity in a most sensitive area.[19]

"No doubt for good practical as well as ideological reasons, [Ferdinand and Isabella had] turned their attention first to the Jews, the most threatening to Christian teachings, and the most vulnerable to Christian power."[20]

Torquemada had urged the king and queen to rid Castile and Aragon of the Jews. Yet Isabella hesitated. She had never harbored a personal dislike toward Jews; high-standing Jewish individuals served the crown. Moreover, she understood the important financial role Jews played in Castile and Aragon. However, the queen received disturbing information on supposed ongoing attempts by Jews to bring *conversos* back to Judaism. "By the end of 1491 the monarchs seem to have become convinced that unbaptized Jews, even when subject to these laws, were having such a bad influence on converts that they should either become Christians themselves or leave."[21] The king and queen decided on drastic measures: the Jews must leave. Added to Isabella's desire to have uniformity of religion in the land was a belief that this uniformity would lead to greater stability. Expelling the Jews "was relatively safe and easy. It also provided useful experience for the later, greater, more difficult, and vastly more important task of expelling the Muslims."[22]

The order to expel the Jews was signed in April 1492 and gave them only three months to decide their fates. The expulsion was not unprecedented in Europe. King Edward I of England had expelled Jews from his kingdom in 1290, compelling some sixteen thousand to leave. King Philip IV ordered Jews expelled from France in 1306, confiscating their belongings in the process. These Jewish expulsions paled in comparison, however, with that of Spain. The expulsion there was a wretched chapter in Spanish history and darkened Isabella's otherwise unparalleled achievements.

No one has agreed on the exact number of Jews who were expelled. Some estimates put it between 150,000 and 800,000. However, a respected historian of Spain believes that "out of a likely total Jewish population in Castile of 70,000 and in Aragon of 10,000, many accepted baptism and others left the country only to return again, so that the figure for those who left permanently could not have been more than about 50,000."[23]

Once the Jews were expelled, Ferdinand and Isabella continued implementing religious uniformity. They zeroed in on the Moorish population, specifically the *elches,* who were "converts from Christianity to Islam, or Muslims of Christian descent."[24] Here, as with the *conversos,* the problem of apostasy ranked high with the monarchs. Again, questions of loyalty or power loomed, but it was, above all, "sadness at the loss of their souls [which] was a source of great personal grief to the monarchs."[25]

After Hernando de Talavera became Archbishop of Granada in 1492, he directed a concerted effort to bring Muslims into the Christian fold. Talavera promoted a policy of persuasion, even learning Arabic so that he could communicate the tenets of Catholicism more easily to the Moors. "Doubtful of the merits of the Inquisition" and realizing that "converted Moors would need time to assimilate their new faith," Talavera even managed to get the Moors exempted from the Inquisition's investigation for forty years.[26] His policy of persuasion brought conversions but at a slower pace than others, including the more rigid Archbishop Cisneros, would have preferred. Cisneros's arrival in Granada in 1499 would signal a major change.

Isabella nominated Francisco Jiménez de Cisneros, a Franciscan, as Archbishop of Toledo. Many found Cisneros a religious hard-liner. To others, he was a religious leader sincere about his faith but necessarily dogmatic for the good of the Church and for the sake of others. The archbishop was a powerful force who enjoyed the full confidence of the queen. Impressed by his reputation for sanctity, Isabella asked Cisneros to be her confessor. He accepted on condition that he not reside at court, lest he become corrupted by life away from his monastery. Forbidding and austere, Cisneros was an ascetic who fasted and denied himself all but the very basic necessities in life, often sleeping on the ground and subsisting on bread and water. Queen Isabella would continue to look to him as a valued adviser.

By the end of the fifteenth century, Cisneros played an active role in the Moorish situation in Granada. Impatient with the pace of conversions, Ferdinand and Isabella ordered Cisneros to help Talavera. In the end, the archbishop convinced the queen that Granada's Moors had to be given the choice of converting or expulsion just like the Jews. The king and queen hoped their Moorish subjects would eventually convert. In practice, however, the Moors were forced to convert, with few being allowed to leave. By the beginning of the sixteenth century, the *moriscos,* or Christian Moors, had come into being. In their dealings with the Moorish and Jewish peoples who inhabited their realms, King Ferdinand and Queen Isabella remained focused on the centrality of "constructing the Spanish nation-state around the principle of religious homogeneity, or *máximo religioso.*" This concept was not a novel one. "The *máximo religioso* has a clear medieval origin: [whereby] Christian doctrine is not an opinion man can choose to support, but rather an eternal truth; one and absolute, it makes whoever possesses it the son of God and inheritor of heaven, and denies the unfaithful eternal salvation."[27] By the early 1500s, Ferdinand and Isabella had clearly done their utmost to implement the concept of *máximo religioso,* exacting a heavy price in the process. Ferdinand and Isabella's defense of the faith plus their actions on behalf of the Papacy against King Charles VIII of France had earned them the title the Catholic Kings (*Los Reyes Católicos*) from Pope Alexander VI in 1496.

Four years before Ferdinand and Isabella received this title, Christopher Columbus discovered a new continent when his expedition arrived at a small island (in what became part of the Bahamas) in October 1492. The discovery delivered a new frontier for Isabella's cherished Catholicism. During Columbus's first voyage, he also discovered Cuba and Hispaniola. He named the lands he found Santa María de la Concepción, Fernandino, Isabella, and Juana. Columbus returned to a hero's welcome and met Ferdinand and Isabella at court in Barcelona in April 1493. The monarchs, accompanied by their son, Prince Juan, were seated in splendor under a gold canopy. In rising to greet Columbus, they bestowed a rare honor, one usually reserved to princes of the blood. The explorer, accompanied by an exotic mix of live parrots and six natives adorned in gold, regaled a rapt audience with stories of his expedition. Impressed by Columbus's accomplishments, Isabella approved a second expedition, this time involving seventeen vessels and over a thousand men, consisting of adventurers, farmers, soldiers, and priests.

By the mid-1490s, Isabella was the triumphant queen. Spain was recognized internationally as a power to be reckoned with. She accomplished what so many generations of Castile's monarchs had tried to achieve: the completion of the Reconquista, and in the process Isabella subjugated the Moors. She imposed religious homogeneity, reformed the Spanish Church, raising its moral tone to new heights. She had succeeded in her goal of creating a robust and muscular Roman Catholicism within Castile. And finally, Columbus, whom Isabella had commissioned on his monumental voyage, had discovered new lands beyond the Atlantic. In understanding what Queen Isabella had accomplished to this point, it is important to recall that "when viewed from the depressed position of her early days ... the achievements of her reign seem scarcely less than miraculous."[28]

5

DESTINED FOR ENGLAND

After over twenty years of marriage, Queen Isabella was as devoted to King Ferdinand as ever. Even his occasional roving eye and the siring of several illegitimate children did not dampen the queen's love for her husband. When, at the end of 1492, King Ferdinand nearly died from stab wounds inflicted by a would-be assassin, Isabella's dedication to her husband was apparent. In informing Archbishop Talavera of the incident, the queen recounted her shock, saying that, "the wound was so great . . . I could not find the courage to look at it."[1] King Ferdinand's brush with death had awakened in Queen Isabella a new sense of mortality, prompting her to write, "Thus we see that kings too may die."[2]

Ferdinand recovered, but the assassination attempt had opened an even more conscious awareness of spiritual development within the already pious Isabella. From this time onward, she dwelled increasingly on the state of her soul, exhorting her spiritual adviser, Hemando de Talavera, to guide her in the right direction. Isabella told Talavera that "greatness and prosperity had made me think of it [death] and fear it more." It was essential, the queen noted, "to prepare to die well."[3]

Talavera took his order to counsel Isabella to heart. As her spiritual adviser, he did not hesitate to admonish the queen when he thought it necessary. Although the queen preferred to dress modestly in private, there were times when her desire to illustrate the splendor of her position resulted in what might have been perceived as an extravagant show. A contemporary once noted how a dress Isabella wore was so opulent "that there is no man who can well imagine what could be the value of it."[4] When Talavera chastised the queen about the court's lavishness, she explained that she had only one silk dress made for her and it was not an extravagant one at that.

Meanwhile, after Queen Isabella's greatest triumph, the fall of Granada, disparate Spanish peoples long accustomed to mutual jealousies bonded as a nation. This unity, along with Spain's enhanced international reputation, prompted the royal couple to look beyond their borders, largely to address Ferdinand's concerns about France, a perennial thorn in Aragon's side. Ferdinand had for many years risked his life fighting for Castile's causes. Isabella knew she owed her husband much and, once Granada was secured, willingly went along with his wish to focus on Europe.

Central to a successful foreign policy was a set of agreements between foreign powers. In the days of Ferdinand and Isabella, these agreements generally consisted of alliances secured by marriages between progeny of the monarchs who had reached formal accord. Therefore, to expand Spanish power and influence throughout Europe, Ferdinand and Isabella jockeyed to secure dynastic marriages for their children. Through a series of brilliant matches, Queen Isabella's children linked Spain to Portugal, England, and the Holy Roman Empire. These carefully planned nuptials had one main objective—to isolate France, then the great power of Europe.

No less determined to see France encircled was Henry VII, the first Tudor king of England. Henry had won his crown in 1485 by defeating King Richard III, who died at the Battle of Bosworth Field. This was the last important battle in the decades-long civil war known as the Wars of the Roses. Richard III's death marked the end of the Plantagenet dynasty's hold on the English throne. When Henry VII, the Lancastrian contender, assumed the crown, it signaled the rise of the Tudor dynasty. Henry knew he needed to secure his tenuous hold on the newly won crown. His marriage to Elizabeth of York, Richard III's niece, was designed to secure the crown at its center. Henry also needed to unite his family in marriage to another powerful one with links to England if possible. In his careful search for a consort for his son Arthur, the Prince of Wales, Henry's choice fell on Isabella and Ferdinand's youngest child, Catherine of Aragon. Spain, the new power on the Continent, would both add luster to the Tudor dynasty and hem in France.

Henry VII worked quickly. He had only assumed the throne the year Catherine was born, and before Arthur's birth. Yet the intrepid new monarch had already decided that a commitment to marriage between the two youngsters was a shrewd move, both dynastically and politically. As early as 1488, when Catherine was in her third year, King Henry proposed that his two-year-old son and heir marry her as soon as the two came of age. The alliance would see England and Castile defend each other from their common enemy, France, as well as aid each other in reclaiming properties held by France. These consisted of Cerdagne and Roussillon for the Spanish and Normandy and Aquitaine for the English.

Henry VII, eager to secure this proposed match, dispatched two representatives, Richard Nafan and Thomas Savage, to Ferdinand and Isabella's court at Medina del Campo. The queen and king treated Nafan and Savage to a spectacular welcome. Eager to impress Henry's emissaries, they ordered a glittering court reception. The monarchs both dressed sumptuously in gold and sable, welcoming the envoys while seated under a grand canopy sporting the arms of Castile and Aragon. Isabella made an especially dazzling impression on the representatives. Looking every inch the queen, she also wore velvet and ermine and a stunning array of rubies, pearls, and diamonds. One ruby was said to be the size of a tennis ball. No less lavishly dressed were the royal children, who donned velvet and cloth of gold. In the days that the emissaries were at Medina del Campo, Ferdinand and Isabella treated them to displays of dancing, jousts, and bullfights. Though Isabella was not a fan of the bullfight, she understood the importance of the bloody sport to the Andalusians and allowed them to enjoy it.

When the time came to meet the object of their visit, little Princess Catherine, Nafan and Savage could not have been more pleased with her. Dressed in brocade and adorned with jewels, Catherine was a healthy-looking child of whom her mother was inordinately proud. At one point, Queen Isabella held up little Catherine for all to see during a tournament in which knights fought in an impressive reenactment of their battle engagements against the Moors. The Englishmen described her as "a singularly beautiful child."[5] The lavish welcome accorded the representatives showed Castile to be a wealthy power, with which Henry VII would be proud to ally himself. Before Nafan and Savage left, they concluded the cherished treaty allying England with Castile. King Ferdinand and Queen Isabella agreed that their youngest should become the Princess of Wales and later the Queen of England. Thus, as Spain reoriented its foreign policy toward England and England did the equivalent toward Spain, the fate of a Spanish princess was cast. At a tender age Princess Catherine was already destined for England.

Spain's royal alliances did not end with Catherine. In 1490, her eldest sister, the infanta Isabel, was given in marriage to the royal house of Portugal, in a bid to maintain peace and friendly relations between the neighboring countries. The blond-haired Isabel traveled with the queen when possible, including those famed visits Isabella made to bolster her troops during the Granada War. Before sending off their daughter to Portugal to wed Prince Afonso, heir to King John II, Ferdinand and Isabella ordered festivities lasting for days. But within six months after the wedding, Afonso died after his horse fell and crushed him. The distraught young widow returned to the family fold. Unlike six-year-old Catherine, the twenty-year-old Isabel suddenly faced an uncertain future. Queen Isabella would have to see if there was another match on the horizon that would benefit Spain.

Since the conquest of Granada, the royal family had lived in the Alhambra whenever possible. The most beautiful of their palaces, the Alhambra was also Princess Catherine's most exotic home, with its long ties to Islamic history. Here, among the brilliant mosaic-covered halls, heavily pillared terraces, and arches intricately carved in the Moorish style, Catherine and her family lived and played. Fountains spouted delicate streams of water into lily-covered pools. Trees and bushes in emerald green and fragrant flowers dotted the lush gardens. Inside, Catherine and her sisters had as their apartments what had been the women's quarters during the palace's Moorish days. Around the city of Granada itself, orange and olive trees grew in profusion along with pomegranates. It was an enchanting paradise for Catherine, who would later choose the pomegranate as her personal symbol.

Within her own family, Catherine could count her mother as a special hero. Here was her own flesh and blood who had spent a decade fighting the Moors and ultimately conquered them. Just six years old when her parents took possession of Granada, Catherine could not have been unimpressed by the great drama surrounding the completion of the Reconquista. The young infanta grew to observe and learn from the woman who was not only her mother but was also a person of singular importance on the world stage. Princess Catherine needed only to look around the Alhambra for reminders of her mother's greatest triumph. Having spent her youth by Queen Isabella's side, Catherine had naturally imbibed some of her mother's well-known traits: her intelligence, her piety, her resilience, her stubbornness. Catherine also "grew up conscious from her earliest years of the dignity to which she had been born as a daughter—an infanta—of Spain; it was an awareness of being a true royal princess . . . which never left her."[6]

Catherine also grew up with a lasting image of her parents living up to their motto, *"Tanto monta, monta tanto."* Before her was an example of a true royal marriage, in which Ferdinand and Isabella epitomized the vision of a "king and queen working in harness."[7] As the child of two remarkable parents, Catherine would always be proud of their accomplishments.

Isabella was preoccupied with Castile, but she did not by any means neglect her role as mother. Her children's welfare was always uppermost in Isabella's mind. The queen had a special place in her heart for her only son, Juan, who received extra attention because of his position as the future king. Because his health was delicate, doctors and caretakers watched the fair-haired prince closely. To groom Juan for his role as king, the queen sent eminent councilors and lawyers to teach her son about statecraft.

Prince Juan may have been singled out for special attention and care, yet this did not mean that Isabella's daughters lacked attention. Recalling her limited training as a child, the queen was determined that Isabel, Juana, María, and Catherine receive a fine education. She demanded that they be developed to their fullest potential. Instruction in the classics was foremost in the princesses' curriculum. To this end, Isabella employed some of the finest humanists of the day, such as the poet Antonio Geraldini and his brother, Alessandro. Under the direction of the Gerladini brothers, Catherine and her sisters read an impressive list of authors that included the Roman statesman, dramatist, and philosopher Seneca; the Christian poets Prudentius and Juvencus; and great doctors of the Church: Saints Ambrose, Augustine, Jerome, and Gregory. The princesses were also tutored in canon and civil law as well as history and Latin. In fact, "so well grounded in the classics" were they, that when they were older, the sisters "were able to reply to the speeches of ambassadors in ex-tempore Latin, fluent, classical, and correct, and Catherine appeared to Erasmus and to Luis Vives [the famed humanist scholars] a miracle of feminine learning."[8] So impressive was Catherine of Aragon's education that Erasmus declared her "egregiously learned."[9] This was high praise indeed since in Italy two famous aristocratic contemporaries of Catherine—Isabella and Beatrice d'Este—were among the most accomplished and educated women in Renaissance Europe.

In educating her daughters, Queen Isabella had not neglected other, more practical arts. Embroidery, spinning, weaving, sewing were introduced, as were music, drawing, and dancing. By the time Isabella's daughters had finished their schooling, she could feel satisfied that she had done well in educating Spain's infantas. Of the four sisters, Juana and Catherine were justifiably among the most accomplished. Juana was highly musical and praised by a contemporary as having "for her age and sex" a high ability in composing and reciting verses, while Catherine, "proficient on keyboard and harp," was also "learned in philosophy, literature, and religion,"[10] having a command of French and German besides Castilian and Latin.

Isabella had never forgotten the inadequacy of her own education in Latin, then the language of the learned and of diplomacy. She set herself the task of learning Latin under the tutelage of Beatriz Galindo, a professor of rhetoric, philosophy, and medicine at the University of Salamanca. Queen Isabella may have never reached the fluency that Catherine and her sisters attained, but she managed to improve her Latin enough to understand documents and even "read with pleasure the Vulgate and Caesar's *Commentaries*."[11]

Isabella's love of reading and learning stayed with her throughout her life. The queen's personal library, housed in the Alcázar of Segovia, provides a glimpse of her interests. Composed of 250 books chosen by the queen, the library consisted of works by Livy, Virgil, Plutarch, and Boccaccio; books on Spanish history, law, science, hunting, riding, and medicine; and especially treasured by the queen were religious volumes.

Spurred by the queen's example, an appreciation of learning infused the Isabelline court. In this, Isabella was very much a part of the world of Renaissance humanism that emerged at the end of the Middle Ages. A new spirit of discovery and learning permeated Europe during Catherine's childhood. Humanism, with its emphasis on classical antiquity and on the human potential as well as reasoning, swept the Continent. The high and mighty, such as Lorenzo de' Medici, sponsored artistic greats such as Michelangelo and Leonardo da Vinci. Giovanni Bellini, Sandro Botticelli, Raphael, and Titian were other artists who made their mark at the time and whose works continue to resonate today. Other notables of the time include the astronomer Nicolaus Copernicus, the writer Baldassare Castiglione, the philosopher and scholar Giovanni Pico della Mirandola, and Niccolò Machiavelli (who featured Catherine's father, King Ferdinand, in his famous work, *The Prince*).

Queen Isabella, who placed a high value on virtue, also imposed a strict moral discipline on her court. This extended to curtailing vices such as gambling that had been rampant under Enrique IV's reign. Religion, not surprisingly, reigned supreme in the home and at court. Isabella inculcated in her children a devotional nature and urged them to discern what was right and true. A life steeped in God, where conscience was to be a guiding force, was fostered by Queen Isabella and taken to heart by Catherine.

As queen, wife, and mother, Isabella offered the young Catherine an example to emulate. Isabella "knew that marriage was no enchanted land of endless romantic bliss and like everything else to which she addressed herself, it required . . . thought."[12] Isabella therefore approached her marriage to Ferdinand realistically. To her, he was neither "a god nor a demon" but "a man with certain weaknesses . . . [and] knowing his weaknesses, she never expected the impossible of him. The good in him she recognized and fostered; the bad she did her best to neutralize. If he served her well, she served him even better. When he rebelled and lost hold of himself, it was her steady hand that soothed him and brought him back to his senses. Throughout her life she was his anchor, his stay, his good genius—a fact clearly proved by the almost total collapse of his character and conduct after she was dead."[13]

But if Isabel steered the marriage firmly, she never attempted to dominate. " 'Con blandura'—with tact, with graciousness—was one of her favorite phrases," and it was this blandura she exercised when dealing with her husband.[14] This is not to say that Isabella felt little or no jealousy. She was jealous of Ferdinand's mistresses. But because Isabella had a profound respect for the sacrament of marriage and herself could never countenance being unfaithful, she contained her feelings. The queen may have tried her hand at keeping the occasional attractive woman from Ferdinand's orbit, but when she could not prevent her husband from straying, she "simply bore the affair until it wore off."[15] Moreover, reproaches for the king's lapses, if any, were kept away from prying eyes. Publicly, Isabella supported her husband, scrupulously avoiding scenes of rage and envy. She forgave him his infidelities and remained devoted to him. Her wifely devotion was evidenced by her sewing the shirts he wore. If Ferdinand "complained that she replaced the sleeves many times before making him a new one, his very tone of affectionate jocularity, to say nothing of the fact that he would wear no others, amply reveals the esteem in which he held her."[16]

This long-lasting and harmonious matrimonial partnership sadly eluded most of the royal couple's children. Already, Isabel, Catherine's eldest sister, had seen her marriage ended after only six months. The widowed Isabel, only in her twenties, exhibited signs of melancholy as she continually mourned her dead husband. Her excessive fasting and religious fervor worried even her highly devout mother. Though her parents wished for a new marriage, Isabel preferred to take the veil. Ferdinand and Isabella finally persuaded their eldest daughter to transfer her allegiance toward another marriage. In 1497, the rail-thin infanta consented to remarry in Portugal, this time to the country's new king, Manoel I. Remembering the comely princess from Castile during her brief stay in Portugal years earlier, Manoel asked for Isabel's hand in marriage, preferring her to her younger sister María. As part of her agreement to marry, Isabel secured Manoel's promise to expel the Jews from Portugal. He reluctantly agreed, and Iberia witnessed another group of persecuted Jews fleeing their homes for strange new lands.

Before Isabel's second marriage, King Ferdinand and Queen Isabella secured a double alliance that joined two of their children to the Habsburg dynasty. As much as a pact with the powerful Habsburgs was sure to help Ferdinand and Isabella in their quest to isolate France, an alliance with the new, powerful Spain was also bound to be to the advantage of the Holy Roman Emperor Maximilian, ruler of Austria and Burgundy and head of the Habsburg dynasty. Infanta Juana would marry Archduke Philip, then Prince Juan, at seventeen years of age, would marry Archduchess Margaret. These marriages would make Maximilian father-in-law to Isabella's children.

Juana stood out among the children. Darker in coloring than her siblings, Juana also had a strangely brooding character that manifested itself early in her life. Catherine found it difficult to relate to this brilliant but mercurial sister, whose moods swung from great heights of happiness to abysmal depressions. Catherine found it much easier to get along with her sister María, a cherubic character but the least talented of Isabella's daughters. Catherine also idolized and enjoyed the company of the family favorite, the much adored Prince Juan.

In 1496 Queen Isabella, accompanied by Catherine and her other siblings, saw seventeen-year-old Juana off from Castile in a fleet that included over one hundred vessels and ten thousand armed men. It headed to Flanders, where Juana was to become the bride of Archduke Philip. On the return trip to Spain, the fleet was to bring Margaret, Philip's sister, so that she could marry Juana's brother. Juana eagerly welcomed the chance to flee from Isabella's strict upbringing and so showed no sign of sadness at leaving her mother. Isabella, by contrast, viewed her daughter's departure with some trepidation. She cried, wondering if she would ever see Juana again. Isabella also feared for this unstable child and for the future. After a harrowing journey, Juana arrived at her destination and immediately fell in love with her new husband. She became obsessed with him. Philip, though at first enamored of his attractive bride, soon returned to his feckless and irresponsible ways. Such a combustible combination was bound to end in disaster. Trouble lay ahead for this infamous daughter of Isabella and sister to Catherine of Aragon. The couple went down in history as Juana la Loca (Joan the Mad) and Philip the Handsome.

The late 1490s were years of great trial for Queen Isabella, nearly all of which involved her children. The first of a string of tragedies took place on October 4, 1497, perhaps the darkest day in Isabella's life. The happily married Prince Juan, Isabella's precious son and heir, died of fever at Salamanca after being married for only a few months. King Ferdinand was with his son when he died. In Juan's final hour, Ferdinand comforted the young man, telling him to "have patience, since God calls you, who is a greater King than any other, and has other kingdoms and seigniories greater and better than any we might hold or might hope to give you, and they will last you forever. Therefore be of good heart to receive death, which comes once inevitably to all, with hope to be immortal henceforth and to live in glory."[17] Ferdinand had the unenviable task of breaking the news to Isabella. When she saw her husband upon his arrival, she asked right away: "Tell me the truth, Señor! . . . 'He is with God,'"[18] came the reply. Then, bowing her head in sorrow and resignation, Isabella uttered: "God gave him, and God has taken him away. Blessed be His holy name!"[19]

Prince Juan's death was more than a personal tragedy for Ferdinand and Isabella. Its dynastic implications changed European history. For now the succession devolved on the couple's surviving children, all female. First in line was Queen Isabel of Portugal. Yet here too great sorrow awaited. In 1498, the second knife of sorrow pierced Isabella's heart: her favorite daughter died in her mother's arms after giving birth to Prince Miguel of Portugal. Strangely enough, the moody Isabel had predicted her premature death. A distraught Queen Isabella was laid low for weeks afterward. Incredibly, the ill wind that carried the seeds of catastrophe blew into Isabella's life anew, shattering her hopes for the future. In 1500 her frail, two-year-old grandson, Prince Miguel, under whom the whole Iberian Peninsula might have been finally united, also died. Again, Ferdinand and Isabella showed fortitude before others. But inside, the couple felt this latest loss very keenly. Spain's future now lay in the hands of Queen Isabella's increasingly mentally unstable daughter Juana. That same year Juana had given birth to a son, the future Emperor Charles V, who was one day to rule an empire stretching from Spain to Burgundy and the Low Countries as well as Naples and Sicily and the German lands of the Habsburgs. As if predicting what lay ahead, Isabella had murmured to Ferdinand upon hearing the news of this grandson's birth on the feast day of St. Matthias: "The lot falls on Matthias."[20]

The infanta María was the next of Queen Isabella's children to marry. The widowed King Manoel, who wished to make another alliance with Spain, asked to marry María this time. After obtaining the necessary papal dispensation, the Spanish princess married King Manoel. María, who became the mother of eight children, turned out to be the most fortunate of Isabella's children, escaping a premature death like those of Isabel and Juan. She was also devoid of the mental instability that increasingly gripped Juana. Finally, María also escaped the marital woes for which her sister Catherine would become famous.

Through these tumultuous years, Queen Isabella and King Ferdinand continued to be embroiled in European conflicts. France's King Louis XII aimed to wrestle as much territory as he could from Ferdinand's dominions. Ferdinand went to war against Louis, which upset Isabella, who was not happy to see her husband fight a fellow Christian king.

As the 1490s unfolded, Queen Isabella remained preoccupied by many events, not least Christopher Columbus's voyages of discovery. They were not proving to be as profitable as had been hoped. That would come later. The issues of slavery and the native populations also concerned Isabella. Columbus was a proponent of enslaving the natives, sending four ships full of captives to Spain in 1495. At first Ferdinand and Isabella agreed to their sale, but days later, Isabella had a change of heart, ordering that the sale be suspended.

Between 1493 and 1500, Columbus embarked on two more voyages. This time the explorer discovered Jamaica, Puerto Rico, and Trinidad, and established settlements on Hispaniola. These colonies turned out to be disastrous. The colonizers were unprepared for the arduous task before them. The fortunes they sought were elusive, and they soon fought among themselves as well as with the native population. In Spain, feelings against Columbus ran high as Spaniards trickled home from the Indies with highly unpleasant stories. Soon enough Ferdinand and Isabella felt compelled to send an official to investigate. They trusted a courtier, Francisco de Bobadilla, to fulfill their mandate. In Santo Domingo, Bobadilla was shocked at what he found. Bad administration by Columbus and his brother had set the inhabitants against them. When Bobadilla confronted Columbus, the explorer insisted he was still the supreme authority on Hispaniola, undermining Bobadilla's royal authorization to become the new governor. Bobadilla promptly ordered Columbus arrested. The explorer returned to Spain in November 1500, manacled and paraded in humiliation before the king and queen at the Alhambra.

When Columbus fell on his knees before Isabella, she took pity on him. She and Ferdinand allowed him to go on his fourth and final voyage in 1502; he was not permitted to visit Hispaniola. Sensitive to the explorer's failure as an administrator, the king and queen did not restore him to his position as governor of the Indies. Columbus ended up shipwrecked on Jamaica for nearly a year. When he returned to Spain in November 1504, much of the luster that had shone on the intrepid explorer in the heady days of his first voyage was gone. Nevertheless, this inglorious ending did not take away the fact that "Columbus' dream and Isabella's breadth of vision had begun the most extraordinary, the most splendid, and the most terrifying chapter in Spanish history. Between them, they gave Spain a fabulously rich and powerful empire, although the discovery that led to Spain's greatness also carried the seeds of the country's decay."[21]

The Americas took on "a life of their own and became the envy of Europe."[22] Queen Isabella took an interest in these faraway lands and "saw to it that proper government, courts of law, and church institutions were established in Santo Domingo, the first capital of the Indies, and forbade the enslavement of American Indians. In 1503 she chartered a House of Trade (Casa de Contratación) in Seville which included royal officials, leading merchants, and ship owners, to regulate commerce with the Indies."[23]

An empire unprecedented in history took root thanks to Columbus and Queen Isabella. Half a millennium after the empire's founding, Spain's impact is still felt there today. Large regions of Central and South America continue to speak Spanish, the Castilian language of Isabella's realm. Millions continue to adhere to Roman Catholicism, the faith she and Columbus so ardently championed.

At the same time that Columbus's troubles captured the Spanish court's attention, another pressing issue preoccupied Queen Isabella. By the beginning of the sixteenth century, all of Isabella's children had left her side through death or marriage, with the exception of Catherine. The queen had to steel herself for the day soon coming when her beloved youngest child would have to leave the nest.

As a girl, Catherine had witnessed much of the drama of her mother's reign. Present at Zubia in the final battle of the Granada War, Catherine saw the chaos, fear, and victory surrounding the Christian soldiers in their fight against the Moors. She could not have been more impressed when her parents took the city of Granada and went to claim the magnificent Alhambra. Upon his return from his first voyage to the New World, "when a triumphant Christopher Columbus, that self-styled Admiral of the Ocean, stood before Their Most Glorious Majesties, King Ferdinand and Queen Isabella, and exhibited the trophies of his exploration, somewhere nearer the throne stood a young and eager eight-year-old. From the comforting familiarity and tradition of the Old World, she viewed with wonder the dazzling images of the New."[24]

As the years passed, that impressionable eight-year-old grew into an obedient teenager. She had none of the remoteness of her sister Isabel, and none of the volatility of her sister Juana. Instead, Catherine appeared to have inherited her mother's intense piety and strength of character. Physically, Catherine did not resemble her darker Aragonese ancestors except for their more pronounced chin. She did inherit Queen Isabella's coloring: her fair complexion, bluish eyes, and reddish gold hair. Nearly medium in height, the princess from Castile also had a pleasant looking face, oval in shape, and clearly possessed an innate sense of royal dignity. This combined with her family background and intellectual accomplishments made Catherine of Aragon a fine catch for any European prince.

In 1498 King Henry VII had already expressed to the Spanish ambassador, Dr. Rodrigo González de Puebla, his pleasure at seeing the marriage alliance between Arthur and Catherine come to fruition. De Puebla reported to King Ferdinand and Queen Isabella that Henry was generally envied on account of this marriage, stating: "He swore by his royal faith that he and the Queen are more satisfied with this marriage than they would have been with any great dominions they might have gained with the daughter of another Prince. . . . Begs that the Princess of Wales may be soon sent to England."[25]

The years drew Catherine ever closer to England when, on Whitsunday 1499, she and Arthur, Prince of Wales, were married in a proxy ceremony at Bewdley Manor in Worcestershire, England. This important stage having been completed minus her physical presence, it was only a matter of time before Catherine had to take that all-important step of leaving for England. It was an unavoidable moment that Queen Isabella nevertheless tried to delay as much as possible. Not only was the queen hesitant to let the thirteen-year-old Catherine go too soon but she also harbored some misgivings about Henry VII, who had a reputation for being stingy.

If Henry seemed to have had some deficiencies in his character, his wife, Queen Elizabeth, appeared to be the opposite. The Prior of Santa Cruz had advised Ferdinand and Isabella that Queen Elizabeth impressed him as "the most noble woman in England. He thought she suffered under great oppression, and led a miserable, cheerless life." The prior also begged Catherine's parents "to write a letter to the poor Queen sometimes, for charity's sake."[26]

Already, Arthur and Catherine had been exchanging letters in Latin, written in formal, somewhat stilted style. In one letter, the prince wrote: "My dearest spouse . . . I have read the most sweet letters of your Highness lately . . . from which I have easily perceived your most entire love to me. . . . Let your coming to me be hastened, that instead of being absent we may be present with each other, and the love conceived between us and the wished-for joys may reap proper fruit."[27]

Ten months before Catherine left for England, Ferdinand and Isabella wrote instructions to de Puebla to reassure Henry VII and to "tell the King of England that our intentions are unchanged. We love him and the Prince of Wales, our son, so much that it would be impossible to love them better. We appreciate the union with him, and his friendship so much that we wish to see the Princess as soon as possible married and living in the home of her husband the Prince."[28]

The excitement over Catherine's impending arrival was not limited to the royal family. De Puebla reported his meeting with the Bishop of London to Ferdinand and Isabella with enthusiasm, saying that "it is impossible to describe how much he and the whole nation desire to see [Catherine]. In all parts of the kingdom preparations are making for her festive reception."[29]

Debate persisted, however, as to whether Catherine was ready to be sent away. Some, including her parents, felt that she was too young to go to a strange land and a new court, fearing that her morals might be corrupted without their personal influence. However, some thought that this might be the right time for Catherine to go, before she became too set in her ways in Castile. If that occurred, she might never be able to assimilate completely in England. And so, in a spirit of compromise, a date for Catherine's departure was finally fixed for 1501.

Ferdinand and Isabella heard of the excitement surrounding their daughter's impending arrival in England and were happy about it. However, the queen was concerned about the money being spent on it and wrote a letter in March 1501 from Granada regarding this: "I am pleased to hear it because . . . demonstrations of joy at the reception of my daughter are naturally agreeable to me. . . . Rejoicings may be held, but we ardently implore him that the substantial part of the festival should be his love; that the Princess should be treated by him and by the Queen as their true daughter, and by the Prince of Wales as we feel sure he will treat her."[30]

Queen Isabella could not delay the inevitable any longer. The time had arrived when she and King Ferdinand had to part from their youngest child. The teenage Catherine prepared to leave the family fold for a new and uncertain life in faraway England, for a "glorious marriage" that would be "of great advantage to the whole of Christendom."[31]

6

THIS ROUGH AND WEARY WORLD

*I*t was time for fifteen-year-old Catherine of Aragon to bid her parents farewell. Catherine had caused no grief over this longed-for marriage alliance. Like her siblings, she accepted that her role as princess required parting from her family in order to make a new dynastic alignment with another royal family. Acceptance, though, did not make the last good-bye any easier. Catherine, after all, had been her mother's faithful companion, the last offspring at home. A child of fine character, she was a mainstay during the family's most trying years, when death had snatched so many loved ones in so short a space of time. The fateful day, May 21, 1501, at last arrived.

Isabella could not have felt anything but deep sorrow at being parted from her daughter. She had accompanied her other daughters to the borders of Castile as they made their way for their new countries but could not accompany Catherine because the fifty-year-old queen was weak from a fever. Isabella, instead, had to say good-bye at the Alhambra. The parting for mother and daughter was heart-wrenching. Perhaps both had a premonition that this might be the last time they would see each other.

Among the many items Catherine took with her were gowns, jewels, plates, and coins. She "herself packed her own small personal possessions—her missal, her crucifix, her books and her needlework materials, for her mother had stressed she must continue with her embroidery at which she already showed considerable skill."[1] Accompanying Catherine on the journey were Doña Elvira Manuel, chief lady-in-waiting, and an assortment of servants (numbering 150), including a chief cupbearer.

Catherine and her escorts traveled from the south to Coruña, in northwest

Spain, in a journey that took over two months. Intense heat dogged the royal party as they wound their way from the sunny south through the scorching Meseta. Before arriving at Coruña, Catherine visited Santiago de Compostela, one of the most important pilgrimage sites in Christendom. Inside the city's cathedral, Catherine witnessed the famous *butafumeiro* being swung. The rope holding the massive censer filled with incense broke. It was an ill omen for the princess, for the story went that whenever the rope of the *butafumeiro* snapped while the censer was swung, bad luck would follow.

Catherine finally reached the port town of Coruña. She had traversed broad valleys and mountainous passes to reach the Bay of Biscay. From there, she embarked on a ship to take her to her new country. As it turned out, Catherine's travails did not end at Coruña. Treacherous waters awaited. Boarding their ships in August, the royal party encountered a fierce storm and had to return to Spain. The princess was taken ill again, and when she wrote to her mother, Catherine admitted that "it was impossible not to be frightened by the storm."[2] At the end of September, they embarked again for England. Constant thunderstorms thwarted the sea crossing. Finally, on October 2, 1501, Catherine of Aragon landed at Plymouth harbor.

Here was England, a land of rolling verdant hills, hazy skies, and damp, chilly weather, all so unlike the familiar sunbaked plains of Castile. Greeting the bewildered princess was a crescendo of voices in an unfamiliar tongue. Never before had Catherine heard so much English spoken. An excited group of local dignitaries welcomed her, and though she was taken aback by everything, Catherine "set foot on English soil with the proud and regal bearing expected of a Spanish princess. She won the hearts of all who clustered near her as she accepted their greetings with touching modesty."[3] As befitted the pious daughter of the pious Queen Isabella, Catherine's first act upon disembarking was to attend Mass, to give thanks for her safe arrival after such arduous travels.

Catherine of Aragon's reception was rapturous. From Plymouth she made her way to Exeter, where nobles and commoners alike strained to catch a glimpse of their future queen. Catherine was enveloped in celebration marked by cheering, fanfare, bonfires, and processions. Two days after landing in Plymouth, one of the Spanish retainers who accompanied Catherine wrote to Queen Isabella with the satisfying news that "the Princess could not have been received with greater rejoicings had she been the Saviour of the world."[4]

Queen Isabella had wished that her daughter not meet Prince Arthur until their wedding day. However, an impatient King Henry ignored this stricture. He and Arthur met the teenager who was the hope of the Tudor dynasty and the nation. Amid shy glances and formal greetings in foreign tongues, Catherine swept a curtsy to her future father-in-law, who eyed her approvingly. Here at last was the girl of whom the king had told de Puebla, Isabella's envoy: "He would give half his kingdom if she [Catherine] were like her mother."[5]

Shortly after the introductions between Catherine and the king, Prince Arthur arrived and came face-to-face with his bride. More polite exchanges in Latin flowed among the dignitaries while the two young people eyed each other hesitatingly. Catherine saw a blond-haired prince who was shorter than she and appeared younger than his fifteen years. There was also a sallow look to the lad, who did not appear as robust as his bride. Relieved to have met the two most important individuals in England, Catherine was emboldened to inject some gaiety into the proceedings by dancing before her august guests. The unfamiliar strains of Castilian music wafted through the English air as Catherine and her ladies moved gracefully through their Spanish dances. With the formalities of meeting done, the trip to London for the wedding was next on the agenda.

Before arriving in London, Catherine met the bridegroom's mother. Queen Elizabeth's brothers included the young boys King Edward V and Richard, Duke of York, known to history as the Princes in the Tower. In 1497, Queen Elizabeth had written comforting words to Queen Isabella about Catherine, "whom we think of and esteem as our own daughter."[6] The English queen's kindly disposition made her appear to be the ideal mother-in-law for Princess Catherine. Perhaps once they came to know each other better, Catherine could find, in this new and unfamiliar land, a second mother in the Queen of England.

Queen Isabella did not receive information about the goings-on in England until the beginning of January 1502, when she was relieved to hear that all had gone so well for Catherine. In a letter to Isabella and Ferdinand, Henry VII had told them of his impressions of their daughter and the festivities surrounding her arrival, of his having "much admired her beauty, as well as her agreeable and dignified manners [together with] the acclamation of such masses of people as never before had been seen in England."[7]

This was in marked contrast to Catherine's sister Juana's emerging life in Flanders. After bidding her a tearful good-bye, Isabella never ceased worrying about her most troubled child. If Archduke Philip had been as good as he was handsome, there might have been great hope for the marriage and for Juana. Philip, however, pursued a profligate life, ignoring how this might affect the emotionally fragile Juana. Scenes of raging jealousy mixed with pathetic begging on Juana's part soon became the talk of the Continent. Juana's erratic and disturbing behavior scandalized Europe. This tragic family situation was a tremendous blow to Ferdinand and Isabella.

After the deaths of the couple's eldest child, Isabel, and their son, Prince Miguel of Portugal, Juana's imbalance took on greater ramifications. Juana was now heir to Isabella's realm. Reacting to his sudden good fortune, Philip proceeded to bully his wife even more. Despite the violent arguments between them, she remained completely under her husband's sway. The petulant and unreliable Philip, meanwhile, became more hostile toward Spain and placed Flanders closer to France's orbit. Queen Isabella increasingly desired that Juana and her infant son, Charles, who would inherit Isabella and Ferdinand's realms, come to stay for a protracted period with her in Castile.

Back in England, Catherine's entry into London was tumultuous. In the procession, the princess, who looked fetching with her hair streaming down her shoulders, was escorted by the ever-present Doña Elvira and another member of the Tudor dynasty, ten-year-old Prince Henry. Already a head taller than Arthur and Catherine, Henry was a study in contrast to his delicate older brother. Fair-haired and with a broad frame for his age, Henry showed promise of being a strapping young man. His easy manner and congeniality, evident already, touched Catherine.

Catherine and Arthur were married at St. Paul's Cathedral on November 14, 1501. Wearing a white gown and mantilla decorated in precious stones and pearls, Catherine was escorted by young Prince Henry, proudly dressed in white velvet. In reading what King Henry VII had to say about the wedding and Catherine, Queen Isabella must have been eager to hear of all that concerned her daughter. "Great and cordial rejoicings have taken place," notes Henry VII's report, where he "begs them [Ferdinand and Isabella] to banish all sadness from their minds. Though they cannot now see the gentle face of their beloved daughter they may be sure that she has found a second father who will ever watch over her happiness, and never permit her to want anything that he can procure for her."[8] Moreover, "the union between the two royal families, and the two kingdoms, is now so complete that it is impossible to make any distinction between the interests of England and Spain."[9] As for Prince Arthur, he sent a reassuring and touching letter to his new parents-in-law telling them that he "had never felt so much joy in his life as when he beheld the sweet face of his bride. No woman in the world could be more agreeable to him."[10]

After celebrating the nuptials with much merrymaking, the young couple were ceremoniously bedded together for the night. According to Catherine years later, nothing happened between her and Arthur that night or over the next several months. Owing to the couple's youth, neither set of parents pressed their children into fulfilling this delicate obligation. Catherine's parents let it be known that they would " 'rather be pleased than dissatisfied' if consummation was delayed for some time, in view of Arthur's 'tender age.' These were the 'instructions relayed to Doña Elvira, which, as a resolute duenna, she could be trusted to carry out.' "[11] No one then knew that decades later Catherine's future would hinge on one sticking point—the consummation or nonconsummation of her marriage with the Prince of Wales.

There was some talk of Catherine staying with the royal family instead of living with Arthur in his establishment, but by the end of the year, she complied with King Henry's wish that she accompany her husband to Wales. Ludlow Castle, Catherine and Arthur's home in Wales, was positioned on a hill by the river Teme. The castle was Norman in origin and built of local limestone, the gray of its stone combining with the frequently raw weather to make this a somber first home for the princess. With mists clinging to the castle's forbidding walls and pervasive dampness, Catherine and Arthur fell ill in no time. The prince, with his weak constitution, succumbed to sweating fever and on April 2, 1502, died. The news reached Catherine in her chamber, where her faithful Spanish attendants were nursing her back to health. Her husband of less than five months was dead. In the space of just ten months, the teenage Catherine of Aragon had undergone tremendous changes. From the sunny, warm climate of southern Spain, where she lived with her mother and family in the Moorish wonder that was the Granada, sixteen-year-old Catherine was now alone, save for some attendants, widowed, and convalescing in the dank, austere castle of Ludlow in the Welsh Marches. Catherine, who understood barely any English, was completely at the mercy of her father-in-law, the suspicious and crafty King Henry VII.

Prince Arthur's death plunged King Henry and Queen Elizabeth into deep mourning. The queen sought to comfort her husband. They were still young enough to have more children, she reassured him. And, true to her word, she gave birth in February 1503 to a baby girl. But tragically, the baby was dead. A week later Queen Elizabeth followed her to the grave. Catherine was saddened by the death of her mother-in-law. Queen Elizabeth had shown her kindness and sympathy since her arrival in England. Now the only close adult member of the royal family left was her father-in-law, who increasingly made life difficult for Catherine, the Dowager Princess of Wales. With communications as they were at the time, Catherine could not even turn easily to her mother for counsel.

Back in Spain, Isabella and Ferdinand worried over their remaining children as well as their country's fate. Not until May 1502 did Juana and Philip visit Ferdinand and Isabella. At the time, Isabella was at Toledo, expecting reports about a battle between her soldiers and the French. There the shocking news of Arthur's death reached her. Added now to her anxiety over Juana were fears over Catherine's fate.

These two daughters—both pawns in their parents' political chess games—were vastly different. On the one hand was Juana, the sultry, irritable princess with the fiery temper and unbalanced mind, whose future could have been so brilliant as the Queen of Castile and wife of the successor to the vast Habsburg domains. Juana, also mother of a male heir, was a stark contrast to her youngest sister. Newly widowed and childless, Catherine was now saddled with an uncertain future. But unlike the difficult and rebellious Juana, Catherine continued to be the obedient child, awaiting instructions from Spain.

Juana's father-in-law, Holy Roman Emperor Maximilian, was unpredictable. Therefore, the Habsburg alliance that Ferdinand and Isabella had carefully cultivated through the double marriage of their children, was proving to be less reliable than expected. Should Maximilian's flirtations with France develop into something more concrete, Spain would become highly vulnerable to French ambitions. Should Spain and England become disentangled as the result of Catherine's widowhood, there would be no stopping France from extending its power at the expense of Spain and the states on the Italian Peninsula, which fell under Spain's sphere of influence.

Juana's volatility exacerbated the anxiety. Her husband tired of Spain and his in-laws, and left for Flanders as soon as he could. He also left Juana, who by now showed disturbing signs of insanity, with her parents. Continually tormented by thoughts of her absent husband, to whom she wanted to flee, Juana caused Queen Isabella such worries that one contemporary vividly described the situation as "tearing at her mother's entrails."[12] Juana reminded the queen of her own mother, Isabel, who had also suffered from insanity. Juana's pattern—crying endlessly for Philip followed by silence, then making rude replies to everyone—had an unnerving impact on one and all. Her disturbed mind drove the queen to distraction. Juana and Isabella's arguments had reached such a point that "there were scenes after which mother and daughter were so exhausted by their reciprocal animosity that both had to go to bed as if stricken with fever."[13]

Little wonder then that the energy for which Isabella had become legendary started to desert her. Illness and exhaustion grew to envelop the suffering queen. This made it even more difficult to deal with her troubled child, but Isabella continued to do her best with Juana. Isabella also, along with Ferdinand, had governing obligations. She worked well into the night to compensate for the hours lost in the day when she attempted to minister to Juana. Not surprisingly, all this took a toll. At one point the queen's concerned doctors reported to Ferdinand, then away in Aragon: "We believe that the Queen's life is endangered by her contact with Madame Princess who staged scenes every day. . . . [Juana] eats little and at times nothing at all, she is very sad and weak . . . reason and persuasion do not relieve her . . . she cries a great deal . . . and all these worries fall heavily upon the Queen. . . . We pray humbly that the fire that consumes her Highness [Juana] disappears. Her life and condition has long affected the life and health of our Queen."[14]

Juana's bizarre behavior was not limited to immediate family or court circles. In one astonishing scene, she clung obstinately for thirty-six hours to the iron gates of the imposing La Mota castle, half-naked and barefoot in the cold November weather, refusing to be coaxed by pleas from her retainers, prelates, and crowds of onlookers. Juana was, according to a chronicler, "like an African lioness . . . flung against the bars and shook them in impotent wrath."[15]

Isabella tried to convince her disturbed daughter that she and Ferdinand did not wish to separate Juana from Philip. Nevertheless, "a furious scene between mother and daughter" ensued that some believe "helped to cause Isabella's premature death."[16] Queen Isabella admitted that she endured insults from Juana "such as I could never have accepted but for the poor state of her health."[17] Even after Juana returned to her husband in Flanders, her bizarre behavior continued unabated.

Far from enjoying a peaceful life, Ferdinand and Isabella were consumed by anxieties over an unstable Juana, an unreliable Philip, a menacing France, and now Catherine's uncertain future. The king and queen followed the unfolding events in England after Arthur's death. They urged de Puebla, their ambassador there, to ensure that Henry VII fulfilled his part of the marriage contract, that "as King Henry retains the marriage portion, he is the more bound to provide for all the wants of the Princess of Wales. It is to be hoped that the English will not act dishonestly."[18] This was similar to another missive: "It is not to be supposed that such a Prince as the King of England would break his word at any time, and much less at present whilst the Princess is overwhelmed with grief."[19] King Ferdinand and Queen Isabella pointedly reminded de Puebla that Catherine must not under any circumstances borrow money for any expenses since it was King Henry's duty to pay for them. The King of Portugal had covered the expenses of their daughter Isabel when she was widowed, while Ferdinand and Isabella did the same for Archduchess Margaret when their son, Juan, made her a widow. Therefore, Henry must follow the custom with Catherine, for it was only right and natural. Ferdinand and Isabella insisted that, if Catherine had to borrow money, "it would reflect great dishonour on Henry."[20] Yet the stingy and indifferent English king was at loggerheads with the cunning and suspicious Ferdinand over Catherine's monetary situation, and an unseemly squabble over money ensued between the Spanish and English courts. Ferdinand and Isabella knew that the miserly Henry would be more amenable to seeing Catherine betrothed to Prince Henry if under pressure. They asked that the 100,000 *scudos* they had paid to Henry VII (which was half the dowry promised), her dower rights (which also had a cost), and Catherine herself be returned to Spain. They also were emphatic that Henry honor his part of the bargain by granting Catherine, as Dowager Princess of Wales, revenues from Chester, Cornwall, and Wales. Alternatively, they encouraged the idea that Catherine be betrothed to Arthur's surviving brother, Henry. There had, after all, been immediate precedent for this within the family when María married her sister Isabel's widower, King Manoel of Portugal.

Ferdinand and Isabella's entreaties to their ambassador regarding Catherine were continuous. In May 1502, they told him that she was suffering and needed to be moved from the unhealthy place she was living in. They continued to insist that their daughter be returned to them. Queen Isabella was especially forthright about this, ordering de Puebla and her other envoy to England, the Duke of Estrada, to see that the princess returned. "Press much for the departure of the Princess of Wales, my daughter, so that she may immediately come home" went one missive.[21] "You must say that the greater her loss and affliction, the more reason is there for her to be near her parents, as well for her consolation on account of her age."[22] Isabella went on: "You shall say to the King of England that we cannot endure that a daughter whom we love should be so far from us when she is in affliction, and that she should not have us at hand to console her; also it would be more suitable for a young girl of her age to be with us than to be in any other place. . . . Add that we greatly desire to have her with us."[23] Queen Isabella also expressed her opinion about King Henry's failure to act promptly regarding Catherine's financial straits, stating: "We cannot believe that he will refuse to do and perform towards us and the Princess all that he has promised."[24]

At the same time, Isabella ordered the duke to promote an engagement between Catherine and Henry, telling him to "bring the betrothal to a conclusion as soon as you are able, and in conformity with the directions given you respecting it. For then all our anxiety will cease, and we shall be able to seek the aid of England against France; for it is the most efficient help we can have."[25] Here, Isabella reveals one of the main reasons behind wanting to see Catherine engaged to Prince Henry: to maintain the Anglo-Spanish alliance so necessary to keep French ambitions at bay. Queen Isabella told Estrada "how great has been the effrontery shown us by the King of France in making war upon us . . . in sending a large body of troops to our frontiers, with the covetous desire to seize upon our possessions."[26]

A year after Catherine was widowed, she still had not left England for Spain. This spurred Queen Isabella to order de Puebla that "preparations must be made for the return hither of the Princess of Wales, our daughter, for there must be no delay about her departure."[27] De Puebla, whom Ferdinand and Isabella did not trust completely, appeared to have wanted to curry favor with Henry VII. With their confidence in him at an ever greater ebb, de Puebla then suggested that Henry VII might wish to marry Catherine himself. The idea intrigued King Henry but infuriated Ferdinand and Isabella. The indignant queen told the Duke of Estrada that "this would be a very evil thing,—one never before seen, and the mere mention of which offends the ears,—we would not for anything in the world that it should take place. Therefore, if anything be said to you about it, speak of it as a thing not to be endured. You must likewise say very decidedly that on no account would we allow it, or even hear it mentioned, in order that by these means the King of England may lose all hope of bringing it to pass."[28] Queen Isabella found the idea of Catherine marrying King Henry unacceptable on several levels. What would be her young daughter's future if she again became widowed in no time, since Henry, in his forties, was far from robust? If Catherine ended up marrying Henry VII, the best she "could hope for from such a marriage was a brief reign as queen consort, then a long widowhood, commencing perhaps in her twenties, with no political influence. Marriage to Prince Henry would assure her of a far more stable and glorious future."[29]

Meanwhile, Princess Catherine—the royal pawn and the subject of all the disputations flying between England and Spain—continued to pray and hope that all would be right in the end. For a while after her widowhood, the teenage princess lived in Durham House in London, where she was watched over like a hawk by Doña Elvira. Once again, the stiff Spanish court etiquette prevailed under the unyielding duenna. All of Catherine's days, however, were not spent in rigid isolation. Outings on the Thames and visits by the royal children eased

Catherine's isolation. Prince Henry and his young sisters, Margaret and Mary, occasionally enlivened Catherine's days with their good humor, despite the language gap that still hampered Catherine.

During this time, the all-important question concerning the consummation of Arthur and Catherine's marriage preoccupied a number of individuals in both the Spanish and English courts. But Doña Elvira, who had close access to the princess, was emphatic. Catherine was still a virgin; she and her ladies would swear to this.

Queen Isabella continued to try to get her daughter back to Spain, telling Estrada, "should the King of England not be willing immediately to settle the betrothal of the Princess of Wales with the Prince of Wales . . . in that case, the Princess of Wales shall depart at once for Spain. She shall do so, moreover, without waiting to recover the 100,000 *scudos* of the portion of which the King of England has to make restitution."[30]

King Henry VII's conduct regarding the money exasperated Catherine's mother, who complained that "it would not be consonant either with reason, or with right, human or divine, but would, on the contrary, be almost barbarous and dishonest proceeding, if the King of England, provided he could, were to keep by force that which the Princess of Wales took with her, and which belongs to her. Likewise, it would be an action the most opposed to virtue that was ever seen, if, over and above the loss and affliction with which God has visited her, and in addition to the great trouble of mind which she had to suffer both on leaving us and on her return, the King of England were to deprive her of whatever consolation and compensation could be given her for her losses."[31] Toward the close of her very long letter to Estrada, Queen Isabella again reiterated her wish to have her daughter at her side, indicating both a maternal concern and anxiety over Catherine's future status. "Take care," Isabella emphasized, "that there be no delay in the betrothal [between Catherine and Prince Henry], because, in addition to the injury and shame which result, it would cause us combined pain and grief to see her remain in the state in which she is."[32]

After nearly two years of negotiations, the treaty sealing the betrothal of Catherine and Henry, Prince of Wales, was finally signed. In the treaty, Ferdinand and Isabella and Henry VII agreed to try to obtain the papal dispensation necessary for their children to marry. This dispensation was needed owing to the facts that Catherine became related to Henry in the first degree of affinity through her marriage to Arthur and that the marriage was solemnized according to the rites of the Roman Catholic Church. It is interesting that the treaty also stated that Catherine and Arthur's marriage had been consummated. In a letter to his ambassador in Rome, King Ferdinand mentioned this, saying that "in the clause of the treaty which mentions the dispensation of the Pope, it is stated that the Princess Katharine consummated her marriage with Prince Arthur. The fact, however, is, that although they were wedded, Prince Arthur and the Princess Katharine never consummated the marriage. It is well known in England that the Princess is still a virgin. But as the English are much disposed to cavil, it has seemed to be more prudent to provide for the case as though the marriage had been consummated, and the dispensation of the Pope must be in perfect keeping with the said clause of the treaty."[33]

When the necessary dispensation was granted by Pope Julius II, in December 1503, stability and happiness seemed within Catherine's reach. Henry, a jovial and strapping youth whose company Catherine enjoyed, was turning out to be an intelligent individual, full of spirit, a gifted musician and mimic. Marriage to him might be an ideal partnership for Catherine. At eighteen years of age, the princess from Castile was showing signs of adapting to English ways, relishing the greater freedoms found in England, and even resenting Doña Elvira's restricting care. Yet these newfound freedoms proved few and far between. A black cloud soon descended upon Catherine, and it concerned her own mother.

Queen Isabella's final years were darkened by pain and anxiety. Exhausted by work, incessant travel through difficult terrain, the deaths of her loved ones, Juana's insanity, and Catherine's troubles, Isabella's health finally collapsed entirely. The chronicler and humanist Peter Martyr, who spent time at Isabella's court, recorded her final days. In October 1504 he wrote that "her whole system is pervaded by a consuming fever. She loathes food of every kind and is tormented with incessant thirst, while the disorder has all the appearance of terminating in a dropsy."[34] In spite of her illness, Isabella continued to work until the end, receiving people while reclining on a sofa. To those who wept at her bedside, she said, "Do not weep for me, nor waste your time in fruitless prayers for my recovery, but pray rather for the salvation of my soul."[35] Peter Martyr, along with other devoted retainers, kept vigil as the illness weakened Isabella. Of the ordeal, Martyr wrote: "We sit sorrowful in the palace all day long, tremblingly waiting the hour when religion and virtue shall quit the earth with her. Let us pray that we may be permitted to follow hereafter where she is soon to go. She so far transcends all human excellence, that there is scarcely anything of mortality about her. She can hardly be said to die, but to pass into a nobler existence, which should rather excite our envy than our sorrow. She leaves the world filled with her renown, and she goes to enjoy life eternal with her God in heaven. I write this between hope and fear, while the breath is still fluttering within her."[36]

Isabella knew death was near and signed her will. In it, the queen characteristically called on God, the Virgin Mary, and the saints, and gave specific instructions on her burial. Through these instructions, Isabella also gave insight into her thoughts and feelings about Ferdinand, saying: "Let my body be interred in the monastery of San Francisco, which is in the Alhambra of the city of Granada, . . . but I desire and command that, if the King, My Lord, should choose a sepulchre in any church or monastery in any other part of place of these my kingdoms, my body be translated thither and buried beside the body of His Highness."[37] Queen Isabella explained that she wanted her body to lie beside King Ferdinand's "in order that the union we have enjoyed while living, and which (through the mercy of God) we hope our souls will experience in heaven, may be represented by our bodies on earth."[38] The queen also left her jewels to King Ferdinand, "that they may serve as witness of the love I have ever borne him, and remind him that I await him in a better world, and so that with this memory he may the more holily and justly live."[39]

Queen Isabella also asked that her daughter and heir, Juana, and her husband, Philip, continue the fight against the Muslims: "I beg my daughter and her husband . . . that they will devote themselves unremittingly to the conquest of Africa and to the war for the faith against the Moors."[40] Three days before she died, Isabella added a codicil. Among the instructions she gave was one pertaining to the Indians in the New World. The queen urged her successors to treat the Indians with kindness and to continue converting them to Christianity. She also wished to ensure that her debts were repaid, that provisions were set aside for the poor and other less fortunate individuals, and that some of her goods be distributed to hospitals and convents.

Shortly before she breathed her last at Medina del Campo, Queen Isabella prayed and consoled those who came to say farewell. Dressed in a Franciscan robe, she received the Last Rites of the Roman Catholic Church. On the morning of November 26, 1504, as the friar intoned the final prayers, "at the phrase, *in manus tuas,* it is said, she sighed and made the sign of the cross and when he said, *Consummatum est,* she died."[41] Queen Isabella was fifty-three years old.*

The day after, Isabella's body was brought in a stately procession to begin its journey from Medina del Campo to Granada, her final resting place. Wind and

---

In manus tuas is Latin for "into thy hands," from the seven last words of Christ. *Consummatum est,* words uttered by Christ, is Latin for "It is finished."

rain lashed at the funeral cortege as it struggled through mud to its destination. Only when the cortege arrived at Granada did the clouds lift and the sun shine. Isabella was buried, dressed in her Franciscan habit, in the cathedral at Granada, the site of her greatest triumph.

King Ferdinand was bereft. He told the chief citizens of Madrid: "It has pleased Our Lord . . . to take to Himself the Most Serene Queen Doña Isabel, my very dear and well-beloved wife; and although her loss is for me the greatest heaviness that this world held in store . . . yet, seeing that her death was as holy and catholic as her life, we may believe that Our Lord has received her into His glory, that is a greater and more lasting kingdom than any here on earth."[42]

Christopher Columbus, on hearing of Queen Isabella's death, wrote to his son, Diego, that the queen was gone from this rough and weary world and, since her life was holy, she was likely with God. Peter Martyr wrote eloquently of Isabella to Archbishop Talavera, echoing the feeling of many of her contemporaries: "My hand falls powerless by my side for very sorrow. The world has lost its noblest ornament; a loss to be deplored not only by Spain, which she has so long carried forward in the career of glory, but by every nation in Christendom, for she was the mirror of every virtue, the shield of the innocent, and an avenging sword to the wicked. I know none of her sex, in ancient or modern times, who in my judgment is at all worthy to be named with this incomparable woman."[43]

7

THE GOLDEN COUPLE

On the day Queen Isabella died, Catherine had written two letters, one to her father saying she had not heard from him, and the other to her mother: "I have written three letters to you, and have given them to Doctor de Puebla to forward with all care. I wish to know above all things else how your health is. . . . I cannot be satisfied or cheerful until I see a letter from you. I have no other hope or comfort in this world than that which comes from knowing that my mother and father are well."[1]

Isabella's death left Catherine bereft of a loving mother and powerful champion. Gone forever was the woman "who had been a legend in her lifetime."[2] Catherine's future now hinged on two men, King Henry and King Ferdinand. In the coming months, Catherine's attempts to win Henry VII's goodwill would be continually undermined. She would also have little support from her father. During this time, Catherine deteriorated "into a woman much weathered by her isolation in a country that forgot the courtesies due to her royal state. She sorrowed in lonely exile."[3] And it was very much a life of exile, since Catherine still had not mastered the English language and felt her isolation keenly thanks in large part to the language barrier. What few communications she had directly with Henry VII were in Latin. Further, she had none of the influential advisers who had helped keep her mother from being marginalized years earlier in Spain. She was obliged to rely on Dr. de Puebla and Doña Elvira. De Puebla was untrustworthy or ineffectual or both, and Doña Elvira would prove herself opportunistic and treacherous.

Queen Isabella's death diminished King Ferdinand's prestige and domination. Many Castilian nobles still harbored suspicions about Ferdinand II of

Aragon, whom they found difficult to accept as one of their own. He had been consort to the Queen of Castile, but upon Isabella's death, the succession to Castile (not Aragon) went to Juana. Isabella had invested Ferdinand with the power to act for their daughter in the event she could not reign, an understandable move considering Juana's mental state. Now that Juana was Queen of Castile, a number of the country's nobles switched their allegiance, believing that, if they sided with Juana and Philip, they might be able to recover some of the prerogatives they had lost during the previous reign.

Isabella's death diminished Catherine's value to King Henry. Spain was quite suddenly no longer the great power it had been when Ferdinand and Isabella ruled as the Catholic Kings. Henry VII thought it prudent to find a more advantageous bride for his only son and heir. King Henry accordingly coaxed his son to make a speech before the Privy Council and Bishop of Winchester in June 1505, in which young Prince Henry repudiated his betrothal with Catherine. This act cast Catherine's fate into the unknown. King Henry was also unhappy with Ferdinand, who would not pay the rest of Catherine's dowry. Henry VII therefore stripped Catherine of the hundred-pounds-a-month allowance he had granted after she waived her dower rights on becoming betrothed to Henry. With no source of funds, Catherine had barely enough money to buy food and could not pay her servants, who struggled to remain helpful to her. One of Catherine's closest and most helpful Spanish friends was Maria de Salinas. "She has always faithfully served me, and in the hours of trial has comforted me," wrote Catherine to her father.[4] Catherine never stopped despairing for her faithful servants and always tried to alleviate their lot by begging money for their wages and dowries.

By April 1506, Princess Catherine's situation had deteriorated so much that she sent the following lengthy letter to her father explaining her difficulties:

> I have written many times to your highness, supplicating you to order a remedy for my extreme necessity, of which (letters) I have never had an answer. . . . I am in debt in London, and this not for extravagant things, nor yet by relieving my own (people), who greatly need it, but only for food; and how the king of England, my lord, will not cause them (the debts) to be satisfied, although I myself spoke to him, and all those of his council, and that with tears: but he said that he is not obliged to give me anything, and that even the food he gives me is of his good will; because your highness has not kept promise with him in the money of my marriage-portion. I

told him that I believed that in time to come your highness would discharge it. He told me that was yet to see, and that he did not know it. So that, my lord, I am in the greatest trouble and anguish in the world. . . . I have now sold some bracelets to get a dress of black velvet, for I was all but naked: for since I departed thence (from Spain) I have nothing except two new dresses. . . . On this account I supplicate your highness to command to remedy this, and that as quickly as may be; for certainly I shall not be able to live in this manner.[5]

Catherine's fate sank into greater uncertainty as the days passed. King Ferdinand, preoccupied with his own problems, wrote infrequently and continued to insist that King Henry was responsible for Catherine. King Henry occasionally gave her some money, but the amounts were few and far between. When Doña Elvira proposed a plan, little wonder then that Catherine jumped at it. As Queen of Castile, Juana might be able to mitigate Catherine's plight, the duenna suggested. Why not write to Juana, inviting her to England? Upon receiving Catherine's invitation, Juana and Philip replied that they could not visit her but that Catherine was certainly welcome to come to see them at Calais. They added that she should bring King Henry with her. Dr. de Puebla got wind of the letter and convinced Catherine that a meeting between Philip and Henry was the last thing King Ferdinand, Spain, or Catherine needed. If Philip and Henry came to an understanding at the expense of King Ferdinand and Spain, there was no telling the impact on Spain's future, as well as Catherine's. For all her distrust of de Puebla, Catherine understood his point. She tried to convince King Henry, who had by then learned of the idea, not to proceed with the meeting.

Catherine soon discovered that Doña Elvira's brother, the Spanish ambassador to Flanders, had pressed her to get Catherine to write the invitation. He had his own agenda, believing that Castile's future was better served by turning away from Aragon and reorienting toward Henry and Philip. When Catherine saw through her duenna's duplicity, "a seething fury replaced her anxiety. She knew she had been played for a fool and she inwardly writhed at her own ineptitude and folly."[6] The event "marked the hour when Catherine came of age and the last of her innocence and naïveté was discarded like a worn-out mantle."[7] She confronted Doña Elvira and dismissed her immediately. From then on, Catherine would tread carefully in a world flush with conspiracy. And aptly so, since nowhere was the art of dissimulation and intrigue going to be more evident or more challenging than in the Tudor court of England's next king.

In 1506 the meeting between Philip and Henry VII took place after all, not in Calais but in England, thanks to the vagaries of the weather. Juana and Philip were traveling from Flanders to Castile to be crowned king and queen in their new kingdom. However, a violent storm unexpectedly sent the ship carrying them to England. King Henry VII welcomed the couple as they disembarked. Catherine met her sister Juana but was never left alone with her, save for a very brief period, during which Isabella's two daughters found nothing in common. Hence, little came of the encounter between the sad sisters.

In October 1506, in an unexpected turn of events, Philip died from typhoid fever, though rumors of poisoning inevitably emerged. A distraught Queen Juana, already besotted over her husband, now transferred her obsession to his dead body. In a macabre turn of events, Juana traveled about Castile with Philip's corpse, refusing to be separated from it.

Across the channel, Henry VII began to entertain the idea of marrying the widowed Juana. He had been impressed by her beauty during her brief visit to England. Henry VII also had been negotiating a marriage between Prince Henry and Juana and Philip's daughter, Archduchess Eleanor, who seemed a greater dynastic and political catch than Catherine of Aragon. Another marriage uniting the Tudors with the Habsburgs, this time Eleanor's brother Archduke Charles with Princess Mary, King Henry's daughter, was also discussed. All these negotiations illustrate the trajectory that the Habsburgs were following. Thanks to Philip and Juana's marriage, the Habsburgs were set to rule Spain for generations and were now well on their way to becoming the most powerful and envied dynasty in Europe.

Catherine wondered when her situation might improve. The constant wrangling over funds, plus her uncertain status in a land still foreign to her, was oppressive, a far cry from her childhood at the Alhambra. There was, however, one person in the English court whom Catherine was getting to know better and who brought some light into an otherwise demoralizing life. This person was none other than Prince Henry.

Born on June 28, 1491, at the Palace of Placentia in Greenwich, Prince Henry, like Princess Catherine, received a first-rate education, becoming fluent in several languages. His paternal grandmother, Margaret Beaufort, the Countess of Richmond, oversaw his education. The miserly Henry VII in the end spared no expense in getting for his son the best tutors, including the poet laureate John Skelton. Prince Henry thrived and excelled at his studies. Healthier than his elder brother, Arthur, Henry was athletic as well as musical and scholarly. By the time Henry was fifteen, he had grown into a handsome young man, tall and muscular, with reddish brown hair and a charming personality. He was turning out to be a fine catch for any woman, and Catherine was not immune to his charms. By the time Catherine was twenty, she and the adolescent Henry had developed a mutual fondness, much to King Henry's annoyance. He kept the two apart, and for three months in 1507, Catherine did not see the prince, prompting her to tell her father that "it seems to me a great cruelty."[8] Despite the king's attempts to loosen the bond that had grown between them, the prince's affection for Catherine had taken hold.

Catherine's maturity prompted her father to bestow an important role on her. King Ferdinand had enough confidence in her to appoint his daughter as his ambassador in England in 1507. As his diplomatic agent, Catherine saw her status improve. Her letters to King Ferdinand became much more than personal opinions; they took on the tone of official views. They were reasoned compositions, evidence of the princess's intelligence. However, never far from her analyses were pleas for help. In one report to her father, Catherine again emphasized where Henry VII stood: "As long as he is not entirely paid [the other half of my dowry], he regards me as bound and his son as free. . . . Thus mine is always the worst part, and what he does now is glorify himself for his magnanimity in waiting so long!"[9]

In spite of the constant penury, Catherine's appointment as her father's envoy invigorated the princess. For the first time since she arrived in England, she was seized with energy. She actively sought out any kind of information about Henry VII, the court, and the political situation. Catherine lobbied King Henry more than ever and "learned too, though this was a hard lesson, to keep her head and her temper, to be patient, wary, closemouthed, to endure without a sign insult, humiliation, open rebuffs and sly persecution, to be spied upon and lied to, and brow-beaten without betraying herself, without abandoning for an instant her sense of the larger issue, her relentless pursuit of her one aim. Her father had told her that on her marriage to the Prince of Wales depended the friendship between England and Spain, perhaps the very safety of her house. If the driving force of a single will could achieve that marriage, Catherine would do it."[10]

When King Ferdinand granted Catherine's request for another Spanish ambassador to England, he came in the person of Don Gutierre Gómez de Fuensalida. However, Fuensalida disappointed Catherine with his grandiloquent ways and insensitive dealings with King Henry. By now, the princess from Castile had become a discerning judge of character. Her unpleasant experience with Doña Elvira had been the first in a long line of incidents that alerted Catherine to insincerity and duplicity. The lonely and desperate years at Henry

VII's court had awakened in her a sharp awareness of the real world. Naturally upright in character, Catherine now understood that political and personal survival depended on courting those in power. But to what extent would she have to dissemble? And would there come a point when she would have to compromise her principles completely?

Throughout this time of crisis and throughout her life, Catherine, like her mother, remained constant in her religious devotions. Like Isabella, Catherine was insistent on having a spiritual director or confessor who could help her form her conscience in accordance with the Church's teachings. In time, Catherine found a most acceptable confessor in the person of Fray Diego Fernandez. A member of the Franciscan Order, to whom Queen Isabella was especially attached, Fray Diego was an intellectual, a Spaniard who spoke English, and above all, a kindred spirit whom Catherine admired and trusted. It was understandable that she came to rely on Fray Diego. Here was an undisputed champion of her cause, cultivating in her much needed mettle. Fray Diego counseled Catherine to hold her ground, urging her to stay strong and to fight for her rightful position as the future wife of the future king of England.

Despite Catherine's attempts to improve her lot, her irregular situation continued. She was at an impasse. Likewise frustrating, the princess felt a growing attraction to the seventeen-year-old Henry, who by now had grown into a splendid-looking prince with his broad physique, great height (over six feet tall), and easy charm. Clean-shaven, with a fair and clear complexion like Catherine's, Henry also possessed handsome features, including a rich head of hair, a fine, long nose, arched eyebrows, and penetrating eyes that cast a playful twinkle. Henry, in sum, was turning into a princely Adonis, and Catherine was succumbing, as any woman would to a handsome and charming young man who paid her flattering attention.

King Henry continually obstructed her betrothal to the prince as he sought a match that might bring greater advantages to England. By the early part of 1509, Catherine's spirit finally broke. She decided to leave England and return to her native land, where "she could spend the rest of her life serving God. This was the final expression of despair on the part of Queen Isabella's daughter, who had been trained to believe that life on the throne, not in the convent, was the destiny for which God had sent her on earth."[11] However, at this, her lowest ebb, fate suddenly took another turn.

For months, Henry VII had been in declining health. His appetite was failing him, his cough became more troublesome than ever, and his constitution was weak. Henry's thoughts turned to Elizabeth, his wife. Clearly the time was nearing when he would join her in peaceful repose. After planning a chapel in Westminster Abbey for himself and his queen, Henry prepared for death, requesting innumerable Masses to be said for his soul. He died on April 22, 1509. The new king, Henry VIII, was two months shy of his eighteenth birthday.

King Ferdinand, upon hearing the news, acted quickly. Not knowing the extent of Henry's desire to marry Catherine, he advised Fuensalida and Catherine that he would grant all the concessions, including the outstanding dowry, in order to facilitate the marriage. One of Henry VIII's first acts was to declare before his councilors his intention to marry and that, in marrying Catherine, he was fulfilling his father's dying wish. Catherine was, he stated, the only woman he desired to marry. He had longed to wed her, the woman he loved, and now that he was king, he was determined to make her his wife in no time.

Upon hearing the news she had so ardently desired, Catherine was overcome with gratitude. All the years of uncertainty, of poverty and humiliation, were not for naught. Fray Diego had been right in counseling her to fight for this, and now she had won. At last Catherine was to become Queen of England.

The longed for day arrived on June 11, 1509, when Henry and Catherine were wed privately at Greenwich. The Archbishop of Canterbury asked: "Most illustrious Prince, is it your will to fulfill the treaty of marriage concluded by your father, the late King of England, and the parents of the Princess of Wales, the King and Queen of Spain; and as the Pope has dispensed with this marriage, to take the Princess who is here present for your lawful wife? The King answered: I will. . . . The Princess answered: I will."[12] The happy bride wore white, with her hair flowing loosely as a symbol of virginity. They then sealed their union with a Mass at the church of the Observant Friars. Catherine would have likely taken comfort in the thought that what God had put together through the sacrament of marriage, no man can put asunder. Only death could part her and Henry now. Unlike Catherine's previous marriage, there was no doubt that her marriage to Henry was consummated soon after their wedding, with the king even boasting that Catherine had indeed come as "a maid" to him, unblemished.

The marriage was popular with the English, who had not forgotten the excitement they felt when Catherine had arrived eight years before as Prince Arthur's bride. The English people had also been aware of her plight after becoming Arthur's widow. Now that Henry VIII had come to the damsel's rescue, all was sure to end happily. Trade between Spain and England would boom, prosperity would smile upon the English. Catherine, though a bit older looking than the bride of fifteen, still possessed a prettiness that charmed many, including the new king.

For weeks after Henry and Catherine's wedding, festivities went on, and Catherine joined in the celebrations. She had told her father as much, writing to him: "Our time is ever passed in continual feasts."[13] Ferdinand was pleased to hear the news, writing to Catherine that he was "thankful to God for the conclusion of her marriage. [He] loves her more than any of his other children. She has always been a dutiful and obedient daughter to him. Her marriage is a very grand and very honourable one."[14] In another letter, he tells Catherine that he "is exceedingly glad to hear that she and the King her husband are well and prosperous, and that they love one another so much. [He, Ferdinand] hopes their happiness will last as long as they live. To be married is the greatest blessing in the world. A good marriage is not only an excellent thing in itself, but also the source of all other kinds of happiness."[15]

Henry VIII proudly wrote to his father-in-law. He expressed much affection for his bride of six weeks, "whose virtues increase, shine and flourish more day by day," adding that he would not have chosen another woman over her for a wife.[16] Nearly a year into the marriage, King Henry could still write to his father-in-law that "he and his Queen are perfectly happy, and that his kingdom enjoys undisturbed tranquility."[17] Catherine also wrote to her father, assuring him that "our English kingdoms enjoy peace and the people love us, as my husband and I love one another."[18]

Soon after Henry and Catherine's wedding, as part of the wedding festivities, a kind of castle was constructed near the palace of Westminster. The rose and pomegranate, Henry's and Catherine's symbols respectively, as well as the initials *H* and *K,* were prominently displayed throughout the castlelike structure. Catherine's choice of the pomegranate as her symbol was highly charged with meaning. She chose the emblem of Granada, which her mother had conquered in 1492. The pomegranate also was associated with fertility, and as Henry's consort, Catherine's first duty was to provide him with children. In no time, the Tudor rose and pomegranate decorated the couple's palaces, so that courtiers and visitors alike needed only to glance at a wall or ceiling to be reminded of the royal couple's deep bond of affection.

In the king and queen's honor, jousts and tournaments were held. King Henry was particularly skillful at playing the knight in these events. He not only reveled in his abilities but also relished promoting a chivalric court. Catherine was his ladylove, and the king was her champion-knight, who proudly wore their initials on his armor during jousts. The young queen delighted in these revelries and supported her husband by her presence.

Henry was a fine horseman who liked to hunt and go hawking. Catherine,

also passionate about hawking, joined her husband in this pastime, courageously riding her horse as hard as she could to keep up with the king. Henry
was also an excellent and avid player of royal tennis and enjoyed archery. There
were few days in the early years of the couple's marriage when King Henry did
not participate in some kind of physical amusement, both as a form of exercise
and as a way of flaunting his prowess, for he was always a boastful creature.

Sumptuous times called for sumptuous clothes, and Henry VIII ensured
that his court dazzled. Velvets and satins, cloths of gold, and heavily embroidered material adorned the king and queen and members of their court, as did
ostentatious jewelry. The jewels in particular caught many people's attention,
because of their size, sparkle, and exquisite cut. With so many saints' days in an
England still steeped in Roman Catholicism, there was plenty of opportunity to
parade in such finery, be it Easter Sunday, or the days celebrating the feasts of
St. George (England's patron saint), Corpus Christi, St. Thomas of Canterbury,
the Nativity of the Blessed Virgin Mary, or Christmas, among many others.

Tudor Christmases were a highlight of court life. They culminated on the
feast of the Epiphany, or the Three Kings, twelve days after Christmas Day, in a
special banquet. Christmas gift exchanges took place on New Year's Day. During
her first Christmas as his wife, Catherine received an exquisite illuminated missal
from Henry. He inscribed it with the words "If your remembrance be according
to my affection, I shall not be forgotten in your daily prayers, for I am yours,
Henry R., forever."[19] Moved by this, Catherine inscribed her own message beneath it, saying: "By daily proof you shall me find to be to you both loving and
kind."[20]

Queen Catherine could not help but be dazzled by this dynamo of a husband. Whatever Henry embarked on he did with vigor and panache. "When a
royal ship was to be launched, he himself acted as pilot, in a sailor's coat and
trousers of cloth of gold, and a gold chain with the inscription 'Dieu et mon
Droit' on which hung a whistle, 'which he blew as loud as a trumpet.' "[21]
Catherine and Henry threw themselves completely into their merrymaking—a
refreshing change from the sober final years of Henry VII's reign. Catherine
herself was occasionally the target of Henry's merriment, but his pranks were
always done in good jest and with good intentions. The couple was obviously in
love, and it was easy to see why Henry and Catherine fell for each other. To
Henry, Catherine was the intriguing princess from a faraway land, demure and
in distress. Each had been lonely in his or her own way, Catherine because of
her predicament as well as being a foreigner, while Henry, though outwardly
jovial, was under the scrutiny of his demanding father and bereft of the loving

presence of his departed mother. Little wonder, then, that the two gravitated toward each other. For Catherine, Henry represented the epitome of a prince. The new queen was not the only one dazzled by this magnificent specimen. A foreigner at court had penned similar thoughts: "His majesty is the handsomest potentate I have set eyes on . . . with an extremely fine calf to his leg."[22] Handsome and athletic, accomplished and intelligent, gentlemanly and religious, Catherine could not have asked for more in a husband. His undivided attention to her was very gratifying, especially after all the years she had to endure in limbo while King Ferdinand and King Henry VII haggled over her future.

Henry VIII and Queen Catherine shared many pastimes. They were both passionate about music and danced together with great enjoyment. Henry was adept at playing musical instruments, including the organ and lute. He also dabbled in composing music, including some for Masses. Piety was among their common interests. Both had a sincere attachment to the Church, scrupulously observing the feasts and holy days and attending Mass frequently. Henry would also join Catherine in her apartment for vespers. As a devout Christian who dreamed of fighting a crusade in the Holy Land one day, King Henry also came to see Catherine in a special way. His wife was, after all, the daughter of the incomparable Queen Isabella. And because Henry's beloved Catherine "had lived in a land conquered by the Infidel and whose mother had driven them away and raised the Cross in their Moorish palaces," she "assumed an almost mystical light in his eyes."[23]

Catherine and Henry were also united by their love of learning. Few, if any, kings and queens in all Europe could compete intellectually with the couple. Henry was gifted with languages, and in order to communicate better with Catherine, he learned Castilian, which he added to his already fluent Latin, Italian, and French (Catherine at last mastered English but continued to speak it with a distinct accent that betrayed her Iberian origins). Henry's intellectual interests also encompassed the sciences and theology. His compositions, which he sent to the Vatican, were much admired for their cogency and elegance.

Intellectually curious like Queen Catherine, King Henry sought to fashion his court into a haven where the promotion of scholarship took center stage. Only five weeks into the new reign, Lord Mountjoy, a humanist and future chamberlain to the queen, wrote with enthusiasm to his friend Erasmus about Henry: "If you could see how everyone here rejoices in having so great a prince, how his life is all their desire, you would not contain yourself for sheer joy. Extortion is put down, liberality scatters riches with a bountiful hand, yet our King does not set his heart on gold or jewels, but on virtue, glory and immortality. The other day he told me 'I wish I were more learned.' 'But learning is not what we expect of a King,' I answered, 'merely that he should encourage scholars.' 'Most certainly,' he rejoined, 'as without them we should scarcely live at all.' Now what more splendid remark could a prince make?"[24]

The English court opened its doors to Europe's greatest scholars. Among the most famous was the Spanish humanist Juan Luis Vives. Other intellectuals who were close to the king were the prelate and Greek scholar William Latimer and the lawyer and author Thomas More, as well as the physician and scholar Thomas Linacre, all of whom stood out for their erudition. The celebrated Erasmus declared that the English court under Henry and Catherine's patronage had no rival. Erasmus also praised Catherine to her husband, telling the king, "Your noble wife spends that time in reading the sacred volume which other princesses occupy in cards and dice."[25]

King Henry VIII and Queen Catherine's presence on the throne of England augured well for the future. The couple themselves exuded a triumphant and optimistic air. Catherine was proving to be a valuable helpmate to her husband. A fine adornment at court, a growing confidante of the king's, an able organizer who "had her mother's gift of producing magnificent effects when she chose,"[26] Catherine, in sum, was the ideal wife for Henry VIII. With so much going for this golden couple, it was not surprising to find King Henry VIII and Queen Catherine basking in their subjects' adulation. As Henry wished, soon after their marriage, Catherine was crowned queen. Alongside her husband at his coronation, she looked suitably regal. Dressed in white and gold satin, she wore a gold crown with sapphires and pearls, her auburn-reddish hair streaming down her back. Queen Catherine made her way in a litter of white and gold to Westminster Abbey. Beside her rode Henry in cloth of gold and bloodred velvet. The coronation ceremony and her wedding were the culmination of a hard-won battle and long supplication for Catherine. At twenty-three, she was the cherished bride of a loving husband, and she, the daughter of Isabella of Spain, was now Queen of England.

8

THE STRUGGLE FOR THE TRUTH

*A*lmost overnight, Queen Catherine had gone from suffering the indignities of penury to a life of comfort and wealth. At her disposal were eight main residences, in and around the small medieval walled city of London as well as in the countryside. Her future seemed bright, the more so when she became pregnant. However, in January 1510, she gave birth to a stillborn daughter, casting a pall where there should have been a joyous event. Catherine became pregnant again in no time, but troubles ensued.

Given all the affection Henry had showered upon her, Catherine was taken aback by the news that he was paying too much attention to Lady Fitzwalter, sister to the Duke of Buckingham. Philandering was not unusual among royal husbands at the time, and King Henry could not understand why Catherine would be so irritated. He accused his wife of meddling and intriguing against him. The Spanish envoy at the time reported: "Everyone can see that [the king] is vexed with Catherine and that Catherine is vexed with him. No one knows how it will end. The storm is at the height."[1] Henry's roving eye caused this, the first real quarrel between them and may have brought about Catherine's miscarriage. Catherine wrote to her father "that her child was still-born [and] is considered to be a misfortune in England . . . [she] begs him not to be angry with her, for it has been the will of God."[2]

Like her mother before her, Catherine of Aragon would have to endure the indignity of being married to a philandering husband. Catherine now saw a new side to Henry—a temperamental side from which even she was not immune. The king's temper was unpredictable, and his wrath extreme. Catherine, though, through thick and thin, would stay devoted and unswervingly loyal to her king and husband. But the truly trying days of the marriage were still far off. For the present, the queen was preoccupied with trying to give Henry children, which they both longed to have.

After weathering the first big fight with Henry and reconciling with him, Catherine was again pregnant, and on January 1, 1511, at Richmond, she gave birth to a healthy baby boy, whom the couple named Henry. The country broke out in celebration. The infant prince was toasted in dancing, songs, and pageants. Again the letters *H* and *K* were displayed prominently in homage to the king and queen. But then tragedy struck. Less than two months later, little Prince Henry died. Queen Catherine was devastated. King Henry too was sorrowful, but with characteristic gusto, he immersed himself in preparation for war. He was eager to prove his prowess on the battlefield.

Like Catherine's parents, Henry VIII wanted to participate in the fight against Islam in defense of Christianity. His father had wholeheartedly approved of such measures and even sent his hearty congratulations to Ferdinand and Isabella during their Granada War. Even in his dying days, King Henry VII had enjoined the soon-to-be Henry VIII to fight for Christendom by telling him: "My son, be a soldier of the Cross; oppose the enemies of God; sustain the Church and her appointed chief; strive to liberate the Tomb of Christ."[3] But in the summer of 1512, it was France, not the Holy Land, which was the object of Henry VIII's aggression. Henry allied himself with Catherine's father in a convenient maneuver that would pit England, Spain, and the Pope against Louis XII of France.

In the end, the English expedition to France was a failure. Some two thousand soldiers died. Mutinous soldiers also made their way back to England. It was an inglorious defeat for Henry. Undeterred by this humiliation on French soil, he led the army himself the next year in another campaign. The Holy League, composed of King Henry, King Ferdinand, and the Pope, was now augmented by the arrival of Holy Roman Emperor Maximilian. The alliance seemed to be an unbeatable combination, but unfortunately for Henry, Ferdinand, in order to keep Navarre, negotiated with King Louis XII. In return, Spain was to desist from fighting France for a year. This, however, did not deter Henry, who left Dover in June 1513.

Queen Catherine, again with child, bade her husband a tearful farewell. As a token of his appreciation for his wife and her abilities, he left Catherine in charge of England in his absence and created her captain of his forces. Henry VIII's appointment of her as regent and governor of the realm in his absence was a significant gesture. Catherine, after all, had acquitted herself well as King

Ferdinand's ambassador and shown an aptitude for politics. Her intelligence was undoubted, her loyalty to Henry, absolute. As his chief confidante, Catherine could be relied on to give him her honest opinion and now to rule well in his stead. The queen's loyalty was never really divided. Though she loved her father, she was not completely blind to his political machinations. And though her heart may have tilted toward Spain, England was now her country. It was England and Henry VIII to whom Catherine owed her first loyalty. Luis Caroz, the Spanish envoy to England, noted as much, saying at one point that "her confessor has persuaded the Queen to forget Spain, and gain the love of the English."[4]

Henry's confidence in Catherine was not mere bravado. She had to ensure that the running of the kingdom went smoothly with the king absent, for England was vulnerable to attack in the north from Scotland's King James IV (the husband of Margaret, Henry's sister). Meanwhile, in France, King Henry saw action in August, when he besieged Thérouanne. French forces arrived to relieve the town, but Henry and his soldiers defeated them in what became known as the Battle of the Spurs. Henry was easily victorious since the French fled in retreat. Another battle, however, proved far more glorious and significant to the English, though to Henry's chagrin, he did not participate because the conflict took place in England while he was still in France.

As expected, King James IV crossed the border into England. Catherine dispatched forty thousand men to fight off the Scots. In rallying troops to the cause, she emulated her mother. Queen Catherine entreated her men to defend their country, and to "remember that the Lord smiled upon those who stood in defense of their own! Remember that the English courage excels that of all other nations upon earth!"[5] As the queen prepared to march north, King James and his troops attacked and fought the Earl of Surrey and his soldiers at the Battle of Flodden Field in September 1513. The English decimated the Scots, killing the king and many of the Scottish nobility, along with ten thousand soldiers. The Battle of Flodden neutralized the Scottish threat to England for at least a generation. In relating what had happened in a letter to her husband, Catherine was careful not to upstage Henry. She reminded him that it was God to whom he owed England's triumph: "To my thinking this battle has been to your grace, and all your realm the greatest honour that could be, and more than should you win all the crown of France. Thanked be God of it; and I am sure your grace forgetteth not to do this . . . praying God to send you home shortly; for without this, no joy here can be accomplished, and for the same I pray."[6] Victory against the Scots did not cause Queen Catherine to forget or ignore her newly widowed sister-in-law, Queen Margaret. Catherine dispatched a Franciscan friar to Henry's sister to assure her that her regency over her young son would be honored as long as peace reigned between the two countries.

To Thomas Wolsey, the ambitious and able administrator who accompanied King Henry to France, Queen Catherine wrote about Flodden as well, revealing how she immersed herself in the fight against the Scots: "Ye be not so busy with the war as we be here encumbered with it. . . . My heart is very good to it and I am horribly busy with making standards, banners and badges."[7] Catherine also could not resist telling Wolsey: "The victory hath been so great, that I think none such hath ever been seen before."[8]

Wolsey, the wily cleric from Ipswich, had begun his ascent early in life, though only the son of a butcher. The young Thomas showed signs of great abilities and graduated from Oxford at fourteen. Seeing the Church as a path to prosperity, Wolsey studied for the priesthood and was ordained in 1498. He made his mark as a talented and industrious worker, eventually getting a foothold in Henry VII's court. Wolsey went on to impress the next king. Since he showed an aptitude and penchant for handling the minutiae of government that tended to bore the king, Henry VIII appointed him the royal almoner. During this time, Queen Catherine did not need to worry about Wolsey, even though he replaced her as Henry's great confidant. After all, the queen had seen close working partnerships between prelate and monarch in her mother's court, where Queen Isabella relied heavily on able men of the Church as advisers and administrators. Wolsey just might play the same role for Henry VIII.

The ambitious Wolsey secured his place by the king's side and had the king's ear when it came to many matters of state. Wolsey's meteoric rise cast an ominous shadow on Catherine's fate. In 1515, to Wolsey's great satisfaction, he became Lord Chancellor and a cardinal of the Church. As befitted his powerful position, he began building a spectacular palace, Hampton Court, on the river Thames some miles from London. Three years later, his power was still in the ascendant as he was named the Papal Legate in England. By this time, Wolsey's positions in government and his influence with Henry made him the most powerful person in the kingdom after the king.

Mere weeks after the spectacular English victory at Flodden and not long before Henry VIII returned from France, Catherine gave birth to another son who did not live. When Henry returned, Catherine became pregnant again, but the king's confidence in his wife began to shake. Central to his increasing coolness toward his wife was the fact that she had still failed to produce an heir. Not one of their children had survived. Catherine herself suffered from the absence of children and desperately yearned to give Henry his coveted heir.

When her second baby son died, a dazed and grieving queen sat beside the empty cradle and was heard to murmur the words of one who cleaved her suffering to Christ: "You must love me, Lord, to confer upon me the privilege of so much sorrow!"[9]

At the same time, King Henry had come to delight in the affections of a certain Bessie Blount, a kin of Lord Mountjoy. Because mistresses were common in the lives of kings and easily discarded, Catherine took comfort in the fact that she was Henry's wife and queen. They were still very much on speaking terms; she had learned to keep her temper in check and to greet him lovingly when he came to her apartments. With no children to lighten her life, and most of her closest confidants gone from court, the queen increasingly took to spending much time in prayer and religious devotions. Like Queen Isabella before her, Catherine also spent much of her leisure time embroidering and mending her husband's shirts and linen, and producing exquisite altarcloths. These activities all helped to keep her mind away from things such as Henry's infidelities.

Besides the annoying presence of mistresses in Henry's life, there was another, more troubling sign that he was tiring of Catherine. Suddenly and unlike before, she was on the receiving end of King Henry's wrath over her father's political intrigues. Determined not to see Henry go through with his anti-French policies and dethrone King Louis XII, King Ferdinand and Emperor Maximilian now refused to come to the English king's aid. Ferdinand's perfidy infuriated Henry, and he became consumed with the thought that Spain had been treacherous to him. He could not help but see his wife as the daughter of the king who had double-crossed him.

From then on, Henry VIII brought England closer to France at the expense of the Anglo-Spanish alliance that Catherine had hoped would flourish. This volte-face was a defeat for the queen and clearly a victory for Wolsey, who had espoused a pro-French policy for England. Mary Tudor, Henry's sister, who had been affianced to Archduke Charles (grandson of, and heir to, Ferdinand and Maximilian), was now to be married promptly to the sickly, fifty-two-year-old Louis XII. When the pretty and vivacious, eighteen-year-old Mary was sent across the channel to become Queen of France, Catherine was at Dover to see off her sister-in-law, whose friendship she had enjoyed these dozen or so years. Mary was unhappy at the prospect of becoming Queen of France, for at the time she was in love with Charles Brandon, one of Henry VIII's closest friends. Henry assured his sister, of whom he was fond, that should the sickly King Louis die soon, he would allow her to marry the man of her choice. For the time being, however, the celebrations commemorating Mary's marriage to Louis underscored that England's previous friendship with Spain, which Catherine had hoped would last a long time, was in tatters.

By marrying off his sister to King Louis, Henry hoped to exact revenge on Catherine's father. Henry aspired to the French king's help in wrestling Navarre from Ferdinand, then in conquering Castile. Capturing Castile was his right, Henry felt, because of his marriage to Catherine. These plans were put aside, however, when much to Mary's relief, King Louis died. Mary then promptly married Charles Brandon without gaining her brother's consent. The couple managed to get Henry to forgive them; these were still the days when there was room in Henry's heart to feel magnanimous.

Having lived in England for some fifteen years, Catherine had developed an affinity for the English people. She was well aware of the role that Catholicism played in both countries. As in Spain, the Roman Catholic faith was still predominant in England. Reform of the Church had been in the air in the fourteenth century with the appearance of the Lollards, but in Catherine's day, Roman Catholicism still held sway in England. There, the late medieval Church had burgeoned into "a large and complex organization." Its "most visible manifestation" was "the proliferation of church buildings across the land. In 1500 England and Wales had twenty-one cathedrals, about 88,000 parish churches, about 265 houses of monks, 306 houses of regular canons, 183 houses of mendicant friars and 142 houses of nuns and canonesses."[10]

Though the Spanish form of Catholicism stood out for its rigorous and somewhat forbidding nature, the less austere form found in England made no less an impact on the inhabitants. Christianity thrived in England, in Spain, and in many parts of Europe. Devotion to the saints was widespread, and "reminders of them were everywhere in late medieval England—engraved on drinking-cups and bowls, carved on lintels and gable-ends, their very names given to children at baptism. Their images filled the churches, gazing down in polychrome glory from altar-piece and bracket, from windows and riches."[11] Among the holy days in England were the anniversaries of the martyrdom of Thomas Becket, Archbishop of Canterbury, and the public flogging King Henry II endured as penance for ordering Becket's killing. Even three hundred years after Becket's death, "kings, noblemen and great numbers of the common people came to Canterbury on horseback and on foot from all over England and Western Europe . . . to lay priceless jewels or humble pennies on St. Thomas's tomb."[12] Devotions centered on the Virgin Mary also proliferated in late medieval England and Europe, "and indeed Englishmen were encouraged to think of their country as being in a special way 'Mary's Dowry.' . . . Her cult came second only to that of Christ himself, and towered above that of all other saints."[13]

Devotion to Christ, particularly the devotion to the Wounds of Jesus, was "one of the most popular cults of late medieval Europe, and in England it was growing in popularity up to the very eve of the Reformation."[14] For the faithful—such as Queen Isabella, Queen Catherine, and their contemporaries—this devotion, which prepares the soul for death was critical, because the ensuing providential judgment would decide whether the soul was to spend eternity in damnation in Hell or in glory with God in Heaven. The last of the seven short sections of prayer in the devotion to the Wounds of Jesus deals with the supplicant's soul at the hour of death, when the prayer intones: "O Lord Jesus Christ, I ask you for the sake of that most bitter suffering which you bore for my sake upon the cross, and above all when your most noble soul left your most holy body: have mercy on my soul at its departing."[15] The preparation of the soul for death preoccupied laymen and royals alike in the England of Catherine of Aragon's time. John Fisher had preached his funeral sermon for Henry VII with a moving deathbed account of Catherine's father-in-law. Fisher spoke of Henry VII's "humility before the Blessed Sacrament 'with suche a reverence,'" and on his devotion on the day of his death toward the Crucifix. Fisher recounted how "the ymage of the crucyfyxe . . . he dyd beholde with grete reverence . . . often embracyncge it in his armes & with grete devocion kyssyng it, & betynge often his brest," so that "all stode aboute hym scarcely myght conteyne them from teres & wepynge."[16]

With the passage of time, Catherine's own faith increased in intensity. Yet far from shutting herself away in prayer, the queen also practiced Christian charity toward her subjects. Catherine visited the poor and sick, often leaving supplies for the less fortunate. She later encouraged lace making so that impoverished women could earn some money. This industry grew in the Midlands, centering in Bedfordshire, Buckinghamshire, and Northamptonshire. Queen Catherine also used the revenues she was entitled to from estates owned and from the rights derived from lumber, forests, and certain abbeys to help the poor and elderly. On bended knee, she pleaded with her husband to spare four hundred prisoners who had been set to be executed. Henry VIII spared their lives and granted the prisoners pardon. Her subjects always remembered these acts of kindness and generosity. They regarded their queen as a munificent angel.

Apart from her faith and concern for her English subjects, Catherine's other great interest was scholarship. England at the time was immersed, as were many parts of Europe, in humanism and a spirit of discovery and learning. Like her mother before her, Queen Catherine was a patron of education and welcomed eminent men of letters into her circle. Thomas More was a favorite with both Catherine and Henry. More, the author of *Utopia,* was renowned for his writings on theology, law, and poetry as well as translations (he had an excellent grasp of Latin and Greek). Eminently qualified to be among the king's counselors, he was one of the most erudite and able. Catherine did not hesitate to remind her husband that More was the only one truly worthy to be called counselor. Erasmus counted More as a friend and, like More, had a high opinion of Catherine. Erasmus declared that "the queen is astonishingly well read, far beyond what would be surprising in a woman, and as admirable for her piety as she is for her learning." He also declared: "We have in the queen of England a woman distinguished by her learning."[17] Erasmus gave credit for Catherine's education where it was due by saying "that she was imbued with learning by the care of her illustrious mother, from her infant years."[18] When he produced an edition of the New Testament, Catherine eagerly gave the humanist her support, and when he wrote a treatise titled *Institutio Christiani Matrimonii (The Institution of Christian Matrimony),* he dedicated it to the queen. Lord Mountjoy, another humanist, student, and patron of Erasmus, became a close member of Catherine's inner circle as her chamberlain. Other learned men whom Catherine favored included the educator John Colet (whom she supported in founding St. Paul's school for underprivileged boys) and the physician William Linacre, whom she encouraged to found the Royal College of Physicians. The queen also supported scholars associated with Oxford and Cambridge universities.

Even though she had spent many years in England, Queen Catherine had not forgotten her mother. During a picnic to celebrate her sister-in-law Mary's marriage to Charles Brandon, Catherine chatted with a Venetian in Spanish. The Venetian guest noted how passionately Catherine spoke about her mother. Catherine longed for this same mother-child relationship, and with every passing year her need to give Henry a child who lived became more imperative, for she was already thirty years old.

Finally, on the morning of February 18, 1516, Catherine's dearest wish came true when she gave birth to a healthy daughter at Greenwich after a long labor. The child was named Mary and baptized in the church of the Observant Friars. Grateful for a living child though disappointed that it was not a male, King Henry VIII did not feel this setback was serious, proclaiming that sons would follow.

Just weeks before Princess Mary's birth, Catherine's last link with Spain was severed when her father died. The news was kept from the queen until after Mary's birth. With King Ferdinand dead, "Catherine's sense of reverence for the Spanish royal house from which she had sprung transferred to her nephew, Charles of Austria."[19] With Ferdinand's death, Charles became King of Spain. Already Archduke of Austria, Charles was also the ruler of the Burgundian lands and German king as well as King of Spain, Naples, and Sicily. Added to these titles was Holy Roman Emperor. As one of the most important personages of the era, Catherine's nephew Charles was bound to be involved in any major dispute involving Europe's monarchs, as Henry VIII was to find out in the not too distant future.

Queen Catherine's preoccupation with intellectual and religious activity took on greater urgency after 1517, when Martin Luther's Ninety-five Theses catalyzed a revolutionary movement that led to the Reformation and the birth of Protestantism. His call for reform and argument against indulgences spiraled into more intense denunciations of the Church. These views were, in Rome's eyes, increasingly heretical, prompting the Pope to excommunicate Luther. Many in Germany and Europe sided with Luther, precipitating a tumultuous conflict that engulfed the Continent for years to come. The previously impregnable Church was under attack.

As Luther's tracts gained hold, Catherine encouraged Erasmus to produce works that argued against Luther. With the same goal in mind, the queen commissioned works from her chaplain, Fray Alfonso de Villa Sancta. Fray Alfonso gladly complied, writing a number of works, one of which he dedicated to Catherine. Overall, Catherine distinguished herself in promoting the new learning and, in so doing, showed herself to be a true daughter of Queen Isabella. Moreover, like her mother, Catherine found reason and religion highly compatible and defended her faith through reasoned arguments.

Henry VIII joined the kings and princes who took sides. An amateur theologian, Henry was dismayed not only by Luther's pronouncements but also by the impact his actions might have on society. The king accordingly took pen in hand to defend Catholicism from the assault hurled on it by the German monk. In his tract of 1521, *Assertio Septem Sacramentorum Adversus Martinum Lutherum (Assertion of the Seven Sacraments Against Martin Luther)*, Henry staunchly repudiated Luther. The work was composed largely by Henry with the help of Thomas More. In gratitude for his efforts, the Pope granted Henry VIII the title *Defensor Fidei* (Defender of the Faith).

It is interesting to note that, in this work, Henry questioned Luther's assertion that marriage could not be a sacrament unless it was so stated in the Bible by writing: " 'You admit no sacrament unless you read its institution in a book!' Marriage, wrote Henry, was the first of the sacraments to be instituted, because the first man, Adam, was married; and it was at a wedding that Christ performed his first miracle. . . . But why, asked Henry, 'search we so many proofs in so clear a thing? especially when that only text is sufficient for all, where Christ says 'Whom God has joined together, let no man put asunder.' O the admirable word! which none could have spoken, but the Word that was made flesh!' "[20]

Henry VIII's defense of the Church was in keeping with his role as champion of the papacy. He had regularly sided with the Pope in foreign policy disputes and had gone so far as to admonish Emperor Maximilian in 1511 for defying the Pope's authority and airing his faults in public.

Besides Emperor Maximilian, King Francis I of France was the other major player in European politics. Like Henry VIII in his youth, Francis was admired for his looks and intelligence. A man of letters, Francis I was a patron of artists, purchasing works by Titian, Raphael, and Michelangelo. He brought Leonardo da Vinci to France and was said to have cradled the great artist's head in his arms when Leonardo died, in 1519.

Catherine and Henry went to France to keep England in Francis's good graces. Wishing to come to an understanding, Francis I and Henry VIII met on a field outside Calais in June 1520 in an encounter that came to be known as the Field of Cloth of Gold. As befitted two monarchs who wished to impress each other, Francis and Henry tried to outdo each other in lavish entertainments. For three weeks, the two courts feasted and jousted, reveled in balls and masques.

King Francis was decidedly unimpressed by Catherine's looks. He noted that "the King of England is young" and declared, "But his wife is old and deformed."[21] Within the short span of ten years, Queen Catherine had lost the luster and looks that had attracted Henry to her. The fresh prettiness that had blossomed during her new marriage was replaced by a matronly image, exacerbated by a tendency to retire from the boisterous life that her husband still liked to pursue. Instead, Catherine increasingly took solace in her faith, rigidly adhering to fasts and prayers. Her religious devotions took many hours daily. Rising at five in the morning, she dressed herself in the habit of the third order of St. Francis, over which she wore her regular clothes. This order, founded in 1221, was for those living not in convents but within the world. Members, both married and single people, followed exercises in piety. Fridays and Saturdays were days of fasting for Catherine; she confessed her sins once a week and had an attendant read to her books of devotion after dinner. As Catherine entered midlife, there was no doubt that "the strain of piety which had made Isabella's last years seem those of a crowned nun was beginning to show in the daughter."[22]

With Catherine becoming increasingly ascetic, Henry felt her six years' seniority as never before. Though she gave birth again in 1518, that child died soon afterward too. In contrast, Henry's mistress, Bessie Blount, had given birth in 1519 to a healthy baby boy, Henry FitzRoy, who thrived. King Henry VIII began to question his situation. With each passing year, the chances of the queen giving him that coveted male heir decreased rapidly. Were he and Catherine condemned to have no male children who lived?

Despite the fact that Henry genuinely loved his daughter, Mary, her existence did not compensate for the fact that he still did not have a son to inherit the throne. Nevertheless, when Mary was very young, the king played the proud father, carrying the little princess in his arms and bragging to visitors in Latin, saying: *"Per Deum immortalem ista puella nunquam plorat* (This girl never cries)."[23] The princess was of delicate health and her eyesight was not very good, but this did not prevent her from becoming a good student. Like her mother, Princess Mary took to learning, and her accomplishments made her parents proud.

As the King of England's daughter, Mary, like her mother before her, became a pawn in the game of European politics. Subsidiary agreements between France and England led to Princess Mary becoming affianced to Francis I's young son and heir, the Dauphin of France. Queen Catherine was not a great supporter of Mary's betrothal to the dauphin. Instead, Catherine wanted Mary betrothed to Catherine's nephew, Holy Roman Emperor Charles V, Juana La Loca's son, who ruled vast tracts of Europe. Catherine's wish came true when the French engagement was renounced and then replaced by young Mary's betrothal to Charles. However, that engagement too was eventually broken, and there was talk that the princess might marry the widowed Francis I or his son, Henri.

The fact that Princess Mary continued to be an only child rankled Henry VIII. The lack of a legitimate son did not sit well with the egocentric king. Moreover, England's stability would likely degenerate into civil war again if a fight over the throne ensued. Though there was precedent for a female sovereign ruling in her own right in the form of the Empress Matilda in the twelfth century, war had erupted over Matilda's right to rule. Then there was the possibility that Mary's marriage might also destabilize England. If she married someone from the English nobility, factionalism was bound to ensue. A marriage to a foreigner might suborn English interests. Should one of their children succeed Mary on the English throne, it would also mean the ascendancy of another dynasty or family at the expense of the Tudors. For all these reasons, Henry VIII was increasingly obsessed with the need for a male heir.

More than ever, King Henry VIII and Queen Catherine drifted apart. Cardinal Wolsey had the king's ear, leaving Catherine increasingly in the background. Meanwhile, Henry, only the second in the Tudor line, had inherited his father's wariness. In the beginning of his reign, in order to garner support from the public, Henry VIII had ordered the execution of two hated courtiers who had implemented Henry VII's fiscal policies. To the scaffold went Sir Richard Empson and Edmund Dudley. Henry VIII then had the Yorkist claimant, the Earl of Suffolk, executed in 1513. By 1521 doubts that Catherine would give Henry his male heir had redoubled, making the king even more leery of other families that might claim the throne. The Duke of Buckingham, a descendant of Edward III, had a legitimate claim to the throne. Wolsey disliked Buckingham and fed Henry's innate paranoia, convincing the king that Buckingham was a dangerous opponent who might usurp his reign. Even though Buckingham was Catherine's friend and she begged Henry to spare his life, the king ordered his execution, greatly upsetting the queen. It also galvanized Wolsey's sway over the king. The 1521 execution of Buckingham ushered in a new and terrifying era in Henry's reign. Tyranny now took hold of the king, a ruthless tyranny that was to bring down the lives of many. It would soon become apparent that no one who stood in the way of his whims was safe. Sir Thomas More, who was later to pay the ultimate price for his king's whims, was well aware that the same king who walked in friendly chatter with him, with his arm around the scholar's neck, would also strike off that head if doing so "could win him a castle in France."[24]

The king now conveniently reasoned that some kind of providential curse had been placed on him and Catherine for her failure to provide him with a son. He found justification for this supposed punishment in the Book of Leviticus, where chapter 18, verse 16, stated: "Thou shalt not uncover the nakedness of thy brother's wife." Even further ammunition fell into Henry's way in chapter 20, verse 21, of the same book, which said: "If a man shall take his brother's wife, it is an unclean thing: he hath uncovered his brother's nakedness; they shall be childless." These words convinced Henry that he had offended his Maker. The papal dispensation that had permitted his marriage to Catherine was wrong, thought Henry, who now believed he was being punished for his transgression with the absence of male offspring. In order to remedy this, Henry convinced himself that his marriage to Catherine must be declared invalid.

Another equally strong impulse drove Henry to be rid of Catherine as a wife—a new infatuation. After Bessie Blount, his attentions fell on Mary Boleyn, whose flirtatiousness attracted the king just as Bessie's outgoing personality had done. And as with Bessie, Queen Catherine neither displayed public disapproval nor played the injured party with Mary Boleyn, though she must have been relieved to find that the liaison with this Boleyn girl did not last long. The same, however, could not be said of Mary's dark-eyed sister, Anne. Her appearance on the scene in the spring of 1526 set in motion a series of cataclysmic events that would have grave repercussions not only for Queen Catherine but also for England and the Church. Once Henry VIII became infatuated with Anne Boleyn, Henry and Catherine's marriage unraveled in earnest.

The Boleyns were courtiers; Anne's father was as ambitious for himself as he was for Anne. After receiving a first-rate education at the French court, where her father had been ambassador, Anne returned to England in the early 1520s, when relations between England and France deteriorated, and entered the service of Queen Catherine. Anne's relationship with Henry VIII started in 1527, when the thirty-six-year-old king became captivated by the charming and witty Anne, who was in her early to mid-twenties. Queen Catherine, at forty-one years of age, was no longer physically attractive to Henry and past her child-bearing days. Her health problems suggested that she might do him the favor of dying. The queen herself thought at one point that she was near death, even admitting to Cardinal Wolsey of the "uncertainty of my life."[25] But Catherine lived, and soon enough Henry agitated to be rid of her.

The king sought not a divorce but an annulment of the marriage from Rome. An annulment meant that, though a wedding ceremony may have taken place, the actual sacrament of marriage did not occur, thus meaning that there was no valid Christian marriage to begin with. A declaration of the nullity of the marriage was thus technically different from a divorce. Henry's request proved difficult to obtain. He continued to insist that the marriage should be annulled, while Catherine was adamant that it should not, because the proper papal dispensation had been given. Furthermore, Catherine insisted that her marriage with Prince Arthur had never been consummated, and therefore could not be regarded as a proper marriage. Frustration and anger on Henry VIII's part soon turned into an obsession. For all his intelligence and magnificence, this Tudor monarch possessed a ruthless streak, compounded by willfulness and great impatience. His appetite to get his way grew, as did his girth. Even Martin Luther was to say of Henry: "Squire Harry wishes to be God and do as he pleases."[26] Henry had transformed from the Renaissance king full of great potential into a despot intent on getting his way, no matter the cost.

By this time, Cardinal Wolsey and the queen's relationship had deteriorated. The ever-ambitious Wolsey sided with Henry in his quest to rid himself of Catherine. Wolsey set spies on the queen. Catherine, with Henry, had twice met with her nephew Charles V, the Holy Roman emperor, near the time of the royal couple's trip to France in 1520. She determined to contact Charles about her plight. However, when Catherine sent a faithful servant to Spain to consult Charles on the ongoing tussle between her and Henry, Wolsey announced that her servant "feigns to go to visit his mother, now sickly and aged; but your highness taketh it surely in the right, that it is chiefly for disclosing your secret matter to the emperor, and to devise means and ways how it may be impeached."[27] Upon hearing of his aunt's predicament, Charles V wrote promising to support her, and wrote to Henry requesting that he desist. What had essentially been a domestic issue had now widened into an international one. Catherine, in turn, sought learned and legal judgments to support her cause. She consulted with her confessor, John Fisher, Bishop of Rochester, retaining him as her counsel in the event the case underwent a full ecclesiastical inquiry.

By 1528, the case known as the King's Great Matter was headed in that direction. That year, Cardinal-Legate Lorenzo Campeggio arrived from Rome to inquire into the validity of Catherine and Henry's marriage. The stage was set for a confrontation the likes of which England had never seen before.

9

THE FINAL BREAK

*L*ike most women who have ardently anticipated a son or daughter, Queen Catherine found much joy and consolation in her only surviving child, Princess Mary. As Henry VIII became more distant and hostile toward Catherine, the queen felt an even closer bond with Mary. Catherine, therefore, paid close attention to her daughter's marital prospects. In this regard, the queen still cherished the hope that Mary's betrothal to her nephew Emperor Charles V would materialize. If Charles and Mary had children, then Queen Catherine could conceivably have a grandchild who would inherit vast territories, incorporating Spain, England, and the Habsburg domains. But closer to Catherine's heart was the thought that, as Charles's consort, Mary would sit on the Spanish throne. Thus was Catherine "in favour of educating her daughter to be Queen of Spain, as once Isabella had educated Catherine to be Queen of England."[1]

Queen Catherine approached this task in earnest. She employed the Spanish humanist Juan Luis Vives to produce a program of instruction. He did so in a work entitled *De Ratione Studii Puerilis (On a Plan of Study for Children)*. At Catherine's request, Vives, who taught law and classical literature from 1523 to 1526 at Oxford, had already written a work on women's education: *De Institutione Feminae Christianae (The Education of a Christian Woman)*, which he dedicated to the queen. Of Catherine, Vives wrote that he had been "moved by the holiness of your life and your ardent zeal for sacred studies."[2] Vives also enthused that "you have so conducted yourself in all these various states of life that whatever you did is a model of an exemplary life to others."[3] A cursory examination of *De Institutione Feminae Christianae* reveals not only Vives's philosophy but also Queen Catherine's views on what a good Christian woman should learn. Among the numerous topics Vives brings up are the following:

The indulgence of parents is very harmful to children, since it offers them free access to a thousand vices.[4]

Her whole motivation for learning should be to live a more upright life.[5]

It would be to our advantage to have at least a knowledge of good to protect us from the constant onslaught of evil.[6]

If you do not pass on the knowledge of good, it cannot be known. Whereas evil, even if you conceal it, cannot be hidden; it is ubiquitous and in full view, and does not allow itself to be confined to the darkness.[7]

So powerful is the kingdom of Satan in this world here below, so great is the conspiracy for evil that thrives in it, so obstinately do the common people defend their own vices that no one can venture forth into public without his soul being assailed immediately through his senses by things pernicious to virtue and piety. It was wisely said by our forefathers that through all the senses as through windows, death bursts in upon the soul or stealthily penetrates its defenses. For which reason we must keep constant watch over the soul, and man's life on earth must be thought of as a warfare.[8]

I think it abundantly clear that chastity is . . . the queen of female virtues. Two inseparable companions follow: modesty and sobriety, which it engenders, and from these two the whole chorus and firmament of female virtues is composed and fashioned.[9]

As Catherine wished, Mary's education conformed to Vives's philosophy by word and deed. Besides the need to instill virtues and a strong piety, Vives urged the introduction of writings by Seneca, Livy, and Plutarch as well as the New Testament. The Bible and the classics were the foundations of his intellectual education for the princess. Not forgotten were works by Erasmus as well as Thomas More's *Utopia* and Plato's *Republic*. Moreover, Christian poets were included, as well as languages. Written and oral exercises in Latin and Greek included a good smattering of memorization of passages in these languages. Catherine herself taught Mary Latin early on. When she relinquished this role to another, the queen still urged her daughter to send her Latin exercises so that Catherine could read them, telling Mary that "it shall be a great comfort to me to see you keep your Latin."[10] By the age of nine, Princess Mary was highly proficient in Latin. Later, when Mary was queen, it was acknowledged of her Latin: "Her idiomatic command of it in conversation with learned foreigners was considered even in the time to be remarkable."[11] Mary also inherited a love of music from her father. A gifted student, the child was universally acknowledged as an exceptional performer on the virginal and lute.

Catherine saw to it that her daughter's education was steeped in Christianity, as befitted the grandchild of Isabella the Catholic. Thus did Mary come to know "that God was truth and that He would not hold them guiltless who took His name in vain; and as she progressed from rote to ordered exposition, not only were the duties of honesty, purity and fidelity laid down for her but related through her unfolding intelligence to the great sacramental scheme of salvation transmitted by Christ to His Church."[12] Queen Catherine also introduced Princess Mary to the convent of Syon in the lower Thames, near the royal palace of Richmond. This convent of the Bridgettine order, which housed both men and women, was marked not only by its piety and strictness but also by the scholarship of its members, many of whom came from England's great families.

As her daughter grew older, Queen Catherine could no longer shelter Mary from Henry's increasing animosity. The princess could not help but notice the pained expression on her mother's face or the whispers about her father's obsession with Anne Boleyn.

Henry plied Anne with attention and letters declaring his love for her. "I will take you for my only mistress," he wrote in one, "rejecting from thought and affection all others save yourself, to serve you only."[13] Anne kept the king at bay, which made her even more irresistible to Henry. By the end of 1528, Anne Boleyn had such a hold over the king that the French ambassador to England wrote, "Greater court is paid to her every day than has been for a long time paid to the Queen."[14]

As she aged, Catherine found court life more and more frivolous. It was almost as if she was taking a cue from Vives, who wrote: "The virtuous woman, when she is free of domestic cares, will choose for herself—daily, if possible, but if not, on feast days—a secluded part of the house, apart from the noise and bustling. . . . Then with the help of some divine reading she will raise herself to the thoughts and contemplation of divine things. Finally, having confessed her sins to God, she will suppliantly beg for pardon and peace from him and will pray first for herself. Then, having found more favor with God, she will pray for her husband, her children, and finally, her whole household, so that the Lord Jesus will inspire a better mind in all of them."[15]

Signs appeared as early as 1525 that Henry might have thought of pushing Queen Catherine and Princess Mary into the background. He ennobled his bastard son, Henry FitzRoy, granting him precedence over all noblemen. The Venetian envoy noted that the queen was outraged. However, as with the many injustices that she had faced in the past, Catherine swallowed this latest indignity too. But the indignities did not stop at FitzRoy's ennoblement. In fact, a new, sinister phase unfolded in relations between Henry and Catherine.

A campaign of intimidation and misinformation ensued. Among those leading the charge was a pliant council of the king's ministers, who declared "that the queen had not shown, either in public or in the hours of retirement, as much love for the king as she ought . . . [that] the king concluded that she hated him . . . [so that] his council in the consciences thought his life was in danger, they advised him to separate himself from the queen . . . and above all to take the princess Mary from her."[16] For Catherine, these scenes were hauntingly like her early years in England. She might as well have repeated the words she had written to her father during her uncertain and despondent years at Henry VII's court as the widow of his son Arthur: "They tell me nothing but lies here, and they think they can break my spirit."[17]

At first Henry VIII's public face during the crisis was of one whose conscience was troubled. He liked to explain that he esteemed Catherine but that, because his conscience bothered him, he believed the marriage was invalid and needed to have it investigated. For a while King Henry appeared in public with Queen Catherine, but he eventually tired of the charade. Catherine's insistence that she was his rightful wife and queen was irksome. Her obduracy infuriated Henry, who was accustomed to getting his way. A pattern of pitiless actions toward Catherine had taken hold. Henry ordered that she surrender her jewels. She tried to avoid this and even daringly told the king that "it would be a sin to allow her jewels to adorn 'the scandal of Christendom' [meaning Anne Boleyn]. This thrust forced a typically self-righteous reply from the king, and the vulgarity of a direct order to send the jewels."[18]

If Henry VIII had thought getting the Pope's cooperation in the annulment would be easy, he was mistaken. In Catherine's struggle against her husband, she could at least take comfort in knowing that she had the support of her nephew. Charles himself exerted a strong influence on the papacy because of the sacking of Rome. In 1527 Rome was sacked by undisciplined troops of the emperor, forcing Pope Clement VII to flee to nearby Castel Sant'Angelo. Appalled by what his troops had done, Charles V nevertheless saw the Pope's predicament as a boon to his own plans, since the Pope was now effectively the emperor's prisoner. Because he was sympathetic to his aunt's cause, Charles exerted pressure on Clement not to declare the King and Queen of England's marriage unlawful. When the imperial forces began to withdraw from Rome, Clement started to show some sympathy toward Henry's representatives. This was how Cardinal Campeggio ended up in England in 1529. But Campeggio was not given carte blanche in the matter. He was instructed to stall as long as possible and not to make any binding decisions without discussing them with the Pope.

Mortified to find her husband bullying one and all, the queen dug in her heels for what was turning out to be a battle royal. She had already formally requested that her case be heard not in England by the legates but by the Pope himself in Rome. Henry VIII had publicly acquiesced in so many words to this request. Nonetheless, in May 1529, Cardinals Wolsey and Campeggio presided over a solemn court at the great hall of the Dominican Friary of London known as Blackfriars. Catherine entered, accompanied by four bishops and her ladies. The queen's stay was brief; she stated that she would accept only the Pope's decision in the matter. As the crisis proceeded, Catherine continued to hold her ground, insisting that she was the king's wife. She adamantly proclaimed this to Cardinals Wolsey and Campeggio, the two papal legates, who requested an interview with the queen before they held their court of inquiry. Catherine, in her reply, even had some sharp words for Wolsey, whom she rightly viewed as one who completely sided with Henry:

> "Alas! my lords," answered the queen, "is it now a question whether I be the king's lawful wife or no, when I have been married to him almost twenty years, and no objection made before? Divers prelates and lords, privy councillors of the king, are yet alive, who then adjudged our marriage good and lawful—now to say it is detestable is a great marvel to me. . . . The king, my father, sent to the court of Rome, and there obtained a dispensation that I, being the one brother's wife, might without scruple of conscience marry the other brother lawfully, which . . . makes me say and surely believe (as my first marriage was not completed) that my second is good and lawful. . . . But of this trouble," she continued, turning to Cardinal Wolsey, "I may only thank you, my lord of York, because I ever wondered at your pride and your glory, and abhorred your voluptuous life, and little cared for your presumption and tyranny; therefore of malice have you kindled this fire, especially for the great grudge you bear to my nephew the emperor, whom you hate

worser than a scorpion, because he would not gratify your ambition by making you pope by force; and therefore you have said, more than once, you would trouble him and his friends—and you have kept him true promise, for all his wars and vexations, he may only thank you. As for me, his poor aunt and kinswoman, what trouble you put to me by this new-found doubt, God knoweth, to whom I commit my cause."[19]

Weeks later, on the morning of June 21, 1529, the Legatine court again convened to hear the case that was so consuming the English court and the Roman Catholic Church. The event was filled with high drama. "Nothing like it had ever been seen in England, or, as far as men could remember, in Christendom: a reigning king and queen appearing themselves in answer to the summons of a court set up in their own land."[20] After Henry addressed the assembly under a gold canopy, his wife's turn came. Queen Catherine answered the summons of the crier, who proclaimed, "Catherine, queen of England, come into the court."[21]

The queen personally pleaded her case in one of the most amazing scenes in English history. Moving from a dais opposite the king, Catherine approached Henry and fell to her knees. Twice Henry VIII tried to get his queen to her feet, but to no avail. With many eyes, both lowly and prominent, including those of the crimson-clad clergy and counselors on both monarchs' sides, fixed upon her, Queen Catherine, still on her knees by Henry's side, spoke in her foreign-accented English:

> Sir, I beseech you for all the love that hath been between us, let me have justice and right, take of me some pity and compassion, for I am a poor woman, and a stranger, born out of your dominion. I have here no assured friend and much less indifferent counsel. I flee to you, as to the head of justice within this realm. . . .
>
> I take God and all the world to witness that I have been to you a true, humble, and obedient wife, ever comfortable to your will and pleasure . . . , being always well pleased and contented with all things wherein you had any delight or dalliance, whether it were little or much. . . . I loved all those whom ye loved, only for your sake, whether I had cause or no, and whether they were my friends or my enemies. This twenty years or more I have been your true wife, and by me ye have had divers children, although it hath pleased God to call them from this world.[22]

Then, the queen pronounced the critical words: "And when ye had me at first, I take God to my judge, I was a true maid, without touch of man. And whether this be true or no, I put it to your conscience."[23]

Henry did not answer this crucial matter. He did, however, try to excuse his long silence about the supposed invalidity of their marriage because, he claimed, of his love for the queen. Catherine left the court after her impassioned plea. She curtsied deeply to Henry VIII and walked out. When the court crier called her three times, Catherine replied that the court was not an unprejudiced one and left.

During this time, there was little doubt about how the English felt toward Queen Catherine. Ordinary women "greeted her at her departure, 'telling her to care for nothing and other such words,'" prompting Jean du Bellay, the French ambassador, to remark: "'If the matter were to be decided by women' the English King 'would lose the battle.'"[24]

The court continued to hear the case. During one session, John Fisher, Bishop of Rochester, braved Henry's wrath by forcefully defending the marriage. Fisher dramatically declared that he would give his life for this cause. Finally, at the end of July, Campeggio adjourned the court, declaring that the case was to be heard by the Pope. During his stay in England, Catherine emphatically denied that she was going to enter a nunnery as implied by Henry's representatives. When Campeggio hinted to Catherine that this might be the best course, she replied that, though she was "'very religious and extremely patient,' she would not in the least accept this suggestion."[25] Cardinal Campeggio had already come to view Catherine as not hysterical but restrained, telling the Pope: "I have always thought her . . . a prudent lady, and now more than ever."[26]

The longer the matrimonial crisis persisted, the more speedily Catherine of Aragon hurtled toward its devastating conclusion. Her refusal to enter a convent, plus her appearance at Blackfriars, show clearly that she did not make this fight easy for the king. But this did not stop Henry, whose passions had been so inflamed by Anne Boleyn. Nothing and no one—not Catherine, not the Emperor Charles V, not Pope Clement VII—was going to prevent him from marrying Anne.

Though she understood herself to be legally married to Henry VIII and accepted the union, for better or worse, as sacramental and therefore sanctified by God, Queen Catherine's intransigence also demonstrated an element of pride. After all, she was a daughter of the incomparable Queen Isabella, and to have to yield to Henry VIII's wish now, "and agree for convenience sake—his convenience—that she, a Castilian princess, had been the King's 'harlot' all these years"[27] was simply too much. Moreover, "to be supplanted by a rival who was not only much younger but also of infinitely lower rank was not easy for the daughter of the 'Catholic Kings' to endure, although she was too clever, and too well-trained to say so."[28]

Forced to live increasingly in isolation, with spies watching and listening for clues that might be used against her, Catherine could do little but keep her counsel. She informed Emperor Charles of her predicament in a letter in 1531, saying: "My tribulations are so great, my life so disturbed by the plans daily invented to further the King's wicked intention, the surprises which the King gives me, with certain persons of his Council, are so mortal, and my treatment is what God knows, that it is enough to shorten ten lives, much more mine. As far as concerns this business, I have offended neither God nor the King, to whom I have always shown obedience as a true wife, and sometimes more so in this affair than my conscience approved of. Yet they treat me in such a manner that I do not know what to do, except to complain to God and your Majesty, with whom my remedy lies, and to beg you to cause the Pope to make such a speedy end of the matter as my truth merits."[29]

Catherine may have felt alone at times and devoid of friends, but she had her fair share of supporters and champions. The people had steadfastly cast their lot with their queen. The Venetian ambassador in England wrote of Catherine at this time, noting, "The queen is of low stature and rather stout; very good and very religious . . . more beloved by the Islanders than any queen that has ever reigned."[30] The Spanish ambassador, Diego Hurtado de Mendoza, wrote to Charles V in a similar vein: "The people here are much in favour of the Queen."[31] Catherine, the wronged wife, appealed greatly to her subjects. In the face of humiliation after humiliation, her dignified behavior also earned her praise. Foreign ambassadors agreed that Catherine's demeanor had an effect on her subjects. The Venetian ambassador added "that the Queen is as beloved as if she had been of the blood royal of England."[32] The Spanish ambassador to England, meanwhile, wrote to Charles V: "If 6,000–7,000 people were put on the coast of Cornwall prepared to espouse Catherine's cause, they would be joined by 40,000 Englishmen."[33]

By contrast, the French ambassador noted that, when it came to Anne Boleyn, "the people remain quite hardened (against her), and I think they would do more if they had more power."[34] Moreover, Henry's move to get the country gradually accustomed to seeing Anne as queen—by allowing her to lodge in sumptuous apartments in another establishment so as to avoid Catherine—backfired. So outraged was the populace that the king thought it necessary to "conciliate and intimidate" the nation by calling an assembly of nobles.[35] The king spoke of Queen Catherine's nobility and virtues, insisting that he would marry her again but that his conscience bothered him. He ended the speech with a warning, however, saying that he would show opponents who was master. The speech "utterly failed to deceive anyone" and even incited more disgust thanks to the king's "audacious hypocrisy in speaking so warmly in the Queen's praise, and in pleading conscientious scruples, which were belied by his shameful display of vice."[36] Revolt was in the air, prompting an anxious Henry to order an arms search. He even demanded the deportation of foreigners, though in the end he did not carry this order out.

Within the royal family, Catherine could count on Mary, Henry's sister, as a true friend. Then there were the Observant Franciscans who preached in support of the queen. William Peto, the provincial of the Friars Minor, even did so directly to Henry VIII, infuriating the king. Fierce outspokenness on behalf of Queen Catherine earned them the king's enmity. Two cartloads of friars were sent to the Tower for their troubles; others were forced to leave their friaries and imprisoned in chains. Catherine's fellow Spaniard Juan Luis Vives was another supporter and wrote a book defending the queen. At court, the Duchess of Norfolk sympathized openly with the queen; so did Reginald Pole, son of Margaret Pole (Princess Mary's tutor and Catherine's great friend). This caused Henry VIII grief because he had taken charge of young Pole's education. Catherine's chaplain, Thomas Abell, likewise braved the king's fury by supporting the queen through reasoned arguments in print. Clearly, the lines were being drawn in the King's Great Matter.

Two of Catherine's staunchest, bravest, and most learned supporters were Sir Thomas More, the soon-to-be Lord Chancellor, and John Fisher, the Bishop of Rochester. More was, according to John Colet, the kingdom's one true genius. Erasmus had described More glowingly, saying: "He seems born and framed for friendships, and is a most faithful and enduring friend. . . . In a word, if you want a perfect model of friendship, you will find it in no one better than in More."[37] Catherine had always highly esteemed More, united as they were by a shared piety and deep interest in learning. She was deeply gratified that he sided with her in her trials.

Catherine's other great supporter, John Fisher, did not stop with his defense of the marriage at Blackfriars. Fisher was no less impressive intellectually than More and had earned international recognition for his lucid tracts against Luther. Fisher's defense of the queen surpassed all. "He wrote at least seven books on Catherine's behalf and their clarity and range of learning are remarkable. He had an eagle eye for the essential and the decisive, his command of sources was staggering. Several times he exposed crucial misquotation and misrepresentation . . . and showed himself as much at home in Hebrew textual exegesis as in the intricacies of the Canon Law of affinity. Having declared himself an opponent of Henry at the very beginning, in 1527, he sustained his opposition for eight years, flailing the king with his pen, devastating new works of the latter's party as they came out, providing the backbone of Catherine's defence in court and eventually, when he had no more to write, carrying on the campaign from the pulpit."[38] "It was Fisher who threw the first spanner into the works, pointing out that the scriptural argument against the marriage was by no means clear. For the book of Deuteronomy contained a divine precept commanding a man to marry his deceased brother's wife when that brother had died without children (Deut. 25:5)."[39]

Henry VIII too had supporters. In the early 1530s Henry sent his agents scouring Europe for support. They succeeded in securing the judgments of Oxford and Cambridge universities in Henry's favor, but not without violent objections, since "there was fighting at Cambridge and great obstinacy at Oxford" over the issue.[40] On the Continent, disputes also arose over Henry's assertions about his marriage. There, the king's agents were in competition with Charles V's. The Pope, "yielding at last to Imperial pressure, . . . issued a bull forbidding individuals to write or speak against the royal marriage."[41]

What had thus started as a dispute between a husband and wife had turned into a protracted, very public international struggle with ecclesiastical and political dimensions. An impressive array of scholars was marshaled in the battle. "Men great and small rallied to defend Queen Catherine, meeting tract with tract, opinion with opinion. By 1529–30 the king's divorce had occasioned an international debate as violent and swift-moving, though on a much smaller scale, as the contemporary conflict between Catholic and Protestant."[42]

Catherine's representation of marriage accorded with Church teachings, namely that once a marriage was lawfully contracted, it was indissoluble. The queen had already informed Cardinal Campeggio of this, for "come what may, she would live and die in that vocation to matrimony to which God had called her."[43] This echoed what Vives had written in *De Institutione Feminae Christianae*: "Marriage is a knot that cannot be untied."[44] Vives's words afford a deeper understanding of Catherine's intractable stand:

> When a woman marries, she must call to mind the origins of marriage
> and frequently review its laws in thought and meditation. She must so

prepare herself that, having first understood this great mystery, she may later fulfill its obligations.[45]

God brought woman to man, which means that God himself was the chief author and mediator of marriage. Therefore, Christ in the gospel refers to them as joined by God.[46]

[The] first and perhaps only law of marriage: "They shall be two in one flesh." This is the hinge of marriage, the bond of *a most sacred fellowship*. If a woman will direct her thoughts, words and deeds to this goal, then it follows of necessity that *she will guard and protect the holiness of marriage with honor and integrity*. . . . May she so live that she both plainly appear to be and truly be one with him. On the contrary, she who does not do this will be entirely without virtue. This precept is very similar to that which Christ often declared was the only one he left to his disciples that they should love one another.[47]

The duties of a wife to her husband, difficult to set out in words, were summarized, as I mentioned previously, in one word by our Lord. Let a woman remember what I said, that *she is one person with her husband* and for that reason should love him no less than herself. I have said this before but it must be repeated often, for it is the epitome of all the virtues of a married woman. *This is the meaning and lesson of matrimony: that a woman should think that her husband is everything to her* and that this one name substitutes for all the other names dear to her—father, mother, brothers, sisters.[48]

Vives was not alone in expounding the holiness of matrimony. Even King Henry VIII had written similar things, as this passage shows: "Who does not tremble when he considers how he should deal with his wife, for not only is he bound to love her, but so to live with her that he may return her to God pure and without stain, when God Who gave, shall demand His own again."[49]

By 1529, Henry no longer espoused such beliefs, determined as he was to be rid of Catherine. When Campeggio announced that the Pope would hear the case, Henry became explosive. Henry VIII and Anne Boleyn turned their anger on Wolsey, whom they felt had failed to speed the process along. No longer indispensable, the cardinal was arrested for treason, avoiding the executioner's block only by his natural death in November 1530. Catherine was undoubtedly relieved to see the last of Wolsey, who had fomented so much trouble for her. Stepping into his place as Lord Chancellor was none other than the fifty-one-year-old Sir Thomas More, who accepted the post with a heavy heart.

As the showdown between Henry VIII and Catherine of Aragon dragged on, Europe remained transfixed. Whereas some four decades before, Queen Isabella of Castile had captured Europe's attention by driving the Moors from Granada, her daughter Catherine elicited the same degree of attention from a new generation of Europeans, though for much different reasons. "What puzzled Henry VIII's European contemporaries most [however] was that he went about his divorce the hard way. Wanting Anne as a wife instead of a mistress was eccentric in the first place, but determination to bludgeon the pope into guaranteeing in advance not only the outcome he wanted but also his own distinctive interpretation of the law, was unprecedented."[50]

Henry remained adamant about ridding himself of Catherine. The queen, meanwhile, was equally intransigent, refusing to succumb to intense pressure, though it was not always easy to maintain such a stand against Henry. For "the lonely decision to fight her case to the last was the most difficult Catherine had made since she told Fuensalida, twenty years before, that she would die in England before she gave up her marriage with the Prince of Wales. In its consequences for England and for Christendom it was the gravest she was ever to make, one of the gravest in history."[51]

It was in Catherine's blood to fight for what she felt was right. For the validity of their marriage, she fought Henry VIII unswervingly. She fought for the right to be his queen. And she fought for the succession rights of their daughter, Mary, to the throne of England. This strong sense of conviction was Queen Isabella's legacy. For "Catherine had been brought up in the midst of a crusading war in which she had seen the apparent Will of God manifest in her own family. She had assumed—like her mother before her—those rigid principles which were to govern her many future actions and, in some ways, make her life more difficult, for compromise was never easy for Catherine."[52] She stayed the course under increasingly difficult circumstances, which entailed ostracization, most painfully from her only child. Henry ensured that mother and daughter were increasingly kept apart. Eustache Chapuys, the Spanish ambassador who arrived at the English court in 1529, noted the difficulties Catherine faced. He assiduously reported the goings-on at court in letters to his master, Charles V. In one letter Chapuys wrote, "The treatment of the Queen continues as bad, I might even say worse than ever. The King absents himself from her as much as possible, and is always here with the lady [Anne Boleyn] whilst the Queen is at Richmond. He has never been so long without visiting her as now. . . . He has also resumed his attempts to persuade her to become a nun."[53] The industrious Chapuys ardently supported Queen Catherine and Princess Mary throughout their ordeal and was assertive when it came to Mary's interests.

Even Anne Boleyn's uncle the Duke of Norfolk "observed to the Marquis of Exeter, that it was a wonder to see [Catherine's] courage—nothing seemed to frighten her: 'the Devil and no other,' he said, 'must have originated so wretched a business.' "[54] Catherine's courage did not fail her even when she faced Henry directly. In one confrontation, she fought back. He was not her husband, Henry told her, as numerous educated doctors including his almoner, Dr. Edward Lee, Archbishop of York, had stated to him. " 'Doctors!' Catherine cried. 'You know yourself, without the help of any doctors, that you are my husband and that your case has no foundation. I came to you as much a virgin as I came from my mother's womb, and you, yourself, have often said so. I care not a straw for your almoner or your doctors. Your almoner is not my judge, thank God, but the Pope. He will decide.' "[55] Henry replied that he had lawyers and theologians who supported him and was awaiting confirmation of their views from the University of Paris. " 'Then,' with a defiant flourish, 'if the Pope does not decide in my favor, I shall declare the Pope a heretic, and marry whom I please.' "[56] Catherine was unshaken. "You know best what opinions you have from Paris, and where not, and how much they are worth. And you know, too, that the best lawyers in England have written on my side. Let me but collect opinions as you have done, and for every doctor or lawyer of yours, I dare say I could find a thousand to hold our marriage good and indissoluble."[57]

Catherine obviously possessed her mother's indomitable spirit and was not about to bow to Henry's whims, despite his constant bullying. She was also on the receiving end of vitriol from the woman who was intent on usurping her as wife and queen. The temperamental Anne, impatient to become queen, lashed out. In 1531 Chapuys reported that Anne "is becoming more arrogant every day, using words in authority towards the King of which he has several times complained to the Duke of Norfolk, saying that she was not like the Queen who never in her life used ill words to him."[58] Chapuys also noted how Anne that year had come to despise Catherine, saying, "She said to one of the Queen's ladies that she wished all Spaniards were in the sea. The lady told her such language was disrespectful to her mistress [the queen]. She said she cared nothing for the Queen, and would rather see her hang than acknowledge her as her mistress."[59]

In May 1531, eminent men of the land, including the Bishop of Lincoln, tried to persuade the queen to give in to Henry. Catherine refused. " 'I love and have loved my lord, the King,' she told them steadily in conclusion, 'as much as any woman can love a man, but I would not have borne him company as his wife one moment against the voice of my conscience. I came to him as a virgin, I am his true wife, and whatever proofs my lord of Lincoln or others may allege to the contrary, I, who know better than anyone else, tell you are lies and forgeries.'"[60]

Among those who tried to coerce the queen, most were either ashamed of their conduct or impressed by Catherine's reply. Charles Brandon, Henry's brother-in-law, reported the meeting to the king and told him that the queen was ready to obey Henry, "except for the obedience she owes to two higher powers." At that, Henry replied, "The Emperor and the Pope?" "No sire, God and her conscience," replied Brandon.[61]

Throughout all the attempts to break her spirit, Catherine maintained a dignified and defiant façade. The fact that she had visibly aged was the only hint that she suffered intensely from her ordeal. Privately, the queen was anxious to get a final verdict from the Pope. In one letter to Charles V, Catherine complained of the delay and also of her frustration with Henry: "I am amazed at His Holiness. How can he allow a suit so scandalous to remain so long un-decided? His conduct cuts me to the soul. You know who has caused all this mischief. Were the King once free from the snare in which he has been caught, he would confess that God had restored his reason. Pity that a man so good and virtuous should be thus deceived! God enlighten his mind!"[62]

In 1532, events moved apace. In January, the Pope exhorted King Henry to take Catherine back and dismiss Anne, but to no avail. Fisher and More remained unswervingly loyal to the queen. Then Henry VIII appointed two individuals, one secular and one religious, to be his closest collaborators: Thomas Cromwell and Thomas Cranmer. Both were intent on doing the king's bidding. Cromwell, as chief minister, was the king's secular tool, while Cranmer was his religious right-hand man. They proceeded to draft and help enact legislation that would end Catherine and Henry's marriage, even if Rome insisted otherwise. Henry, meanwhile, moved to separate the English Church from Rome. In May, the Convocation of Canterbury passed the Submission of the Clergy, whereby the Church in England gave up the right to make new laws without the monarch's ratification, thereby strengthening Henry's hand and weakening Rome's influence in England. Henry's action in browbeating the clergy prompted Catherine to fear "that, since the King was not ashamed of doing such monstrous things, and there being no one who could or dared contradict him, he might, one of these days, undertake some further outrage against her own person."[63]

In September 1532, Henry VIII created Anne Boleyn a peeress in her own right when he granted her the title Marchioness of Pembroke. Anne was now Henry's mistress, and in December she learned she was pregnant. This news led to even more trouble for Catherine. Henry felt it imperative to be rid of her in order to make Anne queen and secure the succession of Anne's unborn child. To this end, Henry made Cranmer Archbishop of Canterbury in March 1533.

In May, Cranmer did his king's bidding by pronouncing Catherine and Henry's marriage null and void. Henry had secretly married Anne in January 1533, and to make up for the subdued wedding, the king had her crowned as Queen of England in June in a brilliant pageant. At the moment of her greatest victory, Anne's venomous attitude toward Catherine reached new extremes. Even Henry was incensed when he learned that she appropriated Catherine's barge for the coronation water pageant and had Catherine's coat of "arms ignominiously torn off and hacked."[64] In spite of the availability of other barges, Anne wanted Catherine's, a symbol, no doubt, of "her spiteful triumph over her rival."[65]

That Henry's subjects continued to support Catherine was clearly evident during Anne's procession among the people. In spite of the splendid attire that gave Anne the appearance of a queen, "there were hardly ten persons who greeted her with 'God save your Grace,' as they used to when the sainted Queen Katharine went by."[66] In fact, "so great was the outcry that rewards were offered to those who should denounce any person speaking of it in a derogatory manner, and priests were forbidden to preach without the licence of the bishop of London who was favourable to the marriage."[67]

Henry's attempts to browbeat Catherine continued despite the people's support for her. In another humiliating gesture, Catherine was ordered to hand over the magnificent baptismal robe that she had brought from Spain so that Anne might use it for her baby. Catherine refused. In September 1533, Anne gave birth to a daughter, Elizabeth, again dashing Henry's hopes for a male heir.

That same year Henry symbolically rejected Catherine. He ordered her arms and symbols removed from the palaces, making it plain that she was no longer his wife. With Anne crowned, King Henry ordered that Catherine be styled no longer "queen" but "princess dowager." Her chamberlain, Lord Mountjoy, had the unenviable task of breaking the news to Catherine. She replied as if she were speaking to "the King, the Council, the Bishops—indeed to all England."[68] Catherine did not cower, for all this also amounted to a threat to her daughter. If Catherine backed down now, there was no telling what might happen to Mary. In her obduracy, Queen Catherine became the "dauntless woman, no more Henry's dutiful wife, but the daughter of generations of desperate fighters. . . . Mary was, she declared, 'the King's true begotten child, and as God had given her unto them, so for her part she would render her again to the King, as his daughter, to do with her as shall stand with his pleasure, trusting to God that she will prove an honest woman.' That was courage; the iron courage of Spain."[69]

The following day Catherine received Mountjoy in audience again, and upon reading the report of their previous meeting that was to be given to King Henry, Catherine used her pen to strike out the words "princess dowager." Then she announced to the assembly: "I would rather be a poor beggar's wife and be sure of Heaven, than to be Queen of all the world and stand in doubt thereof."[70] Catherine went on, saying emphatically she could never agree that her marriage was unlawful, for to do so would mean she would have "to confess to have been the King's harlot this twenty-four years."[71] Furthermore, "no daughter of Isabella and Ferdinand could be degraded into accepting the fact that she had lived in incest with her brother-in-law; Catherine felt such an admission would place her soul in eternal damnation."[72]

Catherine emphatically declared that "neither for her daughter, her servants, her possessions, nor any worldly adversity, nor the King's displeasure, that might ensue, would she yield in this cause to put her soul in danger; and that they should not be feared that have the power to kill the body, but He only that hath the power over the soul."[73]

As befitted the daughter of Queen Isabella of Castile, Catherine's courage never vacillated during her prolonged trial. " 'She was of such high courage,' even King Henry said, 'that with her daughter at her side, she might raise an army and take the field against him with as much spirit as her mother Isabella."[74] Cromwell too admired the queen's fighting spirit, confessing that "nature had injured [the queen] in not making her a man, but for her sex, she would have surpassed all the heroes of history."[75]

To ascribe Catherine's unyielding stand simply to Mary's legitimacy and right to the throne is to ignore her deep-seated piety, nurtured by her mother. Giving in to King Henry was tantamount to going against God and being complicit in corrupting the souls of Henry and those who would carry out his bidding by damaging irreparably one of the Church's seven sacraments. That, Catherine could not have on her conscience. When it came to her faith and the impact on it and on others that her marital conflict with Henry engendered, Queen Catherine took her responsibilities seriously. Since Blackfriars, she had come to the conclusion that she "was fighting the devil and all his minions for her husband's soul and the souls of all his people."[76]

In all this, it would not have been surprising if Catherine had harkened back to an old saying from Spain. " *'La Piedra que es Cristo'* ('the rock which is Christ')—her mother Isabella had been fond of the expression—was Truth, the foundation of the Church. Only on that rock could the Church stand firm. . . . On the fight to defend the fortress and to safeguard the sacraments on which the life of the Christian community was based, on the moral leadership of Europe—Catherine could see the issue."[77] Giving in to Henry would contribute to the destruction of the Church. This is why, when Catherine handed Mountjoy back the paper with the words "princess dowager" struck through, she repeated her message, saying: "Not for a thousand deaths would she consent to damn her soul or that of her husband, the King."[78] This also helps to explain the defiant opposition taken by other like-minded souls, a stand that ultimately cost them their lives.

In 1534, nearly five years from the time Catherine formally appealed her case to the Holy See, Rome rendered judgment in her favor. Catherine's marriage to Henry was valid. Henry VIII had already ignored Clement's exhortation to take back Catherine and dismiss Anne Boleyn. Thus, it came as no surprise that the king ignored the Pope again and instead had Cranmer invalidate his marriage to Catherine and recognize the one with Anne. The Pope's move to excommunicate Henry did not sway the king. He continued his assault on the Church within England to undermine the Pope's position. Parliament passed several acts that enforced the breach with Rome in 1534. The Act in Restraint on Appeals confirmed the Submission of the Clergy passed two years before but also forbade judicial appeals to Rome. The other law, the Act of Supremacy, declared Henry VIII the supreme head of the Church in England. The Act of Supremacy was significant, for it "separated the English Church from Catholic Christendom, and surrendered it to a king who, as Supreme Head, claimed even the power to determine doctrine. This was a power which was unprecedented, and which shocked even Luther."[79]

An acquiescent Parliament also passed the Act of Succession that bastardized Princess Mary. Mary had already been stripped of the title "princess," which was replaced with "lady" when Henry ordered that Catherine be called "princess dowager." By removing Catherine's daughter from the English succession, the act replaced her with Anne's children. Moreover, in his plan to break Mary's spirit, Henry took away her servants "and compelled her to perform the office of lady's maid to his newly born daughter, to whom Chapuys referred as 'this new bastard.' "[80]

Already, for years, Catherine had had to endure being separated from her only child. For Henry now to treat their daughter so cruelly was for Catherine yet another agonizing blow. She tried to lift her daughter's spirits. In a long letter to Mary after the title of "princess" was withdrawn from her, Queen Catherine urged her daughter to obey "the King your father in everything, save that you will not offend God and lose your own soul." Catherine added, "I desire you, for the love you owe unto God, and unto me, to keep your heart with a chaste mind, and your body from all ill and wanton company." As a loving mother, Catherine gave her daughter some encouraging words: "I perceive very well that God loveth you. . . . I beseech Him of His goodness to continue it." She then ended the letter with more sobering words, reminding Mary that "we never come to the Kingdom of Heaven but by troubles."[81]

The Act of Succession not only bastardized Princess Mary but also required every man in the kingdom (over fourteen years of age) to swear an oath accepting the act. Anyone who swore to this act rejected the Pope's supremacy, accepting in his place King Henry's. Catherine was asked to swear to the Act of Succession but refused. Even when threatened with treason and the frightening punishment attached to it, she still refused, saying to the party of men who had come to extract the oath from her, "If one of you has a commission to execute this penalty upon me, . . . I am ready. I ask only that I be allowed to die in the sight of the people."[82] She was willing to die if that was the price she had to pay for not compromising her faith. "I am told, she wrote, "that the next parliament is to decide whether I am to suffer martyrdom. If it is to be so, I hope it may be a meritorious act. . . . I do not fear . . . for there is no punishment from God except for neglected duty."[83] In the end, Henry VIII dared not create a martyr out of his first wife.

Thomas More and John Fisher also refused to obey the king. Sir Thomas More immediately resigned as Lord Chancellor. Both men stayed faithful to Catherine and to the laws of the Church of Rome and would not defy their consciences. By now, refusing to comply with the king's laws had become a terrifying prospect. Thanks to the Treason Act of 1534, dissenters who would not recognize Henry as supreme head of the Church in England or called him an infidel, heretic, schismatic, tyrant, or usurper of the crown could be put to death, with no recourse to claim sanctuary. The law applied to all the king's subjects, both highborn and low.

More had further infuriated Henry VIII when he refused to attend Anne Boleyn's coronation. His response was a far cry from the days when Catherine of Aragon had arrived in London as the bride of Prince Arthur. Back then, More was full of hope, saying of Catherine: "She thrilled the hearts of everyone; she possesses all those qualities that make for beauty in a very charming young girl. Everywhere she receives the highest of praises; but even that is inadequate. I do hope this highly publicized union will prove a happy omen for England."[84]

Imprisoned in the Tower of London for defying King Henry, Fisher and More became the most prominent martyrs of his reign. The elderly Fisher was the only bishop who refused to swear to Henry's supremacy. He suffered for his defiance, left in ragged clothes in the cold and deprived of the ministrations of a priest. He had been created a cardinal in 1535 by Pope Paul III, but this only enraged Henry, who "said that as Fisher had been given a cardinal's hat, he would cut off Fisher's head and send the head to Rome to have the hat put on it."[85] On June 22, 1535, John Fisher, one of Catherine's staunchest supporters and her onetime confessor, went to his execution. Fisher "said a few prayers which were not long but fervent and devout,"[86] and in one stroke, the executioner's blade fell on the old man's head.

Following Fisher to the executioner's block was Sir Thomas More. More had eloquently stated the dilemma facing those who refused to swear to Henry's supremacy above the Roman Catholic Church, describing the act as a "a sword with two edges, for if a man answers one way it will destroy the soul, and if he answer another it will destroy the body."[87] Also physically weakened from his imprisonment, More tried to keep a calm countenance. He drew inspiration from his faith and that of others facing the same sentence. From the window of his cell, More had witnessed several Carthusian priors going bravely to their deaths for refusing to acquiesce to Henry's tyranny. Sentenced to be hanged, drawn, and quartered, the Carthusians were "dragged on hurdles from the Tower through the city of London . . . to Tyburn. . . . There the full sentence of the law was carried out. One by one, while their fellow-sufferers watched, they were hanged, cut down while still alive, and castrated; their bellies were cut open, and their bowels pulled out and burned before their eyes, while they were still living; and then they were beheaded."[88]

On July 6, 1535, Sir Thomas More met his death, declaring he died a servant of the king, but God's first. He asked the assembled crowd "to pray for him and to bear witness that he died in and for the faith of the Catholic Church."[89] Like that of John Fisher before him, Thomas More's head was displayed for all to see on London Bridge.

Catherine was deeply distressed to hear of Fisher's and More's executions. She shed tears and prayed for them and others who had accepted martyrdom rather than acquiesce to the king. Catherine was mortified over the violent persecutions unleashed in England. She wrote to the Pope of her concerns: "What things are done here, what great offence is given to God, what scandal to the world . . . [of] ruined souls and martyred saints . . . [of] the deaths of these holy and good men and the perdition of so many souls . . . these evils which the Devil, as we see, has sown among us . . . [of] the martyrdoms of these admirable persons."[90]

Catherine's closing years were marked by much sorrow. Not only was she pained by the imprisonment, torture, and execution of those who refused to submit to Henry's tyranny but she was also dismayed at the dismantling of the old faith in England. Henry banished Catherine from court with little money to live on. She moved to different homes, living a life of exile, attended by a few servants. Catherine was also deeply wounded by the prolonged absence from her life of Mary. At Henry's orders, Catherine never saw her daughter in the last five years of her life, nor did Catherine ever see Henry again. By separating mother and child, "Henry VIII's disgust at the unwillingness of either woman to bow her neck in submission [to his will] had found its most effective form of expression. He pretended to believe that Catherine was 'so haughty in spirit' that she might take the opportunity of raising a number of men and making war 'as boldly as her mother, Isabella, had done.' This was fantasy. The reality was the cruelty of a thwarted man, visited on an aging, sick woman."[91]

Though Catherine could not speak to Mary directly for some time, her influence on the young woman had been strong. As the grandchild of the dauntless Queen Isabella and the daughter of the equally fearless Catherine, Mary stood firm in refusing to recognize Anne as Queen of England. Anne sought her vengeance on Mary by reducing her to near destitution. Anne's animosity toward Mary and Catherine did not abate. At one point, Eustache Chapuys could not resist telling Charles V: "When this accursed Anne has her foot in the stirrup, she will do the Queen and the Princess all the hurt she can. She boasts that she will have the Princess in her own train; one day, perhaps, she will poison her."[92] In another missive Chapuys added that he and many others believed Catherine's life was in jeopardy, noting that everyone "fears that mischief will now befall her [Catherine]; the concubine [Anne] has said she will never rest till she is put out of the way. It is monstrous and almost incredible, yet such is the King's obstinacy, and the wickedness of this accursed woman, that everything may be apprehended."[93] At one point, Anne "became even more spiteful and vindictive towards Mary and demanded that her ears be boxed 'for the cursed bastard she is.' "[94] Catherine could be forgiven if she had felt nothing but rancor toward Anne. Yet even in her darkest days, Catherine had expressed more charitable feelings, admonishing someone who had cursed Anne Boleyn by saying: "Hold your peace. Curse not—curse her not, but rather pray for her; for even now is the time fast coming when you shall have reason to pity her, and lament her case."[95] Catherine was to be proven correct in her assessment. Anne's misfortunes would unfold in earnest once Catherine exited the scene.

After eight years of incessant struggle against Henry VIII, Catherine's health deteriorated rapidly. So much had taken place in those years, events that Catherine could scarcely have imagined when Henry first declared his intention to end their marriage. In the end, Catherine had the satisfaction of seeing her marriage declared valid by the Pope. But through it all, Henry had done the unthinkable, cut the long-standing ties with Rome and laid the groundwork for Protestantism to take root in England. Events might have taken a different turn had Emperor Charles V been more forceful in his support of Catherine and attacked England. But Charles, driven by other political considerations, never launched the invasion of England that might have forced Henry to return to Catherine. Moreover, Catherine herself was not truly enthusiastic about such an endeavor, preferring to stay loyal to her adopted country and to Henry as his wife.

Catherine's final residence was Kimbolton Castle. There she shed many tears and spent many hours on her knees in fervent prayer for those who suffered for refusing to swear to the Act of Succession and take the Oath of Supremacy. Catherine was just as dismayed for those who succumbed, for in her view, these souls had been lost. From Kimbolton, she tried in vain (through Cromwell) to get permission from Henry to care for Princess Mary, who had fallen seriously ill. Henry denied her request. Catherine then turned to Chapuys, telling him to "say to his Highness that there is no need for any other person but myself to nurse her; that I will put her in my own bed where I sleep and watch her when needful."[96] Again, it was to no avail. Henry dared not place Catherine and Mary together, for to have mother and child under the same roof was to create "a sort of joint shrine of disaffection for multitudes to flock to on every conceivable pretext."[97]

Catherine's health rapidly deteriorated that winter of 1535. Kimbolton in winter was unhealthy—the dampness seeped through the walls, prompting Catherine's ladies to maintain a fire to keep her warm. Suffering from fever and nausea, and above all, sleeplessness, Catherine knew her days were numbered. She was gratified to find her great friend, the widowed Lady Willoughby (the former Maria de Salinas), at her side near her final days. On her deathbed, Catherine wrote the following final letter to Henry:

My Lord and Husband,
I commend me unto you. The hour of my death draweth fast on, and
my case being such, the tender love I owe you forceth me, with a few
words, to put you in remembrance of the health and safe-guard of
your soul, which you ought to prefer before all worldly matters, and
before the care and tendering of your own body, for which you have
cast me into many miseries and yourself into many cares. For my part
I do pardon you all, yes, I do wish and devoutly pray God that He
will also pardon you.

For the rest I commend unto you Mary, our daughter, beseeching
you to be a good father unto her, as I heretofore desired. . . . Lastly do
I vow, that mine eyes desire you above all things.[98]

The letter was signed "Catherine, Queen of England." King Henry VIII, upon reading it, was said to have wept.

Eustache Chapuys managed to get permission to visit the dying Catherine. When she was lucid, Catherine told the ambassador that she understood why Charles V could not help her, tied as he was to fighting off Luther's followers and the Turks. She spoke of the grievous pain of being separated from Mary and of the turmoil engulfing England. She reproached herself for the suffering caused by the course she took, which had led many souls to be lost through disobedience to the Church as well as lives destroyed through disobedience to the king. Catherine also told Chapuys that Henry had not sent her much money, but she nevertheless hoped there would be enough left "to bury her in a convent of the Observant Friars and to provide 500 Masses for her soul. Chapuys did not enlighten her that the monasteries of her friends, the Observant Friars, had particularly suffered from the King's animosity."[99]

On the morning of January 7, 1536, Catherine heard Mass for the final time. She also received the Last Rites. Then, in the arms of her devoted friend, Maria, Lady Willoughby, Catherine "died unconquered as she had lived; a great lady to the last, sacrificed in death, as she had been in life, to the opportunism of high politics. *'In manus tuas Domine commendo spiritum meum,'* she murmured with her last breath.* From man she had received no mercy, and she turned to a gentler Judge with confidence and hope."[100] The words uttered by Queen Catherine on her deathbed echoed those of her mother, Queen Isabella.

---

*"Into your hands, Lord, I commend my soul," Jesus's final words, uttered just before dying on the cross.

One chronicler of Spain has described Queen Isabella in the following words: "She would have expected to be judged on her own high standards, not by how badly other people had behaved under similar circumstances. One thing, and one thing alone, was her final guide—her conscience."[101] These same words could just as easily be applied to Isabella's daughter. For Catherine to compromise on her faith and principles was impossible. She was simply not raised that way. Catherine was just as unbending and unyielding as Isabella had been in refusing to compromise her religious convictions.

The Church in England, once an impregnable citadel, powerful and influential, had succumbed to the whim of a monarch who dared to defy Rome. Henry VIII had set in motion a movement that would lead to the triumph of the Reformation in England, transforming the realm into a Protestant country. Isabella could never have imagined that Catherine's betrothal to Prince Arthur and later her betrothal to Prince Henry would lead directly to the Church in England's break from Rome, amounting to no less than "the final shattering of that Christian European unity to which" [Ferdinand and Isabella] "had devoted their lives and the lives of their children."[102]

The disorder unleashed by Henry VIII's repudiation of his wife would be repeated in another country and another century, though in a different form. Two centuries later, another set of royal mothers and daughters followed in the footsteps of the legendary Queen Isabella and the tragic Queen Catherine. As Isabella and Catherine cast their shadows over the late fifteenth and early sixteenth centuries, two no less famous royals, the impressive Empress Maria Theresa of Austria and her ill-fated daughter Queen Marie Antoinette of France were set to dominate the eighteenth century.

PART II

EMPRESS MARIA THERESA
and
QUEEN MARIE ANTOINETTE

10

THE PRAGMATIC SANCTION

wo and a half centuries passed before Europe felt the impact of another female sovereign the likes of Queen Isabella of Castile. This time, the formidable force emerged not from the far corner of the Iberian Peninsula but from central Europe—Austria, to be exact. There, in Vienna, the capital of the Habsburg Empire, Holy Roman Emperor Charles VI and his wife, Elisabeth-Christina of Brunswick-Wolfenbüttel, awaited the birth of their second child. Since their infant son, Leopold, had died the year before, much anticipation attended this birth. The emperor, head of the illustrious house of Habsburg, was at Laxenburg Palace, his hunting lodge some thirteen miles from Vienna, on the morning his wife went into labor, May 13, 1717. Upon hearing about the impending birth, Charles rode hastily to his capital. When the announcement was made that the empress had given birth to a girl, disappointment pervaded the populace, but nowhere was the disappointment more palpable than in the emperor himself. Charles VI—who held the titles Archduke of Austria, King of Hungary, King of Bohemia, and Emperor of the Holy Roman Empire—had dearly hoped that this child would be another son. At his daughter's baptism on the evening of her birth, she was given the name Maria Theresa Walburga Amalia Christina. The emperor put on a brave face, but witnesses noticed his cheerless countenance.

The birth of a male heir remained a paramount goal for many reigning monarchs, as it had been for England's King Henry VIII, and Emperor Charles VI was no exception. Charles was especially preoccupied with this lack of sons because he was the last surviving male of his line. A son was highly coveted, not simply to carry on the family name and line but also because a male on the throne would likely mean more stability. Female succession, by contrast, might lead to wars that would disturb Europe's equilibrium and result in the deaths of countless people.

Hence, the newborn archduchess seemed in no way destined for fame or greatness. Her parents, at thirty-one and twenty-five years of age, still held out hope for a male to inherit the Habsburg dominions of the emperor. Only time would tell whether this latest addition—Archduchess Maria Theresa—to Europe's most illustrious dynasty would fade into the shadows of history or take up the mantle of power to make her mark.

The Habsburg dynasty at the time was a major sovereign house of Europe, having dominated many parts of the Continent through the centuries. This dominion began with the dynasty's founder, Rudolph of Habsburg, Holy Roman emperor from 1273 to 1291. In the sixteenth century, the Habsburgs under emperor Charles V, son of Juana la Loca and grandson of King Ferdinand and Queen Isabella, claimed significant portions of Europe as hereditary domains, thanks to wars and judicious marriages. Charles V's territories, however, proved too vast to maintain, even for this dynasty adept at territorial aggrandizement. So in 1556 he divided the Habsburg territories between his brother and his son. Charles's brother became Holy Roman Emperor Ferdinand I, and Ferdinand's heirs became rulers of Austria and kings of Bohemia, Croatia, Germany, and Hungary. To Charles V's son, Philip II, and his heirs went Spain, Naples, Milan, Sicily, and the Netherlands and far-flung lands in the Americas and the Philippines.

Rivalry between the Habsburg Emperor Charles V and King Francis I of France initiated the Habsburgs' long-standing animosity toward their French counterparts. For nearly two hundred years, the Habsburgs ruled Spain, until 1700, when at the death of the childless King Charles II, the throne passed on, as Charles had wished, to Philippe, Duc d'Anjou, grandson of France's King Louis XIV. With Philippe's accession as King Philip V, just seventeen years before Archduchess Maria Theresa was born, Spain had effectively passed from the Habsburg dynasty to the ruling Bourbon dynasty of France, thus shaking up Europe's status quo.

The prospect of France's royal family holding the reins of power in Spain dismayed a number of the European powers, because it made France, under the rule of the Sun King, Louis XIV, suddenly even more powerful. An attempt to counter French hegemony and contest Philip V's accession, therefore, soon became the goal of Europe's powers. In order to stifle France's ambition, the Dutch King William III of Orange created the Grand Alliance in 1701. Joining the Netherlands in this alliance were England and Austria, whose Habsburg rulers refused to cede the Spanish crown. The Grand Alliance precipitated a thirteen-year conflict known as the War of the Spanish Succession (1701–1714). During the course of the war, famous battles such as Blenheim, Malplaquet, and Ramillies were fought under two celebrated generals, the Duke of Marlborough and Prince Eugene of Savoy.

In an attempt to keep Spain in Habsburg hands, Maria Theresa's paternal grandfather, Holy Roman Emperor Leopold I, encouraged his son Charles to be crowned King of Spain in 1703 in Vienna. Charles traveled to Spain, where he lived for some years. Charles had actually left Spain in 1711, when he succeeded his brother, Joseph, as the ruler of Austria's territories and settled back in Vienna as Charles VI. Charles had grown to love his adopted country and was bitterly disappointed to find himself no longer king after the Peace of Utrecht settled the War of the Spanish Succession in favor of the Bourbons in 1713. In place of Spain, the Austrians gained Mantua, Milan, Naples, the Spanish Netherlands, and Sardinia (later exchanged for Sicily), yet Maria Theresa's father never considered these territories adequate compensation for the loss of Spain. The extinction of the Spanish branch and loss of the Spanish dominions did not, however, keep the Habsburg dynasty from having a major impact on Europe. On the contrary, from their capital in Vienna, the Austrian branch of the Habsburgs was to make its mark on history until the early twentieth century.

Responsibility for the Habsburg Empire and anxiety drove Charles VI. Much as Charles would have preferred a son to succeed him, he did not wait to secure the Habsburg succession for his daughter. As early as 1713, even before Maria Theresa was born, the emperor had wrestled with the succession question and promulgated a law affecting the house of Habsburg, one that overturned his father's own house law. Charles VI's new statute, the Pragmatic Sanction, declared that the Habsburg territories would be indivisible and stipulated that the succession issue would pass first upon Charles's death to his descendants in primogeniture and then to his dead brother, Joseph's daughters. The Pragmatic Sanction paved the legal way for Maria Theresa to succeed her father in the event that he never had sons.

This brief review of Charles VI's background and the War of the Spanish Succession sheds light on the deep-seated antagonism between the two great dynastic powers, Bourbon France and Habsburg Austria—an antagonism that greatly affected European history for centuries. It also illuminates what is arguably one of the Habsburg rulers' most persistent and deeply held features, their "iron determination to stay in power, a determination which was upheld by every generation, which never suffered a break. History for the Habsburgs was centered on the Family. Nothing else mattered, or existed, for them. Paraphrasing Louis XIV's 'l'État c'est moi,' the Habsburgs might well have said, 'l'État c'est la Famille.' "[1]

When Maria Theresa's father returned to Vienna from Spain in 1711, he clung to Spanish ways. Emperor Charles VI adopted Spanish dress during court functions, where it was not unusual to find him sporting a plumed hat, red stockings and shoes, and a coat trimmed with lace. In Vienna, Charles also promoted the strict Spanish etiquette that was one of the distinguishing features of the Habsburg court. However, this "Spanish" style was in actuality more a distinctive Habsburg style, which amounted to "a conscious rejection of the dominant French model."[2]

What truly distinguished the Roman Catholic Habsburg court was its emphasis on piety. More rigorous in religious observance than the French court, the Viennese court could make life stressful for those unaccustomed to its practices, as the French Duc de Richelieu found in 1726. As Richelieu wrote to Cardinal Polignac after undergoing a particularly trying forty days of Lent: "I have led a pious life here during Lent, which has not left me free for a quarter of an hour; and I avow that if I had known the life that an ambassador leads here, nothing in this world would have determined me to accept this embassy. . . . Only a Capuchin with the most robust health could endure this life during Lent. In order to give your Eminence some idea, I have spent altogether between Palm Sunday and Easter Wednesday, 100 hours at church with the Emperor."[3] Vienna's inhabitants undertook extraordinary displays of penitence that included posting notices of their sins on their chests as well as whipping themselves. "These fervent displays of public sorrow echoed Holy Week as celebrated in Spain . . . rather than anything native to the city."[4]

Archduchess Maria Theresa was raised with this Baroque piety, marked by its theatricality, and steeped in religious observances. Such displays were "an external expression of the inner spiritual life . . . the reflection of a deep and turbulent belief. The brilliant colors and elaborate decoration of the churches and shrines seem best suited to the expression of joy, but there was a gloomier strain, a persistent awareness of mortality and judgment. Maria Theresa's religious training instilled in her a full measure of faith, and piety became for her a natural attribute. In her youth it gave her meaning; in her mature years it gave her strength, then comfort. In times of joy it sobered her; in times of sorrow it sustained her."[5]

The heavily religious atmosphere found in the Viennese court encouraged

Left: Queen Isabella of Castile (1451-1504), who reigned from 1474 until her death. She and her husband, Ferdinand, were known as "the Catholic Kings." Her youngest daughter, Catherine of Aragon, is her most famous offspring.

Right: King Ferdinand V of Castile and León, also King Ferdinand II of Aragon (1452-1516). As the husband of Queen Isabella of Castile, Ferdinand was joint sovereign of Castile. Together, they united Spain and completed the Reconquista against the Moors. *(Getty Images)*

Monastery of San Juan de los Reyes in Toledo, founded by Ferdinand and Isabella to commemorate their victory over the Portuguese. Isabella ordered that the chains that had held Christian captives of the Moors be permanently attached to the church as a reminder for future generations.

This painting of the capitulation of Granada captures when the Moors surrendered to Queen Isabella and King Ferdinand, the event that marked the end of the centuries-long Reconquista in Spain. *(Getty Images)*

The Alhambra Palace in Granada. Long the seat of the Moors, upon their surrender it became the favorite home of Queen Isabella and her family, including her youngest daughter, Catherine of Aragon.

A monument in Madrid, Spain, to the warrior queen, Isabella of Castile. On the left is a statue of Cardinal Mendoza.

Christopher Columbus before Queen Isabella. Her patronage of Columbus in his voyages of discovery led directly to Spain's colonization of the New World and the growth of the Spanish Empire.

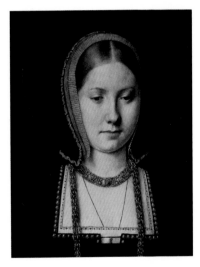

A portrait of the young Catherine of Aragon by Michael Sittow, court painter to Queen Isabella. This painting was done about the time Catherine left her mother for a new life in England as the bride of Prince Arthur. *(Getty Images)*

Henry VIII (1491-1547), King of England and second husband of Catherine of Aragon. Their marriage was a happy one until Henry became obsessed with Anne Boleyn and the need for a male heir.

Maria Theresa (1717-1780), Archduchess of Austria, Holy Roman Empress, and Queen of Hungary and Bohemia. The beginning years of her reign were turbulent, with the War of the Austrian Succession erupting, but she became one of the most successful monarchs of the Habsburg dynasty. *(Getty Images)*

Maria Theresa had sixteen children. A portrait of the empress with her husband, Holy Roman Emperor Francis I, includes their eldest son, the future Holy Roman Emperor Joseph II. *(Getty Images)*

This portrait of the Archduchess Maria Antonia (the future Queen Marie Antoinette) shows some resemblance to her mother at a similar age. *(Getty Images)*

A portrait of the twenty-year-old Queen Marie Antoinette of France.

A portrait of King Louis XVI of France, husband of Marie Antoinette.

A work by the celebrated artist Élisabeth Vigée-Lebrun showing a maternal Marie Antoinette with her three surviving children. *(Getty Images)*

Archduchess Maria Theresa in her devotions. Her very name, given to her in honor of the famed Castilian saint Teresa of Ávila, evoked one of the Catholic Church's most admired individuals. The namesake gave Maria Theresa an unusual link with her devout ancestor Queen Isabella, whom the Venerable Juan de Palafox had associated with the saint.

Not surprisingly, the imperial family undertook pilgrimages to shrines, "preferably those of the Virgin, the *magna mater Austriae,* as she was spoken of in a singular blend of reverence and familial claim."[6] The shrine to the Virgin Mary at Mariazell in the forested mountains of Styria embodied the close bond the Habsburgs always felt with their faith. There, nine-year-old Maria Theresa received her First Communion. The young girl gazed at "the miracle-working Madonna of that fame [who] wore a replica of the dynasty's crown. A life-size effigy of the lamented son of Charles VI, wrought of solid gold reposed at the feet of that statue."[7] Though Maria Theresa may have lived "in the age of cynicism, she always remained a sincere believer, who carried out the forms prescribed by her Church because they meant something to her, and not because these devotional exercises were the proper and expected gestures."[8] Maria Theresa's devotion was reminiscent of the intensely pious Queen Isabella of Castile and her daughter Catherine of Aragon, Queen of England.

Unlike Isabella and Catherine, Maria Theresa did not have a mother who was as devoted to the Catholic faith. Empress Elisabeth-Christina had been a Lutheran. Before her marriage, she had to be coaxed through tears into converting to Catholicism. Doubts persisted about the empress's attachment to her adopted faith, with a rumor as late as 1747 that she was "secretly reading Protestant books."[9] She was widely admired for her beauty, endowed with an exquisite physique, unusual violet-blue eyes, and blond hair. Elisabeth-Christina also possessed endearing charm and an easy manner.

Two more daughters—Archduchess Maria Anna, born in 1718, and Archduchess Maria Amalia, born in 1724—augmented the imperial family. After Maria Amalia, who died at five years of age, there were no more children. Elisabeth-Christina always felt the burden of not giving her husband another son. As the years passed the empress's vivacity and sweetness disappeared, replaced by aloofness. This change might account for the somewhat distant relationship between her and Maria Theresa. They never enjoyed the mother-daughter bond that had united Isabella of Castile and Catherine of Aragon.

Life for the imperial family revolved around their various palaces. The stiff etiquette and ponderous atmosphere at the Hofburg Palace in Vienna contrasted with the more relaxed and casual existence at the Laxenburg and Favorita palaces outside the capital, to which the family periodically migrated. Never taught to ride a horse, Maria Theresa instead enjoyed another outdoor pursuit, shooting targets, on the palaces' wide lawns. Back at Hofburg, "the most strictly measured *grandezza* reigned paramount. It was a strange medley of Olympian revelry, of Spanish monastic severity, and the rigorous discipline of a barrack. . . . The court costume was Spanish, the predominant hue being black. . . . All the court carriages were black."[10] Maria Theresa thus became flexible, able to observe the formal court and religious life under highly rigid rules but equally at home with the relaxed country life.

Antagonism toward France abided, whether in Vienna or in the country. At the Viennese court, the "prohibition on French influence was absolute. In the French dress—especially the white stockings [the Habsburgs always wore red, with red shoes]—even during the time of Charles VI no one dared to show himself at the Hofburg. The Emperor, as often as he saw anyone attired in that way, would at once cry out 'Here is one of those confounded Frenchmen.' "[11]

As a child, Maria Theresa was robust, a blessing she was to enjoy for years to come. She inherited her mother's blond hair and pretty features, while from her father the archduchess inherited the most distinguishing feature of the Habsburgs, a protruding lower lip. An early portrait of her shows a charming looking child with a hint of fierce determination shining forth. She could also be impulsive, such as the time six-year-old Maria Theresa was dazzled by her father's appearance in stately robes during the Corpus Christi procession. Marveling at his majestic bearing, the little archduchess clapped delightedly and exclaimed, "Oh, what a fine papa! Come here, papa, and let me admire you."[12]

Charles VI could be a demanding father who may have been disappointed at his daughters for not having been sons, but he was never cruel to his children. However much Maria Theresa's father loved his eldest daughter, though, he could not accept her completely as his heir. He kept hoping that Elisabeth-Christina would give him the son he so desired. If she had passed the point where she could not, perhaps she would die, and Charles VI could remarry and still father a male child. But Elisabeth-Christina lived, and the emperor never remarried. It became increasingly evident that Maria Theresa was the likely heir.

Preparing Maria Theresa to rule the most complicated inheritance in all Europe, with its myriad lands and peoples, should have been a priority, but the emperor never educated her for this auspicious role. The ever-present shadow of the hoped-for son clouded his thinking. Charles ordered Jesuit priests to tutor Maria Theresa. But the Jesuits, though renowned for giving excellent education, could not teach her to her full potential because the emperor did not instruct them to educate her as he would have a male heir. Instead, he wanted his daughter to become an accomplished woman who would make a good wife and consort. Even when it came to foreign languages, no great effort was made to train her. Maria Theresa's native German remained peppered with spelling and grammatical errors. She was fluent in French, had a good grasp of Italian and some knowledge of Spanish, but her Latin never met the standard of Catherine of Aragon. Unlike Catherine, who was subjected to intense intellectual activity from an early age, Maria Theresa received a far less ambitious education, to some degree the kind her ancestor Isabella of Castile received. Charles VI's eldest child would have to rely on her instincts and natural intelligence to pick up what she could about statesmanship and politics.

The archduchess did, however, excel in music, not surprising considering that her father liked to compose. Maria Theresa became accomplished at the harpsichord; she possessed a fine singing voice and was a good dancer. The young archduchess was also a born diplomat. " 'Always,' [Signor] Foscari, the Venetian ambassador in Vienna once wrote of her, 'she says and does the right thing.' "[13] Otherwise, Maria Theresa's childhood was uneventful. To ensure the Pragmatic Sanction's implementation, the emperor worked diligently to obtain solidarity from as many countries as possible. With claims to Habsburg territories, Bavaria held out from giving its promise, as did France. From the mid-1720s until the early 1730s, Charles VI secured the guarantees of Spain, Russia, Great Britain, the Netherlands, Prussia, and Saxony—though at a high price for Austria. Great Britain, for one, had done exceedingly well in its deal with the Habsburg emperor. In exchange for British support of the Pragmatic Sanction, Maria Theresa's father abolished, in 1731, the lucrative Ostend East India Company, which had challenged British trade in that region.

Charles VI hoped that securing these numerous guarantees would protect the Habsburg succession after his death, keep the dynasty's territories intact, and avert war. Guarantees to the Pragmatic Sanction made Maria Theresa's inheritance seem inviolable. However, Charles VI's lifework was soon to be shredded.

11

ARCHDUCHESS AND QUEEN

*E*ven though Maria Theresa could never compensate for the son he always wanted, Charles VI could take comfort in her value as a bride. As next in line to the throne, his eldest daughter was the heiress to his vast dominions. Anyone securing the archduchess as a bride would gain untold prestige, a valuable alliance with the Habsburgs, and possibly even a claim to the dynasty's territories. It came then as no surprise that there were offers from the royal houses of Bavaria, Poland, Portugal, Prussia, and Spain.

The emperor was inclined, however, to match Maria Theresa with a son of his cousin and childhood friend, Duke Leopold of Lorraine. Leopold's father had served the Habsburgs, fighting with Prince Eugene of Savoy against the invading Turks. Lorraine may have been a French province, but it bordered the Holy Roman Empire and its dukes were generally sympathetic toward the Habsburgs. Duke Leopold was no exception. The first choice was Leopold's son Clement, but when he died of smallpox, the choice fell upon Clement's younger brother, Francis Stephen. Charles VI at first hesitated because Francis Stephen had never contracted the much dreaded smallpox and thus was not immune. But to discount Francis Stephen might mean that Charles would have to look elsewhere, which he was reluctant to do in light of his affection for the family. And so the teenage Francis Stephen of Lorraine was dispatched to the Habsburg court to be inspected as a prospective husband for Maria Theresa, who was only six years old at the time.

Francis Stephen, tall and blue-eyed, soon charmed everyone with his easygoing manner. In fact, he was cautioned to temper his boisterous spirit lest it be misinterpreted as too undignified for one who might marry the heiress to the

Habsburg domains. He bonded with the emperor almost as son and father, over their mutual passion for hunting. The emperor wrote glowingly to Duke Leopold about his son: "I can truthfully say that the young gentleman is quite remarkable for one so young in years; he is clever in everything he does, his manners are good, he is obedient. . . . I can assure you that he is loved and admired by every one."[1] Charles was encouraged enough by what he saw in Francis Stephen that he had the young man live at the Viennese court for the next several years. During this time tutors were called in to turn the Lorrainer into, if not a Habsburg, at least one who would be loyal to the dynasty.

Francis was an obliging student but not a very dedicated one. Sports, especially the hunt, preoccupied him far more than his studies. Francis's lackadaisical attitude was evident in his French and German. The longer he stayed in Vienna, the worse his native French became, but his German never really improved. By the time Francis was a grown man, one contemporary had observed: "His French letters seem to have been written by a German, while his German correspondence might have been written by a Frenchman with a slight knowledge of foreign languages."[2] Subjected to examinations every six months, Francis passed each time, largely because he charmed his tutors.

Maria Theresa too succumbed to Francis Stephen's charms. She grew up by his side and never really remembered life without the handsome young man from Lorraine. Awestruck by his prowess on the hunting field, bedazzled by his charisma, Maria Theresa was swept away with the idea of marrying Francis Stephen of Lorraine. One observer noted that she "sighs and pines all night for her Duke of Lorraine. If she sleeps it is only to dream of him, if she wakes it is but to talk of him to the lady-in-waiting."[3]

In 1729 Francis Stephen's father died, compelling the twenty-one-year-old to return to his homeland as the ruling Duke of Lorraine. While there, Francis proved to be an able administrator who set the duchy's finances in order. After visiting Berlin, where Francis met Crown Prince Frederick of Prussia, who was impressed with the duke's high spirits, Francis returned to Vienna in 1732. There, the eager fifteen-year-old Maria Theresa was unwavering in her resolve to marry the man her father had chosen for her.

Francis found Maria Theresa a delightfully pretty adolescent who had inherited the good looks of her mother's youth. Maria Theresa possessed a longish face and nose, carefully arched brows, and large, bluish eyes. She had a fine, graceful figure and masses of golden hair, her crowning glory. Even more gratifying to Francis was the fact that the archduchess was as devoted to him as she had been the day he had left Vienna. The time for an engagement was close at hand.

The formal engagement took place in January 1736, to the excitement of the young couple, who genuinely loved each other. Shortly thereafter, as they were apart for a brief time, they exchanged written messages. In one, Francis wrote with fervor: "Dearest, it will not be difficult for you to believe that nothing is harder for me than to approach you by letter instead of throwing myself at your feet. Let my dearest of all brides be fully assured that in all the world there is no bridegroom more entirely devoted and reverential than my angel bride's most faithful servant."[4] No less endearing were Maria Theresa's words to her future husband: "It is good that our separation is not for long. I trust there will be fewer partings in our future, much-longed for life together. I assure you that as long as I have any being I will remain your most faithful bride. . . . Farewell, dear Mouse. I embrace you with all my heart. Take care of yourself. Adieu, dear one."[5]

On February 12, 1736, the eighteen-year-old Archduchess Maria Theresa's dearest wish came true when she married Francis of Lorraine. The ceremony took place at the Augustinerkirche, the church of the Augustine friars, adjacent to the Hofburg Palace, presided over by the papal nuncio. The church was lit by thousands of candles, the walls hung with rich tapestries. Dressed in a silver-white diamond-and-pearl-encrusted gown with train, her head and neck covered in sparkling diamonds, Archduchess Maria Theresa looked every inch the imperial bride. Only two days were allowed for festivities to celebrate the wedding because Lent was not far off. Three days after the wedding, the newlyweds went on a pilgrimage to Mariazell, praying at the foot of the statue of the Virgin for their future.

There was a price to be paid for the marriage—and Francis paid it. The French minister, Cardinal Fleury, concerned that the union would bring neighboring Lorraine under Habsburg influence, used the peace treaty ending hostilities over the Polish Succession to strike a blow against the encroaching Austrian power. He did so by requiring Francis to renounce Lorraine as a prerequisite to his marriage to Maria Theresa. Francis was to be given the Grand Duchy of Tuscany as compensation. In order to convince Charles VI to agree to Fleury's plan, King Louis XV's minister offered the emperor a French guarantee to the Pragmatic Sanction. It was an unpalatable offer to Charles, but one that was necessary.

Francis was shocked by the demand. He could not renounce Lorraine, the duchy that had been so near and dear to him and his family. His mother was stunned and urged her son to refuse. Maria Theresa was equally furious. But Baron Johann Bartenstein, Charles VI's most able and trusted adviser, bullied the duke into acquiescing. Bartenstein finally wore Francis down with the blunt words "No renunciation, no archduchess."[6] In the end, Charles VI gained a son-in-law and his precious French guarantee to the Pragmatic Sanction, and Francis got his Maria Theresa and marriage into the Habsburg dynasty. At least his patrimonial name was to resonate through the generations, for their descendants would be members of the house of Habsburg-Lorraine. To his credit, Francis "never in later life reproached Maria Theresa for demanding this sacrifice." As for Maria Theresa, "although she came to detest Bartenstein during the course of this transaction, she later recognised his relative ability and employed him . . . as her mainstay during the first appallingly difficult years of her reign."[7]

By this time, Archduchess Maria Theresa was well aware of her future role and her place not only as a Habsburg and heir to her father but also as a figure of prominence on the European stage. The archduchess began to let people know that she would be a monarch on her own terms and not one at the mercy of advisers. The Venetian ambassador had noted as much in the mid-1730s, saying, "She displays a marked awareness of her future station and leaves people in no doubt that, once she has gained it, the men on whose advice she might call will not influence her decisions."[8]

Soon after Maria Theresa and Francis were married, the archduchess began her remarkable "career" as a prolific mother. In the first four years of marriage, she became the mother of three children, all girls. Unlike many women of her station, Maria Theresa nursed her children herself. Though she took to mothering with great ease, the archduchess did not take confinements lightly. She had written her concerns to her sister Marianne when Marianne was expecting a baby: "Since the first of the month I have not been at peace for a single moment; I think continuously of your coming confinement. I know what it means, and I therefore look forward to it with terror."[9] But this anxiety over childbirth did not deter Maria Theresa from doing her duty and providing the house of Habsburg with numerous archdukes and archduchesses in the years to come.

If Maria Theresa thought she might enjoy the company of her husband these first few years of married life, she was mistaken. Instead, Francis went to war on the Austrian side against the Turks. Russia, in the hope of strengthening its position in the Crimea, had declared war on the Turks. Both Russia and the Turks wanted Austrian aid. Russia, however, had the upper hand. Empress Anna threatened to renounce her country's endorsement of the Pragmatic Sanction if Austria did not support Russia. Emperor Charles VI could not countenance this. And so Austria went to Russia's aid against the Turks. The Austrian army, however, was totally unprepared for the conflict, and hopes that

Francis could distinguish himself on the battlefield were frustrated. Prince Eugene of Savoy, the brilliant general who had devoted his life to the service of the Habsburgs, had recently died and so could not offer his expertise on the conduct of the war. Moreover, the Austrians were hampered by insufficient ammunition, artillery, and supplies. It was a far cry from the days of the Siege of Vienna in 1683, when Austrian forces, along with Polish and German soldiers, defeated the Ottoman Empire in a victory that had great implications for western Europe. Back then, the great Prince Eugene, along with the acclaimed King Jan Sobieski of Poland, had turned back the Muslim invasion, effectively saving Vienna and Europe.

Francis returned to Vienna and to Maria Theresa in defeat, failing to raise his esteem in the eyes of the emperor or in those of his father-in-law's subjects. Accusations of incompetence swirled about him and reached fever pitch. Francis was not the only one within the imperial family who had let down Charles VI. Maria Theresa disappointed her father when she gave birth to her second daughter, Maria Anna (Marianne). Charles VI's torment over having no males in the family grew. With these disappointments, the emperor deemed it prudent to send the young couple to Tuscany, where they took up residence as the ruling grand ducal family in 1739. With a disappointed father and an unpopular husband bearing the brunt of people's anger, leaving Vienna came as a relief. Maria Theresa and Francis did not stay long in Tuscany, however; they were called back to Vienna after only three months.

The Austria to which Maria Theresa returned was in near shambles. The army was in an even worse state, defeated in battles against the Turks. In the humiliating 1739 Treaty of Belgrade, Austria conceded Belgrade and other lands to the Ottoman Turks. During this time, Charles wrote to Bartenstein: "This year took many years off my life, to which only a few are left. God wills it so! He gives me the power to bear it, through it my sins are expiated and where I am wanting it will serve as a correction and warning."[10] Other problems plagued the country, for Austria's "ministry [had] gone up in the smoke of spontaneous combustion; famine, from a failure of crops, was gazing like a gaunt specter at the capital, and the heir to the throne was married to a disgraced husband." Charles VI became despondent. So bad was the state of Austria that, "had the Turks but realized the truth, they might have advanced once more to the walls of the city they hated." Instead, they "looked up the Danube [and] they imagine[d] they saw the shadow of Prince Eugene, and drew back in terror."[11]

Within the Habsburg family itself, sadness and anxiety prevailed. In 1740, Maria Theresa gave birth to yet another girl, Maria Carolina, and in the middle of the year, her eldest daughter, Maria Elisabeth, died of smallpox. This greatly saddened Charles VI, who had become attached to this granddaughter.

The British diplomat Sir Thomas Robinson observed about the Habsburg court and Austria: "Everything in this court is running into the last stages of confusion and ruin; there are signs of the worst folly and madness that ever afflicted a people whom Heaven has determined to destroy, no less by domestic divisions than by the more public calamities of repeated defeats, defenselessness, poverty, famine and plague." Robinson added: "The Turks seem to the Viennese to be already in Hungary and the Hungarians themselves in arms against Austria. They imagine the Saxons are in Bohemia, and the Bavarians at the very gates of the city, while France, the very soul of their opposition is everywhere."[12]

These were not the best years for Maria Theresa either. In her personal life she had the consolation of being Francis's wife and becoming a mother, but elsewhere, the archduchess could find little solace. She was not popular—Francis's reputation as a lightweight contributed greatly here—nor did the nobility or her father's ministers see her as a future sovereign. After all, her father was still in his fifties and might easily live for many more years. Not only did no miniature court grow around Maria Theresa as the future head of the Habsburgs but she was actively shunned by the aristocracy. She recalled these isolated years some three decades later, saying that "no one so much as looked at me."[13]

The one bit of good news to come out in 1740 was that Maria Theresa was again expecting a child. Everyone, most especially the emperor, hoped that this fourth child would turn out to be the long-desired boy. But Charles VI never knew the sex of his latest grandchild. In October that year, after a day of hunting, the emperor fell ill with a cold and fever. Upon his return to his hunting lodge, Charles requested his cook to prepare him his favorite dish of mushrooms. Soon after eating them, he fell violently ill. His physicians bled him but to no avail. The emperor was taken to the Favorita Palace, where he prepared to die. By his side was his wife, the once beautiful Elisabeth-Christina, now incredibly stout. Archduchess Marianne rushed to her father's bedside to say good-bye, but the heiress, Maria Theresa, did not. She had already broken down once in her father's presence during his final illness. Fearing that the shock of seeing him in such a bad state might trigger a miscarriage, Charles VI forbade Maria Theresa to come to him to say her final good-bye. Charles prepared to die as a Catholic by receiving the Last Rites and as Habsburg emperor with the requisite six lit tapers in the room. On his deathbed, he turned toward Maria Theresa's apartments and gave a final blessing. He died on October 19, 1740, the last male in a line of Habsburg monarchs stretching for five centuries. His twenty-three-year-old daughter, five months pregnant with her fourth child, now succeeded him, untrained and inadequately educated for her monumental role as ruler of the Habsburg Empire. Nevertheless, under her reign, history would be rewritten. Cataclysmic shifts would reverberate on the Continent—and Maria Theresa's name would be remembered in the centuries to come.

As the new head of the Habsburg dynasty, Maria Theresa soon discovered what her father's death meant for Europe and for her. The lands that she inherited were vast, but "her inheritance was a dynasty without a firm base. It was not a country, rather a princely house holding disputed sway over many lands and many peoples; Germans, Magyars, Rumanians, Italians, Flemings, a wide and bewildering variety of Slavs."[14] Added to this were lands encompassing present-day Austria and Slovenia, the Czech lands of Bohemia, Moravia, and Silesia; the Austrian Netherlands; Piacenza; Parma; Mantua; Milan and Tuscany, as well as Transylvania, Croatia, and Hungary. This impressive but unwieldy inheritance was bound to cause trouble.

Maria Theresa became the ruler of the Austrian lands and Queen of Hungary and Bohemia. However, because she was a woman, she could not be elected to the seat once held by Charlemagne and most recently occupied by her father. Salic law, which barred female succession, or election in this case, was in operation; therefore Maria Theresa could not become Holy Roman empress of her own accord.*

But Maria Theresa was still a formidable monarch. At her accession, she was very much an enigma to many, but the impression she made those first few hours was positive. Sir Thomas Robinson wrote highly of the new monarch: "Her person was formed to wear a crown, and her mind to give luster to the exalted dignity of her position; she possessed a most commanding figure, great beauty, animation and sweetness of countenance, a pleasant voice, feminine grace with a remarkable strength of understanding, and an intrepidity above her sex."[15] Another eyewitness had similar glowing words: "Had one been given all the women of the world from whom to choose a queen, yet would the choice have fallen upon Maria Theresa."[16]

Maria Theresa's conception of her role as monarch had been fostered by her history tutor, Gottfried Spanagel, the curator of the royal library. Spanagel emphasized to his pupil not so much the divine right of kings but a robust monarchy strongly connected to the state. His "stress on certain simple elements of the

---

*Salic law, derived from the early Middle Ages, was a set of laws that covered among other things, inheritances.

nature of power had great influence on Maria Theresa's approach to her tasks. Specifically, he emphasized the proper 'historical' virtues; the right to rule, not only of monarchs in general, but of queens in particular; and the relationship between ruler and church."[17]

Maria Theresa gave a hint of the kind of monarch she was to become when, within hours of her father's death, she presented herself to her ministers and court at her first formal audience. Upon hearing of her father's illness, Maria Theresa had taken to bed. A combination of sorrow and anxiety worried her doctors that a miscarriage was about to take place. Fortunately her doctors were wrong; Maria Theresa was made of sterner stuff. When the time came to face her subjects, she bravely embraced her new role. Despite her pregnancy and still reeling from the grief at the death of her father, Maria Theresa looked self-possessed and regal as she stood on the steps leading to the throne. Nearby, on the queen's left and away from the throne, stood Francis in the secondary position he would accept for the rest of his life.

Framed by the throne's canopy and wearing dark mourning clothes, Maria Theresa, with her blond good looks and youth, elicited an unusual combination of doubt and dignity. The doubters were none other than her father's ministers, all men in their seventies, save one who was in his sixties. They could scarcely believe that the young mother who stood before them could grapple with the monumental challenges that were bound to come her way. Yet searching eyes also saw a woman who appeared ready to grasp the helm and lead her peoples into uncharted territory.

Holding back tears, the Queen of Hungary and of Bohemia and Archduchess of Austria, among her many titles, recalled her departed father, intoned her trust in God, and declared that she was ready to work with her father's ministers. Slowly and resolutely they approached their new sovereign and kissed her hand. For the time being, there would be not a sweeping away of the old order but a confirmation of it. Maria Theresa knew she was far too inexperienced in the ways of governing to attempt such a drastic step so soon. Instead, confident that, with the help of God, she would quickly learn the art of ruling and statecraft, the queen ensured a smooth transition.

Maria Theresa's accession to the centuries-old Habsburg throne captured Europe's attention, but there was to be no political honeymoon for the new queen. The Pragmatic Sanction, to which so many had agreed, suddenly seemed trifling. Greedy and ambitious powers eyed the young woman's domains, relishing the thought that war might gain them territories at the Habsburgs' expense.

Maria Theresa was not the only new ruler to succeed to an important throne that fateful year. In April 1740, Prussia's king died and was succeeded by his eldest son, Frederick II. Some in Vienna at the time thought this boded well, for the new king appeared to be an intelligent and reasonable man with whom the Habsburgs could come to terms. Yet nowhere was the intention of ignoring the Pragmatic Sanction stronger than in Berlin, the capital of Prussia. The hotheaded young monarch was set to pounce upon the Habsburgs and create misery for the young and vulnerable Maria Theresa. Hence, almost as soon as she ascended the throne, Maria Theresa found herself in a conflagration that was to have great repercussions for the history of Europe. The man who would be known as Frederick the Great would become Austria's—and Maria Theresa's—greatest nemesis.

12

FORSAKEN BY THE WHOLE WORLD

*I*t has been said of Maria Theresa that "no princess ever ascended a throne under circumstances of greater peril, or in a situation which demanded more energy, fortitude and judgment."[1] Yet there was little evidence that the new monarch possessed the qualities to succeed as a sovereign. Even though Charles VI had desperately tried to protect his daughter's inheritance through the Pragmatic Sanction, he had neglected to groom her sufficiently to take over the reins of state. Furthermore, there was nothing in Maria Theresa's young life to show that she had the fortitude, courage, and stamina to take on the challenges ahead. Given the enormity of the troubles, simply holding on to her throne, much less succeeding as a sovereign, would be difficult. And no one was more aware of this than the new queen, who wrote: "I do not think anyone would deny that history hardly knows of a crowned head who started his rule under circumstances more grievous than those attending my accession."[2]

Certainly many of her fellow countrymen wondered if the new Habsburg monarch was up to task. Would the queen leave the governing of the realm to others? Or would she rule effectively? The answer was not long in forthcoming. At Maria Theresa's ascension, she overheard a minister mutter: "Oh, if she were only a man endowed with all that she possesses!" To which she retorted: "Though I am only a queen, yet have I the heart of a king."[3] Her words were almost a paraphrasing of Queen Elizabeth I of England's famous 1588 address to the English army before the invasion of the Spanish Armada: "I know I have the body of a weak and feeble woman, but I have the heart and stomach of a king, and of a king of England too." Queen Elizabeth reigned for nearly forty-five years and is remembered as a decisive and politically astute monarch. Time would tell whether Maria Theresa would emulate Elizabeth I's example.

From the day she held her first audience with her ministers, Maria Theresa was under no illusions. Her ascension as female ruler of the Habsburg dominions was unprecedented and could well bring unwelcome troubles. There were other disadvantages. The ministers she had inherited from her father were elderly, as well as paralyzed with fear over the empire's future. As a whole and without exaggeration, the queen's ministers "presented a picture of creeping senility, . . . [resembling] an array of grizzled patriarchs."[4] The chancellor, Count Philip Sinzendorf, was sixty-nine, while Count Gundacker Starhemberg, president of the chamber, was seventy-seven. Maria Theresa never relied on the unscrupulous, perennially in debt, and self-indulgent Sinzendorf. But the queen trusted the unselfish Starhemberg, though he did not have Sinzendorf's grasp of international politics. In short, the majority of ministers at Maria Theresa's disposal were not outstanding.

The one exception was the haughty but able Baron Bartenstein, who had compelled her beloved husband to give away Lorraine as part of their marriage bargain. Although Maria Theresa could not forgive Bartenstein for his actions, and would have liked nothing better than to be rid of the overbearing baron, she nevertheless let her head rule her emotions. Maria Theresa knew better than to dismiss Bartenstein at this critical juncture. His ministerial experience was crucial to her, so she retained him and listened to his advice. Well aware that the Habsburg dominions rested on foundations that could collapse at a moment's notice, Maria Theresa set about demonstrating that the transition of power in Vienna had gone smoothly. She did not want more uncertainty, though the ministers "all were deeply imbedded in the past. Between them, the members of this cabinet or conference had helped [Maria Theresa's father] Charles to ruin Austria."[5]

Added to this dearth of talent among her ministers, the Habsburg monarchy itself suffered from ineffectiveness. It was in great need of reform and modernization. Troubles abounded in all directions, military, economic, and political. Maria Theresa was dismayed to find that her army was impotent. Its meager eighty thousand soldiers were expected to "defend frontiers reaching from those of the Netherlands and Parma, to those of [present-day] Turkey; the bulk of them, including almost all the cavalry, were in Hungary. There were only 40 pieces of artillery."[6] Desertions were not uncommon. Many soldiers had not been paid because of a near-bankrupt treasury. Only a paltry 100,000 florins were available to Maria Theresa to spend on ruling her lands. Moreover, credit was impossible to obtain; loans from her nobles had already been exhausted. Especially aggravating and potentially dangerous to the monarchy's stability were widespread food shortages from poor harvests that could lead to riots. Nothing, it seemed, went the queen's way.

To her ministers, Maria Theresa put on a brave face, but in private the queen shed tears of sadness and anxiety over these crippling problems. Recalling years later her predicament when she came to the throne, Maria Theresa wrote: "In these circumstances I found myself without money, without credit, without an army, without experience and knowledge, even without counsel, because all my ministers were wholly occupied in trying to discover which way the cat was going to jump."[7] In her new position, however, Maria Theresa willingly admitted her inexperience in governing. She later said of this critical moment: "I resolved not to conceal my ignorance, but to listen to each in his own department and thus to inform myself properly."[8] Seeking help did not come naturally to Maria Theresa. She recalled her "great timidity and diffidence" at the time.[9] But with her abiding faith in God, the queen found the strength to forge on, noting, "From the outset I decided and made it my principle, for my own inner guidance, to apply myself, with a pure mind and instant prayer to God, to put aside all secondary considerations, arrogance, ambition, or other passions, having on many occasions examined myself in respect of these things, and to undertake the business of government incumbent on me quietly and resolutely," for in the end "my duty was not to myself personally but only to the public."[10]

From the day of her accession, though with child, Maria Theresa diligently worked at running her realm. Possessed of great self-discipline and will, the new queen set about making it known that she intended to be an active monarch. Blessed with a healthy constitution, Maria Theresa was determined not to let her pregnancy impede her. Whether pregnant or nursing or recuperating from childbirth, she studied her state papers carefully and met regularly with her government ministers. In this, Maria Theresa acted in the same vein as Queen Isabella of Castile, whose approach to ruling, even while pregnant, was unflaggingly energetic.

Also like Isabella, Maria Theresa had a strong sense of justice. Both queens, after all, had to contend with the issue of crime and revolt; dispensing justice was part of their role as monarchs. Neither tolerated insubordination and so sought to tamp down quickly actions that disturbed the public peace or were a menace to society and the crown. During one such revolt, over food shortages in Vienna in the first year of Maria Theresa's reign, she ordered the condemned leaders to sweep the capital as a penalty, but with a punishing and humiliating twist. Attached to their legs were heavy chains that the men had to drag as they carried out their sentence.

Like Isabella before her, Maria Theresa was determined to be an effective ruler from her earliest days. In order to rule in a world dominated by men, both queens had to dig deep into their reserves of courage, fortitude, and will in order to succeed. Keeping their realms intact was the first step to unifying and strengthening their domains. Unity and strength would allow their subjects to prosper and live in peace. Strength through unity and peace through strength—these were the concepts that Isabella had lived by, and they were the concepts that Maria Theresa too embraced. These goals seemed nearly impossible to fulfill, but Maria Theresa would not let the thought of failure prevent her from doing her sacred duty to her peoples.

Among Maria Theresa's many challenges was the Pragmatic Sanction. The queen believed the sanction, for which her father had worked so hard and sacrificed so much, to be nothing short of a sacred imperial inheritance. " 'God acknowledges my rights,' she said, 'He will protect me as He has done heretofore.' "[11] To "make a reality out of the theoretical assertion of the Pragmatic Sanction" required "a thorough modernization of the Monarchy."[12] But before embarking on the ambitious project of reviving her sclerotic realm, Maria Theresa had to secure her domains. She concluded that, above all, she had to protect her patrimony and buttress her claims to the throne. Yet Maria Theresa knew she could not leave the fate of this sacred inheritance entirely to God. Forceful action was necessary to ensure that the Pragmatic Sanction was inviolable.

This was a task easier said than done. The Habsburg territories were far from secure; in fact, the disintegration of the dominions was a distinct possibility. Certain European countries greeted Maria Theresa's accession with predatory anticipation. The monarchy's instability, insolvency, and poor defensive capability presented opportunities for gaining Habsburg spoils. The queen's own subjects, particularly in Lower Austria, viewed the accession of a woman to the throne with trepidation or disappointment. The German princes disliked the idea of a woman as head of the Habsburg dynasty. Maria Theresa's Bohemian subjects, upset with the higher taxes imposed upon them by Charles VI, resented their reduced influence at court. They were among those whose allegiance to the queen was shaky. In the capital, loyalty to the new monarch was not widespread. Hardly anyone believed that the young and inexperienced Maria Theresa could rule on her own. The Habsburgs were regarded as a spent force. Many thought the queen could command strength only with her husband as coruler, but deep reservations about Francis persisted. As a native Lorrainer, Maria Theresa's husband was seen as being under the influence of France, and France was still Austria's number one enemy.

All these problems did not negatively affect Maria Theresa and Francis's marriage. Unlike most royals, the couple shared the same bedroom and the same bed. By this time, however, whatever illusions Maria Theresa might have had about Francis had been broken. A devoted wife, the queen never begrudged her husband his faults, but her love for him did not prevent her from realizing that she could not lean too heavily on him. Francis did, however, possess one outstanding quality, and that was his absolute loyalty to Maria Theresa as sovereign and to the Habsburg dynasty as a whole. Maria Theresa also recognized Francis's abilities in sorting out finances and soon involved him in the domain's financial situation, which was nothing short of precarious. The queen saw to it that Francis was given responsibilities whenever possible in helping to run her realm, but never to an extent that infringed on her rights as a sovereign. She also reserved great ambitions for him, since Maria Theresa's ultimate goal was to have her husband elected Holy Roman emperor. She was convinced that having her consort occupy that illustrious position would go a long way toward keeping the Habsburg domains intact. At this point, Maria Theresa could only hope that one day her husband would be crowned Holy Roman emperor.* To help his chances, she appointed Francis as coregent of the Austrian and Bohemian lands.

Maria Theresa had hoped for some breathing space from Europe's powers upon her accession, but she soon discovered that this was not to be. None but Russia and the Netherlands offered definitive support, while Britain made only vague noises about being friendly toward Austria. Strong hints from other European powers indicated that her father's much vaunted Pragmatic Sanction stood on flimsy ground. King Louis XV's octogenarian chief minister, Cardinal Fleury, for one, ignored making a firm commitment to recognize the Pragmatic Sanction upon Maria Theresa's accession. The ambitious prince-elector Charles Albert of Bavaria had coveted the Habsburg crown and never recognized the Pragmatic Sanction. Certain segments of Maria Theresa's subjects found the Bavarian a far more palatable ruler of the Habsburg domains. Little wonder then that Bavaria was among the countries that eagerly sought to dismember her

---

*The Holy Roman Empire was a conglomeration of states ruled by royalty, stretching from Charlemagne (crowned in 800) to Francis II, who oversaw its dissolution in 1806. Various rulers elected the emperors, who largely came from the Habsburg dynasty. The empire's territories covered large areas of central Europe, as well as parts of Italy, Belgium, and the Netherlands. Despite their lofty title and claims to temporal suzerainty over Christendom, the Holy Roman emperors' authority was not significant, the title being largely prestigious.

Habsburg territories. Others included Saxony, Spain, and Sardinia. But the most menacing of all was Prussia.

Maria Theresa "all her life was as resolute in defending her own rights as she was scrupulous in respecting those of others."[13] But, unlike her father, who had great faith in treaties, Maria Theresa soon came to think otherwise. She lived in an era—as she was soon to find to her great cost—when treaties meant little, if anything. Leading the charge in this direction was King Frederick II of Prussia.

Five years older than Maria Theresa, Frederick grew up under a cruel and autocratic father. Frederick Wilhelm I, Frederick's father, was known as the "soldier-king." He ruled Prussia ably but was a complete failure as a father. Despotic by nature, Frederick Wilhelm sought to make his son and heir a soldier and brooked no opposition from him, despite the fact that the prince infinitely preferred music and art to the army. The father met Frederick's minor infractions in his highly regimented life with humiliations and beatings. Years later Frederick recalled how "the severities of my father towards me, my sisters and my brothers . . . his ill-treatment, [were] often carried to the extreme."[14] At the age of eighteen, Frederick tried to escape his father's cruelty by fleeing to England with his close friend, Hans Hermann von Katte. Upon their capture, the king imprisoned the pair. Frederick recalled of this time, "I was arrested, broken with blows, smacked in the face. . . . Without my good and excellent mother who came to my rescue, . . . [and] my sister . . . who was also very badly treated, I believe I should have died under the blows I received."[15] Frederick survived his incarceration, but his furious father forced his son to watch von Katte be executed for treason. At one point, it looked as if Prince Frederick might be executed as well, but the intervention of his mother as well as Maria Theresa's father likely helped to spare the crown prince's life.

There were signs that Frederick II might not be the military man his father had so ruthlessly tried to create. Frederick II preferred the company of artists and musicians and aspired to be a philosopher king. Equally at ease in French as he was in his native German, Frederick II championed French culture. He greatly admired the French philosopher Voltaire, who predicted that the king might turn Berlin into the Athens of Germany. With this reputation for culture and philosophy, Prussia's king seemed like a natural ally for Austria. Additionally, since Maria Theresa's father had pleaded with King Frederick Wilhelm I to spare his son's life, Frederick II might have been sympathetic to her. But this was not the case. When the time came to make his move against Maria Theresa, Frederick II of Prussia pretended to be trustworthy. But he was no less eager for the spoils, having, like so much of Europe, carefully planned for this moment.

The new queen carefully assessed the situation. Bavaria was the immediate threat. She mobilized defensive troops for a possible attack and dispatched soldiers to Bohemia, Moravia, Tyrol, and Silesia. Silesia, with its mineral wealth, was of particular importance to the Habsburgs but also of great interest to the Prussians. Possession of Silesia would increase Prussia's geographic borders and resources, enhancing a new German power. Frederick II was poised to order his troops to occupy Silesia (most of which was in present-day southwestern Poland). In December, just weeks after Maria Theresa's accession, Frederick II of Prussia outlined his proposal to the queen. He was willing to support Francis becoming Holy Roman emperor and help the Habsburgs fight their opponents, even throwing money into Austria's near-empty coffers, if she ceded most of Silesia. If she rejected these terms, he would side with her enemies, but above all, Frederick would interpret her rejection as war with Prussia. These were shocking demands, particularly considering Maria Theresa's father's earlier defense of Frederick against his father.

Francis learned of the audacious Prussian demands from Count Gotter, King Frederick's Lord Marshal. Indignant, Francis insisted that Maria Theresa not give up any territory that was her rightful inheritance. "For my part," added her ever-loyal husband, "not for the Imperial crown, not even for the whole world, will I sacrifice one right or one inch of the Queen's lawful possessions."[16] The conversation descended into a loud quarrel, and the queen, who was listening by the door, signaled Francis to end the discussion.

Maria Theresa refused to see Gotter but relayed a powerful message to him and to Frederick that astounded many. She ordered the Lord Marshal to "return to his master and to tell him that as long as one Prussian soldier remained in Silesia, she would rather perish than negotiate with the King of Prussia."[17] Maria Theresa stood her ground. She would not cede any territory to the greedy Prussians. The King of Prussia did not hesitate to march into war. On December 16, 1740, Frederick II crossed into Silesia with his troops, making the richest and most industrialized of Maria Theresa's provinces the first of her territories to be attacked. In January, Frederick told his foreign minister that he had crossed the Rubicon. The War of the Austrian Succession had begun.

Frederick bulldozed his way into nearby Silesia, claiming Prussia's rights to certain principalities. Europe was startled to learn that the King of Prussia had brazenly attacked the Habsburg Empire with only the flimsiest pretext. Yet self-interest characterized the reaction of Europe's powers to Frederick's attack. Britain counseled Austria to come to terms with Prussia. Russia and Poland sent messages of regret. France certainly did not aid Austria but sent feelers out to Prussia. Left to her own devices, Maria Theresa had the choice of giving in to Prussia or fighting back. She fought back. At the Battle of Moll-witz, the Prussian cavalry performed badly, with Frederick II retreating, but his highly trained infantry saved the day. Ultimately, it was a matter of numbers, with 22,000 Prussians outfighting the 16,000 Austrians. The impact of the bat-tle was not lost on Europe: "Little Prussia, a mere upstart, had crossed swords with one of the great established powers of Europe and come off the winner, Silesia was, at least for the time being, lost."[18]

Amid these shocking developments, Maria Theresa, heavily pregnant, also had to contend with tragic events in her personal life. She had been inconsolable when Maria Elisabeth, her eldest daughter, died in 1740 within a few hours after falling ill. Then, seven months later, the terrible scenario repeated when her youngest daughter, one-year-old Maria Carolina, also sickened and died within several hours.* These personal tragedies were difficult enough to deal with on their own, but they—especially Maria Carolina's death—occurred at the same time as grave political problems preoccupied Maria Theresa. When she gathered around her councilors, including Francis, Maria Theresa was disappointed to find that all ex-cept Bartenstein urged her to compromise with Frederick II. Even her husband, who was normally so loyal to her and the Habsburg cause, had given the answer she did not wish to hear. These personal and political blows could have broken the spirit and will of many, but Maria Theresa refused to succumb to self-pity or fear.

Instead, the queen courageously faced her troubles and tried to find solu-tions. She also gave due credit to the source of her strength: her faith. During these dark moments, the queen fervently prayed to her patron St. Teresa of Ávila, and to St. Joseph. Maria Theresa recalled how much she prayed for St. Joseph's intervention. The queen noted of him, "I cannot remember that I ever desired anything by his means which he hath failed to obtain for me." She was grateful too for "the great favours which Almighty God hath done me by means of this blessed saint, and the dangers, both of soul and body, out of which he hath delivered me."[19]

During the final weeks of her pregnancy, Maria Theresa continued to work tirelessly. She met with her ministers while propped up in bed. It was a pattern that she was to adhere to for her many pregnancies. With or without child, the head of the house of Habsburg would always be a diligent worker for her people.

*Maria Theresa named three of her daughters Maria Carolina. One lived from 1740 to 1741, another was still-born in 1748, and the last, who lived from 1752 to 1814, became Queen of Naples and Sicily as the consort of King Ferdinand IV.

Amid the strains of the war, on March 13, 1741, Maria Theresa gave birth to her fourth child, a son. At the baby's baptism that same evening, many had anticipated that the dynasty's male heir would be named after his grandfather Charles VI. Maria Theresa instead named her firstborn son, Joseph, in honor of the saint to whom she prayed to intercede with God for her petitions. After Joseph's birth, the queen quickly returned to the business of ruling. Maria Theresa "had to learn quickly to command. A born worker, she was in her cabinet or at the council table from daybreak until late at night, conferring, planning, dictating, maneuvering, almost literally holding together with sheer strength of will the breaking package."[20]

The conflict against Prussia remained her uppermost priority, but her ministers continued to posture and bicker, doing little to serve their queen. Without a centralized army, Maria Theresa had to rely on her disparate territories to provide soldiers. Even once soldiers were assembled, however, the army was still at a disadvantage. Poorly paid, poorly trained, poorly equipped, they were no match for the highly trained Prussians. General Wilhelm Reinhard Neipperg, Francis's onetime tutor, was sent to the front to command the Habsburg troops but again failed to rout the Prussians.

Within weeks of the Mollwitz defeat, Europe's powers recalibrated their attitudes toward Maria Theresa based, again, upon self-interest. Not surprisingly, their policies were largely aligned with Prussia's actions. France went against Austria formally, siding with Bavaria. Under the direction of Cardinal Fleury and Marshal Belle-Isle, France declared support for Charles Albert of Bavaria's quest to become Holy Roman emperor and his claims on the Habsburg succession. This action prompted other countries, such as Spain, Poland, Saxony, and Bavaria, to go against Maria Theresa too. "It was practically Austria *contra mundum,* for Russia, although an ally since 1726, was too preoccupied with internal dissension, and with a threat from Sweden, to help."[21] Clearly, the Pragmatic Sanction was dissolved and the queen nearly isolated. Only Britain held out, yet its position was delicate because the British had agreements with both Austria and Prussia and did not wish to rock the boat either way.

Instead of giving up hope and conceding to Frederick II, Maria Theresa searched for aid and concluded that an appeal to her Hungarian subjects would help the Habsburg cause. She accordingly ordered that her coronation as Queen of Hungary take place. It was a risky move, as a number of Hungarians wanted greater autonomy from Vienna. Well aware that she needed the strong support of a prominent native Hungarian, Maria Theresa cleverly cultivated the friendship of Count John Palffy, whom she had known for years and always admired.

At seventy-seven, Palffy had enjoyed a colorful life full of wine, women, and horse races. The count, who had fought with the famed Prince Eugene, understood that the Hungarians were better off under the rule of the Habsburgs than under the Ottoman Turks, who had enslaved many of his countrymen. Palffy thus sympathized with the Habsburg cause. Maria Theresa appealed to his chivalry in her hour of need, and he responded with devotion.

Palffy smoothed the way for Maria Theresa's visit to Hungary and coronation. The queen could not afford to bungle before the assembled Hungarians. One slight misstep, one small unintended offending gesture, would set the crowds firmly against her. Of particular concern was an aspect of the coronation that could have gone spectacularly wrong: Maria Theresa, unlike Queen Isabella, was not a natural horsewoman. But the Hungarians placed great emphasis on horsemanship, and a monarch uneasy in the saddle would have been disastrous. Maria Theresa, who was to mount a black stallion at the foot of a hill, practiced her riding assiduously back in Austria. In Pressburg, Hungary, on June 25, 1741, the practice paid off. Maria Theresa did everything right. At the crucial moment, she cut a fine figure and galloped to the top of the hill. She then drew her sword and pointed it to four corners. It was a gesture that announced her intention to rule as queen. This symbolic act echoed Queen Isabella of Castile's coronation, when the sword of state was likewise displayed.

Gestures to secure her crown, however, were not enough. Maria Theresa needed concrete help from the Hungarians to fight off King Frederick II. And so she returned in September that year and appeared before the Hungarian assembly. Addressing them in Latin, which the Hungarian nobles understood, a dignified queen outlined the dangers they faced and asked for help in defending their country, her crown, the Habsburg domains, and her children. Maria Theresa's appeal was straightforward: "The disastrous situation of affairs has moved us to lay before our dear and faithful states of Hungary . . . the very existence of the kingdom of Hungary, of our own person, of our children, and our crown, are now at stake. Forsaken by all, we place our sole resource in the fidelity, arms, and long-tried valour of the Hungarians."[22] When it came to her children, Maria Theresa's normally calm demeanor, which she had already learned to project, suddenly changed. Tears filled her eyes, her voice trembled with emotion.

In reply, some in the assembly protested, but in the end, amid enthusiastic shouting, the nobles agreed to help her. With sabers drawn, the assembled nobles shouted: "We will consecrate our lives and arms; we will die for our queen, Maria Theresa!"[23] Days later, during the swearing in ceremony of Francis as coregent, Maria Theresa made a dramatic gesture by bringing her son and heir, the baby archduke Joseph, before the assembly. The sight of their queen with her young and vulnerable son moved the nobles, who again shouted: "We will die for the queen and her family; we will die for Maria Theresa!"[24]

Maria Theresa took great risks going to Hungary. She went against the advice of her ministers, buttressed only by Francis's support. Her instincts, however, proved correct. Her pleas succeeded beyond her expectations. The twenty-four year-old queen felt confident as never before. She came to believe that she had abilities, including most certainly the power to sway people's opinions. Maria Theresa won the people to her side by the sheer force of her personality. In the process, she got Hungary's powerful nobles to side with her and, just as important, received the pledge of thousands of Hungarian soldiers to fight for her.

Maria Theresa needed all the troops she could muster. The French were on the march, and the Bavarians were making their way into Upper Austria. By mid-September, Bavarian troops occupied Linz, the province's capital, a mere hundred miles from Vienna. This meant that Charles Albert's soldiers were only days away from marching into Maria Theresa's capital, then highly vulnerable because of its weak garrison and poor fortifications. Only French orders prevented Charles Albert from invading Vienna. Instead, he marched to Prague. The French had ordered this to keep the Bavarians from gaining too much power should Charles Albert topple Maria Theresa. At this point, Maria Theresa and Frederick II reached a truce, though the queen made it plain this was only a temporary measure.

Meanwhile, Francis again underperformed as Austrian commander. Prague, the capital of the queen's Bohemian lands, fell to the French (joined by Bavarian and Saxon troops) in 1741. Charles Albert was crowned King of Bohemia in December. When Prague fell, Maria Theresa gave an impassioned message to Prince Kinsky, who had been her Bohemian chancellor:

> So Prague is lost. . . . Here then, Kinsky, we find ourselves at the sticking point where only courage can save the country and the Queen, for without the country I should indeed be a poor princess. My own resolve is taken; to stake everything, win or lose, on saving Bohemia; and it is with this in view that you should work and lay your plans. It may involve destruction and desolation which twenty years will be insufficient to restore; but I must hold the country and the soil, and for this all my armies, all the Hungarians, shall die

before I surrender an inch of it. This, then, is the crisis: do not spare the country, only hold it. Do all you can to help your people and to keep the troops contented, lacking nothing: you know, better than I, the consequences of failure in this. . . . You will say that I am cruel; that is true. But I know that all the cruelties I commit today to hold the country I shall one day be in a position to make good a hundred-fold. And this I shall do. But for the present I close my ear to pity.[25]

Maria Theresa's defense of her realms gained little traction. Worse, Frederick II seized Olmütz, a key fortress on the way to Vienna. The queen reacted to this disconcerting news with steadfastness. She ordered Field Marshal Khevenhüller to proceed with plans to retrieve Upper Austria, even if this meant going in the opposite direction of Vienna at such a vulnerable moment. Less levelheaded individuals would have counseled the queen to save the capital instead. In the end, Maria Theresa proved correct in her assessment. By following her instincts, "she showed herself for the first time a great commander as well as a courageous one by refusing to panic."[26] Khevenhüller, commanding thirty thousand soldiers, marched into Munich, Bavaria's capital, and captured Upper Austria for his queen. This meant that at Charles Albert's moment of glory, when he was crowned Holy Roman emperor in February 1742, he had simultaneously lost his capital to Maria Theresa. The queen was grateful to Khevenhüller for his victory. She sent him a portrait of herself with Archduke Joseph and a message that read: "Dear and faithful Khevenhüller, here you behold the Queen, who knows what it is to be forsaken by the whole world. . . . May your achievements be as renowned as those of your master, the great Eugene, who rests in God. Be fully assured that, now and always, you and your family will never lack the grace and favour and thanks of myself, and my descendants."[27]

But even with this victory, Maria Theresa could not rest. Her enemy, Frederick II of Prussia, broke his compromise agreement with her "quite cold-bloodedly after only a few weeks"[28] and ordered his forces to march into Bohemia. With her troops exhausted, Maria Theresa was compelled to come to an agreement with Frederick, and so the Peace of Breslau-Berlin was signed in July 1742. Maria Theresa paid a bitter price, giving up most of Silesia. The loss of Silesia, "whose million plus inhabitants had been the most productive and heavily taxed of all the Habsburg lands," also meant that "German speakers now comprised no more than a third of the monarchy's 16 million people, a demographic shift pregnant with consequences for the next century."[29]

The loss of Silesia left Maria Theresa completely disgusted by Frederick II's perfidy. She never forgave or forgot his brazen disregard for agreements and what was called the "rape" of Silesia. Decades later she described her archenemy to her son Joseph as nothing short of a "Monster."[30]

13

THE JOAN OF ARC OF THE DANUBE

*A*mid war and all the political difficulties, life at home had its compensations. Both Maria Theresa and Francis delighted in attending plays and dances. They often spent evenings playing cards in her apartments, sometimes for high stakes. Maria Theresa, however, knew when to stop and never incurred huge gambling debts. Yet for all their compatibility, like other royal husbands before him, Francis strayed from the marital bed and acquired a number of mistresses, much to his wife's chagrin. But like Isabella of Castile, Maria Theresa of Austria forgave her husband's infidelities and remained faithful to him. These liaisons may have resulted from Maria Theresa's possessiveness; she greatly disliked being separated from Francis and admitted as much in a letter she wrote to her sister Marianne. Here, she relates a quarrel over Francis's wish to pursue his military obligation: "I was sick with anger and chagrin and made the old one [Francis] ill with my wickedness. . . . At first I only made light of the idea, but finally I saw that he was serious. I resorted to our usual instruments, caresses and tears, as much as one can do with a husband of nine years, but I got nowhere although he is the best husband in the world. I finally resumed my anger which served only to make both of us ill. . . . I gave up fighting him, but shilly-shallied from day to day to win time, but if he does go I shall either follow him or shut myself in a convent."[1] Maria Theresa won this round: Francis stayed at home.

Certainly, the queen's early illusions about Francis had been stripped away. Much as she loved her husband, Maria Theresa found she needed additional support. Francis could not give his wife unbiased advice on matters regarding herself. That unenviable task fell instead on Count Emmanuel da Silva-Tarouca, a Portuguese nobleman who enjoyed an unusual relationship with Maria Theresa. She had known him since she was a child, as Tarouca had served in her father's court. Upon her accession, Maria Theresa asked her old friend to take on the role of mentor.

Tarouca, a man of eminent discretion, was to give his candid and sage advice on many matters. It was a thankless task, one that could easily invite jealousies or suspicion from other courtiers. Nevertheless, Tarouca accepted. As the queen's mentor, he took on the role of "disinterested spectator . . . [who] helped to develop the latent powers of her nature."[2] Tarouca put order into Maria Theresa's life by devising a regimented schedule: she would rise from bed at eight in the morning, dress, breakfast, and attend Mass, followed by half an hour with the children. At the count's direction, she devoted the hours between 9:30 to 12:30 to the minutiae of ruling. This included audiences, conferring with ministers, studying, and signing documents. Maria Theresa was then to eat her lunch at 12:45. Even when it came to eating, Tarouca urged the queen to follow a regimen: she must eat her food while it was warm and drink coffee before it became cold. After luncheon Maria Theresa was to spend time with the children and her mother. From 4:00 to 8:30 she was to work again, then have dinner at 8:45, after which she must spend the rest of the evening in some kind of relaxation, but never to an extreme. Years later, Maria Theresa noted how Tarouca "brought me to a true understanding of affairs and men." She wrote that she owed the count "a great debt, which I will always seek to repay to his children and enjoin my successors to do likewise."[3]

In her personal life, Maria Theresa had more than her share of tragedies. In 1744, less than a year after her sister the docile Archduchess Marianne married, Charles of Lorraine, Marianne died in childbirth. Her sister's premature death was a terrible blow to Maria Theresa. To Gerhard van Swieten, her new physician, who had also cared for the unfortunate Marianne in her dying days, Maria Theresa stated: "God could have permitted no more terrible trial to befall me than the death of my sister. Every day increases my love for the members of my family. Time, they say, heals griefs of this kind. Time will only make me feel more keenly the greatness of my loss. . . . I believe that God has purposes to fulfill through me. By His great grace I shall be upheld on the path He wills me to tread—a path of disappointment, sorrow, and weeping. I submit to what He has ordained and look for no reward in this life. . . . To Him let me offer in sacrifice all that I ever craved for myself."[4]

One of Maria Theresa's enemies, Charles Albert of Bavaria, exited the international stage the same year Marianne died. Austrian troops occupied Bavaria but were eventually driven out, prompting Charles Albert to return to his capital. Yet a mere three weeks later, he fled Munich after Austrian forces defeated the Bavarians. He died in 1745, after only three years as Holy Roman emperor. The death of Maria Theresa's Bavarian nemesis meant not only a possible easing of trouble from that part of Europe but also that the Holy Roman Empire's crown was again vacant. Charles Albert's successor in Bavaria recognized the Pragmatic Sanction and agreed to vote for the election of Maria Theresa's husband as the next Holy Roman emperor. Francis was duly elected and attended his coronation in 1745 in Frankfurt. Maria Theresa declined to be crowned at his side, using the excuse that she was pregnant. She did, however, watch the coronation procession. From the balcony where she watched her husband pass by, she exclaimed excitedly: "Long live the emperor Francis I!"[5]

Francis's election as Holy Roman emperor was one of the few happy events of the 1740s for Maria Theresa, for the War of the Austrian Succession continued to dominate Europe. The conflagration started by Frederick the Great engulfed the Continent's powers. The war "was in reality a coalition against the House of Austria on the part of France, Prussia, and Spain, and was the first round in the great struggle of Austria and Prussia for the leadership of Germany. It was, at the same time, one round in the greater battle of France and Britain for mastery of America and India and the world's commerce."[6] Frederick's conquest of Silesia emboldened Maria Theresa's enemies to make a bid for her other territories: the Saxons coveted Moravia, Sardinia tried to wrest Milan, Bavaria succeeded in obtaining the Bohemian crown, and Spain coveted all the Habsburg lands. France, meanwhile, sought to weaken the Habsburgs by trying to break up Maria Theresa's empire. The empress, in turn, harbored strong apprehensions about the French.

Great Britain, which had signed the Pragmatic Sanction and initially pursued neutrality, now sought action. England's King George II, who was also Elector of Hanover, went to war in defense of Maria Theresa's authority in 1742, at the head of a "Pragmatic Army" consisting of British, Hanoverian, Hessian, and Dutch soldiers, and won a victory at Dettingen against the French. After the Peace of Breslau, the French found themselves in more trouble. Only two years after the French had moved into Prague, French Marshal Belle-Isle and his troops fled the city with Maria Theresa's forces putting on the pressure. Cardinal Fleury then wanted to negotiate peace. But the empress was not easily taken in, replying: "I will grant no capitulation to the French army. I will receive no proposition, no project from the cardinal: let him address himself to my allies."[7] As to Belle-Isle, Maria Theresa remarked: "I am astonished that he should make any advances; he who, by money and promises, excited almost all the princes of Germany to crush me. . . . I can prove, by documents in my possession, that the French endeavoured to excite sedition even in the heart of my dominions; that they attempted to overturn the fundamental laws of the empire, and to set fire to the four corners of Germany; I will transmit these proofs to posterity, as a warning to the empire."[8]

After the French withdrew, Maria Theresa's troops marched into Bohemia victoriously, and she was crowned Queen of Bohemia amid much applause and cheering. Silesia may have been lost, but Maria Theresa now had a firm hold on three important territories—Bohemia, Austria, and Hungary—and her troops occupied Bavaria. The empress had accomplished the seemingly impossible, holding on to most of her domains.

By this time, Lord Carteret (Earl Granville), the British prime minister, had taken a decidedly sympathetic view of Maria Theresa. Soon, in England, the thought took hold that, with the addition of British might, "Maria Theresa could conquer the whole Continent. The British press was calling her the 'Joan of Arc of the Danube,' and chanting her beauty, cleverness, and virtue in harmonious refrains."[9] Like Joan of Arc, Empress Maria Theresa was courageous and a born leader. These qualities overcame the impression that she did not have "a shred of intellectual brilliance. . . . But she had three things even more important in a ruler: sound judgment, a generous spirit, and an enormous store of physical and spiritual stamina."[10]

The War of the Austrian Succession was fought on many fronts, including the Italian Peninsula, where Maria Theresa had been at war since 1741. Fighting continued after she moved her forces from Silesia to the Italian front. Spain's ambitious queen consort, Elizabeth Farnese, sought to seize Maria Theresa's domains in the peninsula, prompting the empress to side with King Charles Emmanuel of Sardinia for help. In return, Maria Theresa had to cede some of her territory to Sardinia. The empress still needed the British as allies, but their support unexpectedly proved dodgy. Great Britain's recent enthusiasm for her suddenly cooled, since they feared that Austria might become too powerful on the Italian Peninsula. Britain's primary enemy was France, and they wanted Maria Theresa's Austria to focus on that front, not on Italy, or on Prussia. The British supported Charles Emmanuel's request that Austria cede territory to Sardinia. They forced her hand. All this had the effect of souring Maria Theresa's views of the British.

France was still Austria's enemy, but now Prussia supplanted the Bourbons as the Habsburgs' enemy number one. When war in the Netherlands in 1744 and 1745 went badly for Maria Theresa, the British urged her to make peace with Prussia. This further infuriated the empress, who was looking to come to terms with the French. A significant shift was taking place in the complicated diplomatic landscape of mid-eighteenth-century Europe, a shift that would have tremendous consequences for one of Maria Theresa's daughters. As the empress began to rethink international strategy, she concluded that, to gather strength, she would have to deal with the dreaded Prussians. A temporary peace with Frederick II would allow Austria to fight Prussia again later, from a stronger position. Maria Theresa accordingly, in 1745, signed the Treaty of Dresden, whereby Frederick II, in return for keeping Silesia, recognized Francis I as Holy Roman emperor. For the time being, Austria and Prussia stopped fighting each other.

Elsewhere, three more years of battles exhausted the European powers financially and politically. Talk of a cessation of hostilities began again. Maria Theresa understood that this period of peace was essential to Austria. She sent Count Wenzel Kaunitz, who was to make his mark in the empress's service in the coming years, as envoy to the negotiations in Aix-la-Chapelle. Kaunitz had his hands full. As he jockeyed to secure as good a deal as he could for Austria, France, Britain, and Spain secretly met in the hope of gaining the greatest advantages for themselves. France and Britain dominated the congress, which met for nearly six months. The empress resented the manner in which the British cajoled her to do as they wanted. When the British ambassador to Vienna urged her to accept the terms imposed on Austria, she indignantly retorted: "Why am I excluded from transactions which concern my own State? My enemies will give me better terms than my friends. . . . All I ask is to have the land which I had before the war in Italy . . . Yes, truly, all these circumstances tear old wounds and inflict new ones into the bargain."[11] In the Treaty of Aix-la-Chapelle, which was signed in October 1748, Maria Theresa was compelled to sacrifice Silesia to Frederick II of Prussia; to cede territories in western Lombardy to the King of Sardinia; and to cede the northern Italian duchies of Parma, Piacenza, and Guastalla to Spain.

The Treaty of Aix-la-Chapelle ended the War of the Austrian Succession. It may have rewarded Frederick II's belligerence by granting him Silesia, but Maria Theresa could still count herself fortunate. For one "must take into account not only what was lost, but what was snatched from the very brink of perdition, and by comparison with what its enemies had intended, and all but achieved in 1741, the condition in which the 'House of Austria' emerged in 1747 was well-nigh miraculous. The great bulk of its territories were, after all, still intact. It had recovered the Imperial Crown. It stood an undisputed Great Power, and for another 150 years there was to be no more talk of dismembering it. And this was very largely Maria Theresa's personal achievement. Alone, she had stood firm when all around her counselled yielding to the Prussians."[12] And "to Maria Theresa herself belongs almost the sole credit of accomplishing what she did in this long, bitter struggle."[13]

Like Isabella of Castile, Maria Theresa of Austria possessed a conquering spirit. Both were contemptuous of weakness. Neither woman, in the darkest days of her reign, sank to self-pity, self-doubt, or defeatism. Faith in their causes and in their God sustained them, as did their understanding of the significance of their actions—or inactions, for Isabella and Maria Theresa were visionaries too. War to them was an unavoidable and sometimes necessary tool, for only through strength could either monarch hope to bring peace and other benefits that accrue with that strength. Maria Theresa admitted that, in these first years of her reign, "I acted boldly, shrank from no risk, and spared no effort," driven as she was from "the conviction that no more unhappy fate could befall my poor dominions than to fall into Prussian hands, indeed, had I not been nearly always *enceinte,* no one could have stopped me from taking the field personally against my perjured enemy."[14]

During this time Count Otto Podewils, the Prussian envoy to Vienna, wrote to his master, Frederick the Great, his impressions of Maria Theresa and left a vivid portrait. "She has a sprightly gait and a majestic bearing. . . . She has a round, full face and a bold forehead. Her pronounced eyebrows are, like her hair, blond without any touch of red. Her eyes are large, bright, and at the same time full of gentleness, all accented by their light-blue color. Her nose is small, neither hooked nor turned up, the mouth a little large, but still pretty, the teeth white, the smile pleasant, the neck and throat well formed, and the arms and hands beautiful. She still retains her nice complexion, although she devotes little time to it. She has much color. Her expression is open and bright, her conversation friendly and charming. No one can deny that she is a lovely person." As for Maria Theresa's popularity, Podewils noted, "Full of enthusiasm, everyone stood by her and rushed to sacrifice himself for this best of all princesses. People deified her. Everybody wanted to have her picture. She never appeared in public without being greeted with applause."[15]

Maria Theresa may have gained some breathing space on the international level; however, on the domestic front, a whole different set of challenges awaited. The empress had largely weathered the diplomatic and military storm that threatened to annihilate her and, in so doing, emerged as the recognized sovereign of Austria, Bohemia, Hungary, and many other lands scattered across Europe, whose subjects spoke ten different languages.* With no strong central authority overseeing her realms, ruling was extremely challenging. The three main kingdoms—Austria, Bohemia, and Hungary—had competing chancelleries and differing laws. Ever active and desirous of ruling well, Maria Theresa also turned her attention to resolving internal problems.

The empress's first set of reforms—directed at streamlining and centralizing the state apparatus, which was an unmanageable mass of confusion—occurred between 1746 and 1756. To Maria Theresa, whose main preoccupation was protecting the integrity of Austria and her other realms, success in developing an efficient state meant that the vast Habsburg territories could be more easily defended and kept intact, especially when it came to what the empress described as "two so mighty enemies, Prussia and the Turk."[16]

She implemented administrative reforms that eliminated some of the rivalry between the Austrian and Bohemian chancelleries. These reforms included forming a supreme court and according criminal law with the *Constitutio Criminalis Theresiana,* named after the empress. Maria Theresa also ordered the creation of a General Directory of Economic Affairs in 1746, to promote economic growth in Austria and Bohemia. With the aim of inspiring business, the government sponsored tax privileges, subsidies, and loans as well.

Throughout the Continent, including within Maria Theresa's realms, an outmoded feudalistic system of governance was still in place. Petty jealousies between nobles were common, and a great chasm divided the aristocracy from the peasants, who often lived in primitive conditions. Most of the peasants were "still serfs in the sense that they formed the matrix of a feudal society and were bound to provide services in work and kind to their landlords, but not chattels to be bought and sold as, under Catherine II, they came to be in Russia."[17] For the most part, the nobles were unsympathetic toward the peasants, many of whom toiled on the land of the great magnates. Peasants were "attached to their landlords in widely varying degrees of servitude, illiterate and often brutish, liable for conscription on a quota basis, and, until Maria Theresa's first reforms, bearing the whole weight of taxation. The attitude of too many of the landowners was summed up in the saying: the peasants should be cut down like grass, they spring up the stronger for it. It was this attitude that Maria Theresa set herself to change, at first for purely economic reasons (the system was too wasteful

*By the mid-eighteenth century, the population of Austria amounted to close to 4 million, Bohemia a little over 3 million, and Hungary 6 million.

of potentially first-class human material), increasingly, as she grew older, from humanitarian motives too."[18] She took a profoundly serious view of her role as sovereign, always mindful of the fact, as she once put it, that the monarchy was "entrusted to me by God."[19]

The selfish ministers who wanted to keep the empress ignorant of what was really happening lingered on. Only Bartenstein was of any real help. The verbose baron and the empress never enjoyed an amiable relationship, but he was loyal and offered sound advice. He was instrumental in convincing the empress of the dire need for reforms. Meanwhile, Maria Theresa sought more information from a coterie of trusted men. These included her husband, Francis, the indispensable Count Tarouca, and her secretary, Ignaz von Koch.

Fortunately for Maria Theresa, by the mid-1740s, many of the old ministers had died off so that she could bring in new blood to address her ponderous obligations. She relied on three men of action to help carry out her ambitious reforms. These were Count Wilhelm Haugwitz, Count Rudolf Chotek, and Count Wenzel Kaunitz. Haugwitz devised the plans for instituting legal reforms. A native of Silesia, where he was governor, Haugwitz was dull and unpolished but clear-sighted, incorruptible, courageous, and a first-rate worker. Maria Theresa assigned the Bohemian financier Chotek (who did not get on with Haugwitz) responsibility for financial reforms. Kaunitz, meanwhile, a tall, haughty hypochondriac in his forties with a penchant for composing long but trenchant memoranda, was recognized early in his career for his sharp mind. One of Maria Theresa's advisers, Count Ulfield, read the young Kaunitz's first dispatch from Turin, where he was envoy. It had been "drawn in so masterly a manner" that Ulfield sent the dispatch to Maria Theresa's attention with the striking words "Behold your first minister."[20] Ulfield was correct in his prediction. Maria Theresa's trust in and reliance on Kaunitz would grow through the years, for as a servant of the dynasty, he was not only intelligent and loyal but also skilled in negotiation, tireless, and honest.

Together, they pushed through reforms that suppressed the nobility's nearly unchecked influence and power. By increasing the crown's power and influence, Maria Theresa planted the seeds of what was "the political ideal of the time—the establishment of a benevolent despotism, the increase of the powers of the central state, and the supremacy of the sovereign over the local noble."[21]

For a long time, the burden of taxation had fallen on the peasants, but military campaigns were costly, so one of the first areas that underwent reform was revenue collecting. Efficient collection of taxes meant increased revenues to the state. The reforms sought to tax the nobility and the Church. Many of the

nobles fought fiercely for their feudal privileges and disdained their empress's
new plans. Maria Theresa's tenacity paid off, though. The nobility (with the exception of those from Hungary) backed down. There was no doubt that Maria
Theresa's reforms had curtailed their financial privileges, but the reforms did
not "entail a dethronement of the aristocracy as a class . . . [the reforms] did,
however, transform the holders of these offices from servants of their Province
and their classes into those of the State, and this was an enormous change, the
most important internal development of Maria Theresa's reign. They also proved
enduring."[22]

With an improved method of revenue collecting implemented, a new army
could emerge. Again, Maria Theresa's foresight and determination proved beneficial. The number of soldiers increased to some 180,000, far more than the
108,000 Maria Theresa originally was advised to have as a standing army capable of fending off attacks from other powers. The empress and her advisers used
the Prussian model for professionalizing her army. Confusion and disorder gave
way to professionalism and discipline. The regiments were rearranged to be of
uniform size. Officer training became more rigorous, while maneuvers were entrenched in training. Maria Theresa herself visited many of these maneuvers, often on horseback. Military reforms did away with inefficient practices such as
disparate training among regiments, irregular pay, and appointments and pro-
motions based not on merit but on purchase or favors.

The civil service was also reformed. Merit became the main reason for pro-
motions within the branches of the government, which doubled to ten thousand
individuals by the early 1760s. A centralizing and more orderly set of reforms
stopped the chaotic governing that had made ruling her realms difficult.

In education, Maria Theresa sought to raise able future generations, taking
advice from the Dutch physician van Swieten, who advocated sweeping
changes. Instruction in schools improved, while the teaching profession benefited from higher salaries. The empress agreed to the creation of the Collegium
Regium Theresianum, where students were taught foreign languages, history,
and military matters. Both Maria Theresa and van Swieten were devout
Catholics, but van Swieten advised the empress to reassign control of education from the Church to the state. This move not only laicized the system but
also reduced the power of the Jesuits, who had enjoyed sweeping authority.
These changes did not introduce a new age of free and spirited inquiry, either
in the educational system or in general society. On the contrary, state censor-
ship grew. In 1753 Maria Theresa, watchful for heresy, ordered that all works
be scrutinized for unacceptable thoughts and words. She even rejected the

founding of an academy of sciences, out of concern that it would come to promote heretical thinking. Here again were shades of Queen Isabella of Castile.

The empress "had no use for abstract learning, nor for the humanities as such."[23] Two other noted monarchs of the time, Catherine the Great of Russia and Frederick the Great of Prussia, were enamored of the Enlightenment, the movement that dominated eighteenth-century European thinking; not so Maria Theresa of Austria. A letter she wrote to one of her sons years later reveals Maria Theresa's thinking on the Enlightenment:

> Nothing is more pleasant, nothing more suitable to flatter our egos as a freedom without restrictions. "Freedom" is the word with which our enlightened century wants to replace religion. One condemns the whole past as a time of ignorance and prejudice, while knowing nothing of that past and very little of the present. If I could see these so-called enlightened figures, these *philosophes,* more fortunate in their work and happier in their private lives, then I would accuse myself of bias, pride, prepossession, and obstinacy for not adjusting to them. But unfortunately daily experience teaches me the opposite. No one is weaker, no one more spiritless than these strong spirits; no one more servile, no one more despairing at the least misfortune as they. They are bad fathers, sons, husbands, ministers, generals, and citizens. And why? Because they lack substance. All of their philosophy, all of their axioms are conceived only in their egotism; the slightest disappointment crushes them beyond hope, with no resources to fall back upon.[24]

As unimpressed as she was by the Enlightenment, with its emphasis on rationality and science, Maria Theresa's reforms were permeated with the Enlightenment ideals of "government by the humanitarian spirit." This meant that the "practical application of the humanitarian tendencies appeared in Austria earlier than in many of the philosophically 'more progressive states.' Many historians have argued that in terms of the humanitarian ideal Theresian Austria was more enlightened than any other European country of the eighteenth century. The vital characteristic of the Austrian Enlightenment was its empirical bent: reforms were not based on a rationalized concept of the 'popular will' or on the assumption of a 'social contract,' but on the recognition of observable need. . . . The pragmatic and humane dimensions of Austrian government in the mid-eighteenth century were as much if not more reflective of

[Maria Theresa's] personality than of the new wisdom of the age."[25] The empress converted ideas into action while at the same time possessing a "flexible pragmatism that always knew exactly when and where to push for change."[26]

Maria Theresa was a dynamic force and the leading light in introducing much needed changes. Thus, by the mid-1750s, the empress "had already earned an honored place in Austrian history. In less than a decade she had virtually doubled state revenue, restructured the administrative and military system, and begun the process of entrusting it to a more competent, professional elite."[27] Her reforms managed to engage the elites, gaining their cooperation, rather than strictly imposing her absolutist rule on them.

Certainly when it came to taxing the very wealthy and easing the tax burden on the poor, the Theresian reforms were far-reaching, so much so that "it is difficult to exaggerate the importance" of Maria Theresa's "victory in this contest. She did exactly what Louis XV neglected to do in France, and what Louis XVI tried later and failed to accomplish. By her clear statesmanship and dauntless courage she obviated the destruction of the monarchy, or at least a bloody revolution, which otherwise could hardly have been delayed longer in Austria than in France."[28] It was, instead, to be the destiny of one of her daughters to feel the full impact of the revolution that would engulf France in the next few decades.

14

MAGNA MATER AUSTRIAE

*E*mpress Maria Theresa once described the principles of monarchy as she saw them. She explained that she "undertook each enterprise with great determination and strong resolution . . . And dearly as I love my family and children, so that I spare no effort, trouble, care, or labor for their sakes, yet I would always have put the general welfare of my dominions above them had I been convinced in my conscience that I should do this or if their welfare demanded it, seeing that I am the general and chief mother of my country."[1]

The *magna mater austriae,* the Great or Holy Mother of Austria, has been an important religious symbol for Austria for hundreds of years. Empress Maria Theresa's view of herself as *Landesmutter,* the mother of her subjects, paralleled this. Like the statue of the Blessed Virgin Mary on the main altar of the basilica at Mariazell, which she so loved, Maria Theresa had become the symbol of Austria and of the Habsburgs. One of her biographers corroborated: "Although she was neither a lenient enemy nor a sentimental monarch, she was guided by matriarchal instincts. She was the mother of Austria and she usually acted towards her people as if they were a great family."[2]

The empress had taken to the role of actual motherhood with great gusto too. Nearly on a yearly basis, Maria Theresa continued to be blessed with children. After Joseph in 1741 came Maria Christina (Mimi) in 1742, destined to be her mother's favorite child. Another daughter was born in 1743, named again Maria Elisabeth, followed by a son, Charles Joseph, in 1745, Maria Amalia in 1746, and Leopold in 1747. A daughter, Maria Carolina, was born and died in 1748. Then came Maria Johanna in 1750, Maria Josepha in 1751, another Maria Carolina in 1752, Ferdinand in 1754, and Maximilian in 1756.

As her children grew, Maria Theresa looked into educating them. Mindful of the poor preparation she had received as heir, the empress sought to avoid her father's mistake by seeing to it that her eldest son and heir, Archduke Joseph, was educated as a future monarch. Maria Theresa assigned experts to prepare analytical documents for Joseph to study while she herself drew up what became her Political Testament. This was intended for use as a guide to ruling, but it also gives good insight into the empress's political thinking. Central to Joseph's education was a heavy dose of religion. His mother insisted that he as well as his siblings attend daily Mass, read devotional works, and go regularly to confession. She declared that "each day must begin with prayer and the first and most necessary thing for my son is to be certain with a submissive heart of God's omnipotence, to love and to fear Him, and to develop from true Christian practice and duty all other virtues."[3]

Archduke Joseph was not the only one receiving Maria Theresa's maternal anxieties about virtue. The morals of the realm became a real concern for the empress. She may not have been able to convince Francis to desist from his occasional infidelities, but Maria Theresa was determined to keep her subjects from straying from the right path. Intolerant of vice and leading a relatively bourgeois family life, Maria Theresa took on the role of policing her subjects' moral lives. She accordingly set up in 1747 a "special security commission" or chastity commission, whose function was to impose moral values on everyone. The empress, so circumspect in her own life when it came to sexual activity, could not fathom people falling into vice. One visitor to Vienna described the empress as "very virtuous in her conduct, true to her marriage vows, and never has an impure thought, has but little patience with the indiscretions of others. She looks upon every grade of social vice with complete disapproval."[4] Her puritanical streak sought to save her subjects from themselves. Liaisons among the fashionable set in Vienna had been common for years, and Maria Theresa set out to correct this impropriety. Soon enough the chastity police were on the prowl in theaters and at balls. They carried out house searches and arrests. Not surprisingly, prostitutes became a special target. Unescorted females walking the streets were assumed to be up to no good and rounded up.

Maria Theresa's thinking on vice and virtue can be seen in a letter she wrote in 1774 to her youngest son, Archduke Maximilian, when he was seventeen. She proclaims that "the mood that prevails presently in Vienna is just as bad in matters of religion and propriety as it is for the well-being of a family and especially for the upbringing of young people, who here give themselves up to great debauchery. From all this I intend to remove you, for you are at an age when, first stepping out of the bounds of childhood, one is scarcely able to control himself and the passions are the most dangerous. Your spiritual welfare and your future happiness depend on it."[5] She adds: "Allow yourself no indulgence; you are responsible for your salvation and to your calling. Do not be led astray by derision or bad examples which you have seen or heard. Reject all talk that is disrespectful of your elders or injurious to a young heart like yours. Never be ashamed to appear at every opportunity a good Christian in word and deed. This point demands the greatest exactness and attention, now more than ever, because morals have become all too corrupt and frivolous. People want to enclose religion in their hearts without practicing their faith openly because they fear they will be laughed at or called hypocritical and narrow-minded. This is the mood that now prevails everywhere, and which is all the more dangerous because everyone who considers himself part of the 'beautiful world' accepts it."[6] With regard to the opposite sex, Maria Theresa warns her son: "Shun everything that involves passion, especially concerning women. Regrettably, I must say that they are more dangerous than the most dissolute men. . . . Scrupulously avoid the first step and be especially wary of any deception or wickedness which drags so much misfortune behind it; only the most debauched give themselves up to it."[7] Finally, the mother exhorts her son not to "stray from the path of virtue . . . and to provide an example to others by your religious conviction, your flawless morals, and your devotion to your family."[8]

Maria Theresa, who gave birth to sixteen children in nineteen years, always expected the best from her children. This was no less the expectation for her eleventh and youngest daughter. On All Souls' Day—November 2, 1755, the day of the dead for Roman Catholics—the empress again went into labor at the Hofburg Palace in Vienna. Blessed with a healthy constitution and accustomed to labor and birthing, Maria Theresa continued working. The impending birth of an archduke or archduchess of Austria was not to hinder the empress from ruling her realms. In between spasms of pain, the mother of fourteen worked diligently at reading, studying, and signing official papers. Only when the time came to give birth did Maria Theresa stop and beckon her midwife for aid. At eight o'clock that evening, a girl was born to the empress, a small but healthy baby who was given the name Maria Antonia Josepha Johanna. Among the imperial family she was to be known as Antoinette, the French diminutive of Antonia. Thirty-eight years old at Antoinette's birth, Maria Theresa was "wreathed in triumph, admired throughout Europe as 'the glory of her sex and model of kings.' "[9] In fact, of Maria Theresa's numerous children, "Marie Antoinette was the one who was born at the zenith of her mother's glory."[10]

The birth of Maria Theresa's youngest daughter took place amid a shift in alliances for the house of Habsburg. After the Treaty of Aix-la-Chapelle, the empress thought long and hard about reorienting her foreign policy. Unable to fight France and Prussia simultaneously, Austria looked to improving relations with France. Kaunitz impressed Maria Theresa with a long essay on the need to come to an agreement with France. The empress was of the same mind. Both regarded Prussia as more dangerous to Austria, and both agreed that the recovery of Silesia was a prime objective. Therefore, in a decisive break with tradition, Maria Theresa and Kaunitz concluded that Austria and France must become allies. No longer would Austria side with Britain against France, as in Prince Eugene's days. Now it was to be Austria with France against the archenemy, Prussia. This change in thinking ushered in the diplomatic revolution of 1756. Britain's failure to give significant aid to Maria Theresa during the War of the Austrian Succession cemented the shift.

In the early 1750s, the empress sent Kaunitz to France with the mandate to bring about the rapprochement. At first he was received coldly. He eventually gained what seemed like the confidence of France's King Louis XV and his mistress, Madame de Pompadour, but when Kaunitz returned to Vienna in 1753, the much-anticipated agreement did not materialize. Maria Theresa was not daunted. She appointed Kaunitz her chancellor and foreign minister, raising his prestige and profile.

In reversing her diplomatic position toward France, Empress Maria Theresa was going against her natural inclination. She had admitted as much to the British minister to Vienna: "I am far from being French in my disposition, and do not deny that the court of Versailles has been my bitterest enemy; but I cannot conceal, that the cessions which Great Britain extorted from me at the peace of Dresden, and of Aix-la-Chapelle, have totally disabled me. I have little to fear from France, than to form such arrangements as will secure what remains." When the British minister replied, "Will you, the empress and archduchess, so far humble yourself as to throw yourself into the arms of France? 'Not into the arms,' she hastily rejoined, 'but on the side of France.'"[11]

International affairs were turning into a complex muddle of alliances and discord, which was again set to explode into major conflict. France and Britain were struggling for mastery over America. Russia, under Empress Elizabeth, was emerging as a force to be reckoned with, while Maria Theresa's nemesis, Frederick the Great, disturbed the international equilibrium yet again when, in August 1756, he invaded Saxony and began the Seven Years' War.

At home, Maria Theresa encountered opposition to the new agreement with France. Some of her courtiers could not overcome their prejudices toward the Bourbons or the French, and within her own family, Joseph and Francis were highly opposed to the rapprochement. The empress was disappointed to find that her teenage heir was already exhibiting an insolence that she hoped would be tempered with time. When Francis heard of his wife's plans for a rapprochement with France, he was filled with indignation. After all, he harbored much animosity toward the French, who had usurped his homeland, Lorraine. Arguing against the alliance, he pounded the table, exclaiming to his wife: "Such an unnatural alliance is impracticable, and shall never take place."[12] With that, he stormed out of the room. As she had done in so many other matters where her husband objected, Maria Theresa ignored his opposition. Francis had long ago accepted this subordinate role. He once told someone that "the Empress and my children are the Court; I am only a simple individual."[13]

In 1756, Maria Theresa's wish for a diplomatic revolution between her empire and France came to fruition. When Frederick II of Prussia signed the Treaty of Westminster with Britain, France was infuriated. Frederick had been telling the French he would not reach an agreement with the British, and when he went through with it, the French felt duped. King Louis XV made his decision to ally his country with Maria Theresa's Austria. During the negotiations, Kaunitz was worried about the empress's reaction to his discussions with the sinful Madame de Pompadour. But the pragmatic empress wrote back saying: "I by no means disapprove of your having chosen . . . la Pompadour, who enjoys the king's maximum confidence. If one had passed her over, she might well have done the maximum harm."[14] Whatever the means, the diplomatic revolution had occurred. What had been France and Prussia versus Great Britain and Austria became France and Austria versus Great Britain and Prussia.

In the First Treaty of Versailles, France agreed to respect Maria Theresa's domains, while Austria promised to be neutral in the French-British conflict. For the most part, the French approved the treaty, in hope that "the union of the two greatest powers would command the respect of all Europe."[15] The only thing needed to cement this alliance was a marriage aligning the Bourbons with the Habsburgs. Little Antoinette would become the political pawn, and as such, she was to be "the most storied victim of the New System."[16]

This time, Maria Theresa had the support of France, Russia, Saxony, Spain, and Sweden against Prussia and Great Britain. The war became truly global, with fighting taking place in Europe and overseas, as far away as Canada and India. In the European theater, in June 1757, Austrian forces scored a great victory over Prussia at the Battle of Kolin in Bohemia, where Prussia suffered nearly 14,000 dead, wounded, or captured to Austria's 8,100. The empress was grateful to Field Marshal Count Leopold Daun for the victory and invested him with the Order of Maria Theresa, which she founded in celebration of this triumph.

More trouble for the Prussians came two months later at the Battle of Gross-Jägersdorf, when Russian troops attacked East Prussia. Then in November, at the Battle of Rossbach, Frederick the Great scored a significant victory by surprising the Austrians and French. Despite being outnumbered two to one, Frederick incurred minimal casualties of five hundred soldiers to his enemies' seven thousand. More battles took place over the next several years, involving tens of thousands of troops. Frederick the Great suffered setbacks, including his bitter defeat at the Battle of Kunersdorf. Things looked grim for Maria Theresa's enemy, who saw his capital, Berlin, fall into Russian hands.

In Vienna, Maria Theresa was conducting her diplomatic analyses and penning instructions amid a busy home life. Her family offered a charming picture of domesticity. The empress, who always preferred the bourgeois life in private, allowed more informality when possible. She gave a hint of her domestic life when she wrote to a former lady-in-waiting. The empress apologized for neglecting to write more properly, giving the excuse that the letter was "done in four installments, with six children in the room, and the emperor, too."[17] The imperial family captured Europe's attention too, for "no other eighteenth-century court had anything quite like them. A sparkle derived from the youthfulness and vivacity of Maria Theresa's family made the Viennese court stand out from Potsdam, St. Petersburg and Versailles. In Potsdam the hated Frederick kept a strictly male menage, communicating with his wife only by letter. In St. Petersburg the childless spinster Czarina Elizabeth hired lovers to keep her company. At Versailles there was [by that time, the king's new mistress Madame] Du Barry to amuse the aging Louis XV, and a batch of unattractive and unmarried daughters."[18] But in Vienna, life was different. Overseeing the imperial family was Empress Maria Theresa, a formidable mother, mentally and physically strong. "That strength of hers was evident . . . even as she sat upon a chair at evening she seemed to be governing from a throne."[19]

Maria Theresa's two eldest children, Marianne and Joseph, gave her the most concern. Marianne was an invalid who had curvature of the spine. Joseph had already shown signs of being difficult. When he was but four years old, Maria Theresa bluntly stated: "My Joseph cannot obey!"[20] As a teenager, he became mercurial. The empress was not blind to her oldest son's problematic personality. He was intelligent yet listless like his father and obstinate like his mother. His relationship with his siblings was no less easy, for Joseph had a tendency to be sarcastic toward them, even in front of strangers. Maria Theresa urged his tutors to mold him into an ideal prince, firing off instructions on how to deal with the heir, who enjoyed "being honored and obeyed" and found "criticism . . . well-nigh unbearable. Tending to indulge his whims," Joseph was found to be "deficient in courtesy and even rude."[21] No matter how hard Maria Theresa tried to curb her oldest son's obduracy and indifference, he was always to do things his way and cause his mother anxiety.

Archduchess Maria Christina, or Mimi, remained Maria Theresa's favorite child. Alert and quick-witted, Mimi was also pretty, with a fair complexion that she inherited from her maternal grandmother, Empress Elisabeth-Christina. The rest of Maria Theresa's daughters, including Antoinette, were lazy and less inclined to follow their lessons. A French tutor once remarked about Antoinette's "inability to concentrate," adding that her mind was "much keener than people here have assumed, but . . . nothing whatever has been done to develop it."[22] Unlike Isabella of Castile, who saw to it that her daughters, including the youngest, Catherine, were among the best educated in Europe, Maria Theresa neglected to impose rigor on her daughters, especially the youngest girl. Antoinette was, however, an eager student of dancing and music. Of all Maria Theresa's daughters, Antoinette was the one whose star shone the brightest when it came to dancing in the palace theatricals and ballets that were usually performed on birthdays or name days. Her bearing profited from dancing lessons, and she was later to be admired for the grace of her carriage.

Despite her numerous progeny, Maria Theresa was not instinctively maternal. Years later, Madame Campan, one of Marie Antoinette's ladies-in-waiting, made the observation that Marie Antoinette had been taught by her mother to "to fear and respect rather than to love her."[23] Not surprisingly, the empress insisted upon strict discipline. She also ensured that the children were immersed in religion and faithfully attended religious observances. Their meals were simple fare, consisting of two dishes including a soup. The empress ordered the governesses to watch her children's eating habits, telling them that "my children are to eat everything set before them without making any objection. They are not to make any remarks about preferring this or that, or to discuss their food. They are to eat fish every Friday and Saturday and on every fast day. Though Joanna has a revulsion against fish, no one is to give in to her. . . . All my children seem to have an aversion against fish, but they must overcome this."[24] The missives did not end there. Maria Theresa gave instructions that her daughters were "born to obey, and have to learn to do so. . . .

Under no circumstances must they be permitted to feel fear, be it of thunderstorms, fire, spooks, witches, or similar nonsense, and the servants must neither discuss such matters among themselves, nor tell any ghost stories. As [the archduchesses] must not be afraid of illnesses, you will talk to them about any of these quite naturally, even of smallpox. And of death also, for it is well to familiarize them with the thought of it."[25] Indeed, Archduke Charles Joseph died in 1761, and Maria Johanna died in 1762.

Smallpox cast its specter on Europe, taking a toll among commoners, clergy, nobility, and monarchs alike. Joseph's first wife, the beautiful, dark-haired Isabella of Parma, was a victim. She had enchanted the archduke and indeed the whole family. Isabella was extremely attached to her sister-in-law Mimi. Mimi knew of Isabella's preoccupation with death, an obsession so pronounced that it appeared as if she was almost seeking it. While pregnant with her second child, Isabella succumbed to smallpox, dying in 1763 at the age of twenty-one. Joseph never really recovered from Isabella's untimely death. His marriage to his second wife, Marie-Josephe of Bavaria (daughter of none other than Charles Albert), planned by Maria Theresa, was extremely unhappy. The marriage ended when Marie-Josephe too died of smallpox.

In 1767 fifteen-year-old Archduchess Maria Josepha was betrothed to the King of Naples. Before her departure for Naples, her mother insisted that she accompany her to the imperial crypt of the Habsburgs to visit the tomb of Joseph's recently deceased second wife. Maria Josepha did not want to go for fear that she might catch the disease that had killed her sister-in-law. Before they left, Marie Josepha tearfully embraced Antoinette with the message that she would never see her again and was headed not for Naples but for her own burial among their Habsburg ancestors. Maria Josepha did indeed catch the disease and died from it. Maria Theresa too had contracted smallpox while Marie-Josephe was dying of the disease. The empress was so ill that the Last Rites were administered. But Maria Theresa recovered.

Another of Maria Theresa's children, Archduchess Maria Elisabeth, the great beauty of the family, also suffered from smallpox. Upon hearing that she was afflicted, the archduchess asked for a mirror to take one last look at her flawless complexion. She survived the disease, but her disfigured face made it impossible for Maria Elisabeth to find a husband.

Maria Theresa understandably sought to tackle the problem of smallpox. After obtaining information on inoculation from a physician recommended to her by England's King George III, the empress decided to introduce the practice into her domains. To set an example, she had her two youngest sons, Ferdinand and Maximilian, inoculated.

Maria Theresa's attention to her many children did not prevent her from keeping a watchful eye on the international stage. Empress Elizabeth of Russia died in 1762, and Prussia's fortunes turned. Elizabeth's successor, Czar Peter III, a great admirer of Frederick's, suddenly made peace with Prussia and became his idol's ally. When Peter was overthrown and murdered, he was succeeded by his wife, Catherine II (the Great), who declared Russia's neutrality in the war. In the meantime, defeats overseas prompted France to conclude peace with Britain in 1763. The loss of France as a major ally forced Maria Theresa to stop fighting. In the 1763 Treaty of Hubertusburg, ending the Seven Years' War, the status quo remained, meaning that Silesia did not revert to Maria Theresa, as she had so dearly wished. Prussia emerged as a definitive great power, while most of France's overseas possessions fell into British hands, signaling the ascendancy of Great Britain on the world stage.

Still, the Seven Years' War was not as significant as the earlier wars for Maria Theresa. Unlike the War of the Austrian Succession, which had established her right to rule, the Seven Years' War was a global conflict that engulfed a coalition of states in which the empress was not the main protagonist. By the end of the war, Maria Theresa of Austria had grown stout and matronly, more resigned to what fate had in store for her. She had also hoped that, after a life filled with conflicts, her later years would be less combative. Yet in spite of the exhausting years and the bitter loss of Silesia, the empress still "possessed all the dignity, the narrow but strong idealism, and the faith which Frederick [the Great] lacked."[26]

In 1765, a personal tragedy of great magnitude struck unexpectedly. Before leaving for their son Leopold's wedding festivities at Innsbruck, Francis drew his favorite child, Antoinette, to him. Years later, Marie Antoinette described the farewell: "My father took me on his knee and, with tears in his eyes, kissed me. . . . He seemed greatly pained at leaving me: which surprised all those who were present."[27] Was it a good-bye with a premonition? During the wedding celebration, Emperor Francis collapsed in Joseph's arms and died. He was fifty-six years old; the empress was forty-eight. Francis's sudden death stunned Maria Theresa and sent her into deepest mourning. The absence of the man whom she had idolized since she was a child turned the widowed empress into a recluse for months. Even though Francis had lately become infatuated with the much younger and extravagant Countess Auersperg, the empress had continued to love her husband dearly. Maria Theresa was magnanimous in her grief, telling Countess Auersperg, "How much we both of us have lost!"[28] The empress also showed a generous spirit toward the countess. Instead of ruining her, Maria Theresa settled on her a large sum that Francis had promised Auersperg before he died.

The day after Francis died, the widowed empress had her luxurious hair cut short, then shut herself in her room sewing a shroud for her husband's body. For the rest of her life, Maria Theresa wore mourning. Every eighteenth of the month was devoted to remembering the late emperor, while every August was consecrated to devotions, penance, and requiems in Francis's memory. The rooms Maria Theresa lived in were draped in gray and black. She stopped wearing jewelry except for pearls and continued to hold Francis's memory dear to her heart. The empress expressed her profound sorrow to her daughters, saying, "Our calamity is at its height; you have lost a most incomparable father, and I a consort—a friend—my heart's joy, for forty-two years past! Having been brought up together, our hearts and our sentiments were united in the same views. All the misfortunes I have suffered during the last twenty-five years were softened by his support. I am suffering such deep affliction, that nothing but true piety and you, my dear children, can make me tolerate a life which, during its continuance, shall be spent in acts of devotion."[29]

To her son Leopold, Maria Theresa echoed the same message: "Nothing but complete acceptance of God's will can help me to beat this blow. You have lost the best and tenderest father. I have lost everything, a tender husband, a perfect friend, my only support, to whom I owe everything. You, dear children, are the sole legacy of this great prince and tender father; try to deserve by your conduct all my affection which is now reserved for you alone."[30] To one of her friends, the widow wrote: "All that I have left is my grave. I await it with impatience because only it will reunite me with the sole object that my heart has loved in this world and which has been the object and goal of all my deeds and sentiments. You realize the void in my life since he has left."[31] The empress's obsession with her husband was such that she had recorded in her prayer book, in minute detail, how long Francis lived: "Emperor Francis, my husband, lived 56 years, 8 months, 10 days, and died on August 18, 1765, at 9:30 P.M. So he lived: Months 680, Weeks 2,958½, Days 20,778, Hours 496,992. My happy marriage lasted 29 years, 6 months, and 6 days."[32]

The widow thought she was through with the world. She confessed to her old confidant Count Tarouca: "I hardly know myself now, for I have become like an animal with no true life or reasoning power. I forget everything. I get up at five. I go to bed late, and the livelong day I seem to do nothing. I do not even think. It is a terrible state to be in, but I revive a little when I see one of my old friends."[33] The thought of retiring to a convent in Innsbruck was tempting, but Maria Theresa resisted. She wrote to Kaunitz that "I am letting myself be dragged back to Vienna, wholly and solely to assume the guardianship of nine orphans. They are greatly to be pitied. Their good father idolised them and could never refuse them anything. It will be changed times now. I am exceedingly anxious about their future, which will be decided in the course of the next winter."[34]

The grieving mother set about planning marriages for her children. These surviving children, after all, "represented an incalculable political capital."[35] When the ill-fated Archduchess Maria Josepha died after visiting the Habsburg crypt, Maria Theresa lost no time in replacing her with the next sister, Archduchess Maria Carolina, as the designated bride for the King of Naples. This sister, nearest in age to Antoinette, married King Ferdinand IV of Naples in 1768. The empress married off Maria Amalia to Ferdinand, Duke of Parma, despite Maria Amalia's objection that she had wanted to marry someone else. The only one of Maria Theresa's children allowed to marry for love turned out to be Mimi, who married Prince Albert of Saxony. Leopold married Maria Luisa of Spain, and Ferdinand married Maria Beatrice d'Este. Far from being mere quaint weddings between European royal families, five of these marriages were arranged by Maria Theresa to solidify Austria's alliance with the French and the house of Bourbon. Of all these Habsburg-Bourbon alliances, the young Archduchess Antoinette's would be the most famous. Of Maria Theresa's sons, only the youngest, Maximilian, never married.

In her despondency over Francis's death, Maria Theresa extended her maternal impulses and her religious devotion out toward her subjects. The result was the continued pursuit of a monarchy of enlightened absolutism. Maria Theresa never understood Frederick II of Prussia's introduction of religious freedom in his country. Like Isabella of Castile, Maria Theresa held religious homogeneity in her domains to be equal with the salvation of her subjects. When in 1777 Joseph sounded off in favor of toleration, his mother retorted: "To my great grief I have to say that there would be nothing more to corrupt in respect of religion if you intend to insist on that general toleration of which you maintain that it is a principle from which you will never depart. . . . I will not cease from praying myself . . . that God may protect you from this misfortune, the greatest which would ever have descended on the Monarchy . . . you will ruin your State and be guilty of the destruction of so many souls."[36]

The empress's faith tilted toward "strong Counter-Reformation convictions," which were buttressed by her "pragmatic but conservative temperament."[37] Like others of her time, Maria Theresa was uncharitable toward the Jews. Nevertheless, she "had no taste for persecution. Quite simply, she believed that she was doing right: 'I must show no spirit of persecution, but, even more important, no spirit of tolerance, nor recognize all religious opinions as of equal worth. I must conduct myself thus as long as I live, until the moment when I shall descend into the crypt.' "[38]

Despite her strong attachment to Catholicism and her family's past association with Jesuit priests, Maria Theresa was not averse to reining in the clergy when necessary, though the powerful Jesuit order had an extensive influence in Austria and Hungary. The empress was motivated to curtail the Jesuits' obstruction to her reforms (they preferred to teach in Latin, though Maria Theresa wanted German to be the language of instruction). Moreover, Count Kaunitz had made her believe that the Jesuits were encroaching on the monarchy's rights. After the Pope dissolved the Jesuits, a reluctant Maria Theresa suppressed the order in her domains in 1773. Though the empress allowed numerous Jesuits to continue teaching, she "ordered the destruction of all Jesuit papers and manuals, because she considered them obsolete and potentially dangerous if they fell into the wrong hands."[39] Maria Theresa ordered churches and convents to desist from granting asylum to any criminal. She also forbade the presence of ecclesiastics when wills were made and curbed the Inquisition.

This suppression of the Jesuits was part of Maria Theresa's second set of reforms, from 1761 to 1778. During these years, she concentrated on improving the welfare of her subjects in her Austrian and Bohemian lands. Concern about revolution as well as her realm's economic and humanitarian well-being directed her attention. The most striking of the reforms concerned the serfs. Of the serfs in Bohemia, Maria Theresa had written to her son Ferdinand that "the peasants there are crushed under the excesses of the lords, who, in my thirty-six years of rule, have always known how to sabotage changes and how to hold their serfs in bondage."[40] It was not an easy task to ease the serfs' burdens. The empress met with opposition from the nobility and mistrust from the serfs. By the 1770s, the serfs gained some respite through her issuance of the Robot Patent, which softened the payments they were obliged to fulfill through service. By reducing the robot, the Theresian regime "turned back the clock on a century and a half of illegal encroachment by the landed nobility."[41] Maria Theresa also eliminated the use of torture in forcing confessions.

Failing to tackle the numerous problems besetting the Habsburg Empire would have invited disaster. These reforms along with her earlier ones not only strengthened the monarchy but also averted possible rebellion among her varied subjects. France, the other great power on the Continent, was beleaguered by its own set of troubles—troubles that were to have profound consequences for Maria Theresa's daughter, Antoinette.

15

MARRIAGE TO THE DAUPHIN

*T*he archduchess Antoinette was but nine years old when her father died. With her father gone, Antoinette went into her teen years in the shadow of her formidable mother, the "Austrian Elizabeth Tudor."[1] In her role as a mother, Maria Theresa's conscientiousness and domineering personality invariably trumped her affectionate streak, which meant that her children, including Antoinette and the eldest, Joseph, held her in awe.

With Francis I's death, Joseph became Holy Roman emperor and coregent. His mother's sometimes overbearing attitude ran afoul of Joseph's own obduracy, making their relationship volatile. As Joseph matured, his willfulness intensified. Ongoing conflict came to dominate their lives after Francis's death. Their relationship was a "clash between mother and son [that] extended to all fields of thought and action. It was a conflict of opposing temperaments, philosophies, aims—a reflection of the intellectual struggle that went on everywhere in Europe."[2] This intellectual struggle was between those who clung to orthodox faith and those who welcomed the Enlightenment. To Maria Theresa's horror, Joseph II eagerly embraced the Enlightenment's principles, which she perceived as antithetical to his salvation and that of her subjects. As emperor, Joseph "consciously brought [the principles of the Enlightenment] into play, and then Maria Theresa resisted them stubbornly, bitterly sometimes, sometimes despairingly."[3]

Opposing parties inevitably coalesced around the two monarchs: Maria Theresa and her supporters focused on religion, morals, and the impact of radical Enlightenment ideas in society. Joseph and his party, by contrast, were keen innovators who embraced the ideas of the *philosophes* and sought to get society to embrace the Age of Reason. In time, suspicions grew among Maria Theresa's subjects, so that "a deep-rooted class struggle developed throughout the Habsburg dominions, especially in the cities. It was the reverberation of the clash of modern ideas [that had its genesis] in France."[4]

Nowhere did the strained relationship between Maria Theresa and Joseph II collide more fiercely than in religion. Though she could be stubborn, the empress preferred moderation and compromise, except when it came to religion. As it had for Queen Isabella in Spain before her, religious unity (under Catholicism) was nonnegotiable for Maria Theresa. Her position was at odds with Joseph's preference for pluralism. In this, the mother wrote of her anxieties to the son:

> What is at stake is not only the welfare of the State, but your salvation, that of a son who since his birth has been the one purpose of all my actions, the salvation of your soul. . . . You are ruining yourself and dragging the Monarchy down with you into the abyss, destroying the fruits of all the laborious care of your forefathers, who at the cost of the greatest pains bequeathed these lands to us and even greatly improved their condition, because they introduced our holy religion into them, not, like our enemies, with violence and cruelty, but with care, pains, and expense. . . . I only wish to live so long as I can hope to descend to my ancestors with the consolation that my son will be as great, as religious as his forebears, that he will return from his erroneous views, from those wicked books whose authors parade their cleverness at the expense of all that is most holy and most worthy of respect in the world, who want to introduce an imaginary freedom which can never exist and which degenerates into license and into complete revolution.[5]

By 1773, Maria Theresa's conflicts with her eldest son had reached the point that he wanted to be released from his position as coregent. The empress confessed that she felt overwhelmed by her duties and replied, "I offer you my whole confidence, and ask you to call my attention to any mistakes I might make. . . . Help a mother who for thirty-three years has had only you, a mother who lives in loneliness, and who will die when she sees all her efforts and sorrows gone to waste. Tell me what you wish and I will do it."[6] This plea precipitated a brief respite in their battle of wills. Inevitably, however, mother and son continued to clash. Overall, Maria Theresa and Joseph's relationship can best be summed up in a letter she wrote to him in the 1770s, in which she touched upon that lightning rod that so separated them—religion: "It is a great misfortune that, with the best intentions, we do not understand each other. Perhaps my anger is due to the fact that I get neither the confidence nor the frankness which I had hoped to deserve. For thirty-six years I have occupied myself only with you; twenty-six of these have been happy, but I cannot say that now, for I can never agree to such lax principles in religion and manners. You show too much antipathy for the old, especially for all the clergy, and all-too-libertarian principles in questions of morals and conduct. This justly alarms my heart for your position and makes me tremble for the future."[7]

As she aged and her struggles with Joseph continued, Maria Theresa considered abdicating and retiring to a more peaceful life. But she held on, determined to do the best she thought possible for her people. Perhaps the empress had recalled what her faithful Tarouca had counseled her years ago: "Madame, we must banish melancholy, like every other idle frittering of time; for all these faults are damaging and sinful in the eyes of God. If we kick against our duties we betray our calling and render ourselves useless to the millions of our subjects."[8] Maria Theresa almost always took Count Tarouca's advice to heart throughout his long years of service, and the count acknowledged that "he was listened to with a humility that was in keeping with the occupant of a convent cell more than with the occupant of a throne."[9] And so, taking her mentor's advice, Maria Theresa soldiered on, banishing thoughts of abdication. But these later years were lonely ones, for the dedicated Tarouca and many of her friends had died, leaving Maria Theresa increasingly alone. Of her surviving children, many had left the family fold, either having taken religious vows or having married into foreign royal families.

The empress was also preoccupied with other matters. Among her most important concerns were the marriage prospects for her remaining unmarried children, including her youngest daughter, Antoinette. Before joining the royal marriage market, the archduchess spent a few carefree years at her mother's court. Home consisted of several palaces, such as the shooting lodge of Laxenburg in the countryside, where court formality was at its most lax. In winter, the family lived at the Hofburg in Vienna. But it was the family's residence during the warmer months, Schönbrunn Palace, just outside the capital, which was the most magnificent of the imperial residences. Schönbrunn was a fine setting for Archduchess Antoinette to grow up in, presaging life at Versailles. The expansion of Schönbrunn under Maria Theresa's direction had taken some twenty years, but the results were well worth waiting for. The empress had transformed this palace into a Rococo masterpiece, adding a complete floor for her burgeoning family. Inside, the many gilt-decorated rooms were furnished with fine portraits, crystal chandeliers, exquisitely carved wood embellishments, and Gobelin tapestries. Among the most splendid rooms in the palace was the Great Gallery. At 140 feet long, with numerous mirrors that reflected the lights flickering from the chandeliers and wall sconces, the Great Gallery was one of the most dazzling rooms in Europe. Then there was the Million Room, so named by Maria Theresa because of the one million gulden it cost to create. Containing a floor of rosewood imported from the Antilles, the room was also decorated with numerous medallions. The empress preferred to work in her study, decorated in the Chinese style with porcelain and lacquered panels.

Maria Theresa used the Mirror Room to receive newly appointed ministers. Wolfgang Amadeus Mozart performed in this room in 1762. The child prodigy, then only six years old, amazed the imperial family with his dexterity on the keyboard. When the keys were covered, he played just as well as when he could see them. Young Mozart was not at all frightened by the illustrious audience. He delighted the empress when he climbed onto her lap, threw his arms around her neck, and kissed her as if she had been his own mother. After the concert, Mozart played with the younger members of the imperial family, including seven-year-old Archduchess Antoinette. When the little guest slipped on the polished floor, Antoinette promptly helped Mozart get back to his feet. Her eagerness to help so touched Mozart that he complimented the archduchess's act of kindness to her mother.

Archduchess Antoinette's exposure to music did not begin and stop with Mozart. Christoph Gluck, the great opera reformer of the era, was her music master, teaching her to play the spinet and clavichord. Sadly for Antoinette, apart from music and deportment, one of the few areas she excelled in, her education was still lackluster. Intellectual subjects were simply not to her liking, nor was the effort of concentrating on her studies. Moreover, the empress failed to correct the deficiencies in Antoinette's education, an omission that was curious considering Maria Theresa's own experience.

Antoinette, like her siblings, became an instrument of politics. After the détente between Austria and France was achieved through the diplomatic revolution of 1756, Maria Theresa determined that the marriage of her youngest daughter into the French house of Bourbon was necessary to secure the alliance. Prince Louis-Auguste, grandson of France's King Louis XV, was second in line to the throne and thirteen months older than Archduchess Antoinette. A marriage between these two seemed the ideal dynastic match.

The third son of Louis, the Dauphin (heir) of France, and his wife, Marie-Josèphe of Saxony, Louis-Auguste had largely been ignored by his parents in favor of the eldest of his brothers, the Duc de Bourgogne, who died in 1761. Another older brother had died, as did the father in 1765, so that by the time he was eleven years old, Prince Louis-Auguste was heir to his grandfather. As the dauphin, Louis-Auguste was expected to sparkle in Versailles, the magnificent seat of the kings of France. The dauphin, however, cut an unprepossessing figure. Shy and awkward, lacking any self-confidence, Louis-Auguste did not make promising material for a future king. He was not unintelligent—he loved history and literature—but these interests were not cultivated by a fine education. He had a passion for hunting, yet his irresoluteness did not bode well for the future.

Not until 1766 did Maria Theresa's emissary make a formal proposal for marriage between Antoinette and Louis-Auguste. The response was unenthusiastic. Louis-Auguste's mother favored a marriage to a princess from Saxony. France's ambassador to Vienna, the Marquis de Durfort, had instructions to move slowly in the matter. It took two years from Durfort's arrival in Vienna for him to be given the green light to announce an offer from the French court for Antoinette's hand in marriage. Maria Theresa did not fail to drop hints to the French envoy regarding the potential marriage. When Durfort joined the empress in January 1768 to watch a procession of sleighs containing members of the imperial family, Maria Theresa nudged him as thirteen-year-old Antoinette passed, whispering, "The little wife."[10]

With Antoinette's future settled, a rush overtook the Viennese court to mold the guileless archduchess into a future Queen of France. No detail, not even Antoinette's coiffure, seemed too minute to tackle. A Frenchman was dispatched to arrange her hair in order to hide a high forehead. Despite her high forehead, small stature, and the protruding lower lip characteristic of the Habsburgs, Antoinette presented a favorable picture. She had a fine complexion, long nose, wide blue eyes, straight eyebrows, blond hair, and above all, a graceful carriage. She looked a bit like a young version of Maria Theresa.

A Frenchman, the Abbé de Vermond, was requisitioned to teach proper French to the young archduchess, taking over from two French actors who, while on tour in Vienna, had been tutoring Antoinette. The abbé, a pious man, had an unenviable task. He noted of his charge that "she is cleverer than she was long thought to be. Unfortunately, that stability was subjected to no direction up to the age of twelve. A little idleness and much frivolity rendered my task more difficult. I spent the first six weeks in drawing an outline of the construction of 'belles lettres.' She easily understood when I presented my ideas in a connected form: her judgment was nearly always sound, but I could not accustom her to get at the root of a subject, although I felt she was very capable of doing so. I fancied I could only get her to fix her attention by amusing her."[11] Vermond was particularly exasperated by the archduchess's handwriting. He observed that "the style of her handwriting is not particularly good . . . [and] she has acquired the habit of writing inconceivably slow."[12] Antoinette never did learn to write proper German, much less French. Nevertheless, thanks to Vermond's careful tutoring—which included histories of France, the royal family, and the French nobility—she not only learned something of France and the Bourbons but also acquired before she left home a fluency in her adopted country's language, a skill that had eluded her Castilian counterpart, Catherine of Aragon, before her departure for England.

For all her academic shortcomings, Vermond concluded of Antoinette that "she has the most graceful figure; holds herself well; and if, as may be hoped, she grows a little taller, she will possess every good quality one could wish for in a great princess. Her heart and character are both excellent."[13]

By June 1769, all was official. Archduchess Maria Antonia was betrothed to the Dauphin of France. A great and glorious future awaited this child of Maria Theresa. The Viennese court now paid careful attention to Maria Theresa's youngest daughter, while at Versailles, reports trickled in on the progress of this teenager who could well one day become a future qeen consort of France. As the day for her departure neared, Maria Theresa took it upon herself to spend time with her daughter. They went together on a pilgrimage to Mariazell, where the *Magna Mater Austriae* was housed and venerated. Maria Theresa had Antoinette moved into her room so that mother and daughter could have much-needed private time together. For two months, the empress instructed the future Queen of France on the duties of a consort. How much the young archduchess absorbed is difficult to tell. That her mother went to such lengths to tutor Antoinette personally indicates that Maria Theresa was concerned about her daughter and the future.

Antoinette did not have long to wait before she was officially dispatched to France. Two days before her departure, she was married by proxy at the Church of the Augustine Friars, where Maria Theresa had been married over three decades before. The next evening, Maria Theresa wrote to King Louis XV, telling him of Antoinette that "her intentions are excellent, but given her age, I pray you to exercise indulgence for any careless mistake. . . . I recommend her once again as the most tender pledge which exists so happily between our States and our Houses."[14]

On April 21, 1770, the fourteen-and-a-half-year-old Archduchess Maria Antonia began her journey to a new life and a foreign land. From the large courtyard of Schönbrunn Palace, Antoinette bade her family farewell. Saying good-bye to her daughters who married had never been easy for Maria Theresa, but as Antoinette was the last daughter to leave the family fold, this farewell was even more poignant and full of tears. The empress repeatedly embraced her daughter and uttered the words "Farewell, my dearest child, a great distance will separate us. . . . Do so much good to the French people that they can say that I have sent them an angel."[15] After that, accompanied by the Abbé de Vermond and over 150 dignitaries, Antoinette left in an impressive procession of nearly sixty carriages, drawn by over 370 horses. As she departed, a sudden foreboding gripped her. The ladies of her entourage saw tears streaming down the young woman's face and heard Antoinette sigh, "I shall never see her again!"[16]

Antoinette took a few things with her, including instructions written by her father to all his children in which he urged them to be good Catholics by reminding them that "the world where you must pass your life is but transitory. There is naught save eternity that is without end. We should enjoy the pleasures of this life innocently, for so soon as they lead us into evil, of whatever sort it may be, they cease to be pleasures." Francis ended the missive with heavy words: "I recommend you to take two days in every year to prepare for death as though you were sure that those two were the last days of your life; and thus you will accustom yourself to know what you ought to do under those circumstances, and when your last moment arrives, you will not be surprised, but will know what you have to do."[17]

On the first evening of her journey, Antoinette stopped at the beautiful and imposing Austrian Benedictine Abbey at Melk, high above the Danube River, where her brother Emperor Joseph II joined her briefly. Afterward, she made her way toward the French border in a velvet-lined carriage. In her possession was also a letter from her mother with a message that must have been perplexing to the sheltered fourteen-year-old: "The one felicity of this world is a happy marriage: I can say so with knowledge; and the whole hangs upon the woman, that she should be willing, gentle, and able to amuse."[18]

Two weeks after she left Schönbrunn, Antoinette reached the Rhine. The actual moment when the archduchess was handed over to France was steeped in etiquette. On an island near Kehl, Maria Theresa's daughter was formally stripped of her Austrian attire and donned in clothes made in France. It was a highly symbolic act that said to one and all, including the bride, that she was no longer Archduchess Maria Antonia but Marie Antoinette, the Dauphine of France. It was almost too much for the teenage bride, who threw herself unceremoniously upon the surprised Comtesse de Noailles, the senior attendant assigned to her, at their first meeting. There were numerous welcoming ceremonies throughout the journey to Versailles. During one of them, Marie Antoinette met the refined Prince Louis de Rohan, the Bishop of Strasbourg. He was to play a damaging role in her life, but at this first meeting he was full of charm, addressing his future queen with the words "For us, Madame, you will be the living image of that dear Empress, for so long, the admiration of Europe, as she will be in ages to come. The soul of Maria Theresa will be united to the soul of the Bourbons."[19] When she heard these words, tears fell on Marie Antoinette's cheeks.

On May 14, 1770, Marie Antoinette met King Louis XV and his grandson, the dauphin. She fell to her knees before the king. Touched by this humble greeting, King Louis was pleased to see a charming looking young woman with a lovely complexion and fine teeth. And there before her was Louis-Auguste, a shy, plump young man. The unprepossessing groom, who liked to fiddle with locks for a hobby, must have been a disappointment to the curious young bride.

Another wedding ceremony took place at the royal family's sprawling estate outside Paris: Versailles, that "epic poem in stone dedicated to one man's [King Louis XIV's] glory. Even to a girl reared in palaces, Versailles was at once breathtaking and awe inspiring. Schönbrunn with its 1,100 rooms plus, the Vienna Hofburg slowly growing through the centuries in the heart of the old city, faded into insignificance beside the arrogant splendour of Versailles; an isolated world of privilege and pomp, in which the grandest of courtiers were ready to perform the most menial of tasks if it brought him into the presence of the King, and duchesses fought for the honour of sitting for hours on hard stools in the royal antechamber."[20] It was in this curious world, part glorified ceremonial penal colony of the aristocracy, part palace and home to France's kings, that Louis-Auguste and Marie Antoinette took their marital vows. In the palace chapel, resplendently decorated in gold and white, the teenage couple knelt on red velvet cushions. Above them was a silver canopy. Marie Antoinette and Louis-Auguste were pronounced man and wife by the Archbishop of Rheims. After a banquet in which the groom gorged himself but the bride hardly ate, the couple were led to their bedchamber. Even in this private moment, the ceremonial ritual that made life at Versailles so public for the royal family continued. The archbishop blessed the nuptial bed, King Louis XV handed his grandson his nightshirt, and the Duchesse de Chartres helped Marie Antoinette.

Many that night expected that the Franco-Austrian alliance would be consummated. But it was not to be. The dauphin, full from his heavy meal, merely fell asleep by his wife's side. The next day Louis-Auguste wrote in his diary, "Nothing." The pattern of "nothing" was repeated night after night. In no time, everyone at Versailles knew that the marriage remained unconsummated. Eyes soon became fixed on Marie Antoinette. She had to act as if everything was fine as people began to whisper all kinds of stories behind her back. Meanwhile, in Vienna, Maria Theresa was curious about what was going on behind the scenes at Versailles. For news, the empress relied on her confidential informant, her ambassador to Paris, Count Mercy-Argenteau, whose tour of duty stretched from 1766 to 1790. He corresponded nearly every day with Maria Theresa with details about the comings and goings of the French court, and with particular reference to Marie Antoinette. When Maria Theresa discovered that the young couple had not yet consummated their marriage, she counseled her daughter to wait, telling her: "You are both so young! As far as your health is concerned it is all for the best. You will both gain strength."[21]

Marie Antoinette's new life in France was but one of the empress's preoccupations. During the early 1770s, a crisis arose over Poland that greatly agitated Maria Theresa. For many years, Poland had been racked by instability. With no real central authority, nobles fought for control over land and the serfs tilling it. This constant rivalry invited chaos and made Poland vulnerable to the political ambitions of its neighbors, in particular, Catherine the Great's Russia. Catherine was winning territory at the expense of the Ottoman Empire, which added to the impression that the czarist empire was set to grab more land. Worried about the impact of a resurgent Russia on Prussia, King Frederick II convinced Catherine the Great and Emperor Joseph II to partition Poland. Joseph jumped at the opportunity, as did Kaunitz. Maria Theresa, however, was appalled. She vehemently disagreed with Frederick's proposal, which in her eyes was typical of the man of whom she had once admitted that she "detested his false character."[22]

Joseph's actions in the Polish crisis prompted Maria Theresa to write: "I must admit that never before in my life have I been so profoundly troubled. When an unrighteous claim was made on my territories, I stiffened my back and put my trust in God. But on the present occasion . . . I can get no rest."[23] She urged Kaunitz in 1772 to forget the scheme, saying: "Let us consider by what means we can extricate ourselves from our deplorable situation without thinking of territorial gain."[24] But it was all in vain. With the combined pressure of Joseph and Kaunitz working against her, a reluctant Maria Theresa in the end acquiesced and watched. The whole episode embittered the empress, who confided to her son Ferdinand: "You will be duly informed of the dreary course of the affair. . . . God grant that I may not be held responsible for it in another world: I am haunted by it now. It weighs on my heart and tortures my brain and embitters my days. . . . I pull myself up sharply, or the worry of it all will land me in melancholia."[25] By the end of the Polish crisis, Maria Theresa had aged and become an unhappy and solitary woman. Her health had also given way. Now corpulent, she no longer possessed the vivacity and energy she had once enjoyed. There were also the anxieties over her daughters in foreign courts.

Maria Carolina, wife of King Ferdinand IV of Naples, found her husband lazy and ugly. Her initial experience of marriage was traumatic, prompting her to worry about her sister Antoinette: "One suffers real martyrdom, which is all the greater because one must pretend outwardly to be happy. I know whereof I speak and I pity Antoinette, who still has this to face. I would rather die than endure again what I had to suffer. If religion had not said to me: 'Think about God,' I would have killed myself rather than live as I did for eight days. It was like hell and I often wished to die. When my sister has to face this situation, I shall shed many tears."[26] Maria Amalia, who married Ferdinand, Duke of Parma, in 1769, caused her mother endless heartache. As it turned out, Maria Amalia's husband was even less appealing than the unprepossessing Ferdinand of Naples. The Duke of Parma was a fool with a penchant for ringing church bells and eating a delicacy he liked to make, roasted chestnuts. Soon Amalia scandalized her mother and others by taking lovers. Her recklessness created an unbridgeable gulf between her mother and her.

In France, meanwhile, the life of Marie Antoinette was fraught with increasing difficulties. An early letter to her mother made it sound as though life at Versailles was rather straightforward. Her daily routine, wrote the dauphine, consisted of rising at nine, dressing, prayers, breakfast, and a meeting with the king and his daughters. After her hair was dressed came the very public part of her day. "At twelve is my reception," wrote Marie Antoinette, "and all may enter who are not common people. I put on my rouge and wash my hands before them all, and then the men go and the ladies remain, and I finish my dressing before them."[27] Marie Antoinette then attended Mass, spent time with the dauphin, read, wrote, or worked on something such as a vest for the king. Then she called on her husband's aunts again, met with Abbé de Vermond, had music lessons, met with the aunts again, went for a walk, then played some games, supped at nine, and ended the day at eleven.

This rather harmless sounding routine belied a more stressful existence. For one thing, the French court was a kind of gilded cage, "where everyone lived in a close and oppressive intimacy, [moreover] a girl still little more than a child had to fight her way through a jungle of intrigue without a single friend to guide her other than her mother's ambassador, who was also her mother's spy."[28] One of the most galling aspects of living at the court of Louis XV was the fact that so many were aware of the most trifling details in people's lives, including those of the royal family. The precedent set by King Louis XIV—*le roi soleil,* or the Sun King—whereby he lived publicly with his nobles waiting on him ceremoniously, had hardly changed when Marie Antoinette arrived. The court too was different from the more pious Viennese one of Maria Theresa, so that Marie Antoinette, though royal and accustomed to etiquette, was initially confounded by life at Versailles. She and her new husband started off married life "practically at the head of the most splendid, luxurious, dissolute Court in Europe."[29] It was a formidable task for a fourteen-and-a-half-year-old girl.

Marie Antoinette's years as Dauphine of France were further marked by frustration with her marital situation, since she remained married to Louis-Auguste in name only. Several months after her marriage, there was a strong hint from the dauphin that he would attempt to consummate his marriage. "Rest assured that I am not ignorant of what is involved in the state of marriage," Louis-Auguste told Marie Antoinette. "You will find that at Compiègne I shall live with you in the fullest intimacy you could wish."[30] Their stay at Compiègne came and went, but yet again, nothing happened. As time passed with no sign of the young couple becoming man and wife in more than name, an exasperated Maria Theresa despairingly confessed: "If a girl as pretty as the Dauphine cannot stir the Dauphin, every remedy will be useless."[31]

The clumsy and awkward prince who seemed to prefer food to love at first found it difficult to make friends with Marie Antoinette. His locks and the hunt asked so much less of him, but with the passage of time, the dauphin came to appreciate his young wife's qualities. Count Mercy tried to reassure Empress Maria Theresa on this front, telling her: Louis-Auguste "seems charmed with the Dauphine, and shows a sweetness and complaisance towards her that he was not believed to possess. . . . She governs him in all trifles, to which he offers no opposition. So with a little patience all may be well. . . . In this country they wish to hurry everything."[32] Count Mercy was correct in his assessment of the dauphin, who admitted, when it came to his teenage bride, that "she is so graceful, she succeeds in everything; one must admit that she is charming."[33] Perhaps all Louis-Auguste needed was some time. Maria Theresa told Count Mercy: "I preach to my daughter patience, and to redouble her caresses."[34]

Other difficulties plagued young Marie Antoinette. Though there were those who looked out for her interests—such as Count Mercy-Argenteau, the Abbé de Vermond, and the French foreign minister, the Duc de Choiseul, who was pro-Austrian and had engineered the marriage—Maria Theresa's daughter also had opponents who were wary of the power and influence she would wield. Jealousies and fears arose among certain courtiers, including the dauphine's chief lady-in-waiting, the Comtesse de Noailles, as well as the dauphin's former tutor, the Duc de Vauguyon, who tried to sow seeds of discontent between Louis-Auguste and Marie Antoinette. In addition to hostile courtiers, Marie Antoinette had to deal with a new family, with whom she lived in close proximity. Besides King Louis XV, the dauphin and dauphine, the French royal family consisted of Louis-Auguste's brothers: Louis-Stanislas-Xavier, the Comte de Provence, and Charles-Philippe, the Comte d'Artois. The rivalries that riddled Versailles could be seen in the relationship between Provence and his older brother. Though he was outwardly cordial to Marie Antoinette, Provence was intensely jealous of Louis-Auguste, and there was always an underlying suspiciousness about him. Louis-Auguste once said of the Comte de Provence that he lacked "that understanding manner which one expects in one's friend."[35] Provence and Artois married sisters, princesses of Savoy, Marie-Josèphe and Marie-Thérèse. For a time, Marie Antoinette got along with her sisters-in-law and their husbands, though she could never quite let her guard down when it came to the Provence couple. Other family members who lived closely with Marie Antoinette were Louis XV's unmarried daughters, Adelaide, Victoire, Sophie, and Louise. Referred to as the aunts, these women exercised some influence over Marie Antoinette during her early days at court. They disliked the very idea of an Austrian alliance, yet they wanted to incur the dauphine's favor in order to use her in their battle against the king's mistress, Madame du Barry. Frustrated, bored, gossipy, and prone to meddling, the aunts encouraged Marie Antoinette in her unsympathetic view of du Barry.

Born illegitimate, du Barry came from a lowly background. As a curvaceous, abrasive, and ambitious courtesan, she had had several wealthy lovers before catching Louis XV's attention. The king's financial profligacy toward her contributed to his unpopularity. His pious grandson Louis-Auguste found his grandfather's life with du Barry embarrassing and highly immoral. As part of an anti-Choiseul faction at court, du Barry maligned herself in the dauphine's eyes. But above all, as her mother's daughter, Marie Antoinette could not help but dislike du Barry's role as the king's mistress. Marie Antoinette told her mother how "pitiable it was to see his weakness for Madame du Barry, who is the most silly and impertinent creature it is possible to imagine."[36] For as long as she could, Maria Antoinette avoided publicly acknowledging du Barry. The dauphine's animosity toward the courtesan became the talk of the court.

Maria Theresa became concerned that this open war against du Barry would jeopardize the Franco-Austrian treaty. Count Mercy advised Marie Antoinette to talk to the king's mistress, but the dauphine held her ground. Obedience ultimately prevailed, however, and Maria Antoinette confessed to Mercy, "The Empress knows that I will always do what she wants me to do."[37] Finally, in 1772, Marie Antoinette condescended to speak a few words to Madame du Barry, saying simply, "There are a great many people at Versailles today."[38] Many years later, Louis-Auguste candidly recalled the difficulties with regard to du Barry. He noted that Marie Antoinette had arrived at Versailles "when she had barely emerged from childhood. My mother and grandmother were no more; and my aunts had not the same authority over her. Placed in the midst of a brilliant Court in close proximity to a woman whom intrigue had placed there, the dauphine had before her eyes a constant example of profligate display. What opinion was she not likely to conceive of her powers and rights, she who united in her own person so many attractions? To live in the society of the favourite was wholly unworthy of the dauphine."[39]

By contrast, Marie Antoinette had managed to charm King Louis XV. A connoisseur of attractive women first, and an anemic leader second, the king took an even greater liking to the dauphine after the arrival of the two ugly Savoyard brides for his other grandsons. When Marie Antoinette came to France, Louis XV had been king for fifty-five years. Near the end of his long reign, not long before Marie Antoinette came to Versailles, Louis XV was already old, "an isolated and mournful man, fatigued and silent. . . . He felt about him in the society he ruled, and within himself also, something moribund."[40] France during Louis XV's later years also "gave the impression of a great palace, old and in part ruined."[41] The king was better known for his profligate and sybaritic life, and for his association with his two famous mistresses, Madame de Pompadour and Madame du Barry, than for any achievement. Count Mercy wrote of France's troubles to Maria Theresa, saying that "it is almost impossible for your Majesty to form any adequate idea of the horrible confusion which reigns here in everything. The throne is degraded by the shamelessness and the unlimited power of the favourite [Madame du Barry], and by the unscrupulousness of her partisans. The nation breathes sedition in indecent writings, which do not even spare the person of the King; Versailles has become the abode of treachery, hatred, and revenge; everything is worked by intrigues and inspired by personal ambitions, and it seems as if the world had renounced even the semblance of uprightness. . . . I have represented to the dauphine that her only safeguard in these critical times is profound silence on matters and on men."[42] It was into this maelstrom that the teenage Marie Antoinette was thrown.

The exchange of letters between Maria Theresa and Marie Antoinette continued unabated. No news from Marie Antoinette was too trivial for the empress to hear, and no advice was too minor for Maria Theresa to impart. Marie Antoinette sometimes hurriedly dashed off letters to her mother before a courier departed in order that prying eyes might not read what she wrote. Maria Theresa, by contrast, was a tireless writer of letters to her children and thought nothing of composing pages of missives to her daughter in France. The empress must have been gratified when Marie Antoinette would write messages such as "Every day I am aware of how much my dear mother did to place me."[43] Maria Theresa's correspondence, however, though not devoid of maternal feeling, generally took on a nagging tone. One of her first letters to Marie Antoinette hints at this tone: "If one is to consider only the greatness of your position, you are the happiest of your sisters and all princesses. . . . As to the dauphin, I say nothing; you know how touchy I am on that point; the wife must be completely submissive to her husband and must have no business other than to please him and obey him. . . . I urge you, my dear daughter, to read my paper [i.e., the instructions] on the twenty-first of every month. I ask you to obey me on this point."[44] Other topics that generated admonishments were too little reading and improving the mind. Marie Antoinette's letter writing was also wanting, as her mother reminded her: "You seem to be doing nothing but amuse yourself—nothing solid or useful, only killing time by promenades and visits. I must tell you that the style of your letters is every day worse and more incorrect."[45] The empress also urged her daughter to wear corsets so as not to spoil her figure. In one letter she wrote: "I beg of you not to let yourself get careless; at your age it is unsuitable, and in your rank even more so: carelessness brings in its train uncleanness, negligence, and indifference in all other respects, and that would be your downfall. This is the reason why I bother you, for I cannot sufficiently warn you against the little failings that would let you slip into the faults wherein all the Royal family of France have fallen for long years."[46]

As the years passed, Maria Theresa's concerns about Marie Antoinette continued to grow. The empress urged Mercy to inform her always of Marie Antoinette's life, saying, "I am not satisfied with the Dauphine, but these things are difficult to remedy. I will pull a little on this cord again, but I shall touch it delicately. I know my children; preach to them too much and it spoils everything and does not correct them."[47] Marie Antoinette occasionally complained to Mercy of her mother's hectoring. One of the dauphine's early letters, however, showed a tender side to the relationship: "I cannot express how touched I am by the kindness Your Majesty has shown me, and I can swear to you that I have not received one of your dear letters without having the tears come to my eyes because I am separated from so kind and loving a mother."[48]

16

MOTHERLY ADVICE

*N*early a year after Marie Antoinette left Vienna, Maria Theresa received a portrait of her daughter. The empress was not pleased with what she saw. Maria Theresa perceived that Marie Antoinette had lost her youthful air. Clearly the dauphine's bedeviled life among people who constantly gossiped and intrigued was taking its toll. This made the empress all the more determined to send Marie Antoinette letters loaded with counsel. Count Mercy wrote to the empress of the effects of these letters on her daughter: "I observe that anything coming from your Majesty produces the greatest impression and continually occupies her mind."[1] "They say you neglect to single out and talk to distinguished persons," went one letter from mother to daughter. "Follow the advice of Mercy, who only thinks of your welfare, and mix yourself up with no party; if you could even ignore all of them it would be better."[2] Marie Antoinette tried to live up to her mother's standards and amend her ways, telling Maria Theresa, "I am in despair that you should believe it when people tell you that I do not speak to them; you must have very little confidence in me, to think that I should be so unreasonable as to amuse myself with five or six young people, and fail in attentions to those whom I should honour."[3]

As demanding a taskmaster as Maria Theresa was, her maternal side also shone through. In one letter, the empress told Marie Antoinette, "I have received your portrait in pastel: it is very like you and is my delight and the pleasure of all the family; it is in the cabinet where I work, and the picture [by Liotard] in my bedroom, where I work at night, so that I have you always before my eyes, as I have you always within my heart." Maria Theresa also added encouraging words: "I am always convinced of your success when you undertake anything, as *le bon Dieu* has given you charm, and a pretty figure, and you have goodness in addition, so that all hearts are yours whatever you do."[4] And in another message, Maria Theresa wrote: "This letter will arrive too late for your birthday, but you may be very sure that I have not forgotten it, that I thank God daily, praying that He will keep you such that you may save your soul and do good in the country where you are while making your family happy and furthering inasmuch as may in you, the glory of God and the welfare of man."[5]

Much as she hoped for the best from Marie Antoinette, Maria Theresa could never quite steer herself from worrying about "the lethargy into which she is sinking."[6] Hence, the hectoring tone of a letter to her daughter: "Do not think I am merely scolding with such energy; I see you sunk in a subjection from which you must be plucked as quickly as possible and by force. . . . I do not demand a total break with the company you frequent, God forbid! but that you tell them nothing, and learn to act for yourself. Too much compliance is degrading; you must play your own part, if you wish to be valued. If you do not, I foresee great trouble before you; nothing but mischief-making and plots, which will make your life unhappy. Believe the advice of a mother, who knows the world and idolises her children and desires only to pass her sad days in being useful to them."[7] Marie Antoinette wrote back, telling her "very dear mother" that "I especially want to follow the good advice you give me, my dear Mama."[8]

Maria Theresa's dead daughter-in-law Isabella of Parma understood the value attached to the empress's advice as well as her character. Of Maria Theresa, Isabella had noted, "The Empress has an exceptionally tender, clinging, sympathetic disposition. Those whom she loves, she loves in very truth. She would sacrifice herself for any member of her family, or even for her friends. . . . Through suffering she has learned to know life and the world. Her advice is therefore extremely helpful."[9]

Marie Antoinette was not the only one of Maria Theresa's daughters who received advice. If the dauphine thought that her mother sometimes singled her out, she needed only to have read one long letter Maria Theresa wrote to Mimi, which touched upon a myriad of topics:

> Every marital happiness consists of mutual trust and mutual kindness; passionate love vanishes quickly. Each must respect the other, and each must be useful to the other; each must feel true friendship for the other in order to be content in marriage, to bear the tribulations of this life, and to promote life's happiness. . . .
>
> What good fortune for him to find in you a loving wife at home,

a wife creating happiness for her husband, supporting him, comforting him, being useful to him, never presuming to afflict him, allowing him instead to come to her, being satisfied with his frequent visits, and finding herself happy when she can be occupied with him. If you do not realize this immediately, you will certainly suffer the consequences later on.

All marriages would be happy if people followed this advice. But everything depends on the wife, who should pursue the proper course, try to win the attention and trust of her husband, never abuse or boast of it. . . .

The less foolishness you display, the better it will be. That is another modern evil: it consists of a great emphasis upon spirit and the idea that people can play tricks on each other without impropriety. . . . Allow at your court no two-faced talk and no malicious backbiting. Make this clear immediately, so you will keep evil elements at a distance. At every opportunity show your eagerness to maintain virtue. . . .

Neglect none of your religious duties; in marriage prayer and God's help are even more necessary than in single life. Your spiritual lessons should occur regularly. I recommend very strongly that you be exact in this matter. Regularize your devotions as well as your moderate offerings according to your confessor's advice.[10]

Nothing better encapsulates Maria Theresa's motherly advice to Marie Antoinette than one of the messages she sent her daughter: "I hope that my constant repetitions do not bore you but convince you that I speak them because I want to see you happy and help you to avoid the pitfalls of youth."[11] Marie Antoinette never lost the chance to remind Maria Theresa that "I shall never be happy, my dear mother, without the knowledge that I have pleased you."[12] To Count Mercy, though, Marie Antoinette admitted: "I love the Empress, but I fear her even from a distance: even in writing I am never at ease with her."[13]

Maria Theresa was grateful to Count Mercy for his guardianship over Marie Antoinette and his ceaseless work on her behalf. "I see, with grief, the dangers that threaten my child," the empress once wrote to him, and "I put my trust in your discernment and zeal alone. Your task is, in truth, arduous, in view of the indifference and levity of my daughter (with a little obstinacy besides), who is accustomed to content herself with passing amusements, without reflection upon their consequences."[14]

In 1773, Maria Theresa could take comfort in signs that her daughter might be capturing the hearts of her future subjects. In June of that year, Louis-Auguste and Marie Antoinette paid an official visit to the French capital, Paris, where the dauphine created a sensation. At seventeen and a half years old, Marie Antoinette had grown into a graceful and attractive creature with a beautiful fair complexion and sparkling blue eyes. Thousands mobbed the two, even to the point of climbing trees, in order to catch a glimpse of the future of France. From the Tuileries Palace gardens, the Duc de Brissac, governor of Paris, told Marie Antoinette: "There you have two hundred thousand people who love you."[15]

Count Mercy eagerly reported to Maria Theresa the sensation caused by Marie Antoinette, saying, "Nothing was wanting; the public was seized with a sort of delirium for the Dauphine . . . [with] cries of 'How beautiful she is! How charming' "[16] Mercy's descriptions were echoed by an English naval officer who witnessed the royal entrée. He wrote of the "amazing crowd" calling out to the dauphine "in rapture, 'God bless your sweet face!' "[17]

Marie Antoinette could not contain her excitement in her letter to Maria Theresa, telling her mother it was a day "that I shall not forget all my life. . . . They received us with all the honours it is possible to imagine; but it was not this that touched me most; it was the tenderness and eagerness of the poor people who, in spite of the oppressive taxes with which they are crushed, were in transports of joy at seeing us. When we went to walk in the Tuileries there was so great a crowd that for three-quarters of an hour we stood there, powerless to advance or to retreat."[18] Marie Antoinette was "moved to tears"[19] by the reception. "I can't tell you, my dear mother, the transports of joy, of affection, that were shown to us despite all the burdens of these poor people. . . . How fortunate we are, given our rank, to have gained the love of a whole people with such ease," she wrote.[20]

Besides her triumphant appearance in Paris, the dauphine's kindness also made a positive impression. She had once given a thousand écus without fanfare to a fund for victims of a fire at the hospital Hôtel Dieu. Then there was the time she went to give her personal sympathy to a lady-in-waiting whose young son had died. It was unprecedented for a French royal to go far from court to pay a visit, but Marie Antoinette begged Louis XV for permission and received it.

Marie Antoinette also became closer to Louis-Auguste and told her mother excitedly: "I think I can confide to you, my dear Mama, and only to you, that my affairs have taken a very good turn since we arrived here [Versailles] and that I consider my marriage to be consummated; even if not to the degree that

I am pregnant."[21] The empress was beside herself with happiness: "The joy is incredibly great everywhere. What delight!"[22] In reality, some kind of intimacy had been reached by Marie Antoinette and Louis-Auguste, though not to the extent that the dauphine could become pregnant.

Maria Theresa concluded that, by this time, Marie Antoinette was old enough to receive political advice. The dauphine was touched by her mother's confidence, telling her: "I will do my best to contribute towards the preservation of good friendship and alliance; where should I be if there were a rupture between my two families?"[23] A part of the empress, though, still hesitated in getting Marie Antoinette too quickly involved in politics; she told Mercy: "I confess frankly to you that I do not wish my daughter to gain too decided an influence in affairs. I have learned, only too well, by my own experience, what a crushing burden is the government of a vast monarchy. Besides, I know the youth and levity of my daughter . . . [with] her little taste for application (and she really knows nothing), and this adds to my fear for her non-success in the government of a monarchy, so shattered as that of France is at present; and if my daughter could not sustain it, or the condition of this kingdom changed more and more for the worse, I would prefer that the people blame some minister and not my daughter, and that it should be another's fault."[24]

There was one crucial issue—political and personal—that mother and daughter wanted resolved. This was Marie Antoinette's lack of children. Her central role, after all, was to be the mother of an heir, and here she never hesitated to compare herself with others. When Marie Antoinette wrote to her mother about the stillborn birth to someone she knew, she added sadly, "But I would rather have even that, terrible as it is, than be as I am without hope of any children."[25] And when the dauphine learned that her sisters Maria Amalia and Maria Carolina were both awaiting the births of children, she lamented to her mother: "When shall I be able to say the like?"[26]

This nagging issue took on added urgency when, in May 1774, King Louis XV fell seriously ill with the dreaded smallpox, signaling the possible end of his long reign. Count Mercy told Maria Theresa that Marie Antoinette had bravely offered to make the sacrifice of staying with the dying king. But for their health's sake, Louis XV refused to see her or Louis-Auguste. Instead, the king allowed his daughters, physicians, and Madame du Barry to care for him. The king's final days were harrowing. Shortly before he died, Louis XV's body began to blacken and emit a putrid stench. He died on May 10, 1774, after a reign of nearly fifty-nine years. His festering body was placed in a lead coffin and rushed away for burial. Once they became aware of their accession, the new king and queen, in a flood of tears, fell on their knees and exclaimed, "O God, guide us, protect us, we are too young to govern."[27] The royal family and courtiers immediately left Versailles in order to avoid contamination. Over a dozen carriages took the royal family to Choisy. Already seventeen people who had had some kind of contact with Louis XV had died from smallpox. It became imperative that the new king and queen be removed from the danger zone.

From Choisy the eighteen-year-old Marie Antoinette wrote to her mother of her new position: "Although I was placed by Heaven at my birth in the rank I occupy, I cannot help admiring the arrangement of Providence that has chosen me, the last of your children, for the most beautiful Kingdom in the World. I feel more than ever what I owe to my August mother, who took all that trouble and pains to establish me so well."[28] Maria Theresa in turn told her daughter: "You are both very young: the burden is great: I am anxious, very anxious." And to her son Ferdinand, the empress wrote with a heavy heart, "I fear this is the last of your sister's peaceful happy days."[29] This foreboding was not an overreaction. After all, "thirty laborious years had taught [Maria Theresa] how burdensome is a crown, while during the same period as a mother she had learned the weaknesses and defects of her daughters."[30] Where the new Queen of France was concerned, "it was her instability, her lack of firm anchorage, her squandering of energies that were great but incessantly misapplied, which her mother took so much amiss."[31] Maria Theresa had indulged her children with a carefree childhood, but she had expected that, when duty called at adulthood, they would easily shed their disposition toward recklessness and giddiness. She, after all, had transformed herself from happy young bride and mother, unprepared for queenship, into a formidable leader who defended the Habsburg lands from being dismembered. Could she not expect the same kind of tenacity and responsibility from her offspring?

Marie Antoinette grasped the immense responsibility that befell the royal couple during Louis XVI's coronation at the cathedral at Rheims. Dating back hundreds of years, the solemn ceremony that saw Louis crowned king excluded Marie Antoinette, in accordance with ancient tradition when kings were not married. Near the high altar, Marie Antoinette watched her husband touch Charlemagne's sword, prostrate himself as litanies were sung, receive the scepter and ring signifying unity with the people, then have the gold crown of Charlemagne placed on his head. She was so moved that she told her mother, "I could no longer restrain myself; my tears flowed in spite of me, and the people liked this."[32]

Not long after Louis XVI became king, Marie Antoinette and Madame

Adelaide, one of the aunts (all of whom came down with smallpox but eventually recovered), jockeyed for the role of influential adviser. Both suggested candidates for Louis to appoint as his top ministers. Madame Adelaide promoted the Comte de Maurepas, who was seventy-three and had previously served Louis XV but had been disgraced when he incurred the wrath of Madame du Pompadour. Marie Antoinette pushed for the Duc de Choiseul. To the pious Louis XVI, only twenty at the time, there was not much to commend Choiseul. A friend of Voltaire, Choiseul had insisted on the expulsion of the Jesuits from France, an act that earned the aunts' disapproval and Louis XVI's disfavor. The queen lost this battle to Madame Adelaide when Louis XVI chose Maurepas as his chief minister. But overall, the aunts' domination began to wane. No longer appendages at Versailles, they now lived at Bellevue, Madame du Pompadour's former home, which was given to them by the new king.

With the aunts away from court, the new king and queen, now at the apex of the social ladder, were left to their own devices. King Louis XVI, who had increasingly come to view his wife with affection, began listening to Marie Antoinette's opinions and granting most of her requests. Though she did not exercise complete control over him, Louis did not dismiss her opinions. Count Mercy reported to Maria Theresa that "it is now proved that when she really wishes for anything it is hers."[33] But, Mercy cautioned mother and daughter alike that everything would be lost if Marie Antoinette were careless. "Her Majesty, who invariably listens to me . . . agrees with my arguments," he recounted to the empress, "but since dissipation always effaces the serious impressions, I only obtain results in particular cases, never anything systematic or consecutive."[34] The fact that Mercy confirmed Marie Antoinette's influence over the king was no great consolation to Maria Theresa, for she knew that unless her daughter applied herself and paid constant, careful attention to serious matters, little good would come of it. One of Marie Antoinette's letters confirmed her mother's suspicions when her daughter confessed: "I must admit my dissipation and disinclination for serious things. I wish and hope gradually to correct it."[35] Maria Theresa, however, continued to be wary of Marie Antoinette's future, telling Mercy that "I am more and more convinced that I am not mistaken about her whole character and her *penchant* for dissipation. I have noticed, that, despite her deference to your remonstrances, she none the less goes her own way when her wishes are involved. I place all my confidence in your zeal and wisdom, but I cannot conceal my fear that some day she may try to get rid of the Abbé Vermond on some plausible pretext in order to be relieved of an embarrassing observer."[36]

In the meantime, France continued to wallow in crisis. At King Louis XVI's accession, the country's fortunes were at a low ebb. Attempts were made to address the myriad of problems. Another important ministerial post, that of treasurer, went to Jacques Turgot. It was hoped that the able and honest Turgot might help turn the fortunes of France for the better. The 23 million subjects of the king were divided into three estates: the first consisting of the clergy (around 130,000); the second, the nobility (around 500,000); and the third, the commoners (approximately 97 percent of the total population). Unlike the third estate, the first two were exempt from taxation. The third estate was made up of bourgeoisie, or the middle class, and the peasants. Peasants composed the overwhelming majority of the third estate and also carried the heaviest tax burden. Though peasants might still be able to declare their affection for their king, they had no sympathy for those who collected the taxes. "Officialdom" thus became "the people's bugbear"; and it was officialdom's minions "who settled on them [peasants] like locusts devouring the work of their hands."[37] Drought and poor harvests aggravated the hunger and poverty of the peasants, who also had little sympathy for the nobles, absentee landlords who disliked and avoided the countryside. Those nobles who were not impoverished preferred to flee to Paris, where many of them indulged in a dissolute existence. The clergy too had problems. During Louis XV's reign, the nobility had profited from obtaining high Church offices, which allowed them to collect additional tithes and taxes. Some lived profligate lives that bred increasing resentment from the people and other clergy, particularly of the lower orders, against these insincere men of the cloth.

Madame de la Tour du Pin was an eyewitness to the impending revolution. She wrote of society just years before the conflagration, saying, "The rot started at the top and spread downward. Virtue in men and good conduct in women became the object of ridicule and were considered provincial."[38] La Tour du Pin bemoaned the nobility's "instances of every form of vice. Gaming, debauchery, immorality, irreligion, all were flaunted openly."[39]

The turmoil in French society and at court had been brewing for some time. Nothing had changed much since 1771, when the English politician Horace Walpole wrote from Paris, "The distress here is incredible, especially at Court. . . . You never saw a great nation in so disgraceful a position." Referring to the future Louis XVI, Walpole predicted then, "Their prospect is not better: it rests on an *imbécile,* both in mind and body."[40] Awkward and shortsighted, heavily set with a propensity to get his hands blackened from working at his clocks, locks, and forge, the new king had many drawbacks, but he was not an imbecile. Louis may have been poorly educated, but when a subject interested him, he applied himself to learning on his own all he could. He came to know English well, including grammar, and he excelled in geography. Louis XVI's aims for the French people upon his accession were certainly well-meaning. An English contemporary wrote of him, "Never did any prince manifest more rectitude of intention, greater probity, or a warmer desire to advance the felicity of his people."[41] Louis recognized that France was critically in need of changes and wanted to revive the country by introducing reforms. But the task would be huge. It demanded an adroit and strong king.

Marie Antoinette told her mother, in a letter tinged with seriousness and maturity, of her worries: "For the moment there is nothing but praise and admiration for the King, which he thoroughly deserves because he is so honest and so anxious to do good. But I am worried as to how long the enthusiasm of the French will last. From the little I understand of politics, it seems that things are very difficult at present, and that the late King has left the country where the people are so volatile and impatient that they want to have everything done at once. But the King will never be as weak as his grandfather, nor I hope will he ever have favourites."[42] Lord Stormont, the British ambassador to France, noted some hopeful characteristics in Louis XVI, saying, "The strongest and most decided feature in this King's character are a love of justice, a general desire of doing well, a passion for economy and an abhorrence of all the excesses of the last reign. . . . He is eternally repeating the word *economy, economy*."[43]

Unfortunately, despite the queen's support for her husband, she was unaccustomed and uninclined to economize in her own life. Moreover, as if to make up for her barrenness and her desire to break out from the unbearable etiquette and public scrutiny to which she was subjected, Marie Antoinette unwisely indulged in heady frivolity. And now that she was queen, she led a very public life at Versailles for a large part of the day, so much so, in fact, that "she could not make a gesture, take a step, utter a word without triggering a reaction in the attendants who never left her."[44] From morning until late in the day and often at night, eyes were trained on the queen, and etiquette demanded that she conform to protocol.

Even the simple event of dressing in the morning after waking, *"la grande toilette,"* was tightly scripted. One of the queen's ladies had to hand her the chemise she was to wear. If a princess was present, the princess was the one who had to hand the chemise to the queen. If there were two princesses of the royal family present, the senior-ranking was the one who was to hand the chemise, but the precious chemise could not be passed between the two women.

Instead, a lady of the chamber had to take the chemise from the lower-ranking princess and pass it on the higher-ranking princess. The tedious *grande toilette* gives a hint of what the queen had to endure in the gilded goldfish bowl that was Versailles. Next, Marie Antoinette was formally attired in an uncomfortable large hooped gown and train in front of the court. She was also inundated by visits from dignitaries, during which she had to remain attentive and preserve a doll-like countenance. Daily Mass was not kept private but was a court affair. Court dinners were ceremonial and often formal. These ceremonials—in many ways developed to keep the nobility preoccupied—continued while the country was coming unhinged.

Little wonder then that Marie Antoinette, feckless and gregarious by nature, yearned for escapes. The queen appeared at masked quadrilles and fancy dress balls, full of animated chatter. She created a lighthearted life among intimates in less formal settings, such as the Petit Trianon. Marie Antoinette adored the Petit Trianon, given to her by Louis XVI soon after his accession. Located on the grounds of Versailles, the Petit Trianon was a small, square-shaped château decorated on the outside with Corinthian columns. The new queen had an English garden created just outside and a mock temple, known as the Temple of Love, built for her amusement. Ever an enthusiast for music, Marie Antoinette added a theater, fancifully decorated in papier-mâché, where she could act in comic operas by the French librettist Michel-Jean Sedaine. It was in this theater that *The Marriage of Figaro* by Pierre de Beaumarchais was first put on before the royal family.

The queen also entertained her coterie of intimates at Versailles and the other royal palaces of Fontainebleau and Compiègne. Among them was her brother-in-law the Comte d'Artois. A libertine who thought little of paying the proper respects to his brother, Louis XVI, Artois liked to amuse Marie Antoinette by organizing horse races, then a novel amusement imported to France from England. Hence, often accompanied by Artois and the king's other brother and sister-in-law, the Comte and Comtesse de Provence (called Monsieur and Madame), the queen attended not just balls but also horse races, while her poor adopted country quickly descended toward a ruin similar to what her mother had forestalled in her realms. Wherever Marie Antoinette appeared, her unrestrained comportment astonished her countrymen, who expected more decorum from their queen. Count Mercy reported to Maria Theresa that crowds of people watched the royals, "but the Queen was not welcomed with the customary signs of joy and applause. . . . The public sees that the Queen is only thinking of amusements."[45] Already, ominous signs of Marie

Antoinette's unpopularity were appearing. For the present, though, the queen seemed almost oblivious. Instead, she enjoyed diversions with her favorites and lived a life among them buffered from reality.

Marie Antoinette's intimate circle of friends included the Princess de Guéméné, who encouraged the queen's growing appetite for gambling. Marie Antoinette attended parties at Guéméné's apartments in the Tuileries Palace. Soon, late nights during which Marie Antoinette and her friends danced and played fashionable games like *lansquenet* and *faro* for high stakes became a regular part of her life. Marie Antoinette's frenzied nightlife did nothing to improve her intimate marital relations. Unlike his frenetic wife, the king liked a regular routine, eschewed parties and gambling, and was in bed by eleven. Luckily for Marie Antoinette, Louis was patient with her and did not seek companionship as other kings of France had done before him by taking a mistress. Instead, he remained content with his hobbies of hunting and locksmithing.

Marie Antoinette's proclivities left her vulnerable to attacks from pamphleteers and gossipmongers. Her self-indulgent excesses reinforced their criticisms of her, making her less and less popular. Criticisms increased when Marie Antoinette embroiled herself with two close friends and their respective factions. Living in an "age of sentimental friendships, when women who had little to do would exchange long and soulful letters, addressing one another as 'Dearest Heart,' "[46] Marie Antoinette found two favorites who fell into this category. The first was Marie Thérèse de Savoie Carignan, known as the Princess de Lamballe, who came to Marie Antoinette's attention as the twenty-one-year-old widow of the great-grandson of King Louis XIV and his mistress Madame de Montespan. Sensitive and prone to swooning (which Maria Theresa thought were mere affectations), the Princess de Lamballe befriended Marie Antoinette, who in turn felt protective toward her close friend. Marie Antoinette's other confidante was Yolande de Polignac, wife of Comte Jules de Polignac. A brunette of middle height, attractive, with a wonderful complexion, like that of the queen, Comtesse de Polignac was not particularly intelligent or clever. Nevertheless, she possessed a certain charm, which made her a sympathetic creature to many who came into her orbit, including the queen. Even King Louis willingly went to Yolande de Polignac's soirees. Surrounded by interesting and lively people, Marie Antoinette eagerly became drawn to the de Polignac set and happily spent hours in Yolande's company.

Hungry for close companionship, Marie Antoinette clung to Princess de Lamballe and Comtesse de Polignac to the extent that their relationship inevitably invited false accusations about the degree of intimacy they shared.

Marie Antoinette also befriended an Englishwoman and allowed her into her inner circle. Georgiana, Duchess of Devonshire, was a leader of English society and married to one of the country's most influential aristocrats. When she went to Paris, she visited Marie Antoinette. The two discovered "they had much in common, not only in having married a position rather than a lover, but also in their relations with their mothers."[47]

In early 1774, Marie Antoinette befriended another noble who came to play an important part in her life. While attending an opera ball in Paris, incognito with a mask, she met the Swedish nobleman Count Axel Fersen, who was only two months older than she. They talked for a while until Marie Antoinette was recognized. They met several times more, but briefly and in very public settings. The wily Swedish ambassador had warned Fersen to watch himself in the queen's company. However prudent Fersen was, his repartee with the queen was sufficient to prompt individuals who disliked Marie Antoinette to start spying on the two. Again, the ambassador urged Fersen to keep his wits about him and to avoid getting entangled in "the bees' nest of Versailles."[48]

For Marie Antoinette's detractors and the growing numbers who sought revolution, Versailles epitomized all that was wrong with the nobility and the royal family. To them, the headquarters of the house of Bourbon was not a magnificent palace surrounded by beautiful manicured gardens, spectacular fountains, and an assortment of enchanting buildings. Instead, it was the home of Louis XVI's foreign consort, who frolicked and spent money to her heart's content while French peasants toiled endlessly to feed themselves during increasingly trying times. Only a glance at the elaborate wigs the queen began sporting was enough to prove that here was a woman who cared little for her less fortunate subjects. Her outlandish coiffures and headdresses known as *poufs* were proof of her dissipation. Designed by Madame Rose Bertin, the queen's milliner, and Monsieur Léonard, prominent hairdresser to the elite, these concoctions of powdered hair and assorted decorations grew to tremendous heights. What emerged was "an elaborate miniature still-life, intended either to express a feeling (*pouf au sentiment*) or to commemorate an event (*pouf à la circonstance*) of importance to the client."[49] No theme was too bizarre to create and wear. These astounding creations, aped by ladies of fashion, included cornucopias full of fruits, swimming ducks, landscapes, and even the British fleet on a stormy sea.

Because "they were explicitly designed to convey topical messages, Marie Antoinette's *poufs* [also] allowed her to play at politics and look fashionable at the same time."[50] Such was the case with the queen's *poufs* that celebrated her music teacher Gluck's opera *Iphigénie en Aulide*. His success in Paris just before Louis XV's death was thanks to Marie Antoinette's patronage despite Madame du Barry's interference. The *Iphigénie pouf* celebrated Gluck's success and Marie Antoinette's victory over du Barry. Empress Maria Theresa queried her daughter on these strange creations, writing incredulously: "They speak of hair-dressing a *coiffure* of thirty-six inches high from the roots of the hair, with feathers and ribbons above that again! You know my opinion, to follow fashion in moderation, never to excess. A young and pretty Queen has no need of such follies." In reply, Marie Antoinette admitted with defiance: "It is true I am rather taken up with dress; but as to feathers, every one wears them, and it would seem extraordinary if I did not."[51]

The queen's coiffures along with dresses, the gardens at Trianon, gambling, and horses (she had three hundred) were just some of the expenses that caused concern and consternation. Marie Antoinette also spent money on jewelry, such as 460,000 livres on pearl-shaped diamond earrings from the jeweler Böhmer. She also bought a pair of diamond bracelets from Böhmer at a cost of 250,000 livres. Close friends too were on the receiving end of Marie Antoinette's largesse, which did nothing but add to the criticisms against her. In 1775 the queen secured for Princess de Lamballe the position of superintendent of the queen's household. For the obligatory entertaining this entailed, the princess was granted 150,000 livres a year. Thanks to Comtesse de Polignac's close friendship with Marie Antoinette, the de Polignac family was also a beneficiary of the queen's patronage.

Though the king was fairly frugal in his personal life, he tolerated his wife's extravagance. She was stronger willed than he, and it was easier to accede to her wishes than call her to task. He also sincerely loved Marie Antoinette and could not bring himself to deny her anything. His guilt over his inability to father a child with his wife along with the malicious gossip that was hurled at Marie Antoinette for being barren made it even harder to say no to the queen's spending habits. When she approached Louis XVI about her debts, which amounted to over 487,000 livres, the king volunteered to pay them out of his own income, earning her sincere gratitude. Unfortunately, however, far from reining in her spending habits, Louis's lenience only encouraged the queen to continue the frivolities. Considering how indulgent her husband was with her, Marie Antoinette shocked her mother when she flippantly referred to the king as "the poor man" in a letter to a family friend. When Maria Theresa saw this, she was indignant, lamenting to Mercy: "I am cut to the heart. What a style! What a matter of thought! It confirms my dread; she is rushing, by great steps, to her ruin, and she will be fortunate if, in her fall, she retains even the virtue of her rank."[52]

In a moving letter to this wayward daughter, Maria Theresa poured out her disappointments and anxieties in the hope of shaking Marie Antoinette into action:

> All I see is intrigue . . . of a sort that a Pompadour or a Barry would have indulged in so as to play a great role, something which is utterly unfitting for a Queen, a great Princess of the House of Lorraine and Austria. . . . Your too early success and your entourage of flatterers have always made me fear for you. . . . Those excursions from pleasure to pleasure without the King and in the knowledge that he doesn't enjoy them and that he either accompanies you or leaves you free out of sheer good nature—all that caused me to mention in my letters my justified concern. . . .
>
> Your happiness can vanish all too fast, and you may be plunged, by your own doing, into the greatest calamities. That is the result of your terrible dissipation, which prevents your being assiduous about anything serious. What have you read? And, after that, you dare to opine on the greatest State matters, on the choice of ministers? What does the abbé do? And Mercy? It seems to me that you dislike them because instead of behaving like low flatterers, they want you to be happy and do not amuse you or take advantage of your weaknesses. You will realize all this one day, but it will be too late. I hope not to survive that dreadful time, and I pray to God that He end my days sooner, since I can no longer help you but cannot bear to lose or watch the sufferings of my dear child, whom I love dearly till my last breath.[53]

17

L'AUTRICHIENNE

*N*otwithstanding the growing public rage against her and the apprehensions of her mother and counselors, Marie Antoinette was not all dissipation, gambling, and frivolity. King Louis XVI found qualities in his wife so that he could remain attached to her and forgive her follies. Joseph II and Maria Theresa too were aware of how kind and charming Marie Antoinette could be. Count Mercy, who knew Marie Antoinette as well as anyone, remained devoted to her, always trying to mend the queen's wayward ways. Madame Campan, her lady-in-waiting, who observed the queen closely, recalled two valuable attributes that Marie Antoinette "possessed in a high degree—temperance and modesty."[1] There was a moderate side to Marie Antoinette. When it came to eating, the queen liked nothing better than nourishing herself simply on boiled or roasted chicken washed down with water, while breakfast was bread and coffee. Marie Antoinette was also modest in the extreme, bathing in a long flannel gown buttoned all the way to the neck. When she left the bath, a cloth was raised high between the queen and her attendants. But these qualities were known only to a few intimates and had little impact on an increasingly desperate population.

Tragically for Marie Antoinette, opinions had already been formed, and they were overwhelmingly negative. Most considered her a spendthrift whose loyalties were not to France but to Austria and her Habsburg relations. Though the queen had largely forgotten her German by this point and become more French than Austrian, they derisively referred to her as *l'Autrichienne* (the Austrian) and later Madame Deficit.

Perhaps the French people would have been more forgiving of Marie

Antoinette's frivolity if their own predicament had been less difficult. But this was not the case; by then starvation was chronic. Already in May 1775, riots had broken out because of hunger. Shops in Paris, especially bakeries, were plundered by furious mobs that seized everything they could. At the gates of Versailles, throngs covered in rags wailed about their hunger. Passersby on French roads were met by peasants with outstretched hands begging for food. Months later, a brutal winter descended on a country near bankruptcy, redoubling the suffering. For Marie Antoinette the heavy snow in the parks at Versailles was a signal not to despair for the French peasants but to go sledding wrapped in furs. Such outings did nothing to endear her to the people.

Meanwhile, in faraway America, Britain attempted to retain its American colonies. The conflict captured Europe's attention. France sided with the Americans. With revolution breaking out in the colonies, could such a fate be awaiting France? Increasing instability, including deteriorating relations between Louis XVI and Parliament, pointed in that direction. The king and his finance minister, Turgot, tried to initiate reforms that included abolition of the hated *corvée* (a forced labor tax), along with the introduction of taxes on the aristocracy. But Parliament rejected them. And so the kingdom continued to spiral toward chaos. Marie Antoinette had little significant influence on politics. Historically, French queens, such as Marie Leszczynska, Louis XV's wife, tended to remain aloof from politics. The French populace expected the same from their present queen. The Habsburgs, however, still expected Marie Antoinette to promote Austria's interests. Thus, on the one hand, Marie Antoinette was expected to refrain from politics, but on the other, she was expected to immerse herself in it. A political role was one for which she was not suited, at least not in the early part of Louis XVI's reign. As it turned out, the queen "did not really have the intelligence or, to be fair to her, the ambition, to do much more than to reward those whom she liked and punish those whom she disliked."[2]

In the meantime, Count Mercy attempted to strengthen ties between Louis and Marie Antoinette. Wanting the queen to have easy access to the king, Mercy convinced them to construct a connecting passage between their apartments. This way, the couple could meet for whatever reason without coming under the gaze of the court. Besides promoting intimate physical relations, Mercy hoped that these meetings would blossom into political discussions that would serve Austria's interests. But much as he cared for his wife and could forgive her extravagances, Louis XVI was careful to keep Marie Antoinette from interfering in politics early in his reign. He was determined that Austria would not have the upper hand in the Franco-Austrian alliance.

Though Maria Theresa would have liked to involve her daughter more in politics, her letters to Marie Antoinette, which continued to arrive with regularity, instead increasingly tried to disabuse the young queen of her profligate lifestyle. The empress cajoled, pleaded, and employed reason. The severity of some of these admonishments drove Marie Antoinette to become defensive: "My mother sees things but from the distance, she does not weigh them in regard to my position; and she judges me too harshly. But she is my mother, who loves me dearly; and when she speaks, I can only bow my head."[3] As the years passed, however, the daughter's reactions to her mother's remonstrance changed. No longer upset and remorseful, she began to dismiss them as inconsequential. When Maria Theresa rebuked Marie Antoinette about the prices she paid for her diamond bracelets ("this humiliating story of the diamonds!"), the queen simply noted, "So the tale of my bracelets has got to Vienna!"[4] By the end of 1776, the correspondence between mother and daughter had taken on a different tone. An almost nonchalant attitude pervaded Marie Antoinette's replies to her mother's reprimands. At one point, the daughter even forgot to send her good wishes in time for her mother's name day. This carelessness extended to her gambling habits. Mercy deplored the fact (and duly reported it to Maria Theresa) that Marie Antoinette did not cease playing *faro* and gambling in her rooms until three in the morning of November 1, All Saints' Day, a solemn day of remembrance.

Much as she found to criticize in Marie Antoinette, Maria Theresa never accused her daughter of being anything other than capricious and foolish. Cruel rumors about the queen spread through spiteful pamphlets reaching Vienna. The empress indignantly discounted the stories and libels concerning alleged sexual relationships with the Comtesse de Polignac or the Comte d'Artois. A mortified Maria Theresa told Count Mercy, "I would never have believed that such inveterate hate could be held in the hearts of the French against . . . the poor innocent Queen. . . . This is the love they bear to my daughter! Never have I seen anything so atrocious; and it fills my heart with the bitterest contempt for this nation without religion, without manners, and without feeling!"[5]

The obscene pamphlets concerning Marie Antoinette tended to contain untruths, yet one accusation hit home. This was the criticism of the queen's barrenness. When her sister-in-law, the Comtesse d'Artois, gave birth to two sons, the need for Marie Antoinette to produce children became even more urgent. Her main role, as mother of heirs to France, thus far was a complete failure, and this only added to the growing dislike of *l'Autrichienne.* To hide from her increasing unpopularity, the twenty-one-year-old Marie Antoinette immersed herself in more revelry. With little inclination to curb her expenses or behavior, she refused to assume a more serious approach to her role as queen. A worried Maria Theresa wrote to the Abbé de Vermond of how she was "very moved by the state of my daughter, who rushes, surrounded by base flatterers who urge her in their own interests, headlong to her undoing."[6]

Meanwhile, back in Vienna, life for Maria Theresa was increasingly enveloped in gloom. For when Marie Antoinette left the family fold, the light-heartedness of youth at Maria Theresa's court departed with her. The Hofburg and Schönbrunn palaces, once filled with the laughter of children, now seemed empty and dreary. Joseph's only child, the empress's granddaughter and namesake, Archduchess Maria Theresa, died at a young age. The two daughters who remained with the empress—the sickly Marianne, appointed an abbess, and Maria Elisabeth, permanently disfigured by smallpox—were dispirited, doing little to lift their mother's spirits. Maria Theresa herself, increasingly weighed down by age and ill health, still wore widow's weeds and spent as much as three hours a day on her knees in prayer. No doubt much of that time was spent praying about her wayward offspring. The empress had once confessed that "formerly my children were my joy, but now they cause me worry and sorrow."[7]

Maria Theresa's fractious relationship with Joseph II never improved; both were still obstinate toward each other. Joseph's continued enthusiasm for Enlightenment ideals, and what in his mother's eyes amounted to radicalism, made her compare him with her sworn enemy, Frederick the Great. She found her oldest son to be a " 'thoughtless imitator' of the King of Prussia, an 'intellectual coquette' like his hero.' "[8] Leopold, Maria Theresa's third son, remarked of his mother and brother: "When they are together, there is [*sic*] unbroken strife and constant arguments . . . even in the smallest affairs; they are never of the same opinion and fight with each other constantly over matters worth nothing."[9] The broken relationship with her son was one of Maria Theresa's greatest trials. Never did she wake in the morning "without feeling that the day might bring resentments and regrets; she never retired without being conscious of the disharmony which was disrupting her home. Whenever she and Joseph were temporarily drawn together during these unhappy years, it was by a family sorrow, or a national calamity."[10]

Also difficult were Joseph's relationships with most of his siblings, including Marie Antoinette. He reprimanded his sister in his letters and in 1777 visited her in Paris, traveling without the excessive trappings of an emperor. Marie Antoinette was apprehensive about this visit, fearing Joseph's disapproving lectures. Count Mercy concluded that the queen's intimate friends had also shaken her confidence in her brother. However, when Joseph II arrived in April, brother and sister shared a happy reunion, Joseph professing his admiration for Marie Antoinette's charm and attractiveness. The emperor also met with Louis XVI and observed that his brother-in-law was not an idiot but was well-meaning and suffered from indecisiveness. Joseph definitely preferred Louis over his brother Monsieur, whom the emperor disliked. In fact, Joseph II found much to dislike in Marie Antoinette's French relatives and friends. But of Louis, Joseph told Maria Theresa, "I like the King, and if needs be I will fight for him."[11] As for Marie Antoinette, Joseph cared very much for her but grieved over his sister's shortcomings. He told his mother that Marie Antoinette "had a clever understanding and good judgment." But "if she would only follow her intuitions and be less influenced by the gossip of people, she would be perfect."[12] Joseph too could see trouble ahead for his sister if she did not alter her ways. This predicament, coupled with the internal situation in France, alarmed him. Before he left Paris, Joseph gave Marie Antoinette a dire warning: "Believe me, this sort of thing cannot endure much longer. The Revolution will be terrible if you do not prevent it."[13]

During this time, Marie Antoinette and Louis XVI seemed destined never to have children. With so little in common, their opportunities for nearness decreased. Count Mercy noted the opposing personalities in 1777, saying that "he lives a life by routine; she, by caprice. He is bent by every force; she resents even the shadow of domination."[14] But Joseph's visit did much good in getting Marie Antoinette to pay more careful attention to the king. Husband and wife became closer, and by August, the queen wrote to her mother that the marriage had at last been fully consummated. Now there was hope that a new life would stir within her. By the middle of 1778, the queen knew she was pregnant. Louis XVI's brothers were unhappy with this news, for now their chances of succeeding Louis on the French throne diminished. Marie Antoinette was well aware of the ambitions harbored by her brothers-in-law. They were even the source of some of the biting gossip whispered about the queen, but she continued to act civilly to them and their wives.

While she awaited the birth of her child, Marie Antoinette lived a far more sedate life than usual. She became more serious, eschewing gambling and late nights in favor of conversation and music. The pregnancy spurred King Louis to treat his wife with even greater kindness, inciting in her a new affinity with her husband. Though she noted Louis's "extreme weakness" and "lack of confidence in himself,"[15] the queen understood that her husband tried to do his best. Her pregnancy also encouraged the king's ministers to begin deferring to the queen. Back in Vienna, Maria Theresa, understandably thrilled with the news of Marie Antoinette's pregnancy, worried about her daughter and unborn grandchild. The empress confessed to Count Mercy that, had he not been by Marie Antoinette's side, she would have been much more troubled.

At this time, the empress was consumed by a new war, news of which triggered tears of concern from Marie Antoinette. If Maria Theresa had hoped that the partition of Poland was the last international crisis she would have to deal with, she was mistaken. When in December 1777, Elector Maximilian Joseph of Bavaria died leaving no heirs, a new war broke out, sparked by the greed of other German princes. Joseph II was among those who coveted more territory at Bavaria's expense. By this time, Maria Theresa had a decided distaste for political intrigue. Fighting to defend her rightful claims—such as in the War of the Austrian Succession early in her reign—was one thing, but she opposed the latest schemes. She pointedly told Joseph that she refused to take up arms. He ignored her. Her son sent troops to occupy Lower Bavaria, provoking Frederick the Great to order Joseph to withdraw. Maria Theresa, alert as ever, implored her son to wake up to the fact that Austria was not in a good position to fight. Whereas Prussia had Russia as an ally, Austria had only France, and France was in no position to be helpful; it had a multitude of internal problems and was enmeshed with the revolution of the American colonies in the New World while fighting Britain. Thus did Joseph's Bavarian adventure appear in Maria Theresa's eyes to be a recipe for disaster. Her son, though, continued to ignore his mother. When Joseph left for Moravia to join his army, Maria Theresa was desolate. When she heard from him of the dire predicament they were in, she took matters into her own hands and wrote to Frederick the Great without telling her son beforehand. This well-meaning move infuriated the humiliated Joseph, who wrote to his mother: "You have crushed me utterly. Nothing would give me greater pleasure than to learn that the answer you receive from the King of Prussia has frustrated your efforts."[16]

Though neither side won decisive battles, the conflict that became known as the War of the Bavarian Succession ended in a Prussian victory. In the Treaty of Teschen of 1779, which ended the war, Austria received a small piece of territory but in the end had to renounce rights to the Bavarian succession in perpetuity. The Prussians' victory meant that their German state was in the ascendant. The march toward the creation of the German Empire in 1871 at Versailles had solidified. In that palace, presently home to Marie Antoinette, would rise an empire over which Queen Victoria's daughter Vicky would reign ever so briefly as empress-consort.

The result of the War of the Bavarian Succession prompted Maria Theresa to fear for the future. She understood that the rise of Prussia on the world stage might well lead to the demise of the Habsburg dynasty. "I am desperate," the empress wrote to her son Ferdinand. "I am now weakened by my age and by my appalling destiny, and my body has no resistance left. I can master my soul with the help of my Faith, but my power to act has passed completely."[17]

Amid the gloom of war, Maria Theresa did receive one piece of very good news. On December 20, 1778, Queen Marie Antoinette at last became a mother. She gave birth to a girl, named Marie-Thérèse Charlotte, in honor of the child's maternal grandmother. The birth had been an ordeal and a very public one. Rooms adjoining the queen's were packed with curious spectators, including courtiers and commoners alike. Pandemonium broke out in the birthing room. Lack of air nearly suffocated Marie Antoinette. Louis, seeing his wife's life in danger, forced one of the windows open, allowing her to breathe. The king's prompt action most likely saved the queen's life. Though a boy would have certainly been welcomed with greater jubilation, Louis XVI and Marie Antoinette were nevertheless very attached to their daughter. When the queen first took the baby in her arms, she murmured: "Poor little thing, you were not wanted; but you will be my very own the more for that; a son would have belonged to the State."[18]

Marie Antoinette could now give more thought to the manner in which she would rear her offspring. She was determined that they be raised with fewer formalities than royal children of France had been in the past. The old regimen, after all, had done nothing to help her husband or his aunts. Instead, Marie Antoinette proposed an almost radical change that greatly curtailed the trappings of royalty. Madame Campan recalled in her memoirs that "the queen often spoke of her mother, and with profound respect. . . . [Maria Theresa], who inspired awe by her great qualities, taught the archduchesses to fear and respect rather than to love her; at least I observed it in the queen's feelings towards her august mother. She therefore never desired to place between her own children and herself, that distance which had existed in the imperial family."[19] When Maria Theresa heard of her daughter's plans to raise her children simply, she expressed her misgivings, saying that "all luxury, effeminacy, and exaggerated service" should definitely be banished, but striking out all etiquette for children of rank was unwise. "The present gospel according to Rousseau," wrote the empress, "that renders people boors by excess of liberty, does not please me at all; and I can see no good in it, but just the opposite."[20]

The birth of a child to the king and queen brought rejoicing in France, but the country at this time, like Austria, was at war. Its support for the Americans in their revolt against England exacerbated France's financial problems, interrupting trade and increasing hardship. In Paris, the price of bread continued to rise. Discontent among the masses grew. At Versailles, all was not well either. Jealousy was rife. The queen made her favorite, the Comtesse de Polignac, governess to Marie-Thérèse (known as Madame Royale). The Comte de Polignac was created a duke and made director-general of *postes*. Their favored status was cemented by the granting of a very large dowry of 800,000 livres to the Polignacs' daughter. Courtiers resented the increasing importance of the Polignac family to the queen. Some of France's most important families bore grudges against Marie Antoinette for ignoring them and preferring the company of the Polignacs and their coterie. A member of one of these established families was Cardinal Prince Louis de Rohan. He had been an envoy to Vienna, where Maria Theresa found much to despise in him. The dissolute de Rohan, who was no credit to the Church with his womanizing, had given Marie Antoinette upon her arrival in the country years ago an effusive welcome. But Marie Antoinette, like her mother, who had once described de Rohan as "a dreadful type . . . without morals,"[21] disliked the cardinal prince. Marie Antoinette's favoritism for the Polignacs also put her on a collision course with de Rohan that would end in disaster for the queen.

By 1780, Maria Theresa's health was declining rapidly. Dropsy left her inclined to stoutness, which made walking a chore. Asthma challenged her breathing, and her heart was weak. She could no longer descend to visit Francis's vault in the Capuchin Church on her own. Instead, the empress had to be lowered gingerly in a chair with ropes. Maria Theresa thought long and hard about her life and what awaited her in the world beyond. She wrote to a confidante: "It often comforts me to know that the years . . . that are gone will not return, and that every moment brings me closer to death. However, I tremble at the thought of the horrible account I will have to render." In composing a list of "all my frailties and the sins I committed from ignorance and then put out of my mind," Maria Theresa also accused herself " 'before God' of having waged 'war out of pride.' "[22]

Maria Theresa fell ill in November 1780, her lungs becoming congested. Despite pain and discomfort, her work ethic never left her, and she diligently read and signed official papers. But her greatest energy was reserved for preparing her soul for the final journey. The empress knew that she was dying and set out to meet her Maker. She made her confession, then received the Last Rites in the presence of her children who were nearby. As for the children who were absent from her deathbed, the empress blessed them, having raised her hand toward Heaven and named each one. When it was her youngest daughter's turn to receive a blessing, Maria Theresa had paused, "and almost shouted the last name: 'Marie Antoinette, Queen of France!' And she had burst into sobs."[23] The empress knew her death was near, telling Joseph, "God has asked for my life. I feel it."[24] To her crying attendants, the empress gave reassuring words: "You are all so afraid. I do not fear death in the least. For fifteen years [since Francis's death] I have put my trust in Him."[25] She bade her disconsolate children who were present farewell and refused Joseph's suggestion that she sleep. "I do not want to be caught by death unawares," Maria Theresa declared. "I wish to see it approach."[26] At her dying breath, Joseph asked his mother, "Where would Your Majesty like to go?" and raising her eyes toward Heaven, she replied, "To Thou above, I come." And at that Empress Maria Theresa breathed her last on the evening of November 29, 1780, after a reign of forty years. The empress was buried next to her beloved Francis in the Capuchin Church in Vienna. After the funeral, Joseph, who had dueled so long with his mother, wrote to his brother Leopold: "I am so overwhelmed by the horrible ceremony that I can only send you a single word. This is the most *cruel* experience imaginable."[27]

One of the empress's advisers, who had come to admire her, wrote of the empress after her death: "When Maria Theresa ascended the throne, externally Austria was without influence, without honor; internally without courage, without stability; its talents without encouragement, without emulation. . . . At her death she relinquished to her successors a monarchy improved in the essential parts of internal administration, prepared for additional reforms, reestablished in the foremost rank of the European system." One historian has concluded that "in its own right it [Maria Theresa's reign] was the most important in Habsburg history."[28] The empress made her mark, having kept the vast Habsburg domains largely intact after rapacious attacks and introduced reforms that touched her subjects' lives in many respects. As the "greatest moderniser in the history of her dynasty,"[29] she earned her place in history as a true achiever.

As for the tumultuous era in which she lived, Maria Theresa "never succumbed to [the Enlightenment]. . . . Her enlightenment was contained within the limits of her piety; she was bound by the persisting spirit of the Counter-Reformation. Ambitious and possessed of the strongest self-conviction, she yet was not consumed by the spirit of adventure and power as was Catherine [the Great of Russia]. No monarch of her age had such royal bearing or such devotion to her people [as Maria Theresa of Austria]."[30] And when compared with other female monarchs, "among the great queens of history Elizabeth [I] of

England is probably the most famous; Victoria, the most beloved; Catherine [the Great] of Russia, the most brilliant; but for courage, intellect, and sincerity, none surpassed the great Maria Theresa of Austria; while as wife and mother her record is scarcely approached by any other queen."[31]

Eight days after her mother's death, Marie Antoinette received the news. To her brother Joseph II, she wrote: "Crushed by the most dreadful misfortune, I cannot stop crying."[32]

18

THE GUILLOTINE AWAITS

*E*mpress Maria Theresa did not live to see her youngest daughter give birth to the longed for French heir, Louis-Joseph, in 1781. Louis-Joseph's birth was a triumphant moment for Marie Antoinette, who described it as the "happiest and most important event" in her life.[1] The king was moved to tears at the arrival of his son, while all at Versailles broke out in celebration. The dynasty was secured with the birth of another son, Louis-Charles, Duke of Normandy, in 1785; he was followed by Sophie Hélène Béatrice in 1786. Motherhood undoubtedly contributed to a new attitude emerging from the queen. At thirty years old, Marie Antoinette reached a turning point, exhibiting a greater sense of maturity.

She now preferred quieter domesticity, escaping more frequently to the Petit Trianon, where she could avoid the main palace's formality. Gone were her outrageous hairstyles and elaborate fashions. The queen replaced them with unfussy, free-flowing muslin dresses tied at the waist with a wide sash, her hair topped by subdued straw hats. The celebrated painter Élisabeth Vigée-Lebrun painted the queen wearing this favored ensemble and showed the painting in Paris. When the portrait was exhibited to the public, "the understated charms of this unqueenly ensemble, were, however, largely wasted on the crowds, at the Paris Salon who fulminated that the consort had finally gone too far. With this latest affront to the dignity and sanctity of the throne, she had proven definitely what her other fashion follies already implied: Marie Antoinette deserved neither her special standing nor her subjects' respect. . . . The Queen [who] 'dressed up like a serving-maid, wearing a chamber-maid's dust-cloth,' brought the hecklers and critics out in force."[2]

Marie Antoinette gave her enemies more to criticize when she had the Queen's Hamlet built on the grounds near the Petit Trianon. Designed after Normandy farm cottages, the Hamlet gave her a place to pretend at being a milkmaid. The queen's efforts could not help but come off as irreverent considering the hardship, even famine, of the French peasants. Hence, as with nearly everything else she did, Marie Antoinette was widely vilified for building her mock idyll. The queen could do nothing right in her subjects' eyes. The cosmopolitan and urbane Prince de Ligne, who was a close friend of Marie Antoinette, alluded to this, saying that "she could not put a foot right. If she laughed, she was called *moquese*. If she was welcoming to foreigners, it was a sign that she hated the French. If she had dinner with Mme de Polignac in her apartment, she was *familière*. If she gave parties at the Petit Trianon, she was *bourgeoise*. If she walked on summer nights with her sisters-in-law on the terrace at Versailles, she was *suspecte*. When she stopped being frivolous, she was accused of being *intrigante*."[3]

One who was dismayed at the queen's widespread unpopularity was Count Axel Fersen. He had fought in America and returned to France in 1783. The queen was overjoyed to see a favored friend after several years' absence. Fersen's affection for Marie Antoinette had never left him; it had even grown to the point where he could not bear to be apart from her. The queen too felt a strong bond of affection for the Swedish count. Speculation abounded as to the nature of their relationship. Some have believed that Marie Antoinette, for all her frivolity, was essentially a virtuous woman, even sexually frigid, while others have been convinced that the queen and Fersen were lovers. Whatever the exact nature of their relationship, there is no doubt of Fersen's loyalty, especially during the difficult years that lay ahead for the monarchy.

Marie Antoinette's missteps, whether real or perceived, took place amid a backdrop of continuing difficulties. The peasants, continuing to bear the burden of heavy taxation, were under increasing hardship. Meanwhile, the king and his ministers doggedly sought ways of mitigating the kingdom's financial straits. In 1776, Louis XVI dismissed Turgot as finance minister, replacing him with Jacques Necker. Under Louis's direction, Necker implemented reforms such as forcing the court to cut its expenditures by reducing some sixteen hundred "idlers" of the king's household. Critics of the royal family ignored such economies. Instead, they focused on what they perceived to be Louis XVI's and Marie Antoinette's wrongs. When the king purchased the palace of St.-Cloud near Paris (during a time of large-scale repairs at Versailles) and gave it to his wife, many thought that the funds for its purchase came from the public purse. In reality, Louis used his own money. The fact that St.-Cloud was the queen's property also infuriated the people. When Marie Antoinette went to Paris for celebrations of the birth of her second son, she met with stony silence. The perplexed queen returned to her husband, crying, "Why should they hate me? What have I ever done to them?"[4]

Marie Antoinette wanted St.-Cloud not for frivolous reasons but for her children, and in particular the dauphin, whom she thought could benefit from the healthier air. Few people knew or cared that Marie Antoinette suffered privately because of the terrible health of Louis-Joseph, who courageously bore tuberculosis of the spine. His mother could only watch helplessly as his body became increasingly malformed. More unhappiness beset the queen when in 1787 Princess Sophie died a month before her first birthday. She still grieved over the child's death months later. When asked why, Marie Antoinette answered, "She might have been a friend!"[5]

Since the arrival of her children, Marie Antoinette also took religion more seriously. She devoted time to daily prayers and regularly confessed her sins. But this was not widely known to the French public. Instead, people continued to hold fast to the malicious gossip about their queen. In their eyes, Marie Antoinette was an immoral spendthrift, a foreigner with no sympathy for France and too much influence over the king: in sum, everything they did not want in a queen.

Whatever many may have thought of Marie Antoinette's shortcomings, they could not (had they been aware of it) have faulted her for her generosity. She and the king had given money freely to the poor from their own income, especially during times of hardship, such as in 1784, when Louis XVI donated 3 million francs while Marie Antoinette gave 1 million. A few years later King Louis again tried to alleviate the plight of the poor after droughts and hailstorms destroyed crops, sending the price of bread skyrocketing. By this point, however, any good the king and queen did was ignored, or its effect dissipated quickly.

The passage of time did not bring Marie Antoinette closer to the people. Her popularity continued to plummet. In 1785 an unsavory incident that came to be known as the Diamond Necklace Affair irretrievably destroyed the queen's reputation. The powerful Cardinal Prince de Rohan thought he had found a way of ingratiating himself with Marie Antoinette. Forged letters fooled de Rohan into believing that the Comtesse de Lamotte, his onetime mistress, had earned the queen's confidence. The cardinal prince, "whose boundless conceit was matched only by his fatuity,"[6] was so determined to gain Marie Antoinette's approval that he fell for Lamotte's plans to get him to purchase, on the queen's behalf, a diamond necklace of 2,800 carats being offered by the court jewelers. The jewelers surrendered the necklace to de Rohan, who promised them they would be paid. It was too costly for the queen to have purchased the necklace herself without causing a public outcry. De Rohan gave the necklace to Lamotte, whose husband then spirited the prized diamonds to London. When the jewelers demanded to be paid, the theft was uncovered. Marie Antoinette learned of the incident after the theft became known. After being confronted by the king, the cardinal was arrested in dramatic fashion. He was tried, as was Lamotte. The duped de Rohan was acquitted, but Lamotte was found guilty. She escaped to London. From there, she wrote vicious lies about the queen, claiming, among other things, that Marie Antoinette and de Rohan were lovers.

Delighted gossipmongers and pamphleteers eagerly gobbled up and disseminated the lies. The affair "helped to ruin the image of the Royal Family, and the privileged position of the unreformed Catholic Church was deeply resented. Such factors combined with the nature of a country whose philosophers were particularly attracted by the new age of reason and the appeal of science . . . [made] the coming Revolution . . . [an] intensely anti-monarchical and anti-clerical one."[7] That Marie Antoinette was blameless in the affair mattered not to her subjects. They easily believed the malicious lies from Lamotte and other enemies of the queen. Madame Campan recalled that "the Queen's grief was extreme" during this time. In despair, Marie Antoinette told her, "Come and lament for your Queen, insulted, and sacrificed by cabal and injustice."[8] The only good that came out of the affair was that it brought Louis and Marie Antoinette closer, but the damage to the queen's reputation was severe.

After the Diamond Necklace Affair, calumnies against Marie Antoinette burgeoned. Every morning, from the police lieutenant of Paris, the queen requested to hear the latest libels against her. When he paused because of the hurtful words, the queen insisted: "Go on, Monsieur, do not let my tears stop you. It is only natural I should feel the evil that is spoken of me and the false opinion formed of me by a people I hoped would love me and for whose happiness the King and I are ready to sacrifice everything."[9]

Just as Maria Theresa had feared, Marie Antoinette's future became increasingly bleak. Crisis after crisis shook France's stability and boded ill for the monarchy. In order to help sort out the kingdom's financial situation, Charles Alexandre de Calonne, who succeeded Necker as finance minister, also urged radical reforms. Similar to Turgot's measures, they promoted a land tax that spared no one, including the nobility and clergy. To gain support, Calonne convinced Louis XVI to convene an Assembly of Notables at Versailles in 1787.

The notables, though, did not want to pay taxes; they wanted a share of the monarchy's power. The assembly degenerated into accusations between Calonne and the notables. Louis dismissed Calonne and replaced him with Étienne Charles de Loménie de Brienne, the Archbishop of Toulouse, who enjoyed the queen's support. The notables still balked at Brienne's tax, which was essentially similar to the one Calonne proposed. The royal family too tried to do their bit, with the king dismissing half the staff of his household, cutting pensions, and selling some of the royal properties. But these measures were not enough. The treasury was still bankrupt.

Loménie de Brienne's appointment marked a significant stage in Marie Antoinette's life. King Louis, overburdened by the troubles besetting his country, suffered from depression and withdrew from others, leaning heavily on his wife. The queen, at last, became immersed in politics. Now her "ill-considered excursions into politics of the previous decade . . . bore bitter fruit. She found herself isolated and alone at the apex of power, as the winds of unrest began to blow."[10] Marie Antoinette might have weathered her new responsibilities better had she been popular, but she was not. Count Fersen summed up her predicament: "The Queen is quite universally detested. Every evil is attributed to her and she is given no credit for anything good. . . . The King is weak and suspicious; the only person he trusts is the Queen, and they say she does everything."[11] Marie Antoinette was under no illusions regarding her unpopularity and the state of the country. During this time the queen admitted that "everything is going badly, and I realize that finances are in a terrible state and, what's more, I am accused of ruining the kingdom, to my brother's advantage. It's an incredible falsehood."[12]

Like Catherine of Aragon, Marie Antoinette was a foreign-born queen living in an adopted country, and like Catherine's, her life was the worse for it. But there were also marked differences. Catherine of Aragon was always loved by the English people and remained popular, but Henry VIII came to shun her. Marie Antoinette, by contrast, may have been detested by the French people, but she had in Louis XVI a devoted and faithful husband. Her problem lay in the fact that the monarchy was deeply unpopular with the people. Her failure to act with diligent care in exercising her role as queen, combined with Louis XVI's inability to bring about much needed reforms, sealed their fate. A revolution was set to explode.

More instability rocked the government when catastrophic crop destruction from a hailstorm combined with the stock market crash forced Loménie de Brienne to resign in 1788. Marie Antoinette wanted the minister to stay but acknowledged that the more popular Necker had to return to office. The queen feared for the future and was troubled by her political responsibilities and the return of Necker. She told Count Mercy: "I tremble . . . that it is I who am bringing him back. My destiny is to bring misfortune; and if he fails . . . or undermines the royal authority, they will only hate me more."[13] Marie Antoinette proved prescient in that Necker "did almost nothing to equip the crown with a coherent policy towards the Estates [General] once it had been called."[14]

The Estates General consisted of representatives from the realm's three estates: the clergy, nobility, and the majority of the population. They had not convened since 1614, but in response to escalating mayhem, Louis XVI convened them now. Delegates met at Versailles in May 1789. Marie Antoinette's unpopularity was evident in the ceremonies marking the convocation. Applause for her was muted at most while the queen had to sit through a bishop's sermon in which he scolded her for her past extravagance. A courtier noted at the time that "never has there been a queen of France less loved and yet she cannot be reproached for a single wicked deed. We are certainly unfair towards her and much too hard in judging what are only faults of frivolity and thoughtlessness."[15]

While the Estates General met at Versailles, Marie Antoinette put on a brave face. It was a difficult task because of the private heartache she suffered as she watched her eldest son, the seven-year-old dauphin, dying slowly and painfully of tuberculosis. Doctors could do nothing for the prince, who was described by his mother as "a good child, tender and loving."[16] The dauphin faced his ordeal bravely, and when he died, on June 4, 1789, his parents were grief-stricken. So stunned was Marie Antoinette that her hair turned gray. Forbidden by etiquette to attend the funeral, Louis and Marie Antoinette kept vigil all night by their dead son's body. The grieving parents left Versailles for a week to mourn, and while they were away the Third Estate declared themselves the National Assembly. They invited members of the other estates to join but proceeded to undertake the nation's governance without them.

Events now rapidly deteriorated. A seething discontent pervaded Paris and France. The masses clamored for more rights, while many nobles voiced their opposition to the king. Louis XIV and XV had reined in the nobility, but now numerous nobles were emboldened. They attacked the monarchy in a quest to blame it for the nation's ills and to overturn the status quo. Even within the royal family, the king and queen could not contain the hostility of vociferous, contemptuous relatives. These enemies included the Duc d'Orléans, who was the people's favorite, and, more galling, the king's brother and sister-in-law the

Comte and Comtesse de Provence. Even the Polignacs, who owed so much to the queen's friendship, sympathized with the king's other brother, the Comte d'Artois, who at this time had his differences with Marie Antoinette over Calonne.

To Yolande de Polignac, Marie Antoinette wrote about her travails, saying of her life that "it is too heavy a burden and if my heart were not entirely bound up with my husband, my children, and my friends, I would as soon give in."[17] Life, though, was to become even more burdensome, much more than Marie Antoinette could have ever imagined.

On July 11, King Louis dismissed Necker, creating an uproar. Crowds in Paris listened attentively to orators who inflamed them with fiery speeches. On July 14, a mob stormed the Bastille, finding only seven prisoners. The Bastille was an old fortress converted to a state prison where for many years prisoners were sent on the arbitrary orders of the king. It had become the hated symbol of monarchical autocracy. Its fall, therefore, was rife with symbolism. At the time the Bastille fell, conditions for prisoners there had improved, but it was attacked because of what it stood for, and because the mob was intent on acquiring munitions stored there. The assault on the Bastille also sheds light on another ominous sign that the monarchy was in grave danger: the army refused to contain the mobs and began, instead, to fraternize with the revolutionaries. When the Duc de la Rochefoucauld-Liancourt told the king of the Bastille's fall, Louis exclaimed, "Why this is a revolt!" to which the duke replied, "No Sire, it is a revolution."[18] Within days, the Comte d'Artois and his two sons fled France, as did numerous aristocrats, among them the Polignacs. Then in August came the publication of the Declaration of the Rights of Man, which has been labeled "the death certificate of the *Ancien Régime*."[19]

Meanwhile, the angry citizens of Paris demanded that King Louis leave Versailles for the capital. He agreed, despite Marie Antoinette's pleas that he should stay. Once the decision was made, the couple prayed; Louis wrote his will, then left. The queen was consumed with anxiety the whole time Louis was gone, certain that her husband would be murdered. At the first sign that the king's life was in danger, Marie Antoinette was prepared to leave for Paris to plead for his life before the National Assembly. King Louis, however, returned that evening to a besieged Versailles nearly empty of courtiers. Awaiting him were his wife and children. To Marie Antoinette's horror, the humiliated king returned wearing the revolutionary tricolor cockade. She may have flinched at the sight but did not berate him, for "it was not in her nature to denigrate their father in front of the children who adored him. He was a good, weak man, whose religion meant more to him than his crown, and now all he could find to say was, 'Thank God there was no bloodshed.' "[20] But blood was soon shed, in the form of indiscriminate murders of anyone perceived to be an enemy of the revolution. In fact, the summer of 1789 was marked by the "murderously festive action of crowd violence—the evident satisfaction the crowd took from stringing up arbitrarily identified malefactors from the *réverbères* (street lamps) and from parading heads from pikes."[21]

At Versailles, Marie Antoinette tried to continue with some semblance of normalcy. She appointed a forty-year-old widow, Madame de Tourzel, as governess to the royal children. After the deaths of two of her children, Marie Antoinette was left with ten-year-old Marie-Thérèse and four-and-half-year-old Louis-Charles, now the dauphin. Marie-Thérèse had a streak of haughtiness and had not been as close to her mother as Marie Antoinette would have wished, but in the midst of adversity the family had become close. Keeping them together became one of Marie Antoinette's primary goals.

The revolution, which Maria Theresa had feared and Joseph II warned of, now spiraled out of control. On October 5, 1789, a crowd of five thousand, mostly armed women, marched to Versailles. The Duc d'Orléans's son Louis-Philippe recalled that the women "were using the most fearful language about all the enemies of the Revolution, especially the Queen."[22] The mob screamed, "Bread! Bread!" and more ominously about Marie Antoinette: "We'll cut off her head . . . rip her heart out . . . fry her liver . . . make her guts into ribbons."[23] The Marquis de Lafayette, who had fought in the American Revolution, arrived at Versailles with the National Guard and offered to protect the royal family. Within hours, a band of armed women attacked the queen's bodyguards, decapitating two of them. Marie Antoinette barely escaped the vicious mob as she ran barefoot to the king's apartment, frantically banging on the door to be let in. The king and queen heard the terrifying sound of axes hacking against the doors.

They were close to being murdered when guards came to their rescue. With the crowds screaming "To Paris! To Paris!" Lafayette asked the queen about her intentions. Marie Antoinette told him, "I know the fate that awaits me but my duty is to die at the feet of the King and in the arms of my children."[24] The royal family had no choice but to acquiesce to the mob's demands. They were compelled to leave Versailles that day, never to return, and headed for Paris in a gruesome procession that lasted for seven interminable hours. Hundreds of incensed market women, waving the severed heads of the guardsmen killed earlier, proclaimed that they were bringing back the "baker, the baker's wife, and the baker's boy." Throughout this journey, Marie Antoinette kept calm, eliciting the admiration of a number of witnesses. One who watched her recalled: "I saw the Queen maintaining the most courageous tranquility of mind, an inexpressible air of nobility and dignity and my eyes filled with tears of admiration and pain."[25] When the royal family arrived at the Hôtel de Ville, Marie Antoinette acquitted herself well. Poised and dignified, she would have made her mother proud. She appeared in the midst of a hysterical crowd "so calmly and so nobly," said one eyewitness. The queen also commented movingly to the Mayor of Paris: "I have seen everything and discovered everything and forgotten everything."[26]

Count Fersen had been a witness to the terrible events and wrote: "May God preserve me from ever seeing again so heartbreaking a spectacle as that of the last few days."[27] As for the tumult that had taken over Paris, Gouverneur Morris, the future American ambassador to France, wrote: "Everything here . . . has gone to pieces. The army is undisciplined and no longer obeys. . . . It is impossible to imagine greater disorder in an Assembly; no reasoning, no examination, no discussion. . . . The anarchy which reigns is inconceivable."[28] In Paris, the royal family—which included the king, queen, their two children, and Madame Elisabeth, the king's sister—were lodged at the Tuileries Palace, where they were subjected to the whims of a curious public. The gardens were open to everyone, and people did not hesitate to shout complimentary or abusive remarks within earshot of the royals. Marie Antoinette met the people with amiable patience, though she soon longed to escape.

During these difficult times the king and queen's fate became linked to the Comte de Mirabeau, a moderate Assembly member who believed in the ideal of a constitutional monarchy. He urged Louis to flee to the countryside, rally the people, and accept a constitutional monarchy. Louis, though, could not countenance a civil war. The queen too could not bring herself to trust Mirabeau, whose "reputation for vice and atheism obscured his very real patriotism and political genius."[29] Nevertheless, Marie Antoinette did meet with Mirabeau, and charmed the onetime supporter of the Revolution. He pledged to her that he would do what he could to save the monarchy, but Mirabeau died in March 1791, and with his death was extinguished the monarchy's last best hope for help within France.

From her native Austria, Marie Antoinette found no succor. Her brother Joseph II died in 1790, unable to aid his sister. Emperor Leopold II, his successor and brother, hardly knew Marie Antoinette. Leopold II and Frederick Wilhelm II of Prussia produced the Declaration of Pillnitz, in which they proclaimed the French monarchy's fate to be of interest to the European powers.

Prince Louis-Charles of France (1785-1795),
second son of Marie Antoinette and Louis XVI.
He was also known as the "lost Dauphin," but
genetic testing in 2000 proved conclusively that
he died in 1795.

Versailles Palace, home of Queen Marie Antoinette. It was also here that the German
Empire was proclaimed in 1871 in the presence of Otto von Bismarck.

A painting depicting the final farewell of Louis XVI and his family before his execution in 1793. *(Getty Images)*

Balmoral Castle, Queen Victoria's Scottish retreat.

This photograph was taken in Balmoral, Scotland, in September 1855, when Vicky and Fritz became engaged. From left to right: Prince Alfred, Prince Frederick William of Prussia, Princess Alice, the Prince of Wales, Queen Victoria, Prince Albert, and Vicky, the Princess Royal. (*The Royal Collection* © *2007 Her Majesty Queen Elizabeth II*)

Queen Victoria (1819-1901), the longest-reigning monarch in English history, was also Empress of India. The mother of nine children, she carried on a voluminous correspondence with her eldest daughter, Vicky, the Empress Frederick.

Vicky and her son Willy, the future Kaiser Wilhelm II. The fractious relationship between mother and son was a source of frustration and unhappiness for Vicky. *(Getty Images)*

A telling photograph of Vicky looking adoringly at her husband, Fritz. The couple enjoyed a supremely happy marriage, just like Vicky's parents, Queen Victoria and Prince Albert. *(Getty Images)*

The Neues Palais in Potsdam, built under the direction of Frederick the Great, was the home of Emperor Frederick III and the Empress Frederick.

Left: Frederick III (1831-1888), German Emperor and King of Prussia, the devoted husband of Vicky, Queen Victoria's eldest daughter. His reign lasted a mere ninety-nine days.

Right: Prince Otto von Bismarck (1815-1898), the Iron Chancellor, architect of German unification. He was for decades the nemesis of Vicky, Crown Princess of Prussia.

Vicky, the Empress Frederick (1840-1901), the eldest daughter of England's Queen Victoria. A highly intelligent and liberal-minded woman, she felt out of place in the militaristic Prussian court.

Kaiser Wilhelm II (1859-1941) was the eldest child of Emperor Frederick III and the Empress Frederick. He was also Queen Victoria's eldest grandchild. The kaiser's withered left arm can be seen prominently in the photograph.

Queen Victoria and Vicky mourning Frederick III, February 1889. The queen holds a portrait of the late emperor. *(The Royal Collection © 2007 Her Majesty Queen Elizabeth II)*

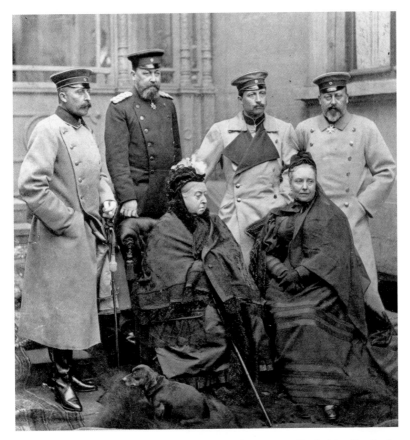

Queen Victoria with her eldest daughter, Vicky, the Empress Frederick. Also in the photograph are Kaiser Wilhelm II (standing between his grandmother and mother) and the Prince of Wales (standing behind his sister Vicky). *(Getty Images)*

The declaration, however, did not advance the French monarchy's cause but helped inflame the revolutionaries, who interpreted it as Austrian and Prussian belligerence. The Pillnitz declaration inadvertently prompted revolutionary France to declare war against Austria in April 1792. Leopold died shortly thereafter, having reportedly said: "I have a sister in France, but France is not my sister."[30] His successor, his son Francis II, who did not know his aunt, also did not come to her aid.

Marie Antoinette was searching for a solution to the dangers facing the monarchy as the revolution continued to wreak havoc in France. Believing that an armed congress of the powers combined threatening (but not attacking) France might be the solution, she wrote in secret to other monarchs, pleading for help. She surprised herself at her efforts, for the carefree creature who had gambled and partied was replaced now by an active and energetic queen who tried to resolve an increasingly impossible dilemma. Marie Antoinette admitted that "it is in misfortune that you realize your true nature." She credited "the blood that runs in my veins," the blood of her mother, the formidable empress Maria Theresa, from whom the queen "found inspiration in her memory."[31]

Marie Antoinette's efforts, however, were all in vain. The powers were driven to act not by altruistic reasons based on the royal family's plight or French turmoil but by purely practical considerations, based upon their own political advantage—and saving the French monarchy did not fall into those calculations.

Back in France, Louis XVI sealed his fate during a showdown with the Assembly. Deeply pious, the king was aghast when the National Constituent Assembly seized the Church's properties and, worse, ordered that the clergy take an oath of obedience to the nation. This denied papal authority, sowing the seeds of schism. Many of the clergy refused to take the oath (they were termed nonjuring clergy), making them enemies of the state. Louis XVI exercised his right to veto the law, but the Assembly bullied the king into signing the decree. His aunts, horrified at the state's brazen attempt to destroy the Church, fled to Rome. Many in France watched Louis with suspicion, wondering if he too would flee. By this time, Marie Antoinette, in contact with the ever-devoted Fersen, had been plotting an escape. Count Mercy had warned her: "Escape has become impossible at this time. Every village could be an insurmountable barrier to your passage. And I tremble to think of the catastrophe that would arise if the enterprise fails."[32] But despite Mercy's warnings, Louis XVI agreed with his wife that they and their family had to leave Paris.

On the night of June 21, 1791, Fersen spirited the family out of the Tuileries, driving the carriage containing the king, queen, their children, Madame

Elisabeth, and Madame Tourzel. Their final destination was a town in northeastern France, Montmédy, where they were sure of strong royalist support. Fersen left the party at the first stop in what must have been a difficult separation for Marie Antoinette. The royal carriage then lumbered across Champagne and reached the small town of Varennes. There, the king was recognized and the royal party captured. They were escorted back to Paris in a four-day-long journey marked by "sufferings physical and moral, nothing was spared them," according to Madame Tourzel.[33] Along the hot, dusty roads, menacing crowds greeted them, some pelting stones. Despite her family's predicament, Marie Antoinette exhibited kindness to the men escorting them. When they complained of hunger, the queen offered some cold meats to them but was greeted by insolent shouts of "Don't touch it, it is poisoned!"[34] As the family neared Paris, the queen clutched desperately at the exhausted and bewildered young dauphin, who with his sister had shared in their parents' ordeals. When the family returned to the Tuileries, the king was allowed to make his way into the palace, but when the queen disembarked from the carriage, people lunged at her. She was barely saved by some guards and carried inside. By now, Marie Antoinette's ordeals had caused a near physical collapse, turning her hair from gray to white. The Spanish ambassador reported that "the Queen is so weak, so broken that those who see her can barely recognize her."[35]

Marie Antoinette wrote to Fersen of their ordeal, saying, "By a miracle I still exist. . . . It is no longer only me whom they are against. They are also plotting to assassinate the King and they do not attempt to hide it. He showed such strength and courage that for the moment it has done some good. But the horrors could repeat themselves at any time."[36] In July 1792, Louis and Marie Antoinette were forced to go the Champ de Mars, where the king had to swear to respect the constitution. Madame de Staël, the famous writer who was also Necker's daughter, commented on what she saw that day: "I will never forget the expression on the Queen's face. Her eyes were swollen with crying; the splendor of her dress, the dignity of her stance contrasted with the cortege that surrounded her. . . . The King walked from his pavilion to the altar set up at the end of the Champ de Mars; that was where he was to swear allegiance to the constitution for the second time. . . . When he walked up the steps of the altar, he looked like a holy victim going willingly to the sacrifice."[37]

Throughout the ordeal unleashed by the Revolution, Marie Antoinette remained by Louis XVI's side and refused to be parted from him or their children. This steadfastness was again evident in August 1792, when it appeared as if the family would die as a mob of twenty thousand were set to carry out an assault on the Tuileries Palace. Marie Antoinette bravely announced to her servants, "You can nail me to the wall before I consent to leave [my family]."[38] While the guards on duty fought desperately to protect the royal family, they fled to the nearby Assembly.

Within a few days, the royal family was imprisoned in the great tower of the Temple, once the headquarters of the Knights Templar. The king was housed on one floor, and the dauphin with the ladies in the one above. Life at the Temple was an ordeal; the rooms, with little furniture, were damp and filthy. Nine-foot-thick walls enclosed the captives, who were under constant surveillance. At first the prisoners, who included Madame Elisabeth and a few servants, were allowed to live out a routine that saw the king teaching the seven-year-old dauphin. Soon, however, Marie Antoinette's ladies, Madame Tourzel and Princess Lamballe, were ordered to leave. Only the king's valet, Hanet Cléry, was left to serve the family. Then, in a horrific turn of events, Marie Antoinette's old friend Princesse Lamballe was murdered, her body brutally disfigured, her head placed on one pike, her heart on another. Then the mob brandished their victim's dismembered body, especially the head, before the royal family. Upon hearing of the horrible deed from officials who held a piece they claimed was the princess's bleeding heart, Marie Antoinette fainted while her children burst into tears.

Her children, Marie Antoinette's great solace during this terrible time, were her paramount concern. Guards became emboldened to act insolently toward the family, taunting them about being executed. Marie Antoinette tried to mitigate their ordeal by reading books to her children and teaching them. And as much as possible, the anxious mother tried to establish some routines, such as listening to the dauphin say his evening prayers. When, without warning, the dauphin was taken from his mother to live with his father, Cléry noted that Marie Antoinette's "distress was extreme" and that she begged him "to watch incessantly" over her son's life.[39]

As for Louis XVI, there was little doubt that he was a marked man. Madame Elisabeth admitted that "the queen and I expect the worst; we make ourselves no illusions as to the fate they are preparing for the king."[40] She was proven correct. In September, the monarchy was abolished, the king becoming simply Citizen Capet. Events continued to go against the royal family. A number of Louis's papers were discovered, and though "the revelations were actually more embarrassing than criminal,"[41] a trial unfolded in December at which he was accused of treason. Given the choice of letting his children see him or their mother (but not both), during the trial, Louis unselfishly gave Marie Antoinette the privilege of having their children with her. He denied the charges of treason. However, there was never really any doubt how the trial would end. On Christmas Day 1792, Louis XVI composed his last will and testament, a document heavily marked with references to his faith in which he begged God for forgiveness. He also pardoned those who had caused him offense. Louis added: "I pray God especially to cast the eyes of his mercy on my wife, my children, and my sister, who have suffered so long with me; to support them by his grace if they lose me, and for as long as they remain in this perishable world." Regarding Marie Antoinette, Louis wrote: "I commend my children to my wife; I have never doubted her maternal tenderness for them; I entreat her, above all, to make good Christians and honest beings of them, to teach them to regard the grandeurs of this world (if they are condemned to experience them) as dangerous and perishable benefits, and to turn their eyes towards the only solid and durable glory of eternity."[42]

In January 1793, Louis XVI was found guilty and sentenced to death, given just twenty-four hours to say good-bye to his family. They were reunited briefly in a scene marked by sobs and embraces, as the king broke the news of his impending execution. When they parted from Louis, "uttering the most sorrowful moans," he assured them they would see him at eight the next morning. "Why not at seven o'clock?" asked Marie Antoinette. "Well, then, yes, at seven o'clock," he replied.[43] Louis XVI never saw his family again, deeming a final good-bye too painful for them to undergo. The next morning, January 21, 1793, Louis attended Mass, then gave Cléry his wedding ring to give to Marie Antoinette. "Tell her," said Louis, "that I part from it with pain and only at the last moment." And with tears in his eyes, Louis told his valet "how much it costs me to go without receiving their last embraces!"[44] He was granted the visit of a nonjuring priest, Abbé Edgeworth, who accompanied him to the guillotine. Moments before the execution, the abbé utterered the words "Son of Saint Louis, ascend to Heaven!"[45] The abbé was standing close to the guillotine, and at the moment Louis's head was severed, his blood splattered the abbé's face.

The morning of Louis XVI's execution, Marie Antoinette had tried to comfort her son, who cried, "Oh papa! papa!" When she guessed that the execution had taken place, Marie Antoinette wept and murmured, "It is all over. We shall never see him again."[46] The queen, now the Widow Capet to her detractors, wore mourning for her dead husband. When the dauphin and his sister saw their mother attired thus for the first time, she sighed: "My poor children, for you it will be a long time, for me it will be always."[47] In July, the dauphin was taken from his mother with her protesting their separation vehemently. Once her son was wrested away from her, Marie Antoinette pined for him, trying desperately to catch a glimpse of the eight-year-old Louis-Charles. She had good reason to be anxious for her son. As it turned out, the dauphin was subjected to brutal treatment by his jailers: the boy was beaten, made to drink alcohol to inebriate him, and taught to become coarse.

Marie Antoinette herself was set to undergo more barbarous treatment. Maximilien Robespierre, one of the most infamous individuals associated with the French Revolution, vociferously called for the former queen to stand trial against the state. In August, she moved a step closer to an official trial when she was taken away from her daughter and sister-in-law. At her final parting from Marie-Thérèse, the former queen entreated her to look upon Madame Elisabeth as her second mother. Marie Antoinette was then taken to the prison known as the Conciergerie. There, the Widow Capet, as she was registered, was held in a damp cell with little light and putrid smells. Throughout her ordeal, Marie Antoinette remained dignified. Toward those few who were allowed to serve her, the former queen showed gratitude and kindness, never uttering a word of complaint. Sustained by her faith, Marie Antoinette grew increasingly religious and "developed into a woman who was markedly pious, much as her mother had been."[48]

The self-possession displayed by Marie Antoinette during her imprisonment never left her, despite her humiliation. Sequestered in a cold, dark cell in the autumn with poor clothing, the former queen soon fell ill. She also suffered terribly from loss of blood as she was hemorrhaging badly. Then, in October 1793, came the inevitable: her trial. Despite her ill health, the former queen answered the accusations—ranging from treason to assassination schemes—in a satisfactory manner. The most vile accusation leveled against Marie Antoinette was supposed "acts of the most licentious debauchery" claimed by her son, who by this time had been abused and brainwashed by his captors. At this, a horrified and indignant Marie Antoinette "won over the hostile crowd" when she exclaimed, "I appeal to the conscience and feelings of every mother present, to declare if there be one amongst you who does not shudder at the idea of such horrors."[49] Order had to be called after this impassioned retort.

Like that of Louis XVI, the outcome of Marie Antoinette's trial was never in doubt. She was condemned to death, a sentence the former queen accepted calmly. She had, after all, once said, "I have learnt from my mother not to fear death."[50] Knowing her fate, Marie Antoinette wrote a final letter to her sister-in-law. In it, the condemned mother commended her children to Elisabeth's care. Marie Antoinette hoped that her son would never forget his father's last words to him: "that he may never revenge our death." She added words that sounded almost as if her pious mother had written them: "I die in the Catholic apostolic and Roman religion, that of my fathers, in which I have been brought up, and which I have always professed. . . . I sincerely demand pardon of God of all the faults I may have committed. I hope . . . that He will deign to receive my soul in His mercy and goodness. I ask pardon of all I know. . . . I forgive my enemies all the harm they have done me."[51]

Empress Maria Theresa's daughter went to her death on October 16, 1793, dressed in white, driven in a cart before a crowd of 200,000. Indifferent to the humiliating howls from the mob, Marie Antoinette made her way to the guillotine with dignity, having "never failed for a single instant either her great soul or the illustrious blood of the House of Austria."[52] The blade of the guillotine came down after noon. She was composed and courageous to the end.

PART III

QUEEN VICTORIA

and

THE EMPRESS FREDERICK

19

DESTINED TO REIGN

In 1818, a crisis over the succession to the British throne compelled three of King George III's unmarried sons to make an unseemly scramble for wives. The goal was to sire a legitimate heir to the British throne. Even though at the time George III had seven surviving sons, there was a dearth of legitimate grandchildren. When Princess Charlotte, George III's granddaughter and second in line to the throne, died in childbirth in 1817, the succession to the throne needed to be secured. Therefore, her uncles—William, Duke of Clarence; Adolphus, Duke of Cambridge; and Edward, Duke of Kent—hastened to marry suitable brides.

The fifty-year-old Duke of Kent married the widowed Princess Victoire of Saxe-Coburg-Saalfeld, nineteen years his junior.* In 1819, the duke dashed back to England from Amorbach, in present-day Germany, with his pregnant wife so that the confinement could take place on English soil. On May 24, 1819, the Duchess of Kent gave birth at London's Kensington Palace to a baby girl. There was a tussle over the names of the baby at the actual moment of christening, which took place at the Cupola Room of Kensington Palace. The baby's uncle the Prince Regent (the future George IV), finally settled the matter by naming the child Alexandrina in honor of her godfather, Czar Alexander I of Russia, and Victoria for her mother. Little Princess Alexandrina Victoria never knew her father, who died unexpectedly when she was only eight months old. From then on, her overprotective mother raised her daughter and became a dominant feature in the future queen's life.

*Upon her marriage, she became the Duchess of Kent and was known as Victoria.

Life for Princess Victoria centered on Kensington Palace, her home in London. Located on the edge of Hyde Park in Kensington Gardens, Kensington Palace was a suitably dignified building that housed a number of royals besides Victoria and her family. She and her mother, the Duchess of Kent, along with the duchess's two other children from her first marriage, Prince Charles and Princess Feodora of Leiningen, were allotted a suite of rooms in the palace by King George IV (Victoria's uncle, who ascended the throne in 1820). The duchess eventually took over more than a dozen rooms of the palace and had them suitably decorated. During her childhood at Kensington Palace, Victoria had few visitors, with the exception of her mother's brother Prince Leopold, Princess Charlotte's widower. Prince Leopold visited his sister frequently at Kensington Palace and took a keen interest in his niece's future. During these years, Victoria looked on Prince Leopold as a kind of substitute father. Another male who figured prominently in the Duchess of Kent's and Princess Victoria's lives during the latter's childhood was the duchess's comptroller, Sir John Conroy. Conroy was an overambitious, scheming courtier who aspired to be the power behind the throne, for as the years passed, it became increasingly evident that Princess Victoria just might become queen one day.

The Duchess of Kent was determined that her daughter be shielded from the influence of her brothers-in-law, Kings George IV and William IV, whose colorful lives made them, in the duchess's eyes, less than stellar examples for her daughter to follow. George was a decadent, womanizing spendthrift who built the exotic Royal Pavilion in Brighton, and William was a gruff naval officer who sired ten illegitimate children with an Irish actress with whom he lived for many years. It was not difficult for the Duchess of Kent to keep Princess Victoria away from court, for neither George nor William cared much for the duchess. And so Victoria's mother raised her daughter in an almost hermetically sealed environment, where the child was allowed few opportunities to mingle with relatives or even people her own age.

Such a lonely childhood left young Victoria susceptible to the influence of her governess, Louise Lehzen. The daughter of a German Lutheran pastor, Lehzen was a dedicated teacher who strove to rein in the willful child and turn her into a well-mannered woman equipped to be a successful monarch. Signs of Victoria's headstrong personality were evident early in her life. The princess's other tutor, the Reverend George Davys, who taught her to read and instructed her in religion, noted of his four-year-old pupil: "She seems to have a will of her own."[1] And when Lady Jane Ellice, one of the few children allowed to play with the princess, came to Kensington Palace and chose some toys on the floor, she was told by the future queen: "You must not touch those, they are mine, and I may call you Jane, but you must not call me Victoria."² All in all, the little princess exhibited signs of being stubborn, passionate, emotional, honest, temperamental, and sensitive—characteristics that were to remain with her always.

A sound curriculum was devised for Victoria that included German, Italian, French, and Latin, though she never achieved the fluency in Latin that Catherine of Aragon was renowned for. Other subjects included history, arithmetic, writing, and religion—all largely taught by Lehzen. Though Princess Victoria's curriculum did not mirror the intense intellectual regimen Catherine of Aragon was subjected to, the British princess at least benefited from a better program of studies than the ill-fated Queen Marie Antoinette.

Lehzen tried to mitigate the princess's loneliness by helping Victoria sort and dress the child's impressive collection of 132 dolls. Besides these dolls, Victoria pampered and played with her pet dogs, including her cherished King Charles spaniel, Dash. A lifelong lover of animals, particularly of dogs and horses, Victoria liked to draw animals as well as people. As a child, she showed an aptitude for sketching and painting in watercolor. Never growing tired of drawing and painting, Victoria honed these gifts, becoming in the end a fairly talented artist. The princess also delighted in the theater and opera, an interest she retained throughout her life.

While studying a table of the kings and queens of England when she was nearly eleven, Victoria came upon an extra page Lehzen had placed in the book. That page contained a genealogical table. Surprised by the information contained therein, the pensive princess declared, "I am nearer to the throne than I thought." After bursting into tears at the realization that she could succeed as queen one day, Victoria gravely noted: "I will be good."³

The princess's proximity to the throne narrowed even further when, in June 1830, King George IV died and was succeeded by his brother William IV. William IV, as George IV before him, eyed the Duchess of Kent warily, a suspicion that was heartily reciprocated. The duchess, therefore, continued to raise her daughter with as little contact as possible with the court and kept Victoria "under ceaseless surveillance. Never was Victoria left in a room without a servant, never was she allowed to go downstairs without someone holding her hand."⁴ Even when she slept at night, Victoria was not alone, because she shared a bedroom with her mother. It all amounted to a kind of gilded captivity. Victoria's constant supervision by the duchess and Conroy came to be known as the Kensington System. The system was designed to promote her popularity by isolating her from the court, and to ensure an eventual regency for her mother as well as a position for Conroy as Victoria's private secretary. Her maternal half sister, Princess Feodora, alluded to this strained existence in a letter to Victoria years later: "I escaped some years of imprisonment, which you, my poor darling sister, had to endure after I was married."[5] Feodora, eleven years older than Victoria, left England for Germany in 1828 to marry but kept in close contact with her half sister.

Several years later, another close relation of Victoria left England when her uncle Leopold became king of the Belgians in 1831. His absence from England did not, however, prevent Leopold from trying to mold Victoria into the ideal monarch. Through a steady stream of letters from Brussels that his niece assiduously read and tried to follow, King Leopold gave sage advice and support. Leopold's close adviser, Baron Christian Stockmar, remained in London, where he continued to advise both Victoria and her mother. The discreet and widely read Stockmar was a medical doctor who could also intelligently discuss law, history, economics, the sciences, literature, and the classics. He remained King Leopold's eyes and ears in London and executed his role ably and faithfully for many years. Stockmar in effect acted to Victoria as Count Mercy-Argenteau had acted to Marie Antoinette.

Both Empress Maria Theresa and the Duchess of Kent exhorted their daughters to live up to their illustrious positions. Whereas the empress's exhortations were largely given after Marie Antoinette left the maternal fold, the Duchess of Kent made hers while Victoria still lived with her. The young princess took her mother's missives to heart. When Victoria was ten, she wrote to her mother: "I must thank you for your *great kindness* to me, and I hope to repay it by being a good and obedient child to my dearest Mamma. I hope never any more to hear Mamma say, 'I am shocked' but to hear her say 'I am pleased.'"[6] When the princess was only eleven, the duchess pointed out: "If you be called to fill the highest Station in the Country,—you will shew yourself worthy of it; and that you will not disappoint the hopes of your anxious mother!—then, only then, can you be happy and make others happy."[7] The duchess was not alone in urging young Victoria to do her best. As part of his good wishes for her thirteenth birthday, King Leopold wrote to his niece: "By the dispensation of Providence you are destined to fill a most eminent station; to fill it *well* must now become your study. A good heart and a trusty and honourable character are amongst the most indispensable qualifications for that position."[8]

By the time she was fifteen, Victoria had shown herself to be a student of history, an appropriate interest in light of her destiny. The princess described reading history as "one of my greatest delights."[9] Among the books Victoria read were Lord Clarendon's *History of the Rebellion and Civil Wars in England* and William Russell's multivolume work, *The History of Modern Europe.* Victoria also enjoyed creating genealogical tables of the kings and queens of England. The princess's preoccupation no doubt helped her recall crucial dates and events of the past. When Victoria was examined on historic battles, she described correctly "the times when they were fought, the commander & situation of the places" as well as military engagements such as: "Marathon, Philippi, Hastings, Neville's Cross, Shrewsbury and the Boyne."[10]

As the princess grew older, she managed to establish a rapport with her uncle and aunt King William IV and his wife, the kindly Queen Adelaide, who had been a German princess like the Duchess of Kent. Both William and Adelaide liked the princess, who was now next in line to the throne, since their two young daughters had died. By this time, King William IV objected to Victoria being kept from his court by his sister-in-law. In August 1836, the king announced publicly his displeasure with Victoria's mother, describing the Duchess of Kent as "a person surrounded by evil advisers and incompetent to act with propriety. . . . I have particularly to complain of the manner in which that young lady [i.e., the Princess Victoria, who was seated opposite the speaker] has been kept away from my Court; she has been repeatedly kept from my drawing rooms, but I am fully resolved that this shall not happen again. I would have her know that I am King, and I am determined to make my authority respected."[11] William continued to dislike the Duchess of Kent because of her desire to dominate Victoria and her uneasy relationship with Queen Adelaide, as well as her dependence on Conroy. He made no secret of his wish to live until the princess came of age at eighteen. If he managed this, Victoria would reign on her own and deny the Duchess of Kent the position of regent. Meanwhile, the duchess and Conroy did not reckon with resistance to their scheme of dominating Victoria from an increasingly independent-minded princess.

In the spring of 1837, William IV's health declined rapidly. But as the old king wished, he held off dying until Victoria reached her eighteenth birthday in May. Just four weeks later, on June 20, William died. Lord Conyngham and the Archbishop of Canterbury dashed to Kensington Palace from Windsor Castle to break the news. The men arrived at five o'clock in the morning and banged on the door of the palace. Victoria was awakened and greeted the men still in her dressing gown and slippers, her hair flowing. Upon hearing the news that she was queen, Victoria dropped on her knees and said to the messengers, "I ask your prayers on my behalf."[12] The young queen was well aware of the heavy burden before her and admitted as much in her first address to Parliament, which was also laden with her reliance on God. "I ascend the Throne," said Victoria, "with a deep sense of the responsibility which is imposed upon me; but I am supported by the consciousness of my own right intentions, and by my dependence upon the protection of Almighty God."[13]

Of that special moment when she learned of her accession, Queen Victoria noted in her journal, underlining the word for emphasis, that she met her visitors "alone." Her accession as queen marked Victoria's first steps toward independence. It also ushered in a new and glorious reign, which remains the longest in English history.

In her journal, the eighteen-year-old queen recorded her sentiments about the momentous event: "Since it has pleased Providence to place me in this station, I shall do my utmost to fulfill my duty towards my country; I am very young and perhaps in many, though not in all things, inexperienced, but I am sure that very few have more real good-will and more real desire to do what is fit and right than I have."[14] Although long kept under surveillance and dependent upon others, Queen Victoria took charge at her accession and, to the surprise of her councilors, appeared at her first Privy Council meeting alone. Neither Sir John Conroy nor the Duchess of Kent was by her side, as some had predicted. Instead, the diminutive queen, who still looked childlike, signaled her desire to reign on her own. Sitting amid politically seasoned and elderly advisers, Victoria impressed them with her demeanor. "She not merely filled her chair," remarked the famed Duke of Wellington, "she filled the room."[15]

Almost immediately, the new queen made plain where the Duchess of Kent and Conroy stood. She would have little to do with their plans of helping her rule her kingdom. Victoria ordered that her mother sleep in separate quarters from then on. Conroy was not granted an audience. But despite her desire to go it alone, Victoria needed a mentor. This role was quickly filled by the prime minister, William Lamb, Viscount Melbourne. Melbourne was a handsome, fifty-eight-year-old aristocrat. To the youthful Victoria, Melbourne, who had both worldly and political experience, became indispensable. Whether it was formal meetings, casual chats, or rides, the prime minister tutored his eager pupil on affairs of state. "Lord M" (as the queen sometimes referred to him) was in turn impressed with his student sovereign, for "he had never met a young woman with more natural command or greater strength of character."[16] Victoria blossomed under Melbourne's tutelage, emerging "more confident, more sophisticated, more determined to do her best. He taught her in short, how to be a queen."[17] Her affection and dependence on the prime minister was the start of a lifelong series of platonic romantic attachments. Passionate by nature, the new queen also hastened to secure a consort. The candidate who appeared best suited to become her husband was Prince Albert of Saxe-Coburg-Gotha.

Albert, Victoria's first cousin, was three months younger than the queen (Victoria's mother and Albert's father were siblings). The younger son of the Duke of Saxe-Coburg-Gotha and his wife, Prince Albert was only five years old when his mother left her husband and children for an army officer, whom she later married. She never saw her children again. This scandal did not prevent Victoria's uncle King Leopold from championing Albert as a husband for his niece. She had first met Prince Albert in 1836, when he and his brother, Ernest, visited England. Victoria thoroughly enjoyed her cousins, finding them both amiable and clever. She was especially pleased with Albert, whom she thought intelligent and handsome with a fine countenance and a good command of English. By the end of the visit, Victoria had fallen under the spell of her attentive cousins. She dutifully reported to King Leopold her impressions of Albert: "He possesses every quality that could be desired to make me perfectly happy."[18] After Baron Stockmar visited the prince in 1836 and reported positive views to Leopold, the king was convinced that Albert would make the ideal husband for Victoria. Leopold ensured a well-rounded education for the intelligent prince, who studied political economy, Roman law, sciences, languages, history, and philosophy at Brussels and at Bonn University.

When Prince Albert visited Victoria in England for the second time, in the fall of 1839, after her accession, the queen's enthusiasm had turned to rapture. Albert had grown into a handsome young man. His cousin was so taken with his good looks that she went into expressions of ecstasy describing his "beauty." Victoria, by contrast, was rather plain. She was petite, standing nearly five feet tall, with brown hair and blue eyes like Albert, and an average looking face. But already, to her vexation, Victoria had a tendency to plumpness that was to turn into the familiar wide girth. In terms of personality, she was the more volatile of the two. The tempestuous and headstrong Victoria's position as queen regnant would always place the shy but intellectually stellar Albert in the background. This role reversal was evident even before the couple married. When it came time to propose, in October 1839, it was Victoria who broached the subject to Albert because she was queen. When she recalled the event, her ardent nature shone through: "Oh! to *feel* I was, and am, loved by *such* an Angel as Albert was *too great delight to describe*! he is *perfection;* perfection in every way—in beauty—in everything! . . . Oh! *how* I adore and love him, I cannot say! *how* I will strive to make him feel as little as possible the great sacrifice he has made. . . . I feel the happiest of human beings."[19] Prince Albert in turn, was taken by Queen Victoria, noting that "the openness of manner in which she told me this quite enchanted me, and I was quite carried away by it."[20] Days before the wedding, Albert penned a few words of endearment to his fiancée, declaring that he would lay himself "right up to your heart, hoping to find it open to me, and remain with unchanging love and attachment, my own dear bride's ever faithful, Albert."[21] Queen Victoria was truly fortunate in finding a man who understood her, for Prince Albert "at once assumed a protective attitude towards his adoring fiancée, immediately deeply conscious of her need for such protection and companionship."[22]

The wedding took place on February 10, 1840, at the Chapel Royal, St. James's Palace in London, on a dull, damp day. Dressed in a white satin gown trimmed on the sleeves and shoulders with lace, her veil of Honiton lace encircled with a wreath of orange blossoms, a radiant Queen Victoria married Prince Albert in a simple ceremony. They spent their honeymoon at Windsor Castle, during which Victoria went into raptures about her husband, admitting that "to look in those dear eyes, and that dear sunny face is enough to make me adore him."[23] In no time, the devoted couple settled in at their desks positioned next to each other. The prince was allowed to view state papers but not to influence the queen on matters of state. Instead, Victoria relegated Albert to running their homes and managing their domestic affairs. As solid as the marriage was, all was not constant bliss. Once Prince Albert settled into a routine, differences between him and Victoria began to appear. The queen remained gregarious, entertaining, and prone to gossip, whereas the prince was far more introverted, preferring intellectual pursuits and discussions. Inevitably, "arguments, in a patois of German-English, developed between the volatile wife and repressed husband as it became apparent that Prince Albert had nothing to do."[24]

A little over nine months after their wedding, on November 21, 1840, at Buckingham Palace, came the birth of the couple's first child. Victoria had been in labor for twelve hours. When the baby was born, the queen's doctor announced, "Oh, Madam, it is a Princess," to which the queen replied, "Never mind, the next will be a Prince."[25] The child was given the names Victoria Adelaide Mary Louise; to her family she was always to be known simply as "Vicky." As the eldest daughter of the reigning sovereign, Vicky was given the title Princess Royal.

The Princess Royal was christened on her parents' first wedding anniversary with water from the river Jordan. Lady Lyttelton, soon to be the royal governess, described the princess as "a fine, fat, firm, fair, royal-looking baby . . . and too *absurdly* like the Queen. . . . They say she laughs, crows, and kicks very heartily, and the Prince tosses her often."[26] The queen was never enamored of babies under six months, with what she called their "frog-like" appearance, and Vicky was no exception. In time, though, the queen delighted in being a mother, calling her daughter "our little lady" and describing her as doing "wonderfully. Growing and becoming more beautiful every day. She has dark blue eyes and a beautiful complexion."[27]

As for Prince Albert, he wrote glowingly of Vicky, whom he described as "very intelligent and observing."[28] Queen Victoria noted the special bond between father and daughter early on, telling King Leopold: "I think you would be amused to see Albert dancing her in his arms; he makes a capital nurse . . . and she always seems so happy to go to him."[29] This bond between father and daughter was to last until Prince Albert's death.

Much change had taken place in the queen's life and household in the little more than four years since her accession. She had put some distance between herself and her mother. She had shown that she would reign on her own and rid herself of the scheming Conroy. Louise Lehzen, Victoria's governess and close companion, was no longer a member of the queen's household either, since she did not get along well with Prince Albert, who viewed the former governess as a negative influence on his wife. The rows between husband and wife over Lehzen had been fierce. After a showdown during which Albert accused Lehzen of driving a wedge between the queen and her mother, Lehzen finally left England for Germany. Victoria and Albert quarreled over other topics as well. These disagreements prompted Albert to complain that "Victoria is too hasty and passionate. . . . She will not hear me out but flies into a rage and overwhelms me with reproaches of . . . want of trust, ambition, envy, etc. etc."[30]

Still other matters went less than smoothly for the queen in her early years. In 1839, she mistakenly believed the gossip about Lady Flora Hastings. Victoria, whose sympathies lay with the Whig party, distrusted Lady Flora, who was part of the Conroy faction and a member of the opposing political party, the Tories. As Lady Flora's abdomen began to swell, rumor had it that the unmarried lady-in-waiting was pregnant. The queen even thought that Conroy was the father. Finally, two physicians attested that the lady did have an enlargement of the abdomen but was not pregnant and was still a virgin. By then, the affair had become public knowledge. Lady Flora died that same year from what turned out to be liver cancer—the cause of the abdomen's swelling. The queen's sterling reputation was damaged because she had believed and had not stopped the scandalous gossip. Victoria was accused of treating Lady Flora badly and was hissed in public.

Soon afterward, what became known as the Bedchamber Crisis illustrated Queen Victoria's naïveté and the partisanship of her affinity for the Whigs. When Lord Melbourne resigned as prime minister in 1839 (after the Whigs lost their hold on the House of Commons), Queen Victoria was constitutionally bound to offer the premiership to the leader of the political party that held the majority in Parliament. She thus reluctantly offered the position to Sir Robert Peel, a Tory. Peel accepted the post, with the proviso that a number of the queen's Whig ladies—ladies-in-waiting at the bedchamber—be replaced by Tories. Victoria, who saw the issue as a personal one, refused his request. Peel was within his rights to request a change in some of the queen's household. After all, past new governments had been accompanied by changes in the monarch's household to reflect the party in power. Queen Victoria's intransigence prompted Peel, who interpreted the queen's actions as a vote of no confidence, to resign. Melbourne, having managed to gain the confidence of enough members of Parliament, became prime minister again. He resigned definitively as prime minister in 1841, his departure a great loss to Victoria.

Many years later, Victoria acknowledged that she was mistaken in her actions against Peel and attributed them to her youth and inexperience. She had allowed her personal prejudices against the Tory party and her obstinacy to overrule her duties as a constitutional sovereign. In time, Prince Albert managed to guide the impetuous Victoria toward a less partisan and more constitutional manner of reigning (though two more prime ministers would cause the queen to reveal her partiality again).

The biggest change during these early years of Victoria's reign came by way of her marriage and ensuing motherhood. Just under a year after Vicky's birth, a boy was born to the couple and named Albert Edward (Bertie). The succession to the throne was thus secured. The births of two children also reinforced Prince Albert's position in England. With Lehzen gone, and the queen very much enamored of her husband, Prince Albert's ascendancy had clearly begun. More significantly, Victoria had firmly entrenched herself as monarch. With the exceptions of the Hastings affair and the Bedchamber Crisis, Queen Victoria had proven herself to be a monarch with sound leadership.

20

VICTORIA REGINA

With both Louise Lehzen and Lord Melbourne departed, Prince Albert became indispensable to Queen Victoria. Far from merely blotting the queen's signature, he soon came to exercise considerable influence on his wife. Unlike Francis of Lorraine, who contented himself with remaining in the background and leaving Empress Maria Theresa to rule her domains, Prince Albert had become Queen Victoria's private secretary in all but name. Victoria increasingly leaned on her beloved Albert for advice on nearly everything. Naturally intelligent and willing to help, he obliged by discussing with her numerous topics and writing trenchant memoranda. Albert carefully tutored his appreciative wife in many fields, including the arts and sciences as well as statecraft, so that Victoria's participation in foreign affairs became more informed. Willingly submitting herself to Albert's encouragement, the queen was fortunate to have at her side a tireless consort who labored for her benefit and that of the British people. So closely did Victoria and Albert work that by 1845 it was observed that "the Prince is become so identified with the Queen that they are one person, and as he likes business, it is obvious that while she has the title he is really discharging the functions of the Sovereign. He is King to all intents and purposes."[1] Albert's influence on Victoria had a salutary effect. The queen, though always passionate and headstrong, came to view her role as monarch with measured clarity and understanding, working with her ministers and gaining their respect for her growing sagacity and authority. Victoria gave credit where she felt it due, telling Albert, "It is you who have entirely formed me."[2]

The royal couple, so obviously devoted to each other, also encouraged a cult of the monarchy. Intent on sweeping away the notoriety of the Hanoverian kings who had preceded her, Victoria and Albert were determined to raise the royal family's reputation. Confirmed constitutional monarchists, they nevertheless believed that "the powers and prestige of the Crown should be somehow enhanced. By the blamelessness of their private life and the high moral tone of their court, the monarchy came to command more respect than had been the case for many years."[3] Prince Albert told Baron Stockmar of this theme, asking rhetorically, "Had we not also to secure the *moral dignity* of the Court? This basis has been obtained. To my mind, the exaltation of Royalty is possible only through the personal character of the Sovereign."[4] Thus did the aura of moral probity and primness associated with the word "Victorian" emerge from the person who gave her name to the age.

Throughout her long reign, Queen Victoria never strayed from the belief that morality and virtuousness could not be separated from a respectable and successful monarchy: that was partly why she came to disparage her eldest son's sybaritic lifestyle. Victoria's maintenance of cherished values was not mere grandstanding; she sincerely held herself and her family to high moral standards. Though she was not devoid of defects and foibles, she tried to live an upright life and reign with the best interests of Britain at heart. The queen was also a prodigious worker. The amount of work she had to get through was immense. In 1848 alone, some "28,000 despatches were sent from and received at the Foreign Office. Every one of those was closely studied, discussed, advised on, as well as annotated by the Queen." Moreover, "an equal number emanated from the Home and Colonial Offices,"[5] more material for the queen to analyze and comment on. Not forgotten were the daily Parliamentary reports. The material was perused by the queen "and not infrequently annotated in her hand before being filed."[6] Added to all this were Victoria's letters to friends and family as well as daily journal entries. More than mere lists of dry facts, these entries were expositions on crises and events of the day, along with often fascinating accounts of individuals the queen had met or knew. Little wonder, then, that Victoria came to rely on Prince Albert's help.

Another reason Queen Victoria easily allowed Albert to work so closely with her in ruling was that she was so frequently with child. Vicky and Bertie were joined in the nursery by Alice (1843), Alfred (1844), Helena (1846), Louise (1848), Arthur (1850), and Leopold (1853). Leopold's birth differed from Victoria's earlier confinements in that she permitted the administration of chloroform to assuage her pain, thereby popularizing the use of anesthetics in childbirth. Tragically, Leopold suffered from the dreaded disease hemophilia.

Of all Queen Victoria's children, Leopold was the most delicate in health, and his mother never ceased to worry about him.

With their growing brood of children, Victoria and Albert yearned for more space and seclusion than was offered by Buckingham Palace or Windsor Castle. Of the latter, the queen complained, "I can no longer go [there] without being followed by a crowd. It makes me feel inclined to become quite like a naughty child."[7] In 1845 this lack of privacy compelled Queen Victoria and Prince Albert to build an Italianate-style palace, Osborne House, on the Isle of Wight, overlooking Cowes Bay. Beyond Cowes lay the Solent (which reminded Prince Albert of the Bay of Naples), which separated the island from the south coast of England. Osborne became a haven where the royal family could relax and enjoy outdoor pursuits such as bathing, walking, and picnics. To amuse and instruct the royal children, a Swiss-style cottage was built on the grounds. Here Vicky and her siblings not only played but learned about nature, housekeeping, and farming.

In the 1850s the royal family found a northern equivalent of Osborne House amid the moors and craggy ridges by the river Dee in Scotland. There Queen Victoria had erected a Scottish baronial castle complete with tartan-clad interiors. As at Osborne, informality reigned at Balmoral. Excursions to nearby lochs and deer stalking were favorite pastimes. The family popularized the distinctly Scottish tartan, often dressing in it during their stays at Balmoral. Through the years, Queen Victoria became enamored of her Highland retreat though her court and government ministers were averse to visiting Balmoral because of its remoteness. For Victoria, the attraction of a strictly private life afforded by Balmoral and Osborne never abated, though the public sometimes grumbled over the family's prolonged absences from London.

Society in Britain during Queen Victoria's reign underwent significant changes. The hundred years from the mid-eighteenth century saw the rise of a prosperous new middle class thanks to the Industrial Revolution. Voting rights were extended twice, allowing the middle and lower classes a greater share of power. Yet millions of other Britons did not benefit from the railways, coal mines, factories, and industrial towns that sprang up. Working conditions were generally miserable and dangerous; moreover, living in slums with poor sanitation encouraged diseases such as tuberculosis, typhoid, and cholera. An anemic British economy plagued the first half dozen years of Victoria's reign. Poor harvests, compounded by an economic slowdown combined with a growing population, made social problems among the poor even more pronounced. Their disgruntlement over conditions brought about by the Industrial Revolution, and their exclusion from its profits, grew.

No less immune to serious problems was Ireland, then part of the United Kingdom, where the potato famine raged during the 1840s, killing an estimated 1.5 million people and forcing another million to emigrate. Victoria was distressed over sufferings she described as "really too terrible to think of."[8] The queen gave large amounts of money to alleviate the famine and supported public charities aimed at doing the same. The plight of the Irish took place concurrently with revolutionary ferment on the European continent. Concerns that such agitations would spill over into England were understandable.

To avert such strife, in 1846 Victoria's government had taken steps such as the repeal of the protectionist Corn Laws, which had kept bread prices artificially high.* The repeal allowed for the importation of cheaper grain, which likely helped to prevent mass unrest. That widespread calls for revolution did not arise was a measure of Victoria's success as a sovereign. The royal couple's visit to Ireland in 1849 might easily have turned into an anti-monarchical, anti-English endeavor. Instead, it proved a success, with the queen saying of the Irish: "I have felt deeply for their sufferings, and it will be a source of heartfelt satisfaction to me if I am permitted to witness the future and lasting prosperity of this portion of the United Kingdom."[9]

Victoria was no less interested in the state of her empire in the far-flung corners of the world. Britain, during her reign, became the undisputed colossus among colonial empires. The countries and peoples under the Union Jack covered one-quarter of the globe's land surface and included Canada, Australia, and numerous countries in Africa, the Caribbean, and Asia. Such scope and influence was unparalleled. The acknowledged crown jewel among British possessions was India. Though Victoria never set foot in India, she always had an affinity for the exotic land. During the Indian Mutiny of 1857, a widespread revolt against the British as represented by the East India Company, the queen "noted a universal feeling 'that India shd belong to *me*.' "[10] India did indeed in some respects come to belong to Queen Victoria when, in 1858, the East India Company was abolished through the India Act and the country was transferred to the British crown. The queen would come to have cherished Indian servants by her side and have one of the major rooms in one of her favorite homes decorated in superb Indian style.

Tremendous changes—political, social, and economic—transpired during

---

*Corn here refers to wheat rather than maize.

the first decades of Victoria's long reign. People understood that they were living through significant times, with society racing toward modernization. To celebrate the many accomplishments of these years, Prince Albert proposed a Great Exhibition of the Works of Industry of All Nations. The Great Exhibition opened in 1851 in the magnificent Crystal Palace at Hyde Park. An astounding 700,000 cheered Queen Victoria and the exhibition's patron, Prince Albert, as they drove to open it. The queen wrote of the event to King Leopold as "the *greatest* day in our history, the most *beautiful* and *imposing* and *touching* spectacle . . . and the triumph of my beloved Albert."[11]

During one of their visits to the Crystal Palace, the royal couple's two eldest children accompanied them. Vicky was ten years old, a precocious child of whom Prince Albert was inordinately proud, and rightly too, especially when she was compared with her plodding brother Bertie. The parents had acceded to Baron Stockmar's forty-six-page memorandum on educating Vicky and Bertie. Stockmar's emphasis on the need to "strengthen the good [and] subdue . . . the evil dispositions of our Nature"[12] greatly appealed to Victoria and Albert. The baron also advocated an emphasis on academics, which suited the intellectually gifted Vicky like a glove but bored and frustrated the slower Bertie.

That the Princess Royal was highly intelligent was evident early on. When she was only three years old, her father reported that Vicky "speaks English and French with great fluency and choice of phrase."[13] Besides French, Vicky had a command of Latin and became fluent in German. Before she was five, the Princess Royal was reading Gibbon's *Decline and Fall of the Roman Empire*. Bertie paled in comparison with his brilliant sister, a shortcoming that Queen Victoria could never forget. As he grew, the heir to the throne felt inferior to his older sister, who reveled in her superiority.

This self-assurance was evident to one special guest at the Great Exhibition: Prince Frederick Wilhelm of Prussia (Fritz). Born in 1831, Fritz was the son of Prince Wilhelm and his wife, Augusta of Saxe-Weimar. Raised in the highly martial atmosphere that prevailed at the Prussian court, Fritz was also a product of the house of Hohenzollern, its most famous member being Frederick the Great. The Hohenzollerns stood out for their pride, their obsession with militaristic matters, and their fierce belief in their imperial destiny, which in the 1850s was in the ascendant.

By this time, the wars for domination that Frederick the Great had unleashed, beginning with his assault against Maria Theresa and the house of Habsburg, had borne fruit. Prussia's prestige rested on its reputation as a military power, so much so that "Prussia was the supremely militaristic society of the post-Napoleonic era." Even in the next generation, military trappings were prevalent: the "dark blue service dress, white ceremonial tunics, epauletted shoulders, long leather boots, flat caps, spiked helmet, fur hats bearing the death's head emblem, iron crosses, the stars and pendants of military distinction, the ribbons and sashes of the great orders."[14] In contrast to this intensely militaristic, swaggering atmosphere was Great Britain, with its liberal democracy and evidently freer society bent on economic success.

When Fritz first set foot on British soil, he was mesmerized by its democratic and open society. He was equally enthralled to find in the British royal family a family life different from his own. That Queen Victoria had raised a close-knit family despite all the trappings of royalty was an eye-opener to Fritz, whose own experience had been of warring parents and a court fixated on martial leanings. But Fritz's upbringing was not colored completely by Prussian militarism. Princess Augusta, who was always at loggerheads with her ultraconservative husband, introduced Fritz to doses of liberalism. Also under Stockmar's influence, she exposed Fritz to enlightened ideas, inculcating in him some of the qualities found in Prince Albert. In fact, Prince Albert and Fritz aspired to something similar: a "strong sense of duty . . . combined with a contempt for cheap joys; a searching after a quality long since out of fashion, masculine virtue."[15]

Victoria and Albert liked Fritz, concluding that he was intelligent and amiable with what appeared to be political sympathies more in line with those of the British couple than with those of his Prussian counterparts. They encouraged a match between the Prussian prince and their beloved eldest daughter, Vicky, which would create an Anglo-Prussian alliance. Moreover, Germany united under Prussian leadership with Fritz on the throne could become more democratic. A liberal-leaning Germany closely aligned with Britain could bring untold benefits to both countries. And who better to guide Fritz and be his helpmate than their precocious Vicky? Thus all hoped that the seeds of affection would be sown between the two young people during Fritz's visit. Much would depend upon the Princess Royal's personality and her impact upon Fritz—a tall order for the child Vicky.

The self-assured princess captivated Fritz. Vicky's aunt, Feodora, accurately described her niece's charm, noting that "it is the vivacity and animation in her countenance and manners which make her so irresistible in my eyes. She is a treasure."[16] Vicky in turn liked Fritz, but "the pleasure she got from Fritz's presence came more from the chance it gave her to instruct—[for] there was always something of the school-marm hidden away in Vicky that did not take much tempting to emerge."[17] Though at this stage in their lives, the nine-year age gap between Vicky and Fritz was glaringly wide (the former was still a child and the latter, at twenty, very much a young adult), Fritz was nevertheless intrigued by his delightful companion. "You cannot form an idea," he was to say later, "what a sweet little thing the Crown Princess was at the time; such childlike simplicity combined with a woman's intellect . . . and . . . dignity. . . . She seemed almost too perfect; so perfect, indeed, that often I caught myself wondering whether she was really a human being."[18] This fascination with Vicky would lead to a devotion that was to remain with Fritz the rest of his life. Queen Victoria could not have asked for a better start to what looked like a bright future for Vicky in Prussia.

21

THE WARRIOR QUEEN

AND THE PRINCESS BRIDE

*P*rivately, Queen Victoria was preoccupied with Vicky as Fritz's prospective bride. The queen did not hesitate to promote Vicky, reporting to Fritz's mother, Augusta, on her oldest daughter's development: "She has grown a great deal . . . has a genuine love of art and expresses opinions about it like a grown-up person, with rare good sense."[1] Queen Victoria's attention, however, was also diverted to the international scene. In 1853 war broke out, with Britain and France attempting to temper Russia's ambitions in present-day Turkey. The Ottoman Empire was slowly crumbling, providing Russia an opportunity to seize more territory. From there, Russia might conquer Constantinople. If Russia were allowed to prevail, the consequences to Britain could be catastrophic. A victory would give czarist Russia unfettered access to strategically significant areas, such as the Mediterranean and the Dardanelles. British imperial interests, not least India, would be in jeopardy. Therefore, Queen Victoria closely followed the war, which was fought on the Crimean Peninsula, declaring that "my whole soul and heart are in the Crimea."[2]

The queen tried to avoid war when possible, but "when forced to it, [she] became [the Roman war goddess] Bellona incarnate."[3] Like the warrior queen Isabella of Castile and the equally pugnacious Maria Theresa, Victoria wanted to be as close to the action as possible, admitting, "I regret exceedingly not to be a man & fight in the war. My heart bleeds for the many fallen, but I consider that there is no finer death for a man than on the battlefield."[4] Ever mindful of war's sufferings, Victoria did not want the fighting to have been in vain. And thus the queen "never ceased to urge her ministers and her generals [during wartime] . . .

to press forward with dogged resolution and not to slacken their efforts until the final goal of victory was reached."[5] So immersed in the crisis was the queen that her secretary of war noted, "You never saw anybody so entirely taken up with military affairs as she is."[6]

The war was not all glory and honor. Insufficient supplies reached the troops, thousands of soldiers were felled by cholera and dysentery, and some eight thousand were killed. Such setbacks for Britain were disheartening, yet Queen Victoria's indomitable spirit carried her countrymen during the low points of the Crimean War. She was no different in this respect from Isabella and Maria Theresa. Victoria was determined to strike a confident tone; anything less from the sovereign might have demoralized her subjects, from statesmen to soldiers and commoners.

By 1855 Queen Victoria had become "a one-woman fighting machine."[7] This is not to say that the queen was immune from doubt and anxiety. On the contrary, she described herself as "being a good deal worried and knocked up by all that has passed."[8] But Victoria refused to be demoralized. The Duke of Argyll recalled how at a "moment of universal depression . . . there was no sign of depression about the Queen, but a cheerful confidence that her army and her navy would yet recover our position." Argyll noted that the queen maintained her composure even though she "knew everything" about the war. He was "struck by the Queen's high bearing under the anxieties of the time," "proud of the courage and tenacity" of her army despite the setbacks.[9] For Victoria, to lead by example and aim for victory would ensure that Britain's best interests prevailed. Victory, and nothing less, had to be the objective.

The British government, under Lord Aberdeen, had been divided over how to deal with Russia's ambitions. Aberdeen favored negotiations through the European powers, which Queen Victoria supported, whereas the home secretary, Lord Palmerston, who had been foreign secretary, favored a more robust response. This reaction was popular with the British public. After France and Britain went to war, Aberdeen's management garnered strong criticism and his government was defeated in Parliament. Victoria was initially resistant to the elevation of Lord Palmerston as prime minister. As a foreign secretary, Palmerston had kept the queen in the dark about discussions and decisions on foreign affairs, and she disliked him for it. However, she eventually invited the infirm seventy-one-year-old to become prime minister, recognizing his foreign policy experience, patriotism, and abilities. Palmerston dominated British politics from the time he became foreign secretary in 1830 until he retired after his second term as prime minister in 1865. At the end of the Crimean War, Victoria conceded that he had earned the Order of the Garter, the most prestigious order of chivalry in England.

The queen, meanwhile, busied herself with buoying the spirits of her soldiers and their families by visiting the wounded. She wrote of the "touching sight—*such* fine men, and so brave and patient! *so ready* to go back and *'be at them again.'* . . . I feel so much for them, and am *so fond* of my dear soldiers— *so proud* of them!"[10] One positive aspect of the war was the improvement in the care for and treatment of sick and wounded soldiers, as well as the founding of modern nursing by Florence Nightingale.

So moved was Queen Victoria by the heroism and sacrifice during the Crimean War that she instituted the Victoria Cross (VC). In 1857, in Hyde Park during a warm day before a crowd of thousands, the queen, on horseback, pinned the first VC medals on sixty-two men. The VC was (and is) open to soldiers of any rank. From its inception, the VC has been awarded "For Valour," the highest decoration for bravery that any soldier of the British Empire (or Commonwealth today) could attain, taking precedence over every British military decoration and order.

As the Crimean War dragged on, Queen Victoria invited her ally Emperor Napoléon III of France and his wife, Empress Eugénie, to pay a state visit to England in April 1855. The excursion, which took place at Windsor Castle, was a huge success. Victoria was flattered by the flamboyantly mustachioed emperor, whom she found to be "a very *extraordinary* man . . . possessed of *indomitable courage* . . . and *great secrecy*,"[11] while the beautiful Spanish-born Eugénie succeeded in impressing the stolid Prince Albert, who was usually impervious to female charms. Eugénie also delighted Queen Victoria, who found the empress amiable and not the intriguer she was supposed to be. So well did the two women get along that they became lifelong friends. Though the dowdier and plump Victoria could never compete in looks with the svelte and ultrachic Eugénie, observers were struck by the queen's commanding presence and innate sense of royalty. When Victoria and Albert paid a return visit to Paris, people watched a brief but telling scene at the opera. After the national anthems were played, Victoria showed she knew she was queen by instinctively sitting down without looking first that a chair was there for her. In contrast, the empress, who was not born a royal, nervously searched for a chair before she sat.

Eugénie's success with the British royal family extended to the Princess Royal. Vicky was dazzled by the empress's elegance. Accompanying her parents to France in August 1855, Vicky thoroughly enjoyed herself. The visit included a magnificent reception at Marie Antoinette's former home, Versailles. Also present was the Prussian statesman Otto von Bismarck. Years later, Bismarck would return to Versailles for an auspicious occasion that would affect Vicky directly.

Flush from her trip to Paris, Vicky returned with her parents to Balmoral, unaware that a life-changing event was about to take place. Prince Frederick of Prussia, who had never forgotten her, was set to visit, intent on deciding if his future marital happiness lay with Queen Victoria's eldest daughter. Still somewhat shy and unsure of himself because of his conflicted childhood, Fritz nevertheless cut a dashing figure. Standing over six feet tall with dark blond hair and a trim mustache, the twenty-four-year-old Prussian prince was bound to set Vicky's heart a flutter. Vicky herself, nearly fifteen, was a pretty adolescent. A petite five foot two, Vicky bore a close resemblance to Victoria but with softer features. She also resembled her mother in temperament. Opinionated, temperamental, and headstrong, the princess was forthright but could be sweet as well. She was also coquettish. On the first evening, Fritz found himself more captivated by her than ever. When Vicky briefly squeezed his hand, Fritz knew he was in love. He hesitatingly approached her parents and stuttered something about wishing to belong to the family. Vicky's parents were pleased, for the couple's marriage meant "the allying of their own happy island kingdom with the increasingly powerful but resolutely illiberal Prussia."[12] Though it was agreed that Vicky was too young to be engaged, her parents conceded that "something would have to be told her and that he [Fritz] had better tell her himself!"[13]

Fritz was allowed to give Vicky a token of his affection. The heather-clad hills around Balmoral provided the romantic backdrop for him to let her know his intentions. After they dismounted their horses, Fritz picked a sprig of white heather for Vicky and kissed her. He then told her that he hoped she would always be with him in Prussia, to which she happily acceded. When she returned to Balmoral, Vicky burst into Queen Victoria's room and both mother and daughter embraced excitedly. Vicky assured her parents that "she would improve" and "would conquer herself" and "hoped to be like" her mother. "My joy, my gratitude to God knows no bounds!"[14] wrote the queen. "Victoria is greatly thrilled," wrote Prince Albert to Baron Stockmar.[15] And in a letter to King Leopold, the queen wrote of Fritz: "He is a dear, excellent, charming young man, whom we shall give our dear child to with perfect confidence. What pleases us greatly is to see that he is really delighted with Vicky."[16] After Fritz's departure for Prussia, Albert told Stockmar, "The young people are ardently in love with one another, and the purity, innocence, and unselfishness of the young man have been on his part equally touching."[17] Albert was correct in relating Fritz's unselfishness, for the eager groom agreed to wait until Vicky was seventeen before they could marry.

For Victoria, there was no doubt that a strong marriage was in store for Vicky and Fritz. The queen expressed her confidence on the matter in letters to Fritz's mother: "I find [Vicky] very good company and this important event in her life has now brought us even closer together."[18] "The young people are as happy as can be here! Fritz is unbelievably in love and shows such a touching faith in our child, which from some one so young was altogether unexpected and is, indeed, very flattering and delightful for Vicky. Her love and trust in him grow daily and yet she is very placid and sensible in herself. *We can see from this fact that here is a relationship, not only of great passion, but based on real trust and understanding such as should assure lasting happiness for them both!*"[19]

Victoria's euphoria over the engagement knew no bounds. "Vicky's joy and simple unaffectedness are quite charming," reported the queen to Princess Augusta. Queen Victoria added Vicky's quote: "Instead of being estranged from you dear Mama, this has brought me closer to you!"[20]

Now that her future was settled, Vicky underwent a regime of tutorials from her father preparing her for her great destiny: to help Fritz usher Prussia into a more democratic phase. While Victoria saw to Vicky's trousseau, Albert honed his favorite child's mind. One hour each evening the teenager eagerly listened to her father, who confided to Fritz that "I put her through a kind of general catechizing, and in order to give precision to her ideas, I make her work out certain subjects by herself, and bring me the results to be revised. Thus she is now engaged in writing a short Compendium of Roman History."[21] Heavy emphasis was placed on her future country and dynasty: Prussia and the Hohenzollerns. It was a daunting regimen for a prospective young bride, but the highly intellectual Vicky thrived on it. Her tutorials were more demanding than the preparations Catherine of Aragon had to undergo before departing for England and were certainly a far cry from the inadequate education Marie Antoinette received before leaving for France. Prince Albert's lessons combined with the Princess Royal's penetrating mind were bound to have a positive effect on Prussia's future. Albert was pleased with his favorite daughter's progress, admitting that "Vicky is very reasonable, she will go well prepared into the labyrinth of Berlin."[22] By the time Vicky's wedding day arrived, she was indeed as prepared a princess as ever was set to become a reigning consort. It was an incredibly weighty burden; Vicky's "special mission" was fraught with "seriousness and difficulty," as Stockmar presciently noted.[23]

In the midst of Vicky's engagement, the Crimean War ended in 1856, with Russia's defeat. Thereafter, imperial Russia no longer dominated the Black Sea. With the hostilities ceased and Russia now weakened, Victoria could focus on her daughter's future. The queen was on an emotional roller coaster during Vicky's engagement. The realization that her daughter was set to leave the family nest for the unknown in Berlin unsettled Victoria. The fact that she was pregnant for the ninth time exacerbated her stress, as Victoria was never at ease being enceinte. Furthermore, the possessive queen felt a twinge of jealousy toward her eldest child, on whom Prince Albert was lavishing such attention. The ongoing difficulties with her exasperating heir, Bertie, who was as listless as ever, aggravated the situation. The patient and forgiving Albert answered his wife's emotional fragility with sympathy. Queen Victoria, in turn, rewarded her husband for his years of loyalty and hard work by creating him Prince Consort in 1857.

Discussions concerning the venue for the wedding ceremony became contentious. The Prussian royal family believed that the wedding should take place in their country. Queen Victoria was indignant. Her imperiousness came through as she declared emphatically that "it is not everyday that one marries the eldest daughter of the Queen of England. The question therefore must be considered as settled and closed."[24] Victoria won. Vicky and Fritz were married on January 25, 1858, at the Chapel Royal in London's St. James's Palace. The seventeen-year-old bride, her hair encircled by orange blossoms, was dressed in white silk trimmed with English Honiton lace. The queen wore a lilac gown and velvet train. Vicky had earlier in the day given her mother a brooch with a message stating that she hoped to be worthy of being the queen's child. The bride and groom spoke their vows clearly and left the chapel to the strains of Felix Mendelssohn's Wedding March. They spent their two-day honeymoon at Windsor Castle, during which touching messages were exchanged between mother and daughter. Vicky sent her mother a note on her wedding day, saying: "I cannot let this day close, which has brought me so much happiness without one more word to you, one more word of the deepest tenderest love."[25] On the morning after her wedding day, Vicky read a letter Victoria sent her in which the mother discussed matrimony as

a very solemn act, the most important and solemn in every one's life, but much more so in a woman's than in a man's. I have ever looked on the blessed day which united me to your beloved and perfect Papa—as the cause . . . of my own happiness (a happiness few if any enjoy). . . . You have also the blessing of a dear, kind, excellent husband. . . . Let it be your study & your object to make his life and his home a peaceful and happy one and to be of use to him and be a comfort to him in every possible way. Holy and intimate is this union of man and wife as no other can be, and you can never give your parents more happiness and comfort than when they know and see that you are a truly devoted, loving and useful wife.[26]

It was a maternal letter that mirrored similar ones written by Empress Maria Theresa to Marie Antoinette. Two days after the wedding, Queen Victoria visited the newlyweds at Windsor and was pleased with what she saw, noting in her journal: "The great happiness of the 2 dear young people, their simple, pure love & affection for one another is truly delightful"—though it was "quite strange" to observe Vicky "walking off with Fritz" at bedtime.[27]

The day of Vicky's departure for Prussia (February 2) was heart-wrenching. The weather—dark and bitterly cold—matched the mood of the British royal family, who now saw their happy family unit being broken up. Copious tears were shed. Upon leaving England, Vicky wrote her father, "I miss you dreadfully dear Papa, more than I can say."[28] On that sad day, the queen wrote to Vicky that "it is cruel, very cruel—very trying for parents to give up their beloved children, and to see them go away from the happy peaceful home." She added, "Dearest, dearest child, may every blessing attend you both. Continue as you have begun in private and public, and you will be happy and succeed in all you undertake!"[29] To King Leopold, Victoria confided of Vicky's departure from the family nest: "The blank she has left behind is *very great* indeed."[30]

The letters between Victoria and Vicky echoed the correspondence between Maria Theresa and Marie Antoinette two hundred years earlier. Motherly advice poured forth from the pen of Queen Victoria as it had from that of Empress Maria Theresa. One letter from Victoria was so similar in tone to Maria Theresa's letters to Marie Antoinette that it could almost have been written by the empress herself. "How right your sometimes not very patiently and kindly listened to Mama was," went Victoria's letter, "when she told you, you could do every thing, if you would but take pains, control yourself and conquer all little difficulties—as you had such great qualities, such a heart of gold!"[31] And in another letter Victoria reminded Vicky: "Only remember that the better you become acquainted with the family and court the more you must watch yourself and keep yourself under restraint. No familiarity. . . . You know, dearest, how necessary it is to have self control, tiresome as it may be.

Kindness, friendliness and civility but no familiarity except with our parents (in-law)."[32]

Unlike Marie Antoinette, who underwent a lengthy wait before consummating her marriage and earning her husband's love, Vicky's new life mirrored Catherine of Aragon's early married days with Henry VIII. Like Catherine, Vicky basked in her husband's devotion and hoped that she might soon give her husband an heir. Queen Victoria was grateful that the huge changes Vicky went through in so short a time went smoothly. Years later, she wrote to Vicky of the dread she had felt at sacrificing an innocent daughter to marriage: "That agonizing thought . . . of giving up your own child from whom all has been so carefully kept & guarded, to a stranger to do unto her as he likes, is to me the most torturing thought in the world. . . . While I feel no girl could go to the altar (and would probably refuse) if she knew all, there is something very dreadful in the thought of the sort of trap she is being led into."[33]

When Vicky arrived in Berlin, she was heartened by the cheers from her husband's countrymen. But the celebrations ended quickly, and Vicky was shocked when she began living in the Berlin Schloss. Instead of comfortable rooms, as in England, the newest member of Prussia's royal house had to contend with old accommodations, which had neither grandeur nor coziness. The place was excessively cold, so Vicky had to bundle up. Simple touches that she had taken for granted, such as cupboards, were lacking; there was no place for the fine trousseau her mother had so carefully chosen. The princess could not heed her mother's counsel to exert self-control; she did not hesitate to question why things were not so or why they did not measure up to English standards.

Vicky was equally aghast over her new husband's family. The nastiness of their quarrels bewildered her. She was shocked by the Hohenzollerns' lack of education, their single-mindedness about all things military, and their overweaning sense of superiority. The Hohenzollerns, in turn, found Queen Victoria's daughter too opinionated and gave no allowances for Vicky's inexperience, naïveté, and youth. Instead, her indiscretion, though not meant to be ill-mannered, quickly marked Vicky as headstrong. Her in-laws' overwhelming impression was that she needed to be checked. To make matters worse, Fritz's family was jealous of Vicky's intelligence. The volatile mixture of personalities and expectations pointed to difficult times ahead for Prussia's newest princess.

Back home, her mother had succeeded admirably as wife, mother, and queen. Whatever doubts there may have been in 1837 at the accession of the eighteen-year-old queen had dissipated by the time Victoria was forty. As a wife, she could still be impetuous and obstinate with Albert, but few royal marriages could compete with theirs. Mutually faithful, Victoria and Albert also worked in tandem for the kingdom's good. Britain had finally come to appreciate Albert's qualities, but his unceasing hard work took its toll on his health. Albert continued as Victoria's indispensable helpmate and, in the process, became increasingly overworked and plagued by ill health. In 1851, he had reported to his grandmother, "I am more dead than alive from overwork."[34]

As a mother on a personal level and to the nation, Victoria had done exceedingly well by giving birth to nine children, including sons. A strict, demanding matriarch who loved her children, the queen kept a close eye on their development, never hesitating to correct them and push them to be morally upright members of society. Above all, notwithstanding some elements of republicanism in Britain, Victoria was respected as a monarch at home and abroad. As for Britain itself, it was a first-rate power, its empire still expanding. The Victorian era was in full bloom, the queen having given her name to a period that was to last many decades.

In faraway Berlin, meanwhile, Vicky could only hope that her life might come to reflect her mother's in some measure. Would Vicky, along with Fritz, be able to steer Prussia toward the liberalism of which her parents dreamed? Would relations between Vicky's native and adopted countries flourish into the twentieth century? Such were the hopes and aspirations of Vicky and her parents.

22

ENGLAND'S DAUGHTER

*E*ven before Vicky and Fritz were married, misgivings were voiced about the union. Otto von Bismarck, the rising Prussian statesman, commented bluntly on the "English marriage": "The 'English' in it does not please me. . . . If the Princess can leave the Englishwoman at home and become a Prussian, then she may be a blessing to the country . . . [but] if our future Queen . . . remains even only partly English, I can see our Court in danger of being surrounded by English influence."[1] Many of Prussia's ruling class shared Bismarck's concerns. They were highly suspicious of England's liberal concepts, such as a constitutional monarchy and expanded suffrage, both of which meant greater democracy. They recognized and were uncomfortable with one of the marriage's main objectives—the promotion of interests advantageous to the bride's country. In this, Vicky's marriage was no different from those of Catherine of Aragon and Marie Antoinette; and ultimately Vicky's task was no easier than Catherine's or Marie Antoinette's when it came to fulfilling those aspirations.

The seventeen-year-old had no illusions about her situation, writing to her father that "my position . . . has its difficulties which require to be considered."[2] Vicky's strongest detractors were the Junkers. Being the landed aristocracy, the Junkers, held a powerful position in Prussia—militarily, socially, and politically. Bismarck belonged to this class, which jealously guarded its privileges. Advocates of Prussia's strident militarism, strong monarchy, and extreme conservatism, the Junkers disdained those who opposed them and their views. As potential disturbers of the equilibrium, liberal-leaning individuals such as Vicky were suspect in their eyes. Whereas Queen Victoria fondly referred to Vicky as *"England's* daughter,"[3] many Prussians derisively called her *Die Engländerin,* "the Englishwoman." It may have been a fitting description for Queen Victoria's eldest daughter, but the Junkers promoted the appellation in the pejorative, feeding nationalist paranoia.

Though Vicky had left her family in England, she was not independent of them. Nor did she find much in Prussia that was equal or superior to England and English ways. Within weeks of her arrival in Berlin, it was evident that Vicky would never shed her Englishness. When the Queen of Prussia reproached Vicky for sneezing in her presence, the princess, "looking rather like her mother," gave her reply in a "clear voice ringing through the room": "We do not have customs like that in our Court at home."[4] Vicky was never truly able to be discreet about her pro-English proclivities; and this indiscretion marked her out early for derision in Prussia. Added to this was the fact that Queen Victoria also wished to continue to have a strong influence over her daughter. Prince Albert concurred, telling Vicky that there was no conflict in her dual role of wife and daughter, but balancing that role would be a lifelong challenge for her. She confided to her father that "if I was to lose sight of my English title and dignity I should do myself and my husband much harm, besides be forgetting my duty to you and England."[5] Fritz himself knew and had always known that Vicky was English to the core. When, before their marriage, he returned to Bonn to further his education, Fritz intensified his English studies. Vicky, after all, "was England and England was Vicky, and if he could not be there he did everything he could to bring England to the banks of the Rhine."[6] Moreover, Fritz's admiration for the British royal family and indeed the British agenda made him all the more supportive. As Fritz's wife, Vicky never lost her pride as an Englishwoman.

The queen's insistence on overseeing her daughter's life mirrored Maria Theresa's attitude toward Marie Antoinette. Confident in their maternal wisdom, both well-meaning mothers firmly believed that their daughters would be eager for their motherly advice. Vicky, like Marie Antoinette, was at once grateful and resentful. This was evident to Baron Stockmar, who, like Count Mercy before him, urged the royal mother to temper her zealous solicitude. Stockmar even approached Lord Clarendon, the foreign secretary, to seek his help in mitigating Queen Victoria's zeal, confiding that "the Queen wishes to exercise the same authority and control over her [Vicky] that she did before her marriage; and she writes her constant letters full of anger and reproaches, desiring all sorts of things to be done that is [sic] neither right nor desirable."[7] Queen Victoria also demanded that Vicky write frequently, once complaining petulantly that "you have not written me one single word, for more than a week!! I am vexed, for you could easily have managed . . . to say: 'I am well. . . . And this could have been done in 1 minute and would have given me pleasure. . . . You seem to think that if you can't write to me a long letter you are not to write at all."[8] A contrite Vicky replied: "I promise never to let such a long time pass again without writing, but will you, dearest Mama, tell me that you have forgiven me."[9] Here again are shades of Maria Theresa and Marie Antoinette.

One year after her wedding, Vicky had accomplished the paramount role required of every female consort—one that eluded Catherine of Aragon and took Marie Antoinette years to achieve. She delivered a male heir who lived. On January 27, 1859, Vicky gave birth to a boy, the future Kaiser Wilhelm II (Willy). Queen Victoria was naturally disappointed at not being able to be with her daughter for the confinement, but she did send an English physician and nurse to her. The birth was excruciatingly painful; Fritz wrote to her mother of his wife's "horrible screams and wails."[10] Mother and child were in grave danger. So traumatic was the birth that the doctor who delivered Willy declared that he never wanted to go through such an experience again. Vicky and Willy survived the ordeal to the relief of many, especially Queen Victoria; however the breech birth caused permanent damage to Willy's arm, making it useless to him.

The news of the future Kaiser Wilhelm II's birth was relayed to Queen Victoria at Windsor Castle with the words "A boy! God preserve mother and child!" And within an hour, the queen replied by telegram: "Is it a *fine* boy?"[11] To the baby's Prussian grandmother, Queen Victoria confessed her disappointment at not being in Berlin, saying, "It is particularly grievous to me not to have been nearer my own beloved child during the most difficult hours of her young life. And now having to sit here far away, unable to see her and her little child even for a moment, this is almost more than I can bear!"[12]

Queen Victoria was again disappointed at being unable to attend the christening. She complained how "it *almost breaks* my heart *not* to witness our *first grandchild* christened! I don't think I *ever* felt *so* bitterly disappointed *about anything* as about this!"[13] It was not until late 1860 that Queen Victoria saw Willy for the first time. When she beheld him, the queen was touched, exclaiming: "Such a little love! He is a fine, fat child. . . . He has Fritz's eyes and Vicky's mouth. . . . We felt so happy to see him at last."[14]

As much as she loved Willy, Vicky was terribly disappointed about his deformed arm. In fact, "her shame on account of the 'mutilation' of her first-born son was so deep in part because she knew how her enemies at court would gloat over this 'flaw' and use it against her."[15] Vicky also lamented the therapies Willy had to endure. For an hour each day, Willy had to wear a ghastly machine that was supposed to help correct a drooping neck, a syndrome brought about by the deformed arm. Vicky bewailed this treatment, writing, "I cannot tell you what I suffered when I saw him in that machine. . . . To see ones [*sic*] child treated like one deformed—it is really very hard."[16]

Willy's handicap and the excruciating birth did not keep Vicky from expanding her family. She soon emulated Queen Victoria in giving birth regularly. Willy was followed by Charlotte (1860), Henry (1862), Sigismund (1864), Viktoria "Moretta" (1866), Waldemar (1868), Sophie (1870), and Margarethe "Mossy" (1872). Vicky delighted in being a mother, particularly of young babies. She wrote to Fritz in 1871 of her joys in motherhood: "To have a baby at one's breast . . . is the *greatest* joy of womanhood." And in another letter: "All the pain of labour is nothing compared to the happiness of having such a dear little creature to hold & to nurse oneself."[17] Queen Victoria, who preferred older children, could never understand her daughter's fuss over small babies. She once told Vicky, "Hardly anyone I know has such a *culte* for little Babies as you have."[18]

Motherhood appeared to bring Queen Victoria and Vicky closer. When the latter visited her mother in England months after Willy's birth, the queen marveled at how she and Vicky could talk almost as equals: "We are like 2 sisters!"[19] Vicky was delighted at this newfound closeness and eagerly wrote of it to Fritz: "Mama shows a kindness & love for me that I have not hitherto known, & which touches me deeply & makes me happy. We are together all day, more like sisters than like mother & daughter. We are more in harmony than ever before.—Everything I do is approved of, even my clothes meet with approval!!!!!!!!"[20]

As closely as she followed Vicky's life, Queen Victoria also considered the futures of Vicky's siblings, especially Bertie and Alice. Bertie's undistinguished showing continued to preoccupy her. She bemoaned his lethargy and interest in clothes, his obsession with theater and parties. Though the strict regimen imposed upon the prince by his parents reaped lackluster results, his training continued. The prince was next sent to Oxford and also undertook foreign tours. Then an earnest search for what Queen Victoria hoped could be his salvation— a wife—was begun. Here, the queen relied on Vicky, who sent lists of candidates to ponder. Vicky's favorite was the attractive Princess Alexandra (Alix) of Denmark. "I never set eyes on a sweeter creature than Princess Alix," wrote Vicky enthusiastically to her mother. "She is lovely! . . . She is one of the most lady-like and aristocratic looking people I ever saw! She is as simple and natural and unaffected as possible."[21] By 1861, Alix was the family's choice, with Prince Albert telling Vicky, "We dare not let her slip away."[22]

Sad events, however, took priority over plans to marry off the Prince of Wales. In March 1861, Victoria's mother, the Duchess of Kent, died. The years had eased the strain that had existed between mother and daughter during the early part of Queen Victoria's reign, so that Victoria sincerely mourned the loss of "that *precious dearly beloved tender Mother* . . . without whom I can't *imagine life.*"[23] In Prussia, death also visited Vicky and Fritz when his grandfather King Frederick Wilhelm IV died in January. This was the first time Vicky faced death close up, and it made a profound impression on her. The king's death signaled the accession of Fritz's father as King Wilhelm I, making Fritz and Vicky the crown prince and crown princess of Prussia and thus but one heartbeat away from the throne. Then, in December, a third death, the most devastating, shattered Vicky and most especially Queen Victoria.

For some time, Prince Albert had been plagued by ill health. Overworked and stressed, the prince also had a far weaker constitution than his wife. He confided to Stockmar that his sufferings were "frightful" and that "sleepless nights and pain have pulled me down."[24] He added, "I am well-nigh overwhelmed by business, as I do my utmost to save Victoria all trouble."[25] Anxiety over Bertie added to Albert's stress. In November he and Victoria were mortified to learn of their son's sexual dalliance with an actress while the prince was stationed in Ireland. Interpreting this as Bertie's downfall, Albert wrote to him and then confronted his son in person. Upon returning home, Prince Albert, who had previously been soaked to the skin during a visit to Sandhurst, fell ill. Typhoid set in. With chills racking his body, Albert's deteriorating condition petrified Victoria.

Prince Albert's final moments came on December 14, 1861, in the darkened Blue Room at Windsor Castle in Queen Victoria's presence. "Oh yes, this is death," the queen murmured, "I know it. I have seen this before."[26] Prince Albert died, making the queen a widow at the age of forty-two. Lady Augusta Stanley, one of the ladies who was with her when the prince died, described what then happened: "The Queen fell upon him, called him by every endearing name; then sank into our arms and let us lead or carry her away to the adjoining room, when she lay on the sofa; then she summoned the children around her, to clasp them to her heart and assure them she would endeavour, if she lived, to live for them and her duty, and to appeal to them from henceforth to seek to walk in the footsteps of him whom God had taken to Himself."[27] Victoria accepted God's will in this, the most heart-wrenching tragedy in her life. Lady Stanley was sure of this, noting, "She felt that the God whose law of love and truth had been so deeply engraved in the heart of that adored husband, is a God of love, and that in love He had taken her treasure."[28]

When Vicky, who had been in Prussia, heard the news, she wrote to her mother: "Why has the earth not swallowed me up? To be separated from you at this moment is a torture which I can not describe." On the same day, the newly widowed queen began her letter to Vicky: "My darling Angel's child—Our Firstborn. God's will be done."[29] Vicky tried to comfort her mother by letter, saying that "Papa's memory, Papa's love shines like a bright star in our darkness and God's almighty hand has poured his heavenly peace into our crushed souls and broken hearts! . . . How I pray that God may support you through it as he has done through the rest! . . . How I long to be with you, to be near you, to speak to you and see you."[30]

On the day after their father's death, Alice sent a telegram to Vicky, saying: "Do come. Mama wants you so much."[31] But Vicky's doctors ordered her to stay in Prussia. Fritz went to England in her stead. Despite her distress, the prince was full of admiration for his newly widowed mother-in-law, whose "greatness of soul in this most terrible of all unhappy times" shone through.[32] One of the queen's ladies noted a similar strength amid the despair, recording, "This frightful blow has left her in utter desolation; she is wonderful, however, saying, 'they need not be afraid, I will do my duty.' "[33]

Queen Victoria described herself to King Leopold as "utterly broken-hearted and crushed. . . . My *life* as a *happy* one is *ended*! The world is gone for *me*! If I *must live* on . . . it is henceforth for our poor fatherless children—for my unhappy country, which has lost *all* in losing him—and in *only* doing what I know and *feel* he would wish, for he *is* near me—his spirit will guide and inspire me! But oh! to be cut off in the prime of life—to see our pure, happy, quiet, domestic life, which *alone* enabled me to bear my *much* disliked position, CUT OFF at forty-two . . . is *too awful,* too cruel!"[34] Days later, Victoria described herself as dragging "on a weary, pleasureless existence! . . . I am also *determined* that *no one* person may *he* be so good, ever so devoted among my servants—is to lead or guide or dictate *to me.* I know *how he* would disapprove it. And I live *on* with him, for him; in fact *I* am only *outwardly* separated from him, and *only* for a *time.*"[35]

Both Victoria and Maria Theresa were widowed suddenly in their forties. The queen and the empress not only reacted strongly to their husbands' deaths but never ceased to mourn the men they loved. Yet in their desire to be left alone in their bereavement—a retreat from public life that Queen Victoria immediately sought—both women never lost sight of their duties as sovereigns. Though neither ceased to mourn her husband, both eventually emerged from their self-imposed seclusion to take their places in the world. Queen Victoria's mourning and commemorating of the Prince Consort went beyond wearing widow's weeds. She had the room he died in made into a shrine, and clothes were freshly laid out for Albert as if he were still alive. Victoria also erected a granite mausoleum at Frogmore, near Windsor, in the form of a Greek cross. There, both their remains would eventually lie together. The most spectacular memorial was the Victorian Gothic structure known as the Albert Memorial in Kensington Gardens, which rose to 180 feet. Consisting of a bronze gilt statue of the prince under an elaborate Gothic canopy, the memorial continues to be one of London's most striking monuments.

A month after the Prince Consort's death, Queen Victoria was still reeling. She expressed her sorrow to Fritz in a letter: "Everything is going as badly with me as possible. I live on from hour to hour in the most horrible dream with my broken heart, and long to follow him soon! . . . I am inexpressibly unhappy."[36]

When Vicky was allowed to visit her grieving mother at Osborne in February 1862, the princess wrote of her impressions and feelings to Fritz: "How madly I long for you, my angel," went the letter. "How I miss you and how I miss *him* whom I worshipped, his step, his dear dear voice, his beloved face. . . . Darling Mama, oh it is touching to see her, she looks so young and pretty with her white cap and widow's weeds; she bears her sorrow so well in a resigned and Christian spirit, it grieves me deeply when I see her crying and think how formerly Papa comforted her, and now she is so alone."[37] Vicky's letters to Fritz at this time illustrate the bond that Queen Victoria and her oldest daughter shared, a bond so rare in royal circles: intensely happy marriages. "Mama is dreadfully sad," Vicky wrote, "she cries a lot; then there is always the empty room, the empty bed, she always sleep[s] with Papa's coat over her and his dear red dressing-gown beside her and some of his clothes in the bed! . . . Poor Mama has to go to bed, has to get up alone—for ever. She was as much in love with Papa as though she had married him yesterday, I see that daily, she feels the same as your little Frauchen . . . and is always consumed with longing for her husband. I should feel just the same. . . . Mama had so desperately longed for another child. The central point is missing, we wander around like sheep without a shepherd."[38]

After the Prince Consort died, Queen Victoria looked to Fritz to help sustain her, telling him: "You alone are my support in my infinite loneliness and boundless sorrow which increases day by day. . . . For I feel so strongly how inferior I am to him, that ingenious man, who was the pride and also the life and light of the house and country."[39]

In the immediate aftermath of Albert's death, the queen leaned heavily on her second eldest daughter, Alice. Victoria's emotions had crashed to precipitous lows. Without the eighteen-year-old Alice's assiduous ministrations and mature countenance, the queen might easily have collapsed into a profound melancholia. Not as brilliant as Vicky, who would have easily helped Victoria had she been by her side in those days right after Prince Albert died, Alice was nevertheless indispensable. From her seclusion, the grieving queen relied on Alice to deal on her behalf with ministers. Alice also tried to rally the queen. In a letter to her mother, who had remained in seclusion at Osborne House, Alice urged: "Take courage, dear Mama, and feel strong in the thought that you require all your moral and physical strength to continue the journey which brings you nearer to *Home* and to *Him*. . . . Bear patiently and courageously your heavy burden, and it will lighten imperceptibly as you near him, and God's love and mercy will support you."[40]

Alice did not stay by Queen Victoria's side for long, since Victoria had given her permission to marry Prince Louis of Hesse in July 1862, largely because this had been settled while Prince Albert was still alive. The wedding ceremony, held in the dining room at Osborne House, was a forlorn event, with a trousseau consisting largely of black gowns. Even Queen Victoria described the ceremony to Vicky as "more funeral than a wedding."[41] The bride looked somber and haggard, far older than her nineteen years.

With Vicky's and Alice's futures settled, concerns regarding Bertie persisted. The queen continued to blame her eldest son for his father's death, albeit indirectly and unfairly, and told Vicky, "Oh! that boy. . . . I never can or shall look at him without a shudder. . . . I try to employ and use him—but I am not hopeful."[42] And in another letter the queen told Vicky: "Poor Bertie!—he is very affectionate and dutiful but he is very trying . . . his listlessness and want of attention are great, and cause me much anxiety."[43] Prussia's crown princess commiserated and also feared for her own son, telling the queen: "Poor Bertie, how I pity him!—but what sorrow he does cause. . . . The education of sons is an awful responsibility and a great anxiety and it is bitter indeed if they do not repay one for one's care and trouble—it makes me tremble when I think of my little William and the future!"[44]

All still perceived the solution to Bertie's dissipation as marriage. After the Prince Consort's death, Vicky continued to champion Princess Alix and acted as matchmaker, motivated by the approval Prince Albert had given the match before his death. The couple married in March 1863 at St. George's Chapel, Windsor, with the queen watching from Catherine of Aragon's Closet above the altar, dressed in mourning. Vicky's four-year-old son, Willy, created a scene when he bit his hemophiliac uncle, Leopold, on the leg. Queen Victoria came to like her daughter-in-law, whom she later described to Vicky as being "calm and sweet and gentle and lovely. Very clever I don't think she is, but she is right-minded and sensible and straightforward."[45]

Since the queen persisted in being the reclusive widow, the Prince and Princess of Wales soon became the leaders of London society. During the early years of her marriage, Alix's increasing deafness and frequent pregnancies did not stop her from trying to keep up with her husband's entertaining. Soon, fashionable society centered on their London home, Marlborough House. Queen Victoria disapproved of the prince's late nights and parties and, later, his infidelities. She was grateful that Alix remained devoted to Bertie through it all, choosing to focus on her children: Eddy, George, Louise, Victoria, and Maud. Pleased to see the succession to the throne secured with the Wales children, Queen Victoria nevertheless confided to Vicky about her disappointment in the first three, describing them as such "miserable, puny, little children (each weaker than the preceding one) that it is quite a misfortune."[46]

The Prince of Wales could never live up to Queen Victoria's ideals as embodied by the late Prince Consort. She complained to Vicky about Bertie and Alix, "both looking as ill as possible. We are seriously alarmed about her—for though Bertie writes and says he is so anxious to take care of her, he goes on going out every night till she will become a skeleton. . . . I am quite unhappy about it. Oh! how different poor, foolish Bertie is to adored Papa whose gentle, loving, wise, motherly care of me when he was not 21 exceeded everything."[47]

Much as she disapproved of the couple's social whirl, Victoria was herself partly to blame. As she remained reclusive—even five years after Prince Albert's death still absenting herself from London—high society hungered for arbiters, naturally gravitating toward her heir. The queen finally began emerging from seclusion when she opened Parliament in 1866—but then only grudgingly. She may have worked assiduously in private, but she still clung to her grief "with all the intensity of her nature" and in the process plunged the court "into its long period of mourning."[48] This mourning largely took place at Osborne and Balmoral, Queen Victoria's favorite homes.

The queen's Scottish retreat, hundreds of miles from London and in a desolate area where Victoria could enjoy the cold, damp weather, was particularly appealing. Impervious to the cold, Victoria, like Maria Theresa, preferred to have windows open even when it was chilly outside. Also at Balmoral was the queen's favorite gillie, John Brown. In his late thirties, the blue-eyed, bearded Brown had an undeniably masculine appeal, and certainly the queen had always appreciated manliness. But it was Brown's bluntness, devotedness, and observations that most struck a chord with the middle-aged Victoria. By 1865 he was a permanent fixture at the queen's side. She told Vicky, "As for Brown I never saw such an unselfish servant . . . and my comfort—my service are really his only objects."[49] His brusqueness seemed like fresh air to the highly circumspect queen. Unperturbed by familiar talk from Brown, Victoria was instead comforted by it. In one such exchange, Brown was heard shouting at the queen after she pricked her chin, "Hoots, then, wumman, can ye no hold yerr head up?"[50]

The unlikely closeness between the rugged Scots gillie and the imposing monarch was such that by 1868 whispers of "Mrs. Brown" could be heard in reference to the queen. Brown remained by Victoria's side for nearly twenty years, until his death. Whatever people thought of the gillie, and many, including the queen's older children, found him unbearable, there was no denying that he helped Victoria emerge from her grief over Prince Albert. Moreover, Brown's support helped Victoria take the reins in leading her family. With Baron Stockmar and King Leopold also dead, Queen Victoria's value as an adviser within the family correspondingly rose.

As monarch, matriarch, and adviser, the queen now had complete command over her family. This was in evidence during a family dinner party, dominated by her awe-inspiring presence. Of that evening, Prince Nicholas of Greece recorded: "Despite the fact that it was an intimate family circle, I noticed that my uncle and aunt and all my other relations seemed somewhat intimidated, and whenever the Queen asked them a question they replied with an expression of the deepest reverence."[51] Prince Nicholas was also struck by Victoria's imposing presence. Despite being small in stature and dressed in her habitual black widow's weeds and veil, the queen had an appearance "marked by a dignity and majesty so great that anyone who saw her for the first time could not help being profoundly impressed." She was, concluded the prince, "a Queen in everything and at all times."[52]

Head of an ever-burgeoning family, Victoria embraced the mantle of matriarch. And nowhere were her attentions more focused than toward Vicky and Prussia. Queen Victoria continued to pay close attention to the situation in Prussia, where she hoped Fritz's father would move toward a constitutional monarchy in the British model, as Prince Albert had envisioned. Vicky and Fritz nearly had their chance in September 1862, when Wilhelm I threatened to abdicate because of a dispute with Parliament. Vicky urged Fritz to accept his father's offer of the throne, but he refused. He was too attached to his father and the Hohenzollern traditions to seize the opportunity. Fritz noted forlornly:

"We are faced with the worst—the idea of abdication! May God help us!"[53] His reticence inadvertently opened the door to Otto von Bismarck's domination of German affairs. Since Fritz would not step into the breach, Bismarck did, becoming King Wilhelm's first minister. It was one of those unheralded roads not taken. Had Wilhelm I abdicated, "the name Bismarck would never have been heard of outside Germany. Thus the third week of September in 1862 may be seen as one of those turning points in history, silent, unnoticed, but almost infinite in their consequences."[54]

The political maelstrom that erupted in 1862 in Prussia placing liberals against conservatives extended to the senior members of the Prussian royal family, pitting the king, who naturally leaned toward the conservatives, against his wife, Fritz, and Vicky. When Fritz daringly opposed his father's unconstitutional leanings, the crown prince and princess found themselves in a quandary. Vicky told her mother of being "in a dreadful position, the country loudly clamouring for Fritz to come forward and he receiving the most peremptory commands from the King and no thanks for the tact and self denial Fritz has been showing the last whole year—only reproaches for having opposed the King."[55] "We are," added Vicky, "in a sad state of perplexity and alarm and quite alone—without assistance or advice."[56] She concluded the letter with the anxious words "Dear Mama, pity us and think of your much tormented and affectionate and dutiful daughter."[57] The princess also confided to her mother that "we are surrounded with spies, who watch all we do, and most likely report all to Berlin, in a sense to checkmate everything we do."[58]

Victoria was beside herself with worry, telling Vicky: "Oh! dearest child! How distressed I feel for you both! And darling Papa, not being here to help us and advise us! If I only could be of any use I would do anything to save you sorrow and anxiety!"[59] The queen added, "This house—your old home—sad and shaken as it is—is open for you. Come here with the children and you can be with us or in town, or in the country or wherever you like—only don't stay in Prussia."[60] Vicky could not help but compare Prussia with her homeland, writing to her mother: "The way in which the Government behave, and the way in which they have treated Fritz, rouse my every feeling of independence. Thank God, I was born in England, where people are not slaves, and too good to allow themselves to be treated as such."[61] And in another letter, Vicky wrote, "If it becomes necessary for us to leave the country, I can hardly say how grateful we shall be to be once again with you, in that blessed country of peace and happiness!"[62] Vicky must have been gratified to read her mother's words: "You are the best and wisest adviser [Fritz] could have. . . . May God bless and protect you and guide you in your arduous and difficult task!"[63] The crisis eventually passed, but the experience confirmed Vicky's suspicions about Bismarck, who did nothing of significance to help Fritz during this trying time.

With Bismarck's fortunes in the ascendant, Vicky saw trouble ahead. Already in 1859, she had warned Queen Victoria that he was a "false and dangerous adversary."[64] And to Fritz in 1862, the princess lamented: "*For God's sake, anyone but him* as minister."[65] Bismarck was, after all, the mastermind of German unification who in 1862 had famously proclaimed that the great questions of the day were not to be decided by parliamentary speeches and majority votes but by "iron and blood."

The arrival on the political scene of Otto von Bismarck as minister-president in 1862 meant increased difficulties for Vicky and Fritz. A proponent of fiercely conservative views, Bismarck was to use every opportunity to undermine the couple. To counter their influence and cement his own, he cleverly cultivated Wilhelm I's natural conservatism. Once Bismarck became a power to be reckoned with, he "played Wilhelm I like a virtuoso. . . . It was a fine performance, signifying a unique talent that Bismarck would use to the awe of his supporters and the despair of his enemies."[66] Vicky saw through it all. The crown princess related Prussia's political troubles to her mother in writing: "Our affairs here are in a lamentable state—indecision, confusion and mistakes of all kinds. . . . The reactionary party get stronger every day and have the King now completely on their side and in their power."[67] Vicky foresaw nothing but trouble in the man who would become the architect of the German Empire. "This country seems to me like a ship tossing about . . . a reckless, inexperienced and short-sighted man (B) at the helm and storms gathering around—ourselves and our children at his mercy!" she complained to the queen.[68]

Victoria sympathized with her beleaguered daughter's plight, urging Vicky to remember: "Always, dear child, write to me anything you hear and are anxious about, just as you did to dear Papa."[69] The remarkably close relationship between Victoria and Vicky was forged during these difficult years, when the crown princess was in her early twenties. Though Vicky was not yet empress and the German Empire not yet proclaimed, 1861 to 1864 "are important years in the history of the [royal] family and of the two countries, for they mark the slow—the pitiably slow—emergence of the Queen from the shadows of sorrow and the alarmingly rapid development of Prussia, bringing in its train the beginning of the rivalry between England and Germany which was to last for eighty years."[70]

Prussia's rising status took on added momentum under Bismarck's leadership. With the goal of unifying the German states under undisputed Prussian domination, Bismarck engineered three wars that would lead to the creation of the German Empire. In 1864, in the first of these wars, Prussia and Austria together wrestled the provinces of Schleswig-Holstein from Denmark's control in an easily won conflict. Within Queen Victoria's own family, the war over Schleswig-Holstein generated heated feelings. Alix, the Princess of Wales, naturally sided vehemently with her father, with Bertie staying loyal to Alix. To the princess, Prussia was the predator bent on stealing Denmark's provinces. Vicky, meanwhile, supported Prussian ambitions. Annoyed at the carping within her family, Victoria finally ordered the subject out of bounds in her homes. Thus, Otto von Bismarck's shadow had extended even into the British royal family.

As the years passed, the battle between Queen Victoria's eldest daughter and the wily Prussian Junker intensified. In some respects Bismarck and Vicky were similar. Though he was twenty-six years her senior, Bismarck, like the crown princess, was perceptive and fought tenaciously for a chosen cause. Neither was docile or unambitious; both were daring and unafraid of provocations. Here then were "two remarkable personalities, each watchful and guarded like two expert duellists who realise the skill of the other."[71] Well aware of Vicky's abilities and forcefulness, Bismarck was always extremely wary of her influence on Fritz and her impact on Prussia. The first minister was correct in this, for Vicky did not hesitate to tell Fritz her political opinions, but she did so always with his and Prussia's best interests at heart. In one letter, Vicky warned her husband: "You owe it to your future, to the country and to your children to keep aloof from everything which might lead the people to have an erroneous idea of your political convictions, or that might shake the confidence which you have won by your liberal attitude and your collaboration with Ministers holding those opinions. This is really your duty and in no way conflicts with that to your father. Please, please, dearest, listen to your little wife who only thinks of your welfare and who lives for you and is so proud of you. I am afraid you are too good and think that you are doing your duty by sacrificing your opinion to that of your dear Papa. You have other duties, which in my opinion, take first place."[72]

Vicky's lot in Prussia was not an easy one. The crown princess may have had a loving husband who shared her political convictions, but they were thwarted in their attempts to promote a liberal agenda, especially with Bismarck watching their every move. In a long letter to Queen Victoria, Vicky had poured out her frustrations: "You cannot think how painful it is to be continually surounded by people who consider your very existence a misfortune and your sentiments evidence of lunacy! . . . Do not think it easy, dear Mama; it costs me many and many a hard struggle. I know what a responsibility I take upon myself in taking advantage of my husband's reliance on my judgement and in giving any advice as positively as I can."[73] Vicky was conscious of her reputation in Berlin and told her mother so: "It is very disagreeable to me to be thought meddling and intriguing. . . . I should like to conciliate all parties and particularly to live in peace with all those by whom we are surrounded, whose affection I know I could gain if I sought it by having no opinion of my own. But I should not be a free-born English-woman and your child if I did not set all those things aside as minor considerations. I am very ambitious for the country, for Fritz and the children and so I am determined to brave all the rest!" However, she also confessed, "I have not a bright prospect before me," especially when she admitted that many look "upon me with jealousy as a stranger and as an Englishwoman . . . continually say[ing] I dislike Germany, I cannot get accustomed to live out of England, I wish to change everything and make everything English."[74] Queen Victoria replied with understanding, agreeing that "your position is indeed a very difficult one."[75] It would not become easier.

Four years later, the tone in Vicky's letters to her mother continued to highlight her struggle at the Berlin court. "Our children," went one, "are universally pitied for having the great misfortune of having me for their Mama with my *'unglücklichen englischen Ideen'* [unfortunate English ideas] and *'unpreussichen Gesinnungen'* [un-Prussian views]. It is supposed they cannot possibly turn out well. This I am so accustomed to hear that I have got quite used to it and do not care a straw for all their 'bosh.' I trust my children may grow up like my Fritz, like Papa, like you—and as unlike the rest of the Prussian royal family as possible; then they can be good patriots and useful to their country, call it Prussia or call it Germany."[76]

In 1870, Fritz confided sadly in his diary that in Berlin, "the order of the day is to vilify my wife."[77] At least Vicky took consolation in the crown prince, as she proudly admitted to her mother: "I have a husband who loads me with undeserved kindness, indulgence and confidence, with whom I live in unity and happiness and whom I daily learn to respect, admire and love!"[78]

23

THE BRITISH AND GERMAN EMPIRES

he Crown Princess of Prussia visited Queen Victoria in England when she could. An English courtier commented on one such meeting between mother and daughter in 1863, noting, the "Pr. Royal is now alone with the Q. and young ones, and I hope it will be very good their being thrown completely on one another. [Vicky] is a wonderful creature, gifted beyond expression, delightful, but with much to contend with to bring those strong impulses and that keen intellect into submission, dear child!"[1]

As Queen Victoria's remaining children grew older, she concerned herself with their marriage prospects just as Queen Isabella and Empress Maria Theresa had done with their offspring. But unlike Isabella and Maria Theresa, Victoria did not seek marriages that were necessarily politically advantageous. Vicky's marriage had been the glaring exception. Next among Victoria's daughters to marry were Princess Helena (Lenchen) and Princess Louise. In comparing these two daughters, the queen bluntly admitted that Louise was "so handsome . . . so gracious . . . so quiet and lady-like. . . . Poor dear Lenchen, though most useful and active and clever and amiable, does not improve in looks."[2] Lenchen married the impoverished Prince Christian of Schleswig-Holstein-Sonderburg-Augustenburg, fifteen years her senior. They lived happily with their children near Windsor Castle and kept their distance from the queen when possible, much to Victoria's annoyance, though Lenchen did her share of attending her mother. In 1871 Princess Louise, the prettiest of Victoria's daughters and a highly accomplished artist, married the Marquess of Lorne (later Duke of Argyll), who became governor-general of Canada. The province of Alberta and Lake Louise were named after the princess. The couple remained childless.

Next to marry was Prince Alfred, Victoria's second eldest son. Arrogant and short-tempered, Alfred enjoyed a career in the Royal Navy and eventually became the reigning Duke of Saxe-Coburg-Gotha. In 1874, he married Grand Duchess Marie of Russia, a formidable woman who could never forget that she was a Romanov with a demoted status at Queen Victoria's court. One of their daughters became the flamboyant Queen Marie of Romania. Prince Arthur, Victoria's third and favorite son, named after the famed Duke of Wellington, who had defeated Napoleon at Waterloo, fittingly chose a military career. In 1874, he married Louise Margaret of Prussia, daughter of Fritz's first cousin Frederick Charles of Prussia.

Of all Queen Victoria's children, her two eldest girls, Vicky and Alice, were fated to lead the most poignant lives. The sisters were close from their childhood days, a bond that did not disappear once marriage sent them both to Germany—Vicky to Prussia and Alice to Hesse. Vicky's future always held out a far more glittering prospect than Alice's, thanks largely to Fritz's position as the future king of Prussia. Prestige and wealth set Vicky apart from Alice. "Vast riches," in fact, were "expected someday to come Vicky's way on her accession as queen of Prussia," whereas Alice's "fiscal situation seemed almost bleak."[3] In comparing their predicaments, one need only look at the cities where the sisters made their homes. Vicky's home, Berlin (capital of mighty Prussia), with its Baroque and Neoclassical buildings and the impressive Brandenburg Gate, easily overshadowed Darmstadt, Alice's home and Hesse's small, provincial capital, dotted by half-timbered buildings and narrow streets.

The sisters' marriages also diverged. Though nearly ten years separated them in age, Vicky had unquestionably found her soul mate in Fritz. Like Queen Victoria, Vicky was passionately devoted to her husband, an affection that was heartily reciprocated, despite the fact that the prince was all too aware of his intellectual limitations compared with his cerebral powerhouse of a wife. Vicky made no secret of her dreams for Fritz, telling him, "I have . . . unlimited ambitions for you & will not rest until you have set an example for the whole world to follow—& through you Prussia has become a worthy example for the others."[4]

Vicky's love for and devotion to Fritz never faltered. She wrote appreciatively of her husband to her mother, saying, "Every day I have a new opportunity of admiring all dear Fritz's sober qualities."[5] The queen agreed with her daughter's assessment. After spending some time with her son-in-law while Prince Albert was still alive, Victoria wrote a glowing letter to Vicky's husband: "Allow me to tell you, my dear Fritz, how fond I am of you, how close you have drawn to us during this long and yet all too short and pleasant visit, and how we have learned to appreciate, love and respect you more and more every day!"[6] Fritz was touched by his mother-in-law's words and wrote to Vicky, "It is a wonderful thing for me to be so honoured by your respected and beloved parents! Since I have called you mine, you have made a different person of me . . . everything, everything only through *mein Frauchen*. . . . If 'marriages are made in heaven,' then God has obviously done so in our case."[7]

The marriage of Vicky's sister Alice, by contrast, was not so blessed. As the years passed, she and Louis drifted apart, prompting Alice to write candidly to him: "I longed for a real companion, for apart from that life had nothing to offer *me* in Darmstadt. I could have been quite happy and contented living in a cottage, if I had been able to share my intellectual interests, and intellectual aspirations with a husband whose strong, protective love would have guided me around the rocks . . . but we have developed separately—away from each other, and that is why I feel that true companionship is an impossibility for us—because our thoughts will never meet."[8]

Vicky and Alice differed in personality, Vicky being far more outspoken and forward than her more tactful sister (though Alice's pro-English inclinations, like Vicky's, were in ample evidence). Vicky understood this difference and uncharacteristically felt at a disadvantage. Alice, Vicky pointed out, "did everything imaginable, or so tells Mama—and Mama believes it all as well—ever increasing Mama's love for her."[9] As for herself, Vicky noted disconcertingly to Fritz: "I unfortunately do not have the talent & am not clever enough to say what I do not think. . . . Alice acts, by contrast, like a smart little lady—& that's why she has a tremendous amount of influence. She is right & I am wrong, for it would be much cleverer to hide opinions that only irritate others & the assertion of which is not of the slightest benefit. During our childhood it was always so—she was always the docile and loveable one, yielding with bonne grace, easy to praise & almost never getting into trouble. How different things were with your little fat girl, who always had the talent for 'putting her foot in it.' "[10]

Differences between Alice and Vicky made their way in to Vicky's correspondence with their mother, tinged with sibling rivalry. Queen Victoria once reproached her eldest daughter for this: "I must scold you dearest child, for a little jealous remark about poor Alice which is not right! . . . Alice's position is a totally different one to yours—she was much more with me than you had ever been, for you married at 17—she only at 19—and beloved Papa was then my blessed companion and support. Then Alice's husband has nothing to do at home now; they are not rich, and their best work is to be a support and comfort to me. If Alice could not be with me much hereafter—why, then Lenchen must be, because, dearest child, your position is too great and high a one ever to be able to be here long at a time or to devote yourself solely to me."[11] In reply, a humbled and defensive Vicky wrote: "I am sorry that I should again have so ill expressed myself. . . . I am not in the least jealous of her. I know the difference of her position and mine quite well, and would not change mine, difficult as it is, for any other in the world."[12]

Relegated at Darmstadt to a less important court than Vicky's, Alice nevertheless diligently worked for her adopted country; for instance, she nursed the wounded during the Austro-Prussian War of 1866. Just two years after the Prussian-Danish War, the opportunistic Bismarck had seized the chance to defeat Austria by fighting over Schleswig-Holstein. This conflict, the Austro-Prussian War of 1866, was the latest in the minister's plans for Prussian aggrandizement. The war proved especially heartbreaking for Queen Victoria, who was perturbed to see two of her daughters with their husbands off to war on opposing sides. Hesse, like most of the German states, viewed Prussia warily because of its aggressiveness and so was not averse to siding with Austria. Alice's and Vicky's opposing sides had added poignancy because Alice had recently visited Vicky in Berlin and told their mother that "Vicky is dear, so loving! . . . There is a reflection of Papa's great mind in her."[13] Alice also told Queen Victoria, "Life with dear Vicky . . . reminds me in many things of our life in England in former happy days. . . . We both always say to each other, no children were so happy . . . as we were; and that we can never . . . give our children all that we had."[14] Alice had a particularly difficult time during the war. There was little food, and she had to watch with trepidation as the Prussians marched into Darmstadt.

Prussia won the war in a mere seven weeks. Bismarck's plan to unify Germany under Prussian dominance at the expense of the Habsburgs' Austrian dynasty was taking shape. Frederick the Great's dreams of Prussian hegemony and the subordination of the Habsburgs were finally coming true.

Throughout this turbulent time, Vicky had her share of sorrows when her son Sigismund, not yet two, died of meningitis. The anguished Vicky told her mother of "the long cry of agony which rises from the innermost depth of my soul."[15] Family tragedies and war were not the only sadnesses that plagued Vicky. Her unpopularity had grown among many Prussians. Vicky, who had so much influence over Fritz, went against the grain of the Prussian aristocracy's "conception of marriage" as being that "in which the wife was expected to be the compliant mate of an omnipotent husband."[16] Outrage over her domineering personality and forthrightness "fatally undermined her attempt to establish a place for herself in Berlin by insisting she was her husband's partner, not his servant."[17] The years had not dampened Vicky's raison d'être in relation to Fritz. When she married, Vicky had "plunged with the zealous ardor of a missionary into the task of combating the influence of [the] army and *Junkers* on her husband."[18] She had not relinquished and would not relinquish that task.

Back in Britain, Victoria gradually emerged from her seclusion, having understood the need to play a public role. Moreover, the queen had at last gained back her zest for life, telling Vicky: "I have learned to wish to live, and try and keep myself tolerably well—for the sake of my people, children, friends and country!"[19] Besides opening Parliament, another event signaled Victoria's reentry into public life: the service at St. Paul's Cathedral held February 1872 in thanksgiving for the Prince of Wales's recovery from a serious bout of typhoid. For some time, relations between Victoria and her heir had been frosty, though they never degenerated into the exasperating battle of wills that beset Empress Maria Theresa and her oldest son, Joseph II. Yet unlike Maria Theresa, who willingly shared power with Joseph as co-ruler, Queen Victoria did not encourage the future Edward VII to learn statecraft and ruling. In fact, "Queen Victoria guarded her prerogatives jealously and did not allow the Prince of Wales to share any part of her work. . . . The Prince of Wales had sought refuge from this enforced idleness in a purely social life, for which the Queen criticized him without offering him any interesting or constructive alternative."[20]

Victoria was as immersed as ever in the minutiae of reigning—the workload of her private secretary, Henry Ponsonby, attested to this—but she had less power than Isabella of Castile or Maria Theresa had had in their days. Her role as monarch was circumscribed by Parliament. Nonetheless, holding strong political views, Queen Victoria sometimes overstepped the bounds of constitutional behavior. Indeed, the queen "rebelled at the notion that her job stopped at the 'criticism of detail.'"[21]

For nearly three of her six decades as queen, Victoria dealt with the two most famous of her ten prime ministers: the goliaths of British politics William Gladstone and Benjamin Disraeli, who alternated their time in power: Disraeli (1868), Gladstone (1868–74), Disraeli (1874–1880), Gladstone (1880–85, 1886, 1892–94). Victoria had a passionate dislike of Gladstone and a deep-seated affection for Disraeli. The two were archrivals, sitting as they did on opposing sides of the political spectrum (Gladstone was a Liberal, whereas Disraeli was a Conservative). They were also polar opposites in almost every other respect; and nowhere were their opposing personas more starkly in evidence than in their conduct toward women. Whereas Disraeli, the Victorian "dandy," was at ease in the great homes of England's political elite, seeking their support and friend-ship, the highly religious Gladstone would seek out prostitutes with the sole objective of trying to rescue them from their life of sin. With his piercing gaze that could turn into a frightening scowl, Gladstone had a forceful personality matched by an impressive intellect, which he did not hesitate to unleash, even on the queen. Disraeli, by contrast, with his pointed face and pleasant countenance, was convivial, flamboyant, and flattering toward his queen. He easily charmed his way into Victoria's heart. Disraeli gained further accolades from the queen because he praised Prince Albert, a shrewd move since she continued to view her dead husband as incomparable. Whereas Disraeli gladly nurtured his relationship with Victoria in flowery language and actions, the deeply moralistic Gladstone could be dour and hectoring. This browbeating tone greatly annoyed the queen. She once famously commented that Gladstone addressed her as if she were a public meeting.

Gladstone understood the need for the queen to be seen more publicly and urged this upon her, to which an annoyed Victoria replied that she was indisposed. The queen complained of Gladstone to Vicky, describing him as "very arrogant, tyrannical and obstinate, with no knowledge of the world or human nature."[22] Nor did Gladstone's support of Irish home rule endear him to Victoria, who interpreted home rule as an attack on the empire. Moreover, Gladstone's tendency to send long-winded memoranda instead of clear, concise ones infuriated her. Added to this were Victoria's and Gladstone's divergent political views. At the beginning of her reign, the queen's sympathies had been decidedly pro-Whig (the Liberals were an outgrowth of the Whigs). But by the time of the Gladstone-Disraeli rivalry, Victoria espoused Conservative views that matched Disraeli's.

Another reason Victoria disapproved of Gladstone was that she believed he was trying to curtail her importance; thus, the queen "was not above threatening abdication to counteract his attempts to reduce her influence."[23] In the end, the "war" between Queen Victoria and William Gladstone "lasted longer and was more dramatic than even the great public conflict between Gladstone and Disraeli."[24]

Though Gladstone was not as hostile to his queen as Bismarck was to the crown princess, Gladstone and Victoria's prickly relationship somewhat mirrored Vicky's antagonistic relationship with the goliath of Prussian politics. Mother and daughter came to see both men as their nemeses. Unfortunately, Vicky was never able to find her political equivalent of a Disraeli. Only Victoria had that good fortune.

If Gladstone was Victoria's bête-noire, Disraeli was her second Lord Melbourne. It was not a one-sided attachment. The adoration was mutual, for Disraeli's "taste had always been for dowagers rather than debutantes . . . his women friends were *'tout grand mères.'* How much more rewarding then, to be dealing with the greatest grandmother of them all. Here, surely, was the culmination of a life-time's association with matrons. Here was the mother-figure to end all mother-figures."[25] Disraeli knew exactly what to say to the queen. When she sent for him in 1874 to form a government, she noted with pleasure: "He repeatedly said *whatever I wished* SHOULD *be done.*" Disraeli also knew how to act before his queen—dropping on his knees to kiss her hand and romantically declaring: "I plight my troth to the kindest of *Mistresses.*"[26] But there was more substance to the couple's special relationship than platitudes and gestures, for Queen Victoria was in complete accord with the robust imperial policies pursued by Disraeli. She instinctively disdained Gladstone's propensity for allowing Britain to " 'swallow insults' and play a negative role."[27] Victoria had once said that Gladstone had "no strong sense of the dignity and power of England abroad."[28] Not surprisingly, the queen celebrated Disraeli's desire "to reassert British power in Europe."[29] Disraeli made no apologies for Britain's greatness and did not retreat from asserting it.

One of his greatest successes was preventing the Suez Canal from falling completely into French hands when the Khedive of Egypt was selling his shares (which amounted to just under half the total). To have allowed France to control that strategic link to India, through which most British ships crossed, would have been an extremely grave forfeiture. In this, Victoria was in complete accord. Disraeli maneuvered so that the British government bought the khedive's shares in 1875, thanks to a 4-million-pound loan from the Rothschild bank. Having concluded the transaction, Disraeli told the queen: "It is just settled. . . . you have it, Madam." Thus did he lay at Victoria's feet the Suez Canal "like some exotic gift."[30] Next, in 1877, the loyal Disraeli handed Victoria the title Empress of India. Though she never visited the jewel of Britain's empire, Victoria paid special attention to India and its peoples, making the title "empress" an especially gratifying one. In gratitude for all he had done, Queen Victoria created Disraeli the Earl of Beaconsfield. His greatest service to the queen was to transform her from the "Widow of Windsor into the Faery Queen, [which] enabled Victoria to develop into the revered, magnificent and almost mythical figure of her old age: the Doyenne of Sovereigns . . . Victoria *Regina et imperatrix.*"[31]

Vicky, ever Victoria's confidante through the years, watched events in England closely and was pleased to see her mother's reign unfolding brilliantly.

Vicky espoused outlooks similar to those of her mother and Disraeli when it came to affirming and exercising British power on the world stage. In the mid-1880s, Vicky explicitly voiced this view, noting, "England is a great deal too humble to foreign Powers! They only misunderstand her. We get no thanks for our modesty and moderation."[32] On another occasion, she stated emphatically: "You know I take so passionate an interest in the progress and development of liberty and culture all over the globe that it is not without the greatest pain that I can even brook the idea of England's abdicating her legitimate part in the work of civilization. *She has no right to do so*, and thereby do incalculable harm to the good cause and . . . to all other nations."[33]

Vicky's appreciation for Queen Victoria's sympathy and advice had also grown, and she admitted it to her mother: "You cannot think what a word of approbation from you is to me! . . . A word from you . . . repays me for oh! so much, so I kiss your dear hand in deep and tender thanks."[34] And in another letter, "As one grows older and lives through more trials and difficulties one's love to one's mother grows and deepens."[35] This closeness contrasted with the strained relationship between Vicky and her mother-in-law, Augusta. The outrageously rouged and wigged Augusta loved to meddle, entertain, and gossip. She expected Vicky to dance in attendance and acted the tyrant, ordering her exhausted daughter-in-law to be at her beck and call. Queen Victoria sympathized with her daughter's predicament in Berlin, confiding to a courtier of the empress: "She is markedly unkind to the Crown Princess."[36] It thus comes as no surprise that, for Vicky, "Queen Victoria and England remained the ultimate refuge in a life dominated by disapproving relations and dynastic jealousies."[37] By the time she had made her home in Prussia for thirteen years, Vicky could hardly be blamed for having definitively concluded that England reigned supreme in her heart. "You cannot think," she wrote to one of her English friends, "how dull and melancholy and queer I feel away from you all and from beloved England! Each time I get there I feel my attachment to that precious bit of earth grow stronger and stronger. . . . Going away and returning here [to Prussia] always causes a commotion in my feelings which want a little time and reasoning to one's self to get over."[38] A large part of Vicky's continuing devotion to England no doubt stemmed from the steady love and support she received from Queen Victoria, though six hundred miles separated mother and daughter.

Vicky's closeness to Queen Victoria meant that she continued to relate her impressions of events and individuals to her mother, especially where her children were concerned. Vicky's relationships with her older children were less warm than those with her youngest brood, a disappointment she did not hide from her mother. Vicky was always frustrated with Charlotte, whom she found dull and possessed of a difficult temper. Willy was "a dear, interesting, charming boy—clever, amusing engaging—it is impossible not to spoil him a little." But Vicky also noted his failings; such as his inclination to be "selfish, domineering and proud."[39] Two years later, when Willy was nine, Vicky still wrote of his potential but added another drawback to his character, laziness. At the time the young prince's schooling began, in 1867, his mother wrote of her concern to her brother Prince Arthur: "Now that Willie's [*sic*] education has begun in earnest . . . I often feel how difficult it is, and what a responsibility is laid on one's shoulders."[40]

Much to Vicky's consternation, Willy's overweening pride became more pronounced with the years. His exposure to Hohenzollern-Prussian militarism inevitably nurtured this arrogance. Vicky tried to soften the edges by sending Willy to England and Queen Victoria as often as possible, visits that he enjoyed. Nevertheless, in the end, Wilhelm was first and foremost a Prussian. He would come to have a love-hate relationship with England, as he did with his mother.

As time passed, Willy became increasingly alienated from his parents. Indulged by his Prussian grandparents, Wilhelm and Augusta, the prince felt a growing affinity for them and came to share their disapproval of his mother. From Willy's teenage years onward, Vicky found less to extol about him to Queen Victoria and more causes for complaint. Just before his eighteenth birthday, the overbearing Willy was packed off to England to be "cut down to size" by his English grandmother. Although the queen and the prince had very strong differences, thanks to Victoria's making allowances and Willy's ability to "take hints," a major clash between the two was barely avoided.[41]

Besides anxieties over Willy, Victoria's and Vicky's attentions were riveted to momentous events beyond their family circle. One of these, the Franco-Prussian War, had far-reaching repercussions. France's Emperor Napoléon III played into Bismarck's hands. In 1870 the wily minister provoked France into fighting Prussia in a war that would determine whether France or Prussia would become the Continent's unrivaled power. And as Bismarck had calculated, the south German states took Prussia's side in the conflict. With victory, a united Germany was set to rise under Prussian domination.

When war broke out, Queen Victoria was aghast, telling Vicky that her prayers were with Germany and that "my heart bleeds for you *all*!"[42] Fritz again went off to war, while Vicky, who had recently given birth to her daughter Sophie, was frantic about his fate. In Berlin, Vicky tended to the wounded in hospitals and near the front. The war lasted less than a year, ending when Napoléon

III and 100,000 French troops were captured at Sedan. Napoléon was then overthrown. Paris, after months of famine, surrendered. On January 18, 1871, Bismarck watched as the German Empire was proclaimed in the Hall of Mirrors at Versailles. King Wilhelm was now the German emperor: Kaiser Wilhelm I. Bismarck became Germany's first chancellor—the "Iron Chancellor." As for Vicky, she was, above all, gratified that Fritz not only had survived the war but had acquitted himself well.

Besides cementing Prussia's position as a European power, the Franco-Prussian War placed Prussia at the fore once and for all among the Germanic states; for "Prussia did not become German. Germany became Prussian."[43] Bismarck's ambitious plans for Prussia had finally borne spectacular fruit. Vicky's nemesis had without a doubt become "a truly Machiavellian figure of astounding political skills."[44]

The outcome of the Franco-Prussian War left Queen Victoria of two minds. On the one hand, she was pleased to see Germany's success and happy for Vicky and Fritz, but on the other hand, she could not help but feel pangs of pity for her friends Napoléon III and Eugénie. The queen sent the former empress a message, saying "that I could not be unmoved by their dreadful misfortune."[45] Napoléon and Eugénie eventually fled to England and lived there in exile. Victoria was impressed by Eugénie's demeanor when she arrived, telling Vicky's mother-in-law that "the Empress bears her tragic fate with dignity. She never utters a word of complaint or bitterness against anyone."[46]

Back in Germany, instability racked the empire as a battle of wills pitting Bismarck against the Roman Catholic Church emerged. At unification, Germany absorbed a number of states with substantial Catholic populations, many of whom were generally represented by the opposition Center party in the Reichstag (German Parliament). When Bismarck could not persuade the Center party to agree to his policies, he sensed the power of a resurgent Church. To preempt this, the chancellor unleashed a campaign of repression against Germany's Catholics, known as the *Kulturkampf*. By breaking the Church's power, Bismarck aspired to consolidate his own power. Harsh laws were passed against Catholics and their clergy in a campaign that lasted for several years. Bismarck's *Kulturkampf* eventually abated and ultimately failed. Within the imperial family, Wilhelm I and Fritz were in agreement with the campaign, while Empress Augusta and Vicky were not, though as the attacks became more vicious, Fritz started siding with his wife. Although Vicky was brought up and confirmed in the Protestant church, she espoused "rational religious views" that "had always scandalized orthodox Christians. Having grown to maturity during a period of religious and intellectual ferment (these were the years of *Ecce Homo*, Renen's *Vie de Jésus* and Darwin's *Origin of Species*) she had not the same blind, unquestioning approach to Christianity."[47] Vicky took the "*side* of science and philosophy—as opposed to real faith," as Queen Victoria put it. This perturbed her, for the queen believed that "both should go *together*."[48] Vicky had little regard for Catholicism and its elaborate rituals. Nevertheless, she believed in religious toleration and opposed Bismarck's *Kulturkampf*.

As for Queen Victoria, she admitted being "a fervent Protestant and hating all that approaches Catholicism."[49] Her preferences were not too theological and not "high church" (which utilizes practices closely associated with the Catholic Mass). When Marie of Bavaria converted to Catholicism, Victoria told Vicky, "One can't understand anyone who has been a Protestant ever submitting to this."[50] The queen also complained to Vicky about the "alarming innovations" of the Protestant churches in England, which were "too Catholic" for her tastes and bordered on being "most dangerous!"[51] Yet like Vicky, Victoria tolerated those whose faith differed from hers and worried about persecution. Earlier in her reign, the queen had written: "I cannot bear to hear the violent abuse of the Catholic religion, which is so painful and so cruel towards the many innocent and good Roman Catholics."[52] And decades later, the queen told Vicky, "Certainly I would never persecute others for their religion and would always respect it."[53]

When it came to her own faith, Queen Victoria, who liked plain sermons, was at home in the Scottish Kirk, especially at Crathie Church at Balmoral. The queen expressed her esteem for the Scottish Kirk to Vicky, telling her, "Thank God the Scotch Church is a stronghold of Protestantism, most precious in these realms."[54] With such staunch Protestant views, it is not surprising that the declaration of Papal Infallability in 1870 and Bismarck's *Kulturkampf* had fired in Queen Victoria a "Protestant militancy" and "the longing to show that in Britain also there was a Defender of the Faith."[55] Thus, as in Isabella of Castile's and Maria Theresa of Austria's times, religion played a personal and political role in the lives of royalty, though less intensely and pervasively.

For Vicky and Victoria, personal milestones matched the significant political changes of the 1870s. Numerous births augmented the family's next generation. Vicky's daughter Charlotte made her thirty-eight-year-old mother a grandmother and fifty-nine-year-old grandmother a great-grandmother in 1879. But the dark cloud of death and family troubles cast its long shadow too. From 1878 onward, tragedy struck the family with unrelenting regularity. That year, diphtheria struck Vicky's sister Alice and her family. Several of her children came down with the disease that eventually killed Alice's youngest daughter, May. During their illness, Alice wrote to Queen Victoria that "knowing all these precious lives [are] hanging on a thread, is an agony barely to be conceived."[56] After kissing her son Ernie, who also had diphtheria, Alice came down with the disease and died on the seventeenth anniversary of Prince Albert's death. A shocked Vicky wrote their grieving mother a thirty-nine-page letter upon hearing the news. After Alice's death, Victoria took her Hessian grandchildren under her wing, becoming almost a second mother to them. Further tragedy struck. In 1879, Vicky's son Waldemar died of diphtheria at eleven years of age, leaving his mother distraught. Waldemar and Sigismund had been her favorite sons, and now they were dead.

As tribulations mounted, Queen Victoria advised Vicky to turn to her faith. The queen assured her eldest daughter that the only way to face their trials was to accept them as God's will, echoing the last line of a favored hymn of Princess Alice, which quoted from the Lord's prayer: "Thy will be done."[57] "It is only by trusting in God's all merciful goodness and in following the precepts of His beloved Son," noted Victoria, "that one can go through the trials, sorrows and difficulties of this life. Without this conviction sorrows and trials will lead to feelings of despair and bitterness, whereas if you can say 'Thy will not mine be done' and 'God's ways are not our ways' you will feel a peace and contentment."[58] Both women would need to cling to this precept, for the coming years were to bring yet more difficulties and heartache.

24

MOURNING AND JUBILATION

Though Queen Victoria had by the 1870s and 1880s emerged somewhat from her seclusion, she had not shaken off the mantle of mourning and consistently dressed in widow's weeds. Her standards and demands when it came to mourning extended to even minute details. Soon after the Prince Consort's death, a government official wrote, "The Queen is very watchful about what people do and how the mourning is observed. She sent back the other day all the papers she had to sign because the black margin was not sufficiently broad."[1] The inch-deep black border "covering almost half the area of every sheet" was never changed in Queen Victoria's lifetime. From 1861 on, the queen wrote her letters on funereal paper; the only concession she granted as the years went by was to "decrease slightly in width" the black borders, or sometimes she tried "a new variation of the monogram V.R. or V.R.I."[2] Such was the somber life that pervaded the English court.

During this time, further personal anxieties gave Victoria cause for concern. Like Vicky's unease over Willy's deformed arm, the ever-present specter of illness permeated Queen Victoria's life, in the form of hemophilia in her fourth son, Prince Leopold. The knowledge that something was wrong with the prince came gradually, and diagnosis did not occur until he was a little boy. In an 1863 letter to Vicky, Queen Victoria told her oldest daughter about Leopold's internal bleeding, explaining that "we can account for it in no way but from his riding which the poor child had just begun to enjoy and which now must be stopped. . . . It is very sad and I miss darling Papa again here so awfully. Oh! how this alarmed and distressed him! I feel all these terrible anxieties are sent, and must be borne with patience!" "But oh!" the queen went on, "the illness of a good child is so far less trying and distressing than the sinfulness of one's sons—like your two elder brothers. Oh! then one feels that death in purity is so far preferable to life in sin and degradation!"[3]

When he was six years old, the queen had confided to a courtier that Leopold had "grown so weak of late."[4] When he was twenty, Victoria told Queen Augusta of Prussia that "he will have to be most careful, which, anyway, must always be the case."[5] By this time, Victoria had come to accept the illness more. Previously, "even though she had spoken to the doctors, she seemed not to accept that Leopold did not walk and stand well because he was ill, and often in pain."[6]

When it dawned on Victoria that her sickly son was turning out to be intellectually bright, like Prince Albert, her views on Leopold improved. "His mind and head are far the most like any of the boys to his dear Father," the queen wrote to Vicky of Leopold. "I think he is happier now because he sees where his course lies, and does not think of what he cannot have."[7]

Queen Victoria tried to keep Leopold at home, but she acquiesced to him studying at Oxford. She also allowed him to travel to North America, though she thought Australia was too far. She told Disraeli that she could not "bring herself to consent to send her very delicate Son, who has been <u>4 or 5 times</u> at <u>death's door</u> . . . to a great distance."[8] Denied a military career because of his health, Leopold served his mother, though unofficially, as her secretary. His marriage to Princess Helen of Waldeck-Pyrmont in 1882 allowed the prince to gain some independence from his mother. Leopold died two years later after a fall, leaving a pregnant wife, a daughter, and a deeply distressed mother. In her journal, the queen poured out her emotions: "My beloved Leopold, that bright, clever son, who had so many times recovered from such fearful illnesses . . . has been taken from us! . . . Am utterly crushed. How dear he was to me, how I had watched over him! . . . The poor dear boy's life had been a very tired one, from early childhood. . . . Oh! God, in His mercy, spare my other dear children!"[9] After Prince Leopold's funeral, the queen confided to Randall Davidson, the Dean of Windsor and later the Archbishop of Canterbury, about her "poor bleeding heart, which has been so cruelly torn."[10]

The specter of hemophilia haunted Queen Victoria's other descendants. Even though she thought the disease "such a rare thing and not in the family,"[11] hemophilia made its mark on succeeding generations. Her daughter Alice passed the gene to several of her children, including her daughter Alix, who became Czarina Alexandra of Russia, consort of Czar Nicholas II. Their only son and heir, Czarevitch Alexei, suffered from hemophilia, paving the way for the appearance of the notorious Rasputin, whose presence at court helped greatly to undermine perceptions of the imperial family, Alix in particular. Alix's sister Irene (who later married Vicky's son Henry) was also a hemophilia carrier. Because of this, two of Vicky's grandsons suffered from hemophilia. In 1873, tragedy hit the Hessian royals when Alice's two-year-old son, Frederick, a hemophiliac, died after falling from a window.

Princess Beatrice also passed the gene on to her descendants. Victoria Eugénie, her daughter, was also a carrier. She became Queen of Spain when she married King Alfonso XIII. Two of their sons suffered from hemophilia. Thus did Queen Victoria's gene affect the royal houses of Hesse, Prussia, Russia, and Spain, cutting a path of misery and suffering.

Meanwhile, Vicky continued to find contentment in her marriage and growing family. Home centered on the Neues Palais, a lovely two-hundred-room Baroque palace set in Sanssouci, a verdant royal park in Potsdam, southwest of Berlin. Kaiser Wilhelm II's childhood friend the American Poultney Bigelow (who had gone to school as a child in Potsdam and played with Wilhelm and his brother Henry) remembered Potsdam as "a wilderness of palaces, barracks, fountains, temples, esplanades with innumerable marble divinities waving their naked arms and legs as though begging in vain for warm clothes in the damp and cold of the Brandenburg swamps."[12] The Neues Palais "as a playground for us boys was unequalled," wrote Bigelow in his memoirs of Prussia.[13] He also noted Willy's pride in his mother's painting abilities and how the prince showed his friend her collection of "paint pots, easels, and canvases" that "proclaimed the earnestness with which she cultivated the painter's craft."[14] Painting, a hobby shared with Queen Victoria, was a pastime Vicky pursued with seriousness through the years. When he was emperor, Wilhelm recalled how he and his mother had shared a hearty laugh in his youth over a favorite book of his, *Frank Fairlegh*. "I always read it aloud to Mamma while she was painting," he said, "and I shall never forget how we laughed over it together. Mamma laughed so much that she couldn't go on painting."[15] Vicky had her own studio, where she spent many hours honing her craft in the vast abode that was the Neues Palais.

Built by Frederick the Great after the end of the Seven Years' War, the Neues Palais was a magnificent home decorated in a highly ornate style. "Protruding from the center of the building and painted black, a shallow dome is set on a tall, windowless drum and topped by three nude female figures holding up a crown. The dome, which serves no functional purpose, is there because Frederick decided a royal palace should have one. The three ladies are said to represent his three chief enemies in the Seven Years War: Elizabeth of Russia, Maria Theresa of Austria and Madame de Pompadour."[16] No less ornate were the interiors, where semiprecious stones and marble abounded. The most unusual room was the Grotto Hall, covered in quartz and thousands of shells. Queen Victoria's homes could scarcely match the splendor of the Neues Palais. Here, Fritz and Vicky raised their family and entertained their guests. The prince and princess were amiable hosts to young and old alike. The young Poultney Bigelow recalled how the royal couple always inquired after his parents and "had a smile and a kind word for each of their little guests . . . the mother in particular had a keen eye for napkins not properly tucked in or any breach in nursery manners."[17]

Ever energetic, Vicky left her mark on the Neues Palais, beautifying and enlarging her home's grounds and gardens. A gentleman attached to her household remembered how "she would discuss with me some alteration or improvement till perhaps twelve o'clock at night, and in the morning at seven I would receive from her a written statement, with all the details and directions worked out—all in her own writing. She must have written it after I left."[18]

The Neues Palais was nicknamed "the Palace of the Medicis" because of Vicky's tastes for the arts and sciences. With wide-ranging interests, she welcomed artists, scientists, and other intellectuals, regardless of their social standing, into her palace. That she did not extend invitations according to "the number of [aristocratic] quarterings,* by which [the Prussians] set so much store, [and which] meant nothing to her,"[19] scandalized Prussian aristocracy.

One of the crown princess's English friends, Sir Howard Elphinstone, left a glimpse of these Prussian nobles, noting that "there is no doubt society here is made up of very small 'sets.' Each set is quite exclusive, and will not even look at the other. The aristocracy is not to my liking, being very vain, small minded and decidedly dull. Of politics they are afraid to talk, of art and literature they know little. Consequently bitter tittle-tattle is their element, in which they excel." To these closed-minded elements of German society, Vicky was both intimidating and dangerous. Elphinstone concluded that "she was generally unpopular in consequence of the free thinking tone she took up."[20]

German society after unification underwent significant changes. As industrial activity accelerated, a new middle class, to whom the Junkers left industry and trade as their domain, prospered. A breed of wealthy industrialists grew out of the middle class—industrialists who expected to be rewarded by "estates and ennoblement which the aristocracy resented."[21] Added to this was an overheated economy that led to overproduction and was exacerbated by foreign

---

*A quartering denoted an aristocrat's ability to show on his crest that he was descended from aristocratic ancestors through various lines.

competition, decreasing the demand for German goods. This, in turn, led to demands for wide-ranging tariffs, including one on imported grain. While this protectionism had the effect of uniting the aristocracy and the new wealthier middle classes, the added costs also had a detrimental effect on the working class, leading to social problems.

In trying to ease Germany's social problems, Vicky became involved with various noncontroversial endeavors, such as nursing schools for girls. But when it came to advancing ideas and causes such as social welfare and prison reform, her critics disapproved. The passing years had not eased the crown princess's unpopularity in her adopted country. She told her mother of her "difficult and trying position" and how "life often appears very hard to me at Berlin." Moreover, "to be friends with the present regime is impossible, and yet to be in opposition is a thing as impossible. I always feel like a fly struggling in a very tangled web, and feelings of weariness and depression, often of disgust and hopelessness take possession of me."[22] Sir Howard Elphinstone saw firsthand this dispiriting existence and admitted that in Germany "there is no one of whom she could make a friend."[23]

Vicky was especially disappointed with the Germans' support for Bismarck, telling Queen Victoria: "Their apathy and servility and want of independence and dignity is [sic] grievous and shows how the German character has deteriorated through the inordinate vanity this man has instilled into people blinding them to better and higher feelings and aspirations."[24] There was no letup in the strained relations between Bismarck and the crown princely couple. From 1881 onward, Bismarck became increasingly open about his hostility toward Vicky, warning her that he would not let Germany be ruled, when Fritz came to the throne, "after the English fashion."[25]

Vicky's life had become even more immersed in troubles and sorrows since the death of Waldemar, her favorite son, who had showed promise of becoming like Prince Albert. She "was in despair and said that the clever ones had been taken, and the stupid ones left: 'good boys,' she said, 'but nothing in them,'" according to one of Vicky's intimates.[26] The sorrows had "transformed her into a Mater Dolorosa . . . and that childlike capacity for enjoyment, which had constituted one of her principal charms, left her, never to return."[27] A good portion of the weight upon her derived from her deteriorating relationship with her eldest son, Wilhelm.

Vicky was partly to blame for Willy's ambivalence toward her, for she too held ambivalent feelings for him. They loved each other but were also highly critical of each other. Vicky never stopped hoping that Willy would measure up to the two paragons of virtue in her life, Fritz and her father, Prince Albert. But

Willy almost always fell short of her expectations. Queen Victoria had similar feelings toward her eldest son, the Prince of Wales. The queen once wrote of the young Bertie: "With the Prince of Wales . . . one had to contend with an unhappy temper, incapacity of concentrating his mind and defective mental qualities. . . . The Prince of Wales really *cannot* be made to *look* at a book un-less during lessons. One cannot fix his attention even on a novel. In fact he would wish to be doing absolutely nothing whatever; throw himself down upon a chair, or else on the good nature of others."[28] Even when the twenty-year-old prince was at Cambridge University, his mother continued to despair and admonish him as if he were a child. Queen Victoria complained to the Prince of Wales about the way he sat, telling him, "You forget and have got into a habit of sitting quite bent, on one side, or lolling on the table. . . . This, dear child will NOT do for *any* person in your position, or any gentleman."[29]

Queen Victoria's disappointment in the Prince of Wales reflected Empress Maria Theresa's views of her son Joseph II. But as rocky as Bertie's and Joseph's relationships with their mothers had been, there were still moments of calm and affection. This was hardly so in Berlin.

As Wilhelm grew older, the question of a wife came to the fore. In the 1870s Willy fell for his first cousin, the beautiful Ella, daughter of Vicky's sister Alice. But Vicky opposed the match on the grounds that Ella was too closely related to Willy, though there was little objection when Willy's brother Henry later married Ella's sister Irene. In the end, Wilhelm married in 1881, to Augusta Viktoria (Dona) of Schleswig-Holstein-Sonderburg-Augustenburg. Unintellec-tual, submissive, undemanding, and an unequivocal supporter of Willy, Dona was everything Vicky was not, which made her ideal in her husband's eyes. She eventually bore him six sons and one daughter. If Vicky had hoped that the presence of Dona in Willy's life would mellow him, she was mistaken, for mar-riage made Willy even more unbearable. The future kaiser continued to ignore his parents and gave his attention instead to Bismarck. Helped along by the chancellor, who flattered Willy and approved of the fawning and insignificant Dona, the prince's arrogance grew.

Bismarck's approval of Dona was in stark contrast to his views on Prince Alexander (Sandro) of Battenberg as a husband for Vicky's seventeen-year-old daughter, Moretta. Moretta was part of the youngest trio of daughters (the oth-ers being Mossy and Sophie) of Vicky's brood, who were the children closest to their mother. Both Vicky and Queen Victoria wanted to see Moretta happy and approved of Sandro, the reigning prince of Bulgaria, as a possible husband. The couple also wished to marry, but Bismarck would have none of it. His objections were such that he sought the Hohenzollerns' support. Sandro had incurred the Russian czar's ire by taking a pro-Bulgarian stance, which meant independence from Russia's orbit. Bismarck deemed Sandro's contrarian line against Russia, an important German ally, potentially dangerous for Germany. To Wilhelm I, Bismarck made a case against Sandro because of a supposed "plot of Queen Victoria to make the young man secure against Russia by an alliance with our court."[30] Politics, therefore, ultimately drove the chancellor in opposing the marriage, the problem being "born in the geopolitical quicksand of the Balkans, and further nurtured by an animosity on Bismarck's part toward Vicky that had settled into a deep and near-unchecked loathing."[31] Bismarck also used the Battenbergs' morganatic blood (making them unequal in rank to reigning royalty) as a hindrance, thus playing to the Hohenzollerns' exalted view of themselves. By 1888 the romance had ended, defeated by Bismarck, Willy, and Wilhelm I. Willy's opposition to the match had so incensed Queen Victoria that she wrote to Vicky of "that very foolish, undutiful and I must add unfeeling boy, I have no patience with, and I wish he could get a good 'skelp'g' as the Scotch say."[32]

Moretta's failed romance was all the more poignant in light of the fact that two of Sandro's brothers, Louis and Henry, married into Queen Victoria's family: Louis to Princess Alice's eldest daughter, Princess Victoria, and Henry to Princess Beatrice, the queen's youngest child. When Beatrice announced that she wanted to marry Prince Henry of Battenberg, the queen was indignant, telling Vicky, "What despair it caused me and what a fearful shock it was to me when I first heard of her wish! It made me quite ill."[33] Queen Victoria, who paid scant attention to matters such as morganatic blood, was opposed to Henry for another reason. She had hoped that her youngest daughter would remain unmarried and stay with her indefinitely. Henry's marriage proposal threatened to scupper these plans. Because of the separation from her that marriage entailed, the queen admitted to Vicky that she thought "a daughter's marriage dreadful, repulsive," causing a "dreadful gulf," which she hoped she "should never have to go through again."[34] But she did go through it again. Beatrice was adamant; for months, mother and daughter refused to speak to each other because of the queen's opposition. In the end, the queen allowed her "baby" to marry, under one condition: that Beatrice and Henry live under her roof. "As she remains always with me," wrote the triumphant and contented queen to Vicky, "I cannot refuse my consent."[35] The wedding took place in 1885; three of the bridal attendants being Victoria's granddaughters the future Queen Maud of Norway, Queen Marie of Romania, and Czarina Alexandra of Russia.

Not surprisingly, when during their honeymoon Beatrice and Henry paid Vicky and Fritz a visit, Willy and Dona snubbed the newlyweds. A furious Queen Victoria wrote to Vicky of their "extraordinary impertinence and insolence" on the matter. The queen added a comment by Lord Granville, "that if the Queen of England thinks a person good enough for her daughter what have other people got to say?"[36] Beatrice's newfound happiness was a far cry from Vicky's life, now sorely tried by her deteriorating relationship with Willy, which increasingly mirrored the crown princess's antagonistic relationship with Bismarck. By the mid-1880s, Willy had come to despise his mother's overt anglomania. He believed too in the outlandish fantasy that Vicky was nothing short of a spy for England, passing highly sensitive information on to Queen Victoria.

In 1887, Victoria celebrated fifty years on the throne, her Golden Jubilee. At sixty-eight, the gray-haired, overweight queen was prone to indigestion and rheumatism in the knees. She had the look of an elderly dowager, with white widow's cap and black mourning gown. Yet she was still relatively healthy and even enjoyed a new holiday destination, southern France, where she vacationed for several years. There she would sometimes meet with Empress Eugénie, who had become a close friend. Their friendship had taken on an air of poignancy after Eugénie's only son, the Prince Imperial, was killed in South Africa fighting the Zulus in 1879 while serving in the British Army.

To her own family, Victoria remained the awe-inspiring autocrat, but she was also a caring and concerned matriarch. She continued firing off letters of advice to children and grandchildren alike. She also liked to have her family visit her, such as the time that her granddaughter Victoria (Alice's daughter) came to Windsor to give birth to her first child. After caring for her during the labor, Victoria was gratified to see the birth of a great-grandchild, named Alice, who was one day to become the mother-in-law of Queen Elizabeth II, Queen Victoria's great-great-granddaughter. Another Alice in the family, Prince Leopold's daughter, recalled living as a little girl in Windsor, where "there was an *aura* about the whole place." Like many a grandparent, Victoria was often more indulgent toward her grandchildren and great-grandchildren than she was with her own children. Princess Alice remembered playing after tea in Queen Victoria's room, where she and her brother were allowed to build "walls with her numerous despatch boxes."[37] These boxes were otherwise used to transport official government documents and were decorated with the sovereign's monogram.

As the queen loved the theater, she encouraged her household and family to perform in plays. In one tableau, Alice and Victoria Eugénie of Battenberg, Beatrice's daughter, mounted a mise-en-scène to imitate King Charles II's children, as depicted in one of Anthony Van Dyck's famous paintings that hung at Windsor. Yet however indulgent she was, the queen also expected a certain decorum from her grandchildren. During lunch with the queen, Alice and her young cousins had to observe "the correct silence or low-voiced conversation"[38] or suffer the consequences of their misdemeanors.

During her Golden Jubilee year, Queen Victoria met with manifestations of resounding loyalty from her subjects. Seas of Union Jacks fluttered, and cheers greeted the queen. Those grumblings of republicanism during her reclusive years had died down. Victoria reigned supreme, as did Britain in the world. In 1859, Lord Palmerston had written to the queen of this, saying, "England is one of the greatest powers of the world, no event or series of events bearing on the balance of power, or on probabilities of peace or war can be matters of indifference to her, and her right to have and to express opinions on matters thus bearing on her interests is unquestionable."[39] By the 1880s, Great Britain's influence in the world had increased. Victoria reigned over a quarter of a billion people. Hers was the largest empire in history, stretching to all corners of the earth. The sun, indeed, never set on the British Empire.

As Empress of India, Victoria took great interest in that exotic part of the empire. In her later years, she employed servants from India, including Abdul Karim (the Munshi), who taught her some Hindustani. Victoria, ever susceptible to a strong male presence, made the Munshi the last of her favorites, in a line that had included Lord Melbourne, Prince Albert, Napoléon III, John Brown, and Benjamin Disraeli. Like John Brown before him, the Munshi attracted hostility from the queen's suspicious household, but Victoria remained attached to him. So entrenched at one point were both sides over the Munshi that a furious Victoria swept the contents of her writing table onto the floor to make her point. Her then prime minister, Lord Salisbury, was called to resolve the friction. Just as the Munshi turned out to be Victoria's last favorite, Lord Salisbury turned out to be her last prime minister. Unlike Bismarck in Germany, who was the bane of Vicky's existence, or Gladstone, who was Victoria's bête noire, Salisbury was on good terms with the queen and remained in office until the end of her reign.

Queen Victoria's reign by 1887 had become a success, though the long list of achievements was blotted by some failures and difficulties. Those that stand out include the negative effects of the Industrial Revolution, which continued to be felt with the growth of urbanization and large numbers of people living in squalor; the Irish Famine; the Indian Mutiny; and most recently, the fall of Khartoum, with the death of General Charles Gordon, in 1885. Nevertheless, Victoria's reign by this time was considered a triumph. Her subjects benefited greatly from an extension of voting rights. The Reform Acts of 1867 and 1884 included in the electorate millions more, such as workingmen and agricultural laborers. The middle class also expanded under Victoria's reign, propelled by the expansion of business and industry. And then there was the empire itself. Nowhere was this global domination more in evidence than in the names given to various places around the world, and the name that dominated was Victoria. Her name resonated and continues to resonate in British Columbia, where the provincial capital is Victoria; in Australia, where two states, Victoria and Queensland, are named after the queen; and in Africa, where the continent's largest lake, as well as the magnificent Victoria Falls, derive their names from none other than Queen Victoria.

Thanks to Britain's achievements on the world stage and to the queen's personal qualities, which had elevated the monarchy to new symbolic heights, Victoria had also secured the crown for her descendants. To many, it was simply inconceivable to separate the monarchy from the greatness of British imperialism.

The Golden Jubilee was a clear manifestation of the triumphs of the British Empire, and many of the queen's subjects lined the streets of London to show their affection for the woman who had been their sovereign for five decades. Queen Victoria's record of the day vividly captures how moved she was:

> The crowds from the Palace [Buckingham] gates up to the Abbey [Westminster Abbey] were enormous, and there was such an extraordinary outburst of enthusiasm as I had hardly ever seen in London before; all the people seemed to be in such good humour. . . . The decorations along Piccadilly were quite beautiful, and there were most touching inscriptions. Seats and platforms were arranged up to the tops of the houses, and such waving of hands. . . .
> When the service [at Westminster Abbey] was concluded, each of my sons, sons-in-law, grandsons . . . , and grandsons-in-law, stepped forward, bowed, and in succession kissed my hand, I kissing each; and the same with the daughters, daughters-in-law . . . , granddaughters, and granddaughter-in-law. They curtsied as they came up and I embraced them warmly. It was a very moving moment, and tears were in some of their eyes.[40]

It was, concluded an emotional Queen Victoria, "a never-to-be forgotten day."[41] A bevy of royals, many of them her family, joined the matriarch in celebrations.

And of all the royals present, Vicky and Fritz were among Victoria's most favored guests.

Unbeknownst to many, a cloud hung over the jubilee celebrations. Vicky had earlier sent troubling news about a growth in Fritz's throat. German doctors, who suspected a malignancy, suggested an operation that involved cutting the larynx. Even if Fritz survived the dangerous procedure, he was likely going to be voiceless. The German doctors had also suggested the crown prince see a British specialist, Dr. Morell Mackenzie. Though the German doctors suspected cancer, Mackenzie thought otherwise at first and advised a nonsurgical approach. He treated Fritz when the prince and Vicky came to London to celebrate the jubilee. In London, Fritz managed to ride in the queen's procession to Westminster Abbey, looking magnificent in his white uniform, shining breastplate, and eagle-crowned helmet. Vicky, who sat next to Queen Victoria in the royal carriage, was proud of her husband but also anxious for him.

When the time came for Vicky to leave Queen Victoria after the celebrations, the mother wrote a touching letter to the daughter: "Darling, Beloved Child, I must write you a few lines and say how truly grieved I was to part from you again. I only pray it may not be very long. The older one grows, especially at my age, one feels it more and more. To feel that this memorable time, this large family meeting is all over is sad. And to part from you, knowing you in the midst of such uncertainty and difficulties . . . distresses me doubly."[42]

In autumn, the couple did not return to Germany but eventually went to San Remo on the Italian Riviera, where the weather was more agreeable than in Germany and the demands upon them less strenuous. Vicky hoped that this respite would help Fritz improve, for by now the pain, swelling, and hoarseness were worse. Back in Germany, people blamed Vicky for keeping her husband away when the aged Wilhelm I was himself declining. She thought this criticism as "unjust and ignorant as it was spiteful and impertinent."[43] After deflecting decades of incessant criticism, Vicky was tiring of it all, confessing, "I am weary of being constantly blamed and picked to pieces by people who have no right and no business to meddle in our affairs. Whenever anything is wrong, it does not matter *what* it be, it is put on *my* back. The Court and official world find me a very convenient scapegoat."[44] For the crown princess's enemies, it was all too easy to hold Vicky responsible for whatever they perceived to be wrong, but above all, she remained to them highly suspect because of her liberal sympathies. To her friend Lady Ponsonby, Vicky confessed that in Germany "there are those who *will not* be pleased I am an English woman, suspected of Liberal . . . tendencies. . . . I am labelled 'suspicious' and 'dangerous' by the

QUEEN VICTORIA AND THE EMPRESS FREDERICK

clique who are all-powerful now. . . . I keep as quiet and make myself as small as I can, but I cannot change my skin to please them, nor shall they tread me underfoot, as they would like to some day."[45]

Vicky was by no means a radical liberal, and she disagreed with many doctrines of modern liberalism, as she expounded in a letter to Queen Victoria in 1880:

> My idea of a liberal is simply a commonsense view of things, and a wish to be fair, and tolerant and charitable, and to improve at all times that which wants improving; in fact to try and raise each branch of existence into something as good as it can be made, not to change and destroy things because they are old and traditional nor to preserve what is no longer useful merely because it is old.
>
> No one can have a greater horror and dread of Communism than I have and I think many measures of Prince Bismarck such as "universal suffrage" "manhood suffrage" utterly foolish, most dangerous and quite destructive of all good government. There are a great many doctrines of modern liberalism I do not and cannot agree with; and were I a man I should feel it impossible to join any party that held them. I hold the British Constitution to be the best and most useful and blessed form of government in the world and yet I feel that the world goes on, things change from day to day, new wants spring up that must be met, many a time-honoured thing becomes senseless and superfluous that was once indispensable. Wild liberals and violent conservatives are alike distasteful to me as their ideas lead to the same mischief. These are my very terrible opinions and always have been—and I suppose always will be as I see more to justify and confirm them every day.[46]

Queen Victoria was more skeptical toward liberalism than her daughter. According to her private secretary's son, the queen "feared and mistrusted [liberalism], closely allied as it came to be with radicalism."[47] In 1885 the queen (writing in the third person) showed her concern over liberals and radicals, saying, "She is most anxious that the Liberals shd be *detached* from those dreadful socialists Mr. Chamberlain [Joseph Chamberlain, Liberal Member of Parliament] & others & that all should try to separate from him, or the country may be ruined."[48] Yet however much she may have had misgivings about liberalism, Victoria did not let her opinions keep her from employing a liberal in a very sensitive position. Her long-standing private secretary, Henry Ponsonby, was an avowed liberal. Ponsonby was good-humored, diplomatic, and above all, a patient servant to the queen, though unlike Victoria he held Gladstone in esteem. Queen Victoria, after all, could be a demanding and imposing mistress, who, according to Ponsonby's son, "was incapable of any pretence or of attempting to conceal the severity or disapproval which her facial expression often very clearly betrayed."[49]

Meanwhile, at San Remo, a drama was being played out that riveted Queen Victoria's attention and preoccupied Vicky. Fritz was indeed stricken with cancer of the larynx. The ninety-year-old Wilhelm I was greatly moved by his son's suffering, saying, "I have only one wish, which I should like to be gratified before I die, and that is to hear my poor son, Fritz, speak as clearly as he used to do."[50] Time was not on the old emperor's side, nor was fate on Fritz's. Within months of those words being uttered, the succession to the imperial throne of Germany was set to change, sweeping in its wake Queen Victoria's eldest daughter, the much tried and much beleaguered Vicky.

25

THE NINETY-NINE-DAY EMPRESS

By the time Fritz's gruesome illness was playing itself out, the fates of Queen Victoria and Vicky had largely been sealed. Queen Victoria was settling into old age, content at the way her reign had unfolded—proud that her empire was respected, feared, and admired. Vicky, by contrast, far from enjoying the same adulation as her mother, had to swallow the bitter pill of unpopularity and vicious accusations. Perhaps if the crown princess had been more tactful and less forthright in her views, some of the criticisms might not have stuck, let alone been voiced. But Vicky, who had many good qualities, was much too plainspoken to charm her way into the hearts of certain people. Lady Ponsonby, who had known both, best summed up the characters of mother and daughter, saying of Vicky: "All her life she remained one of the most undeceitful women I have ever known. I cannot say that she had the same charm as the Queen: in her great seriousness there was too much of the professor about her; all the same she was an exceptionally clever woman and wonderfully loyal to her friends."[1]

Queen Victoria possessed the same loyal streak. She also inspired fear and reverence in many. One contemporary observer, Princess Catherine Radziwill, wrote of the queen: "The eyes are frank and sincere, and they look at you with an expression of intense truth; but they are imperious, and reveal a character that does not brook contracdiction." But, added Radziwill, "perhaps because no other sovereign has understood so well how to appeal" to her subjects' "inmost feelings and to associate [the people] with all her joys and sorrows," Queen Victoria successfully offset this forbidding side by also displaying a highly sympathetic side. "In my eyes," added Radziwill, "Queen Victoria appears in the light of an exceedingly fascinating woman, in spite of her years. There is in her face, even more than in that of her daughter . . . [Vicky], an extreme charm. It is seen too, in her voice; her whole person, in fact, expresses great sympathy."[2]

Victoria, who had a natural gift for eliciting empathy, could also be mystifying. More than the forthright Vicky, the queen fascinated kings and commoners alike—a gift derived partly from the fact that Victoria was a bundle of contradictions. For here was a woman who "deplored the idea of women's rights, yet she appeared to be the most powerful woman on earth. In truth, Victoria was proud yet humble; possessed of common sense yet subject to unreasoned emotional outbursts; demurely feminine yet profoundly imperious; naïve yet shrewdly intelligent; independent yet extremely needy; confident yet insecure—in short, an oddly assembled combination of conflicting elements that coalesced to make her formidable yet charming, aloof yet familiar."[3]

Though criticisms were also voiced about Queen Victoria, such as her reclusiveness after the Prince Consort's death and her dependency on John Brown, the complaints never tarnished the queen to the same extent as those thrown at Vicky. Ironically, one of the longest running objections about Vicky concerned her impact on her beloved husband, a criticism that also had the damaging effect of "cutting off Fritz from his patrimony. [For] in a society as patriarchal as Wilhelmine Germany, the Crown Prince seemed to be manipulated by a domineering wife who took orders straight from her omnipotent mother, the woman the Germans called the Widow of Windsor."[4] This criticism was a widely circulated one and, according to a British diplomat at the time, one that was easily believed. Of Fritz, this contemporary had commented "that his wife had the stronger will of the two," a fact that "seemed evident even to the superficial observer."[5] Little wonder then that Vicky's refusal to bow to Prussian conformity when it came to her role as wife led to one of the most persistent criticisms she had to endure.

By the late 1870s, the crown princess had ample opportunity to observe the patriarchal attitude that so permeated her adopted homeland. Vicky explained to her husband that, in Germany, "the *position* of the *German* woman in general, her *upbringing* & her relationship to men!" was the "main reason" for the rejection of liberal principles. It was not unusual to find that, in Germany, a woman was "*not* the companion, friend & *helper* of her husband in all his business and in everything he does, is not his adviser, his secretary, does not share his level of education, does *not* share men's interests & in the home is neither fully mistress of her house, nor educator of her children!" Inevitably, the crown princess went on to compare this state of affairs with the English model. "If a woman here lays claim to the position she has legitimately held in England for centuries (& that is one of the main causes of the *strength* of the English people & why the civilization there is more developed than here), she is regarded as dangerous, bossy, absurd, crotchety, & *war* is declared on her!"[6]

After nearly three decades in Prussia, Vicky had been unable to endear herself to many of her future subjects. Though she spoke faultless German and tried in her way to become Prussian, the court and many of the people had still failed to embrace her as their own. In this, Vicky came much nearer to Marie Antoinette's experiences in France than to Catherine of Aragon's in England. By the time she was well into her forties, Vicky came to see herself more closely allied to England than ever before, a situation caused by a number of factors. First, the crown princess found that "her belief in Germany as a center of culture and rationality had been trampled—first by the unltraconservative Prussian court, then by Bismarck, and finally by the German people themselves, who seemed all too easily led to believe the worst of *die Engländerin*."[7] This was unfortunate, as Vicky's views about Prussians were not completely negative; she also had positive things to say about her countrymen, telling Queen Victoria in the 1860s of their "sterling good qualities."[8] But in the princess's mind, these qualities seemed to be increasingly overshadowed by faults, including—most painfully—their inability to believe that she always had Prussia's best interests at heart. And thus, "knowing herself to be untrusted and unloved in her adopted country and temperamentally unfit to pay lip service to principles she loathed, Vicky began to turn back to England. This change in attitude can be traced in her letters to her mother; in the early 1880s, the word 'we,' which formerly referred to the Germans, now meant the English."[9]

Nowhere does this attachment to England, and her mother, appear more evident than in the words Vicky had written to Queen Victoria some years before. After a visit to England, Vicky penned the following from Berlin: "Attached as I am to this country [Prussia] and anxious to serve it with might and main, the other [England] will ever remain the land of my heart and I shall ever feel the same pride of being home there, a child and subject of yours."[10]

Vicky's attachment to England would increase even more with the health crisis suffered by her husband. For what was in store for Queen Victoria's eldest daughter would amount to nothing short of the "completion of Vicky's ruination in Germany."[11]

Fritz's deteriorating condition took its toll on his devoted wife. In December 1887, her friend Lady Ponsonby, who was at San Remo with the couple, recorded the following impressions: "Yesterday was the first day she broke down before me. She is generally in apparent excellent spirits, though preoccupied at times: but yesterday it was too much to find [Fritz] reading a recapitulation of the doctor's former opinion, with a paragraph pointing out the difference between this and the present bulletins and leaving their readers to make their own inference. The poor Crown Prince turned to [Vicky] and said, 'Why will they take every ray of hope away? What good is done them by this?' and pointed to the paragraph. She was quite cheerful to him and then came into the next room where I was and cried. She is so wonderful generally that it fills one with pity."[12]

In November 1887, when the crown prince was finally told of the fatal nature of his infirmity, even his eldest son, Wilhelm, who was at loggerheads with his parents more often than not, wrote a moving letter to his grandmother Queen Victoria:

> The final descision [sic] of the Doctors has been taken this morning & the fearful hour has at last after all arrived! They told Papa everything & he received the news like a Hohenzollern & a soldier, upright, looking the doctors straight in the face. He knows that he is irretrievably lost and doomed! And yet he did not move an inch or a muscle, they were immensely moved by this splendid display of character. His great & noble heart did not flinch & he is serene, composed & calm, like a brave captain, who knows that in leading his forlorne [sic] hope he will fall with his brave men, he holds up his head & even tries to cheer us up when we all of us broke down after the doctors had left. It is quite horrible this confounded word "hopeless"! Poor Mama is doing wonders, she is perpetually on the verge of completely breaking down, & yet she keeps on that gigantic struggle against her feelings only not to distress Papa, & not to let the household see her grief. . . . Our doctor is in tears. Besides Grandmama is seriously ill & not fit to hear any bad news & the Emperor very deeply affected by the bad news, so that one is nearly off one's head with anxiety.[13]

The diagnosis of Fritz's fatal illness left no one in doubt that his reign would be very brief. This spurred Bismarck to look at the rising power on the horizon—none other than Prince Wilhelm, Vicky and Fritz's twenty-eight-year-old son—and begin bypassing the dying crown prince. For with the aged emperor in Berlin also seriously ill and weak, there was little doubt that the scepter of power was now devolving onto the next generations. Within a week after Prince Wilhelm wrote his moving letter to Queen Victoria, Bismarck saw to it that he was made deputy kaiser. This meant that, should the sickly Wilhelm I become unable to sign official documents, Willy had the right to do so on his behalf. This action had the effect of bypassing the dying crown prince, who at San Remo murmured rightly to Vicky: "So they already look upon me as dead."[14]

The year 1888 brought opportunities for Queen Victoria to indulge in her preoccupation with mourning, for two significant deaths took place in Germany. On March 9, Vicky's ninety-one-year-old father-in-law, Kaiser Wilhelm I, died, making Fritz, Emperor Frederick III and Vicky his empress. The couple was still in San Remo when news of their accession arrived. As the first act of his reign, Fritz invested Vicky with the insignia of the Black Eagle, Prussia's premier order of chivalry. In characteristic selflessness and humility, the new kaiser, unable to speak, scribbled a note to his doctors thanking them for "having let me live long enough to recompense the valiant courage of my wife."[15]

The new emperor and empress hurried back to a Berlin engulfed in freezing cold and snow. But it was evident that the emperor would not be able to reign for long. Frederick III was a pitiable sight. "Hardly able to breathe, now without the power to speak, his general's uniform collar hiding the excruciatingly painful steel cannula sticking out of his windpipe, the only joy the ravaged man had left in his heart was the satisfaction that his doctors had gotten him through long enough for his wife of thirty years to live out the rest of her life with the style and titles of Majesty, and Empress, and Queen. He knew full well that without Vicky's encouragement, he would never have made it this far. Thus began a reign that history has all but forgotten," one that would amount to a "phantom reign."[16] Vicky knew that their time on the throne was limited. She wrote to Queen Victoria about having "to leave all the work undone which we have so long and so carefully been preparing."[17]

Her words were all the more poignant when compared with Fritz's own message to Bismarck: "May I be destined thus to lead Germany and Prussia in a course of peaceful development to new honours. . . . Not caring for the splendour of great deeds, not striving for glory, I shall be satisfied if it be one day said of my rule that it was beneficial to my people, useful to my Country and a blessing to the Empire."[18] But this was not to be. And because of this "cruel irony of fate," Vicky, after having hoped so much, after having shared so many high ambitions, so many disinterested and humanitarian plans with the husband she loved, . . . [now] found herself in the presence of an inexorable reality which took away from her with one hand all that it had given to her with the other.

Instead of sharing the throne with the companion of her life, she saw herself watching at his death-bed. No tragedy could have been more cruel. Yet the Empress bore herself magnificently, and showed to the world the strength of her admirable character. In those tragic hours when the faltering but nevertheless firm hand of Frederick III took up the reins of the German Empire, she was sublime in her abnegation, in her utter forgetfulness of her own sufferings. She succeeded in hiding from the world the anguish under which she was breaking down, and found the courage to speak in hopeful tones to the poor invalid who knew but too well that no help was left to either of them.[19]

The day after Fritz and Vicky's accession an emotional Queen Victoria wrote to her daughter:

My heart is very, very full. May every blessing be yours and may you *now* be able to see the right thing done for beloved Fritz as it should be, and every possible help and care that is needed afforded. . . . I know how kind and good and forgiving you are, but I beg you both to be firm and put your foot down and especially to make those of your children, who were always speaking of the Emperor and Empress to remember who they are now. Many there are who will have to learn this and I fancy that you will be firm. My own dear Empress Victoria—it does seem an impossible dream— may God bless her. You know how little I care for rank or titles, but I cannot deny that after all that has been done and said, I am thankful and proud that dear Fritz and you should have come to the throne.[20]

A contemporary of Vicky's noted of Frederick III: "He can be an Emperor only in name and how long will he be that? I hear that he and his son are reconciled, but not so Prince William and his mother. The sad spectacle of these family dissensions are given to the whole world for everybody knows about them and talks of them."[21] Several years before, Vicky had written to Queen Victoria about this seemingly unbridgeable gulf between her and Wilhelm. It was the summer of 1880, and by then "the disappointment of the Crown Princess in her son was complete." "Willy is *chauvinistic* and *ultra* Prussian to a degree," related Vicky, "and with a violence which is often very painful to me." In order to deal with this, she added, "I avoid all discussions, always turn off the subject or remain silent!"[22] By the time Vicky and Fritz ascended the throne, mother and son were still in battle mode.

Because of his weakness, Fritz had no choice but to keep Bismarck at the helm of the government. The chancellor himself looked back on this era as a time when "I was an absolute *dictator*."[23] He had, after all, been a commanding and powerful leader during the previous reign, who in "his tendency towards insubordination" had "never behaved as if he had a boss."[24] Wilhelm I himself once admitted candidly: "It is hard being Emperor under Bismarck," adding, "He is more important than I."[25] Now with a gravely ill Frederick III at the helm, there was no reason for Bismarck to temper his ways.

Vicky knew that it would be dangerous to antagonize this powerful enemy. The chancellor understood the extent of his power over the empress, "for what little influence she possessed with [her son] Wilhelm would vanish the moment her consort died, although the chancellor's would continue."[26] That was the future, but for the present, she had to contend with something equally insidious, for "the end result of Bismarck's campaign to isolate . . . [Fritz] and his wife, destroy their reputations, and render them politically powerless was alienation."[27] During Fritz's reign, Vicky and the emperor continued to be alienated by Bismarck and his ruling clique. Her son Wilhelm would likely become kaiser in no time. For the opportunistic, there was thus no reason to rally around Fritz and Vicky.

Queen Victoria was horrified by the situation in Berlin. She was especially indignant about those who circled Vicky and Fritz like vultures, ready to jump on Wilhelm's side as soon as Frederick III died. The queen expressed her concerns to Lord Salisbury about "the terrible *cercle vicieux* which surrounds the unfortunate Emperor and Empress and which makes Bismarck's conduct really disloyal, wicked and really unwise in the extreme!"[28]

Fritz and Vicky's ordeal was nothing short of martyrdom. In early 1888, breathing became nearly impossible for Fritz, thus necessitating the insertion of the steel cannula. Though absolutely necessary, the cannula caused further extreme discomfort. Then there was the friction among the doctors. Mackenzie and the German doctors bickered over Fritz's illness, and even here Vicky was not spared unfair criticism, with Germans wondering why she insisted on having a British physician instead of leaving the diagnosis and treatment to German ones.

Vicky's tribulations redoubled as her relationship with her oldest son degenerated into one long-pitched battle punctuated by the occasional truce. From Willy came the complaint that his mother hated him "more than anything else on earth."[29] Vicky, in turn, said that "what she wrote about him was 'by *no means* exaggerated,' . . . but 'only a third of what happens . . . and I do *not* wish to torment you with a list.' "[30] Though many knew of the antagonism between mother and son, few were privy to the extent of the vitriol that Wilhelm spewed at his long-suffering mother. Vicky may have been occasionally overbearing toward Willy, but she did not deserve his overly narcissistic complaints and cruel behavior. She was especially appalled at his overt impatience and lack of feeling for his dying father. "William fancies himself completely the Emperor and an absolute and autocratic one!" wrote the disgusted empress to her mother, an observation backed by the Austro-Hungarian ambassador to Germany.[31]

Bertie had seen the depressing spectacle that was playing out with his sister and brother-in-law. According to Vicky's friend Lady Paget, "The Prince of Wales on his return from Berlin told the Queen that Bismarck and the other ministers treated the Emperor Frederic[k] as quite *sans conséquence;* he reigns but he does not govern. He is so unhappy he cannot sleep. Knowing the personages of the tragedy so well, one reads between the lines and one cannot help feeling terribly anxious as to what may happen if this uncertain state of things lasts. Poor man, this is the heaviest cross of all for him to bear."[32] Lady Paget added that "the Queen's feeling is that it is a bore always knuckling-under to Bismarck, but she is told that as everybody always is knuckling-under they must go on doing so. . . . It does seem too dreadful that the poor man [Frederick III] is really a martyr and politically his position seems to be getting more and more difficult."[33]

Vicky and Fritz rightly feared for the future. Concerned that Willy might destroy documents they could use to show that, contrary to his assertions, they were not enemies of Germany, they had their personal papers spirited out of the country in several stages. The papers arrived in England for safe storage.

In April 1888, Queen Victoria traveled to Berlin. It was a poignant visit for both mother and child, politically and above all personally. For Victoria was bidding her cherished son-in-law farewell and would be leaving her oldest daughter alone in what amounted to a den of wolves. During this visit, Victoria met with Otto von Bismarck. The Iron Chancellor was evidently impressed with the queen, for when he left their meeting, he mopped his brow and declared: "That was a woman! one can do business with her!"[34]

Vicky was overjoyed to see her mother. "*What* a happiness it was, in all that misery, to catch a glimpse of the Queen!" she wrote to Lady Ponsonby. "Her visit went off so well that I think she was pleased—in spite of the gloom and sadness which pervades everything, to see what pleasure her visit gave. I cannot speak of my own sufferings and trials, they are too great to mention lightly. . . . You know all the circumstances that make my fate *so* hard. I have not the heart to speak of the future."[35] Victoria's own impression of her visit vividly describes her daughter's depth of emotion: "Vicky took me back to my room and talked some time very sadly about the future, breaking down completely. Her despair at what she seems to look on as the certain end is terrible."[36]

The queen's visit to Berlin ended on a sad note for Victoria and Vicky. "Vicky struggled hard not to gave way, but finally broke down," recounted the queen, "and it was terrible to see her standing there in tears, while the train moved slowly off, and to think of all she was suffering and might have to go through. My poor poor child, what would I not do to help her in her hard lot!"[37]

Soon after leaving Germany, Queen Victoria wrote to Vicky, "Most beloved and darling child, How dreadful our separation was I cannot say or *how* my whole heart and soul go out in love and sympathy towards you and our most dearly beloved suffering Fritz. . . . My heart was wrung with grief and pity and yet not devoid of the hope which God mercifully implants into our souls and hearts to enable us to go on."[38] Vicky wrote with gratitude to the queen, telling her, "Your motherly kindness and affection has done me good and has refreshed my aching heart!"[39]

Throughout Fritz's dreadful illness, Vicky nursed him diligently. As her husband was unable to communicate properly, she learned to read his lips. "Tell me," he would pronounce in silence each morning, after having stretched out his arms to his wife. "I always had to tell him," recalled Vicky, "every tiny little thing I had done, seen and heard the day before, what I had thought, hoped and imagined."[40]

As the fifty-six-year-old emperor's life drew to a close, Bismarck paid him a last visit. The chancellor and Vicky faced each other on opposite ends of the sickbed. The dying emperor took his wife's and his enemy's hands and clasped them together in a silent but moving plea for unity. Fritz tried to help Vicky and Germany by imploring the chancellor to promise his help. But Bismarck did not commit to anything. He kissed his emperor's hand and stated simply: "Your Majesty may rest assured that I shall never forget that Her Majesty is my Queen."[41] Vicky broke down.

Count Hugo von Radolinski, who had been Fritz's court chamberlain as well as Bismarck's spy, described what had taken place as "one of the most touching scenes" he had ever witnessed.[42] Vicky, who had been no less moved, nevertheless did not let the exchange compromise her powers of observation. She recounted that Bismarck "did not appear to be affected, his face expressed neither sorrow nor sympathy!"[43]

Another dramatic scene involved Fritz and Vicky's daughter Princess Sophie. On June 14, she turned eighteen, and to celebrate the milestone, the young woman went to her dying father's bedside, where Fritz, who put on a brave face, gave her a bouquet of flowers. "What a birthday for the poor child!" recorded Vicky, "what a recollection for the whole of her life! The last day on earth of her beloved father!"[44]

Emperor Frederick III's agonies and ninety-nine-day reign ended on the morning of June 15. Vicky stayed with her beloved husband until his last breath. The widow then took the withered laurel wreath she had given Fritz after the Franco-Prussian War and placed it on his chest. She placed his sword on his arm and collapsed in stunned sorrow.

It was the end of a solid, passionate, loving marriage. Fritz had once confided his deep, abiding love for Vicky, saying, "She has been the guardian angel of my existence and she has helped me to bear all its sorrows and dark hours. She is perfection itself as a woman."[45]

To Fritz's mother, Vicky conveyed a touching message: "Thy beloved only son is no more. I am proud to have been the wife of that hero. One of his last thoughts was of thee. Support this terrible blow with resignation and courage."[46] Queen Victoria's letter to Empress Augusta was full of sympathy but added: "The tragedy for my poor child is too ghastly—much worse even than mine in 1861."[47]

Victoria, who had awaited the dreadful news at Balmoral, was still taken aback when she learned of Fritz's death. "A terrible day!" bemoaned the queen. "I cannot, cannot realize the dreadful truth—the awful misfortune! It is too, too dreadful! My poor dear Vicky, God help her!"[48]

To her mother—who understood all too well what she was going through—Vicky wrote, "How cruel it does seem—that he should be thus . . . cheated of life. . . . Oh, it is all so terrible, so dreadful. On one of the wreaths was the inscription . . . [God's will does not allow of why] so it is—and so we must bear our Cross."[49] Vicky looked to Queen Victoria for inspiration to go on, telling her mother: "You bore it, and I must bear it! It would not be right, not grateful to mourn against God's decree."[50]

"Darling, darling, unhappy Child," wrote Victoria, "I clasp you in my arms and to a heart that bleeds, for this is a double, dreadful grief, a misfortune untold and to the world at large. You are far more sorely tried than me. . . . May God help and support you as He did me."[51] To her grandson Willy, who was now the emperor—Kaiser Wilhelm II—Victoria wrote: "I am broken-hearted. Help and do all you can for your poor dear Mother and try to follow in your best, noblest, and kindest of father's footsteps."[52]

Wilhelm ignored her. In keeping with his bombastic style, Wilhelm II's accession began with bluster as he announced: "We are bound to each other—I and the army—we are born for each other, and we shall hold together indissolubly whether it be God's will to send us calm or storm."[53] But behind those words of bravado were the actions of a coward, and a cruel one at that. A mere half hour after his father died, Wilhelm II ordered a regiment of hussars to seal off the Neues Palais. They ran roughshod over the palace, overturning furniture, including Fritz's desk, which was disrespectfully taken apart in search of papers. When a uniformed Wilhelm II arrived, he gave his shocked mother no explanation. More high-ranking officers came to ransack the palace and rifle through Fritz's desk again while Vicky huddled with her three youngest daughters, the dead emperor's body still lying nearby.

In a moving letter written not long before his death, Vicky captured the tragedy that had befallen her and her husband:

> When one falls from so high as I have fallen, one's friends are particularly dear to one. Sometimes it seems to me as if all this agony is nothing but a dream from which I must awake; and then anguish seizes me again, and I realize my misfortune in all its depth. And when one thinks that I belong to the number of those who are called the happy ones of this earth! If only all the people who envy me—or, rather, who have envied me—could only guess how often the great ones of this world have to suffer for the high position which is theirs, they would not be in such a hurry to judge or to condemn them. We have even to endure the pain of not being able to talk about our sufferings, and at all costs we must fall and die like kings.[54]

The contrast between Vicky's and Victoria's fates was at no time more glaring than in 1888. Queen Victoria was enjoying widespread popularity, unrivaled and unequaled as a monarch, while her daughter fell to the depths of despair, racked by the demoralizing knowledge that her husband's reign was so brief it had made no positive impact on Germany. Vicky's "assigned role as the missionary of progress,"[55] one she had eagerly embraced as a teenage bride and had such hopes of achieving with Fritz, was now in tatters. With her husband's death went any hope that Vicky could help move Prussia toward the English model. For the widowed Empress Frederick, as Vicky now wished to be called, her life's hopes and ambitions, nurtured by her parents, came to naught. She continued to be derisively thought of as *die Engländerin*—the Englishwoman in the land that never accepted her. It was a painful blow to the Empress Frederick and to Queen Victoria. But if both women thought their torments had ended with Fritz's death, they were sadly mistaken.

26

APOTHEOSIS AND ANGUISH

Queen Victoria lost no time in consoling her oldest daughter in her time of grief, urging her to come to England to recuperate. Vicky, with her three youngest children, arrived in England five months after Fritz's death. Five-year-old Princess Alice of Albany, daughter of Victoria's son Leopold, was struck by the sight of the empress accompanied by Moretta, Sophie, and Mossy, in deepest mourning. All were in black crepe with Mary Queen of Scots–style caps, with their "red eyes, as they were all crying together—and Grandmama Victoria, too."[1] When Lady Paget saw the widowed empress in England, she was taken aback by her friend's state. "She was terribly changed," noted Paget, "her face bore the marks of despair and grief and in her eyes was a look of opportunities lost for ever."[2]

When Victoria and Vicky were first reunited, "many tears were shed," and Vicky was "very much upset when she first saw me," recounted the queen.[3] But the Empress Frederick's visit to her mother had been like a much-needed salve to soothe a deep wound. In her diary, she confided: "Saw Mama again! Very affecting! She was love and kindness itself and it did my broken heart good. . . . Here in my beloved Windsor Castle I feel the peace of protection and love, I am safe, like a storm-wrecked ship—at last in a safe harbour! Dearly beloved home of my childhood! My native country, my home! With broken wings, impoverished, bowed down with sorrow I return home. But the picture of my Fritz accompanies me all the way, he would be glad to know I was here. Am living in the rooms we had at the time of our wedding, which I always shared with him."[4]

Vicky had every right to be upset with so much that had happened in her life. Not only had she lost her husband to an agonizing disease but the attacks on her continued. She and Fritz were accused of passing military secrets to the French during the Franco-Prussian War, but most hurtful of all were accusations that she had contributed to her husband's death because she had supposedly ignored the German doctors. The public attacks on Vicky emanating from the pro-Wilhelm press were vociferous and vitriolic. They prompted Vicky to tell her mother, "I am no longer astonished at any *lies* or impertinence. The most impudent gang in the world, without principles or conscience, is now in power! I feel *utterly without any protection* whatsoever!"[5]

Vicky also decried the campaign "to wipe out all trace of Fritz's reign, as of an *interlude* without importance. . . . William II succeeds William the 1st—in *perfect* continuity."[6] The Empress Frederick was not only astonished at the venom being unleashed against her and Fritz's memory but also aghast at Bismarck's orders to have a list of the royal couple's friends drawn up so that their houses could be searched.

Additionally painful was the way Vicky's son Wilhelm acted. He was openly hostile toward her, ordering the empress to leave the Neues Palais, her home of thirty years, without compensating her with a comparable property, as was due a dowager empress. The situation in Berlin for Vicky and her sympathizers had become intolerable. "I try never to think of William," she confessed in her diary, "so as not to make myself ill with bitterness, indignation and anger."[7] To her mother, the maligned empress could not help vent her hurt and frustrations, agreeing though with Queen Victoria by starting off,

> That William is not quite aware of the insults and injuries I have suffered at his hands, though I certainly did my best to enlighten him! As he does not feel for his mother he cannot be surprised if she who gave him so much love and care, now can only remember with pain that he is her son. Perhaps years may change this, but at present I am too sore and have suffered too much! He has it in his power, if he likes, to change this. I can do nothing, nor will I ever give way and humour him, and bear all in patience and silence. . . . He simply accepts that and thinks he can continue to ride roughshod over me; there he makes a mistake. I think he simply is so wrapped up in himself, his power, his vanity, his plans, his position, that he does not remember my existence.
>
> I so thoroughly and utterly disapprove of all that has been done since that dreadful day [of Fritz's death], with very few exceptions, and have so little hope of its mending, that I strive to hear as little

and think about it as little as I can. But one cannot cease to care for the country and its interests, and it is difficult to become indifferent to things which for thirty years and up to last June seemed of vital importance to Fritz and to me, and which we watched with such anxiety.[8]

Besides her son's outrageous and hurtful directives, Vicky was consumed with anger and disappointment at the way the kaiser ruled Germany—full of bombast, belligerence, and lack of proper vision. Lady Paget also found Wilhelm II pompous, recalling how in one of his "all-too-frequent speeches," the kaiser "advises all those whose opinions differ from his to leave Germany. Then he speaks of God as if he were on the most intimate terms with Him and he ends up by saying that he knows he is quite right in all he does and that in spite of all that is said he will steer his own canoe."[9]

Vicky could not help but mourn the lost opportunities Fritz's death entailed. "We had a mission," she wrote to Queen Victoria, "we were faithful to what we believed and knew to be right. We loved Germany, we wished to see her strong and great, not only with the sword, but in all that was righteous in culture, in progress, in liberty. We wished to see the people happy and free, growing and developing in all that was good."[10] When the queen urged a reconciliation with Wilhelm II, Vicky replied, "He does not understand me. . . . He does not perceive how, during the whole year, he not only cruelly neglected me, but also allowed injuries and insults to be heaped on me."[11]

By the time of Frederick III's death, "the antagonism between mother and son had become so intense that there was no possibility of reconciliation. Both admitted that there were troublemakers at work to separate them, but they could not agree as to who these noxious figures were. Wilhelm's allies were his mother's enemies, and hers were his."[12] Wilhelm himself once admitted bluntly: "My mother will always remain an Englishwoman and I am a Prussian; so how can we ever be in harmony with one another?"[13]

Now that Wilhelm was kaiser, Vicky saw no hope for improvement on his part. She lamented to her mother about what his early accession (Wilhelm was twenty-eight) meant: "I cannot imagine anything worse for his disposition than being Kaiser!"[14] Vicky was not alone in her low opinion. Soon after he ascended the throne, the kaiser reveled in his role, making ostentatious public appearances and foreign visits. All this mortified his grandmother Queen Victoria, who in her letters to relatives "condemned the impious, pleasure-seeking conduct of her grandson."[15] "How sickening it is to see Willy not 2 months after his beloved & noble Father's death going to Banquets & Reviews. It is very indecent & very unfeeling!" wrote the queen to the Prince of Wales.[16]

On another level, Vicky and Willy's fractious relationship did not help Anglo-German relations. During his father's brief reign, Wilhelm wrote, "That our family shield should be besmirched and the Reich brought to the brink of ruin by an English princess who is my mother—that is the most terrible thing of all."[17] His vitriol was not confined to his mother. During Queen Victoria's visit to Berlin in 1888, Wilhelm "said that it was high time that the old woman—his grandmother—died."[18] With his antagonism toward his mother and grandmother inflaming his already volatile personality, it came as no surprise that Wilhelm openly flirted with reorienting German relations toward Russia. Vicky worried about this possible loosening of ties between Germany and England. "Of course—it must be our endeavour, that the relations of England and Germany should *not* suffer in spite of Pce Bismarck's [*sic*] wickedness and William's folly," she wrote to Victoria.[19] An infuriated queen had aired her anxieties to Lord Salisbury, her prime minister, not long after Frederick III's death: "This all engrossing misfortune of poor darling Fritz's death, which is such an untold tragedy,—of the symptoms in William's Opening Speech, of a leaning towards Russia, & there having been no mention of England,—of Pce Bismarck's violent language, when talking to Bertie, which showed how untrue & heartless he is, after all he seemed to promise me, & after poor Fritz had placed Vicky's hand in his, as if to recommend her to him! It is incredible & disgraceful."[20]

Queen Victoria was not blind to her daughter's oppression, telling one of her granddaughters: "The way poor dear Aunt Vicky is persecuted & attacked & the way in wh. those vile Bismarcks & *their crew* attack her & dear Uncle's memory is not to be borne!"[21] Meanwhile the Bismarcks—Otto and his elder son, Herbert, the foreign affairs secretary—dramatically underscored their opposition to the Empress Frederick's influence. Receiving the Prince of Wales during a visit he paid to Germany, the duo thumped the table and declared: "We won't have petticoat government here!"[22] Herbert von Bismarck in particular so incensed the Prince of Wales with his remark that the voiceless Fritz should never have reigned, that Queen Victoria's son nearly threw the younger Bismarck out of the window.

Upon their return from Berlin, the Prince and Princess of Wales related to Queen Victoria the cruelties that had been heaped upon Vicky. The queen passed on the distressing situation to one of her granddaughters soon after Fritz's death: "It is too dreadful to us all to think of Willy & Bismarck & Dona [Willy's wife, Augusta] being the supreme head of all now! Two so unfit & one so wicked. [Bismarck] spoke so shamefully about dear Ant V[icky] to Uncle Bertie & A[unti]e Alix!"[23] To Princess Maria Anna of Prussia, Queen Victoria wrote in July 1888: "The loss of our dear Fritz is quite irreplaceable and a great misfortune for Germany and Europe, and it is fearful for my poor child . . . whose whole existence is quite ruined!"[24]

To Vicky, Victoria wrote sympathetically: "They must be taught that persecution, oppression and wickedness will not and cannot be tolerated. It is beginning to be much talked of here . . . and while, of course, one wishes not to quarrel if possible with the German Government, there is a limit to that, and the way in which the Princess Royal of Great Britain is treated must be known and will be greatly resented."[25] The queen followed this message with another: "Your treatment is a scandal and must not go on."[26]

Of all the three royal mothers—Isabella, Maria Theresa, and Victoria, it was Victoria who had the greatest misfortune to live long enough to witness the tragic destiny of her daughter play out. Isabella had a glimpse of Catherine's early problems after Prince Arthur's death; Maria Theresa experienced to a greater extent Marie Antoinette's tribulations. But it was Victoria who saw the full scope of her daughter's grievous fate in her adopted land.

Vicky's grief, tribulations, and bravery were in full view when her sister Lenchen visited her weeks after Fritz's death. "I never saw such a courageous woman," wrote Lenchen, "for crushed and broken-hearted under a load of sorrow and care such as few have ever had to bear, she always pulls herself together, determined to face whatever comes, and thinking all the time of how she can help others and what she can do for the good of the country."[27] Lenchen was right about Vicky, who "kept a proud and dignified silence, and only her letters to her mother show the seething resentment that consumed her."[28]

Fortunately for Vicky, she was able to move away from Berlin and its noxious politics. A friend bequeathed her money that she used to build a large villa in the Taunus Mountains near Frankfurt. Named Friedrichshof, in honor of Frederick III, Vicky's new home was designed and decorated to her specifications. The architecture was an infusion of Renaissance and the timbered local German style with doses of English Tudor. Vicky filled the house with a huge collection of books, family portraits, and exquisite furniture. One visitor described it as "the most perfect and best appointed residence of its day," where everything "had a quality of its own: the parquet flooring, the oak window frames, the brass door handles—everything was in the most studied taste yet adapted for its purpose." One could not help but be "dazzled by all its treasures."[29] Vicky had plenty of time to decorate Friedrichshof, for her son kept his long-suffering mother away from the corridors of power. Wilhelm II even denied his mother the opportunity to take over Empress Augusta's charitable works when she died in 1890 and gave them instead to his wife, Dona.

By this time, Vicky, at fifty, looked astonishingly like Queen Victoria, especially now that the empress always wore mourning. Moretta, who visited the queen in 1889, was also struck by their resemblance, and told her mother so: "Grandmama so often reminds me of you in all her ways & I am reminded daily of your voice when she calls."[30]

In her grief, the Empress Frederick's three eldest children, Wilhelm, Charlotte, and Henry, continued to remain distant from her. In 1888 Vicky had written of them: "These are not my children."[31] And of Wilhelm in particular, the empress lamented, "This son has never really been mine."[32] Vicky therefore gravitated all the more toward her youngest children, Moretta, Sophie, and Mossy—a fact that did not go unnoticed by Queen Victoria. Thus the queen urged Vicky: "For your three dear girls' sakes you must struggle on bravely."[33] The trio and Vicky did indeed cling to one another for comfort, especially in the face of Wilhelm's callousness. Vicky's precious trio, however, soon broke up. In 1889 Sophie married Crown Prince Constantine of Greece and went to live in Athens. In 1890 Moretta married Prince Adolf of Schaumburg-Lippe, and in 1893 Mossy married Prince Frederick Charles of Hesse.

Vicky's relationship with Sophie was especially close. Though her youngest daughter was in faraway Athens, Vicky emulated her mother and kept up a voluminous correspondence with Sophie, who remained as attached to her mother as Vicky was to Victoria. The tone of Vicky's letters to Sophie differed from that of her correspondence with Queen Victoria, for instead of the "confidences of a troubled daughter to a revered parent," the letters were those of a "fond mother."[34] It was not unusual for Vicky to express her attachment to her daughter, such as in this line in 1892: "You cannot know, you cannot guess, my Sophie, how dear you are to me."[35] More trouble from Wilhelm, however, threatened Sophie's happiness. When she announced in 1890 that she was converting to the Greek Orthodox faith, the kaiser exploded in fury, dragging the Empress Frederick and Queen Victoria into a public quarrel with his sister, whom he threatened to forbid setting foot in Germany. Vicky wrote to Sophie that "William is convinced I had tried to persuade you to become Greek. He is so firmly convinced that I am always in some 'intrigue' against him."[36] When she converted, Sophie sent her mother a telegram saying Wilhelm refused her entry into Germany for three years, adding her opinion: "Mad. Never mind."[37]

During these difficult years, Queen Victoria and the Empress Frederick grew closer, united by the positions they shared and the challenges these positions brought. But it was above all their mother-daughter bond that truly united Victoria and Vicky. "The more my sorrow & loneliness weigh upon me, the more I cling to your love and affection & sympathy which has never failed me," wrote Vicky to her mother a year and a half after Fritz died. "May God bless & protect you for many a year to come," she wrote seven years later, "& spare you to us to whom your love & kindness & sympathy are so inexpressibly precious, & to <u>none more</u> than to me!"[38] Victoria and Vicky were also drawn closer by their mutual experiences as mothers. The queen had alluded to this before, telling Vicky, "The older your children grow, the more our feelings will be in harmony for you are as anxious as I am for the welfare and success of our children, and we both have the same feeling of the trials and difficulties which they entail and of the frivolity and wickedness of the world."[39]

Victoria wholly concurred with Vicky's exasperation over Wilhelm, not only on a personal level but also on a political one, for both women strove for good Anglo-German relations. Wilhelm II may have been able to run roughshod over his mother and had a propensity to brush off his uncle the Prince of Wales, but the kaiser had to be more careful with his grandmother, and hence was always respectful toward her. The queen, however, understood Wilhelm's personality and deplored his pomposity, describing to Lord Salisbury as "perfect madness" her grandson's insistence that he be "treated in private as well as in public as 'his Imperial Majesty.' "[40] Furious at the kaiser's complaint that the Prince of Wales did not supposedly treat him as emperor, Victoria told Salisbury, "This is really too vulgar and too absurd . . . the Queen will not swallow this affront."[41] Salisbury was well aware of Victoria's negative views of Wilhelm, noting that "she thinks very badly of him, resents his conduct to his mother, and has more than once shown her resentment very plainly."[42] Wilhelm's pretentiousness and need for adulation bordered on the ridiculous. One official ceremonious greeting to him began: "Our sublime, mighty, beloved Kaiser, King and Lord for all times, for ever and ever."[43] The words were written by none other than Wilhelm himself.

As for the Empress Frederick and her nemesis, Bismarck, the chancellor never helped the empress as Frederick III had wished him to do. The antagonism between Vicky and Bismarck, which she described as "a quarrel of thirty years' standing,"[44] never abated. Vicky's detractors would ascribe this feud to her stubbornness and inability to compromise, but admirers, such as Princess Daisy of Pless, saw something else. An Englishwoman married to one of Germany's wealthiest aristocrats, Daisy described Vicky as having "certain elements of true greatness." She added that "the very fierceness of the venom with which Bismarck pursued her is to me proof that he recognized her essential qualities and feared them. It was not given to any other woman in history to make the Iron Chancellor put on all his armour and unsheathe his sword. And in those days it was all the more wonderful because in Germany women were absolute nonentities, to be seen, but never heard."[45]

Otto von Bismarck's fall came in 1890. He and Wilhelm differed on many matters, especially domestic policies. Moreover, the kaiser was determined that he be respected as a strong ruler. With Bismarck by his side, Wilhelm appeared not autonomous but more like his father, doing the old man's bidding. And so the kaiser forced Bismarck's hand, prompting the chancellor's resignation. As he saw his power slipping, the elderly chancellor visited the empress, asking if she could intercede for him. "I am sorry," Vicky replied, "you, yourself, Prince Bismarck, have destroyed all my influence with my son. I can do nothing."[46] Nevertheless, they parted in a kind of truce. Vicky wrote to the queen that their good-bye was amicable and "in peace, which I am glad of, as I should have been sorry—having suffered so much all these long years . . . that it should appear as if I had any spirit of revenge, which I really have not." But with a heavy heart, Vicky added her anxiety for the future where the kaiser was concerned: "I fear he will find it very difficult, almost impossible, to fulfill all the duties of his office. . . . I am afraid William is a most thorough despot and has some very queer ideas on this subject in his head."[47]

The dowager empress's fate had by this time become fully steeped in melancholy. For "other than a few women in her retinue and a handful of bluestockings in Berlin . . . [Vicky] had made no friends in the forty years she lived in Germany. She often complained that she had no intimates . . . with Queen Victoria serving as the outlet for her expressions of loneliness and distaste for Prussia. She felt herself superior . . . as an Englishwoman, as an Anglican (she never joined the establishment Evangelical Church of Prussia), as a . . . savant at a court that was intellectually lifeless, as a liberal among political antediluvians."[48]

One of the great tragedies of Vicky's life was that she could never find a close affinity for her adopted country. Catherine of Aragon and Marie Antoinette had both adapted to English and French ways, but not Vicky when it came to Prussia. Her detachment from her adopted country was evident in a letter she wrote to a friend after a visit to Italy: "I cannot tell you how bitterly I feel the contrast when I come back to the heavy dull stiffness, to the cold ugliness of north Germany and the neighborhood of Berlin! The moral atmosphere of the Court, the political and official world seem to *suffocate* me! The ideas, the tastes and feelings and habits are so totally different from mine, that

I feel the gulf between me and them deepen and widen and bitterest and hardest of all is that my son Wilhelm and his wife stand on the other side of this gulf!!"[49] Vicky might have warmed to Germany much more had she been allowed to use her considerable talents and energies, particularly in the political sphere, but this was denied her.

Unlike Vicky, who was politically marginalized, Queen Victoria, even in her seventies, remained thoroughly immersed in her role as reigning monarch, fully cognizant of domestic and international situations. Moreover, in contrast to her daughter's fate, Victoria's "participation [in government] was, in the main, always treated with near-religious respect, and her views granted as much deference as possible."[50]

In 1897, Queen Victoria celebrated sixty years on the throne—her Diamond Jubilee. She had reigned for so long that hardly anyone in Britain recalled being the subject of any other monarch. But the queen did not think of herself as resilient, especially during her early widowhood, when she was convinced that she could not live, let alone reign, without her beloved Albert. She talked of her shattered nerves and, consumed by grief, feared she could not go on. Her uncle King Leopold, after all, had once told Victoria that the task of carrying out the role of a constitutional sovereign, and doing *"it well, is a very difficult one."*[51] Yet the queen forged on despite some missteps and exercised her duties well. She had come a long way from the apprehensive, sensitive, and insecure young Victoria, who leaned heavily on Lord Melbourne and Prince Albert. She was now the redoubtable queen, "masterful in her manner, so uncompromising in her truthfulness,"[52] a force to be reckoned with, buttressed by decades of experience on the throne. Victoria once wrote that she did "not require to be reminded of the honour of England, which touches her more nearly than anyone else" and that "the Queen also knows what her responsibility is, as the Sovereign of this great country."[53] She never deviated from that path, so that her motto became "Still endure."

Victoria was at the helm of an empire the likes of which the world had never seen. The British Empire still dominated the globe as it had during her Golden Jubilee, but it was now burnished with more luster than ever. The queen's great-grandson King Edward VIII captured the impact of Victoria's Britain at the year of his birth, 1894, noting that "British sea power and financial and commercial influence were nearly everywhere supreme. Ships built on Clydeside carried the hardware of Birmingham, the steel of Sheffield, the cotton of Manchester and Paisley, and the textiles of Bradford and Leeds, into every corner of the world. British capital, its home market saturated, was building the railroads of Argentina and Japan, was opening up the Middle East, and turning to the raw materials of undeveloped Africa."[54] Thus, in the twilight of Victoria's life and reign, "the sixtieth anniversary of her accession to the throne was being celebrated as a festival of imperial strength, splendour and unity—a mammoth exhibition of power." Huge crowds lined the route of Victoria's procession through London's streets, craning to catch a glimpse of their queen. They "waited in proud excitement [for] they were citizens of a kingdom which, particularly in its own estimation, was of unique consequence in the world."[55] At the apex of it all stood Victoria, queen and empress. Before setting off on her procession to St. Paul's Cathedral, the elderly queen sent a telegram to her empire. A brief and humble message, it read: "From my heart, I thank my beloved people. May God bless them!"[56] It was, thought the technicians at the Central Telegraph Office, "a supreme moment in her illustrious career."[57] To bring this moment into perspective, one need only recall that "not so long before, when men spoke of Empire they were thinking of Napoleon III, the Tsar or lesser foreign despots. Now they thought only of Victoria, Regina et Imperatrix."[58]

The homage to Victoria was in essence an homage to the British Empire, the revelry amounting to a celebration of Great Britain as the preeminent military and economic power, whose dominions and colonies were united and loyal to the crown.

> The Empire had been growing steadily throughout the century, generally without much public excitement, but since the 1870s, it had expanded so violently that the statistics and reference books could scarcely keep up, and were full of addenda and hasty footnotes. Recalled now from the grand junction of the Jubilee, the separate lines of the Victorian story seemed to have been leading the British inexorably towards the suzerainty of the world—the methodical distribution of their systems, their values, their power and their stock across the continents. Their Empire, hitherto seen as a fairly haphazard accretion of possessions, now appeared to be settling into some gigantic pattern: and like gamblers on a lucky streak, they felt that their power was self-engendering, that they were riding a wave of destiny, sweeping them on to fulfillment.[59]

To celebrate the Diamond Jubilee, a magnificent panoply unfolded in the British capital. A display of empire the likes of which had never been seen before greeted the huge, excited crowds. Some fifty thousand troops from all over the British Empire marched through London as part of the festivities. They provided an exotic touch and gave the crowds a glance at the astonishing extent to which the Union Jack prevailed. For these soldiers of the realm included "Hussars from Canada and Carabiniers from Natal, camel troops from Bikaner and Dyak headhunters from North Borneo. . . . The seventeen officers of the Indian Imperial Service troops were all princes. . . . There were Malays, and Sinhalese, and Hausas from Niger and the Gold Coast, Jamaicans in white gaiters and ornately embroidered jackets, [and] British Guiana police in caps like French gendarmes."[60] In an open carriage, Queen Victoria made her way through the packed streets of London to St. Paul's Cathedral. Because of her frailty, the queen did not go inside, but a thanksgiving service was held outside. To top off this imperial bacchanalia, the Prince of Wales presided over a naval review at Spithead of twenty-one battleships and fifty-six cruisers. The spectacular review underscored the Royal Navy's might and Great Britain's continued dominance of the seas.

In recording her impressions of this momentous day, the aged queen (who by now had shrunk to four feet seven and possessed a forty-six-inch waist) wrote that she "passed through dense crowds . . . who gave me a most enthusiastic reception. It was like a triumphal entry. . . . The windows, the roofs of the houses, were one mass of beaming faces, and the cheers never ceased. . . . All vied with one another to give me a heartfelt, loyal, and affectionate welcome. I was deeply touched and gratified."[61] The next day with a characteristic mixture of humility and pride, she added, "No one ever, I believe, has met with such an ovation as given to me, passing through those six miles of streets."[62]

Queen Victoria, the object of the empire's adulation, was moved by this remarkable milestone, recording that "the crowds were quite indescribable, and their enthusiasm truly marvellous and deeply touching."[63] The Empress Frederick was equally touched, writing to her mother: "I am so thankful I witnessed the ceremonies of your Jubilee. . . . It was a never-to-be-forgotten time."[64] How right Vicky was, for "never did the queen, as fountain of honor, as patron of philanthropy, and as symbol of the Victorian virtues, loom larger in the eyes of her subjects. For Queen Victoria, the decade between her Golden Jubilee (1887) and her Diamond Jubilee (1897) constituted an apotheosis."[65]

If this was a time of apotheosis for Queen Victoria, it continued to be a time of anguish for the Empress Frederick. She never stopped worrying about Wilhelm II's megalomania and Germany's future. Much to Vicky's and Victoria's chagrin, Wilhelm's accession meant trouble for Anglo-German relations, thanks to the kaiser's ambivalence toward England, which echoed his feelings for his mother. Relations between the two powers reached new lows in 1896, when Wilhelm congratulated Paul Kruger, the head of the Boers in South Africa, for foiling a British-supported raid against them. So upset was Queen Victoria at Wilhelm that she had banned him from her Diamond Jubilee celebrations. Nor did she invite him to her eightieth birthday party, which infuriated the kaiser. Victoria was indignant at both her grandson's behavior and his attempts to throw a spanner in Anglo-Russian relations. This state of affairs prompted Queen Victoria to write to Czar Nicholas II in 1899, warning him: "I am afraid William may go and tell things against us to you, just as he does about you to us. . . . It is so important that we should understand each other, and that such mischievous and unstraightforward proceedings should stop."[66]

The German press, heaping scorn upon the English, were as unsympathetic to England as the kaiser. Of this, Vicky noted: "I fear it leads to a distressing conclusion in England, which is that she has no greater enemy than Germany and no more bitter foe than William."[67]

Into the 1890s, the Empress Frederick and Kaiser Wilhelm continued to be estranged. Both stubborn, they rarely gave way to each other, making reconciliation difficult. The empress also admitted to Queen Victoria in 1890 that "I am completely cut off from the official world. Not a single official person ever comes near me!"[68] Vicky's estrangement from officialdom and the German court was to be the least of her troubles, for a painful illness, with echoes of Fritz's suffering, was soon to consume the troubled empress.

27

TO FACE LIFE WITH COURAGE

*W*hat meager joy Vicky experienced during these years centered on family life, as it did with Victoria. Vicky's relationships with Moretta, Sophie, and Mossy, as well as her role as grandmother, sustained her through these otherwise lonely years, which increasingly took their toll as well on her mother. Vicky never hesitated to keep Sophie, in Athens, informed of what went on with the rapidly aging Queen. "How lame and infirm she is breaks my heart to see," wrote Vicky in 1894, "but thank God . . . her mind and intelligence and interest and power of work [are] quite what they were."[1]

In 1897 Vicky's anxieties reached new levels when hostilities broke out between the Ottoman Empire and Greece. Victoria sent money to Vicky for the Greek refugees, but the queen insisted that her contribution be kept a secret. Vicky also begged Wilhelm II to help Greece, but "his hostility was so blatant that Queen Victoria made a formal protest through her embassy in Berlin."[2] Greece lost the Greco-Turkish War of 1897, sending the Greek royal family's popularity plummeting. Vicky counseled Sophie to bear with it, as she knew firsthand how it felt to be unpopular.

As for Queen Victoria herself, who was as popular as ever, she was grateful for having been granted a long life. Gone were the days when she thought she would not outlive her beloved Albert for long. Though she never stopped grieving for her dead husband, Victoria had come to embrace life, despite the many sadnesses she had lived through. In 1897 she admitted: "My poor old birthday again came round, and it seems sadder each year, though I have such cause for thankfulness, and to be as well as I am, but fresh sorrow and trials still come upon me. My great lameness, etc., makes me feel how age is creeping on. Seventy-eight is a good age, but I pray yet to be spared a little longer for the sake of my country and dear ones."[3] It was an echo of the message she had sent the nation upon Prince Leopold's death in 1884, in which she said: "Though much shaken and sorely afflicted by the many sorrows and trials which have fallen upon me during these past years, I will not lose courage, and with the help of Him who has never forsaken me, will strive to labour on for the sake of my children, and for the good of the country I love so well."[4] These trials and tribulations in life were all part of the "difficult road of life as a believing Christian,"[5] words the queen had written at the time of Vicky's confirmation many years before.

With the passage of time, more deaths of friends and family saddened Victoria. It was thus with some trepidation that the queen anticipated her final years, confessing once to Vicky that "as time goes on the love and affection of a mother and her appreciation of one's sorrows, trials and difficulties becomes a greater comfort. My trials are so great and many—the loss of devoted friends and valued advisers is so keenly felt—that I can only foresee that my declining years will be very trying ones."[6] The queen was right. Prince Henry of Battenberg's death from malaria while serving with the British Forces in the Ashanti War in 1896 had been especially hard on the old queen, who enjoyed her son-in-law's amusing company. Victoria felt especially compassionate toward Henry's widow, Beatrice, and her fatherless four young children. These grandchildren, who lived under the same roof as their grandmother all year round, brightened the queen's final years.* She delighted in their presence. Though Victoria could be intimidating to many (she could be simultaneously tyrannical and caring when it came to her servants), toward the youngest in her family, the queen was imposing but not so frightening. King Edward VIII recalled that "such was the majesty that surrounded Queen Victoria, that she was regarded almost as a divinity of whom even her own family stood in awe. However, to us children she was 'Gangan,' a childish interpretation of 'great-grandmama.'"[7] Queen Marie of Romania, daughter of Victoria's son Alfred, saw the queen in a similar light, referring to her as "dear old Granny."[8]

The doyenne of sovereigns, Victoria was also the grandmother of Europe. By the end of the nineteenth century, her descendants reigned, or were set to occupy, the thrones of England, Germany, Greece, Romania, and Russia. Dynastic

*Victoria Eugénie, Beatrice's only daughter, became Queen of Spain upon her marriage in 1906 to King Alfonso XIII.

matchmaking preoccupied Victoria and Vicky in the 1890s as it had decades before. The matrimonial prospects of one of Victoria's favorite granddaughters, Princess Alix of Hesse, were of particular concern. Victoria had great plans for the beautiful but introverted Alix. The queen hoped that Alix would marry the slow-witted Eddy, Bertie's eldest son and thus second in line to the British throne. Alix, however, declined his proposal and instead married Czar Nicholas II of Russia in 1894. The queen accepted the marriage, but ever the Russophobe, who eyed the Russian Empire with suspicion, Victoria always harbored deep reservations about Alix's future there.

After Alix rejected Eddy of Wales's proposal, Queen Victoria and the Empress Frederick began to discuss the suitability of Princess May of Teck as his future wife. Victoria told Vicky, "May is a particularly nice girl, so quiet & yet cheerful & so vy carefully brought up & so sensible," to which Vicky replied, "I wonder whether Eddy—will ever marry May?"[9] Eddy did propose to May, but he died suddenly of influenza in 1892. Afterward, his younger brother married her, and they became King George V and Queen Mary upon the death of King Edward VII in 1910.

Victoria still gave her eldest son little in the way of meaningful training or tasks to prepare him for kingship. Nevertheless, their relationship did not degenerate into the love-hate relationship that plagued the Empress Frederick and Kaiser Wilhelm II. Isabella of Castile and Maria Theresa of Austria, like Victoria, were disappointed by the fates of their eldest sons. Isabella's son, Juan, had grown to be a young man with great potential but died before ascending the throne. Maria Theresa's son Joseph II turned out to be a difficult co-ruler with whom she was always at loggerheads. Victoria's oldest son, who succeeded her as Edward VII, was a bon vivant who never lived up to her high hopes, forever overshadowed by his brilliant sister Vicky.

Vicky and Edward's brother Alfred died in 1900, prompting Victoria to cry out in her journal, "Oh, God! my poor darling Affie gone too! My third grownup child, besides three very dear sons-in-law.* It is hard at eighty-one!"[10] The deaths of three of her children, three sons-in-law, and several grandchildren, along with tribulations such as those experienced by Vicky, were more than enough to try Victoria's Christian faith sorely—yet she never lost her faith and continued to rely heavily on Providence for strength. Victoria's faith had sustained her in her darkest days and continued to do so. "There is so much sadness

---

*The queen's third son-in-law, Grand Duke Louis IV of Hesse, widower of her daughter Princess Alice, had died in 1892.

on this earth," the queen once wrote but added, "God alone can console and strengthen us."[11]

Victoria remained indefatigable until the end. In the autumn of 1865, she had told her uncle King Leopold, "I sometimes wish I could throw everything up and retire into private life."[12] But the queen soldiered on, determined not to let her personal inclinations stand in the way of her duty. At no time was this indefatigable spirit more in evidence than during the Boer War. In South Africa the Boers again went to war against the British Empire. Vicky wrote to Sophie about the crisis, saying, "It is very hard for dear Grandmama, but she neither loses her nerve nor her confidence and feels that in the end the difficulties will be mastered."[13]

Despite her poor eyesight and physical weakness, the queen gallantly cheered on her departing troops, telling them: "May God protect you!"[14] She visited convalescing soldiers, personally awarded medals, and wrote to widows. The queen received government ministers and senior officers in audience, giving advice when necessary. She sent 100,000 tins of chocolate to her soldiers and packages of knitting. What Victoria "could do, she did. It was no coincidence that she became the embodiment of the national spirit."[15] Now, in the twilight of her life, Queen Victoria led by example, buoying the spirits of one and all, especially in times of despair, such as the sieges at Ladysmith, Kimberley, and Mafeking, when the British armies fell into serious trouble. Then, in the course of one week, Black Week as it came to be known, three British generals and their troops were defeated. Upon hearing the news, the aged queen refused to collapse into dejection and surrender. When Arthur Balfour, leader of the House of Commons, went to see the queen at Windsor that week, she greeted him in a defiant and decisive manner, saying, "Please understand that there is no one depressed in this house; we are not interested in the possibilities of defeat; they do not exist."[16] The queen's dogged determination was rewarded in May 1900, when Mafeking was relieved. Victoria wrote to Vicky that the "whole country" was in "wild delight" and that "everything is really going on well now everywhere."[17] The Empress Frederick still had not lost her attachment to her mother and her native land, telling the queen on New Year's Day 1900, "My motto for this century: 'God save the Queen.' "[18]

By the turn of the century, both Queen Victoria and the Empress Frederick faced life with courage—the queen in spite of age and frail health remained a vital force for the empire, rallying her soldiers and subjects in a time of war. Vicky, meanwhile, led a dignified life, not wishing to wreak vengeance on those who had wronged her, Fritz, and Germany. The dowager empress, however, could not help but lament what had happened. In the mid-1890s, Vicky confided to her friend Marie de Bunsen: "Earlier in life, as a young girl, I always thought that Germany was imbued and permeated by all the ideals and talents, and that only relief from government suppression was necessary in order that everything that is lofty and noble might spring into flower. And now?" De Bunsen noted of the empress, "She complained of the lack of political capacity of the Germans." Vicky added, "They talk of 'making politics.' Politics are not 'made'; political issues are matters affecting the weal and woe of the community; consequently every man and every woman, everyone has not only the right but is under an obligation to be concerned in them."[19] Then, of course, Vicky added her own opinions on her eldest son, the kaiser, insisting how different they were, conveniently ignoring the fact that both could be stubborn to a large degree: "There's nothing of me about Wilhelm, but a great deal of Frederick William IV. He himself believes he is most like Frederick the Great."[20] The kaiser, by contrast, when he complained "of the strained relationship with his mother expressed the opinion, 'We are so much alike, of course, and that makes things more difficult.' "[21] Wilhelm echoed this observation: "My mother and I have the same characters. I have inherited hers. That good stubborn English blood which will not give way is in both our veins. The consequence is that, if we do not happen to agree, the situation becomes difficult."[22]

The Empress Frederick never stopped lamenting her strained relationship with Wilhelm II, but she also grieved over how it affected her relationship with Wilhelm's children. "They are kept entirely away from me, though I am so passionately fond of children," noted a resigned Vicky to Marie de Bunsen. Then she added poignantly, "I loved my father and mother ardently; they were my models; when I came to have children of my own it seemed to me a matter of course that they would return my love in the same spirit. How differently things have turned out."[23] Vicky's isolation was complete. Cut off from her eldest son and his children as well as official life, the empress increasingly leaned on her mother and daughter Sophie for support. Only Count Seckendorff, the empress's court chamberlain, could be truly be counted as her friend in Germany. But she had to suffer the indignity of the false stories, instigated years before by Bismarck, that she and Seckendorff were carrying on a clandestine affair.

In her final years, Vicky's greatest battle—in a life full of battles—was the one she waged against death. She was already suffering acutely from the cancer that was spreading into her spine. During the Boer War, she sewed and knitted for the British troops but could not complete as many items as she would have liked because of her illness. Increasingly, Vicky's infirmity kept her from leaving

Friedrichshof. She visited Queen Victoria in England in 1899. At the end of the visit, the queen wrote her daughter a moving letter, telling Vicky: "It is my greatest pleasure and happiness to be of any use to you, my darling, and to help and comfort others is the *one* object in life, when one has gone through so much sorrow as I, and indeed you have too. . . . Let me repeat, come to us whenever and wherever you like."[24]

Mother and child kept up their ardent correspondence. Vicky occasionally told her mother of her sufferings, but not to the same extent as in her letters to Sophie in Athens. To her mother, Vicky wrote of being in bed, "in tortures of pain,"[25] but to her daughter, she elaborated, writing of "the *terrible* nights of agony" and how they "are worse than ever, no rest, no peace. The tears rush down my cheeks when I am not shouting with pain. The injections of morphia dull the pains a little for about a quarter of an hour, sometimes not at all, then they rage again with renewed intensity, and make me wish I were safe in my grave. . . . It is fearful to endure. My courage is quite exhausted and this morning I cried for an hour without ceasing." She added, "I bear this martyrdom hoping to live on a few years more, and see you happy, and the children grow older."[26]

In her letter, written on Sophie and Constantine's wedding anniversary, Vicky showed her tender side as a mother and gave her opinion about life: "May God bless you both, and your darling children and send you many long and happy years of usefulness and success. Thank God great happiness has been granted you in a dear husband and sweet children. Life is *never* easy, it is a struggle at best, but the hours of sunshine, and the blessings vouchsafed, make up for what is pain and sorrow."[27]

In a later letter, the empress again brought up her illness: "I am often in very low spirits and shed many tears, but sometimes when I feel a trifle better I am full of hope, and think of a possible future and better days, though I well know that I cannot be cured, and that my life can never again be what it was. This must be accepted, but I do not find it easy."[28]

When Marie de Bunsen visited the Empress Frederick in December 1900, she found her "horribly ill, the torture had been unspeakable and still almost unbearable." When de Bunsen asked why this had happened to her, Vicky replied, "There is no answer to that. It is so, and has to be endured."[29]

Queen Victoria was naturally perturbed to read of Vicky's illness, telling her: "I am in despair to hear of your having been again so suffering. How I wish I could be of any use!"[30] But there was little she could do, for back in England, at Osborne, Victoria's own health continued to worsen; "the emblem of [the] nineteenth century was dying."[31] There was little doubt that, in the twilight of their lives, "the greatest agony Victoria had to bear was the thought that she might have to survive her own firstborn daughter's death. Most tragic of all the burdens for these two great women was the fact that, though they were united in suffering, they would not be able to see each other during their final illnesses."[32]

Victoria's last letter to Vicky was written on January 6, 1901. In it the queen, wrote touchingly: "I am so grieved to see by your dear letters that your hands trouble you so. It is very troublesome [that they] hurt you so much. I attempt to write myself [instead of dictating]. I don't suffer from my eyes, only the sight is rather bad since I have been rather poorly but I hope it will soon be much better. . . . I must, I fear, end for today. . . . God bless you, darling child."[33]

Sir James Reid, the queen's physician, informed Kaiser Wilhelm of his grandmother's deteriorating condition. He left for Osborne, where he had not visited since being banned a few years before. But he would not be denied being present for the most dramatic event in the British Empire: Queen Victoria's last days.

Toward the end, Victoria was dazed and confused, often asleep, but the queen had her lucid moments too. Her physician was with her, and when Victoria recognized him, she would tell him, "I'm very ill."[34] The queen's family gathered around her bedside, in disbelief that the matriarch was dying. In the queen's final moments, she fixed her eyes upon a painting, the *Entombment of Christ*. At 6:30 P.M. on January 22, 1901, Queen Victoria died in the arms of Sir James Reid and Kaiser Wilhelm, who held her on opposite sides. She was eighty-one years old and had reigned for sixty-three years, the longest in English history.

Queen Victoria's death was a shock to her subjects. The end of her reign seemed simply inconceivable to many. The future Queen Mary captured the mood of the nation: "The thought of England without the Queen is dreadful even to think of. God help us all."[35]

To Vicky, who could not be with her mother at the end, Victoria's death was a bitter blow. "Words cannot describe my agony of mind at this overwhelming sorrow," she wrote to Sophie. "Oh, my beloved Mama! Is she *really* gone? . . . To have lost her seems *so* impossible—and I far away could not see her dear face or kiss her dear hand once more. It *breaks* my heart. . . . What will life be to me without her, the wretched bit of life left to me, struggling with a cruel disease? Now all that is gone."[36]

Queen Victoria's body was taken ceremoniously from Osborne to Windsor Castle. Huge crowds lined the streets in solemn tribute. Silence reigned; a deep and sincere mourning among the late queen's subjects was observed. Upon its arrival at Windsor, men of the naval guard of honor pulled the gun carriage with the coffin up a steep hill from the railroad station. On February 4, the coffin was taken to the mausoleum at Frogmore, and there, Victoria's remains were laid to rest next to Prince Albert's, to repose side by side in eternity.

Back in Germany, Vicky's disease continued to rage. When Wilhelm II returned from the queen's funeral, he found his mother in terrible shape and told his uncle Bertie, now King Edward VII, of Vicky being "weak" and feeling "absolutely miserable. . . . We are all fearfully pained by what we see & hear. . . . Poor mother's simply in a horrible state of suffering & discomfort."[37] Edward VII visited the dying Vicky. Though he had been always unfavorably compared with his eldest sister by their parents, Edward and Vicky had remained close as siblings, and seeing her in such a miserable state greatly moved the king. Accompanying Edward VII on this visit was his private secretary, Sir Frederick Ponsonby, a godson of the empress. After Ponsonby met the empress, he recalled that "she looked as if she had been taken off the rack after undergoing torture."[38] Vicky, though, was lucid enough to ask Ponsonby to fulfill an important task: to spirit her letters away to England for safekeeping. "I don't want a soul to know that they have been taken away," she told him "and certainly Willie [sic] must not have them, nor must he ever know you have got them."[39] Ponsonby agreed. When he received the letters in the middle of the night, he was shocked to find that they were contained in two huge boxes. Ponsonby was at his wit's end about how to smuggle the letters out since Friedrichshof was surrounded by secret police. He finally labeled one box as books, the other as china, pretending that they were items he had purchased in Germany. When the time came to leave Friedrichshof, soldiers were ordered to take everyone's luggage out to be loaded. Ponsonby nervously watched as the two precious boxes were taken away while he talked with Kaiser Wilhelm. Fortunately for Ponsonby and Vicky, the clandestine operation went smoothly.

Vicky's life was nearing its end; the empress was well aware that she had failed in the task she and her parents had set out for her so long ago. The Empress Frederick herself had described her hopes and aspirations for Germany soon after her husband's death: "Why were we then in opposition? Because our patriotism wanted to see the greatness of the fatherland linked with the noble feeling of right, moral behaviour, of freedom and culture, of independence of the individual,—uplifting of the person as a human being and as a German, European and citizen of the world . . . 'Improvement,' 'progress,' 'ennoblement' was our motto!"[40]

Ambition was always a driving force for Vicky, "yet her ambition had never been motivated by selfishness," for "her ambition was to educate Germany . . . towards freedom and culture . . . and for her persistence in these ideals she had been maligned and persecuted. Tact had not been her strong point, but she was always so transparently sincere that it is well nigh impossible to understand the reasons for the persistent hatred which had surrounded her."[41] Vicky had once noted of her life that if all were "made clear in a biography . . . it would be a long plea for the liberal cause—with which the life of a noble and faithful man, the life of a prince and that of a misunderstood princess were intertwined. And yet our tragic fate belongs to German history."[42]

The Empress Frederick's last letter to her beloved daughter Sophie echoed somewhat Queen Victoria's to her written only six months before: "My own Sophie darling, . . . I have been terribly bad these past few days. The attacks of pain so violent, the struggle for breath so dreadful, when in bed or lying down, most distressing. . . . I manage to struggle through the day, I know not how, and am much out of doors, lying down, my arm hung up in a cushion, my head too. . . . What joy it will be to see you and Tino [Constantine] and the sweet children. . . . Goodbye my own darling, God bless you. Ever your devoted, fond and doting, suffering 'Mother, V.' "[43]

In early August 1901, the Empress Frederick lay dying at Friedrichshof. The gardens that she had lovingly designed were in fine form. Vicky liked to gaze upon them from outdoors during her final days, but on August 3, she was taken into her house. During this time, her three devoted daughters Moretta, Sophie, and Mossy were with their mother, taking turns nursing her. Wilhelm and Dona arrived as well. On the morning of August 5, Vicky breathed her last. Mossy and Sophie had just stepped out for some fresh air. Upon returning a minute or two later, they found their mother dead. With her at the end, as he had been with Queen Victoria, was Kaiser Wilhelm II, the son and grandson whom both women loved but who had caused them much anxiety. In a repetition of his actions after Frederick III's death, Wilhelm II ordered that Friedrichshof be searched immediately after Vicky's death for her papers. Soldiers ransacked the place but found nothing. Vicky had ensured that Wilhelm and his soldiers would come out empty-handed.

Even after the end, "calumnies pursued her beyond her death," for the "most scurrilous stories about her dying wishes circulated in Berlin. The empress insisted, they whispered, that she be buried not as a German sovereign, but as an English princess. . . . She was to be laid naked, wrapped in a Union

Jack, in a coffin brought over from England and the body sent back to England for burial at Windsor."[44]

In the end, the Empress Frederick's coffin was taken to the church at the nearby village at Kronberg by torchlight, covered by the Prussian royal standard. Her body was then taken to Potsdam, where it was buried next to her beloved Fritz. Peace had at last come to Vicky, a peace that had largely been denied her in her lifetime.

Epilogue

Grief and pain come alike to all; broken hearts are to be found in palaces as well as in cottages, and the bond of brotherhood seems strongest when love and pity unite all hearts, and reverence for what is good lifts up our souls.[1]   —THE EMPRESS FREDERICK, 1888

The story behind three special pairings of royal mothers and daughters has come to a close. Encompassing three distinct eras, the historical significance of the mothers remains undisputed. Distinguished by successful and celebrated reigns, Isabella of Castile, Maria Theresa of Austria, and Victoria of Great Britain remain prominent figures of great historical significance. But behind their famed roles as leaders, Isabella, Maria Theresa, and Victoria were parents—mothers of three daughters who also made their mark on history. Catherine of Aragon, Marie Antoinette of France, and the Empress Frederick of Germany, though less illustrious than their mothers, each has earned a deserved place in the annals of time.

Like their mothers, the daughters were reigning monarchs. However, whereas the mothers were queens regnant, their daughters were consorts. Both kinds of monarchs faced challenges. Whereas the queens regnant had the double challenge of securing their rights to the throne (in Isabella's and Maria Theresa's cases) and ruling effectively, the consorts faced the equally difficult task of forging new dynastic alliances. These pages have explored the burdensome and demanding lot of foreign consorts. Because Catherine, Marie Antoinette, and Vicky were political pawns in great power politics, much hope and responsibility had been placed upon their shoulders, starting in their teenage years, when they became wives. The daughters were married off with the purpose of advancing their countries' causes abroad. Their task entailed gaining influence in their adopted countries, first by winning over their husbands, then by winning over their courts and subjects, and finally by providing male heirs. Suspicion and jealousy were rife and hard to overcome among courts and people inclined to distrust foreigners, as was the case for Marie Antoinette and Vicky; Catherine overcame this disadvantage. Challenges were fewer if the consorts' husbands were sympathetic to their wives; here, Marie Antoinette and Vicky were supremely blessed (Louis XVI and Frederick III were devoted husbands) but Catherine ultimately cursed.

Catherine's early marital success unraveled when Henry VIII became obsessed by the need to have a male heir. Catherine's misfortune stemmed from her failure to accomplish the greatest role expected of a consort: becoming the mother of a male heir. Marie Antoinette and Vicky fulfilled this role. But even here, Vicky reaped bitter seeds. Though she gave Germany a son, Kaiser Wilhelm II, not only did he cause his mother undue anguish but he also set his country on the path toward World War I. Even the long-awaited birth of a son to Marie Antoinette was politically for naught, for the Bourbon dynasty collapsed as revolution engulfed France. In the end, the daughters and their children contributed little or nothing to advancing diplomacy. Dynastic and political misfortune dogged these daughters of Isabella, Maria Theresa, and Victoria. The alliances they attempted to forge actually weakened Spanish-Anglo relations (in Catherine's case), Austrian-French relations (in Marie Antoinette's), and Anglo-German relations (in Vicky's).

One of Queen Victoria's granddaughters, the English-born Queen Marie of Romania, once wrote of "the sadness we Princesses endure in having to marry into foreign countries."[2] The sagas of three princesses from Castile, Austria, and England attest to this sobering observation. Each of these women endured more than her fair share of sadness in her adopted country. When compared with their mothers' fates, Catherine's, Marie Antoinette's, and Vicky's lives appear that much more poignant.

The mothers' achievements as monarchs, successes realized partly thanks to supportive husbands, stand in contrast. Ferdinand provided Isabella with political and military support; Francis assisted Maria Theresa and gave moral support; Albert tutored the young Victoria in the craft of queenship and acted as her confidential secretary. Of the three husbands, only Albert remained a "prince" after marriage; but even though Ferdinand was King of Aragon and Francis was Holy Roman emperor, like Albert, they subordinated themselves politically to their wives, becoming the junior partners in marriage. That Isabella, Maria Theresa, and Victoria received such support from their husbands reflects positively on the women's characters and personalities. After all, the lot of husbands who must take second place behind their reigning wives has never been an easy one.

King Leopold of the Belgians, uncle to Prince Albert and Queen Victoria, correctly surmised the difficulties male consorts faced when he said: "The position of a husband of a Queen, who reigns in her own right, is a position of the greatest difficulty for *any person* and at *any time. . . .* But," he concluded, "the success *we all desire* will depend on the good sense and right feeling *not of one alone,* but of both parties. It is my most intimate conviction that a really sensible husband may be the most *useful,* the safest and *the best friend a Sovereign Queen can have.*" "Yet," added Leopold, "to enable any man to become this, it seems however necessary that the Queen herself do *take from the very beginning a correct view of* her married position. She ought to see clearly that from the moment of her marriage even her political success will greatly depend upon her domestic happiness, and that by endeavouring to ensure the latter she *increases herself* by her own *power and arguments the chances of a prosperous and honourable reign.* She ought then to be imbued with a strong and deep conviction that it is *as well her own as the Prince's interest to make common cause and to live well together.*"[3] This was precisely what Isabella, Maria Theresa, and Victoria did—they found with their respective husbands common causes to espouse, and in spite of imperfections in their marital relationships, their marriages and political partnerships proved solid, enduring, and invaluable.

In the end, what is most fascinating and moving from the storied past of these unique sets of royal mothers and daughters is that the three daughters, though left in their mothers' triumphant wake, faced their tragic fates with heroism. Catherine, Marie Antoinette, and Vicky each demonstrated courage and dignity. They stood up with principled ideals that their mothers had inculcated in them. If the daughters did not emerge politically victorious, as their mothers had done, they did meet their challenges head-on, unflinching in the face of the hostilities hurled at them; unbowed by the guillotine's blade or the ravages of their final illnesses.

These courageous, dignified responses were the ultimate legacies of their august mothers. In that respect, Catherine, Marie Antoinette, and Vicky prevailed in a manner that would have made Queen Isabella, Empress Maria Theresa, and Queen Victoria ultimately proud—and should qualify the daughters to be placed beside their mothers in history's pantheon of valiant, noteworthy figures.

Notes

Introduction

1. Petri Martyrus Anglerii, *Opus Epistolarum,* as translated and quoted in Peggy K. Liss, *Isabel the Queen: Life and Times* (New York: Oxford University Press, 1992), p. 3.
2. Antonia Fraser, *The Wives of Henry VIII* (New York: Alfred A. Knopf, 1993), p. 9.
3. Antonia Fraser, *The Warrior Queens* (New York: Alfred A. Knopf, 1989), p. 186.
4. Edward Crankshaw, *Maria Theresa: A Biography* (New York: Viking Press, 1969), p. 338.
5. Elizabeth Longford, *Queen Victoria: Born to Succeed* (New York: Harper & Row, 1964), pp. 575–576.
6. Sidney Lee, *King Edward VII: A Biography, Volume II: The Reign* (New York: Macmillan Co., 1927), p. 1.

1. Called to Rule

1. Liss, *Isabel the Queen,* p. 3.
2. Christopher Hare, *A Queen of Queens & the Making of Spain* (London: Harper & Brothers, 1906), p. 57.
3. Luis Suárez Fernández, *Isabel, Mujer y Reina* (Madrid: Ediciones Rialp, 1992), p. 13.
4. Alma Wittlin, *Myself a Goddess: A New Biography of Isabella of Spain* (London: Ivor Nicholson and Watson, 1936), p. 221.
5. Townsend Miller, *Henry IV of Castile 1425–1474* (Philadelphia: J. B. Lippincott Company, 1972), p. 60.
6. *Ibid.,* p. 219.
7. Liss, *Isabel the Queen,* p. 23.
8. John Edwards, *Ferdinand and Isabella: Profiles in Power* (Harlow, U.K.: Pearson Education, 2005), p. 2.
9. Alfredo Alvar Ezquerra, *Isabel la Católica: Una Reina Vencedora, una Mujer Derrotada* (Madrid: Ediciones Temas de Hoy, 2002), p. 191.
10. Nancy Rubin, *Isabella of Castile: The First Renaissance Queen* (New York: St. Martin's Press, 1992), p. 50.
11. *Ibid.,* p. 53.

12. Ierne L. Plunket, *Isabel of Castile and the Making of the Spanish Nation 1451–1502* (New York: G. P. Putnam's Sons, 1915), p. 90.

13. *Ibid.*

14. William H. Prescott, *History of the Reign of Ferdinand and Isabella the Catholic,* vol. I (Philadelphia: J. B. Lippincott Company, 1865), p. 206.

15. Rubin, *Isabella of Castile,* p. 71.

16. Miller, *Henry IV,* p. 251.

17. Hare, *Queen of Queens,* p. 77.

18. Liss, *Isabel the Queen,* p. 80.

2. Consolidation of Power

1. Garrett Mattingly, *Catherine of Aragon* (Boston: Little, Brown and Company, 1941), p. 4.

2. Liss, *Isabel the Queen,* p. 82.

3. William Thomas Walsh, *Isabella the Crusader* (New York: Sheed & Ward, 1935), p. 45.

4. Edwards, *Ferdinand and Isabella,* p. 23.

5. Melveena McKendrick, *Ferdinand and Isabella* (New York: Harper & Row, 1968), p. 28.

6. Liss, *Isabel the Queen,* p. 82.

7. Walsh, *Isabella the Crusader,* p. 58.

8. Prescott, *Ferdinand and Isabella,* vol. I, pp. 239–240.

9. Marilyn Yalom, *Birth of the Chess Queen: A History* (New York: HarperCollins Publishers, 2004), p. 201.

10. John Edwards, *The Monarchies of Ferdinand and Isabella* (London: Historical Association, 1996), p. 5.

11. John Edwards, *The Spain of the Catholic Monarchs 1474–1520* (Oxford: Blackwell Publishers, 2000), p. 20.

12. Walsh, *Isabella the Crusader,* p. 59.

13. Edwards, *Monarchies of Ferdinand and Isabella,* p. 5.

14. Cayetano Rossell, ed., *Cronicas de los Reyes de Castilla, Desde don Alfonso el Sabio, Hasta los Católicos don Fernando y doña Isabel. Coleccion Ordenada por don Cayetano Rosell,* vol. 70 (Madrid: M. Rivadeneyra, 1878), p. 253.

15. Walsh, *Isabella the Crusader,* p. 61.

16. *Ibid.,* p. 62.

17. Prescott, *Ferdinand and Isabella,* vol. I, p. 243.

18. Wittlin, *Myself a Goddess,* p. 233.

19. Walsh, *Isabella the Crusader,* p. 71.

20. Hare, *Queen of Queens,* p. 86.

21. Walsh, *Isabella the Crusader,* pp. 72–73.

22. Rossell, *Cronicas de los Reyes de Castilla,* p. 296.

23. McKendrick, *Ferdinand and Isabella,* pp. 32–33.

24. Liss, *Isabel the Queen,* p. 124.

25. *Ibid.,* pp. 136–137.

26. Felipe Fernández-Armesto, *Ferdinand and Isabella* (New York: Dorset Press, 1975), p. 48.

27. Edwards, *Ferdinand and Isabella,* p. 6.

28. Roger Bigelow Merriman, *The Rise of the Spanish Empire in the Old World and in the New, Volume I: The Middle Ages* (New York: Macmillan, 1918–1934), p. 36.

29. Rubin, *Isabella of Castile,* p. 151.

30. *Ibid.*

31. *Ibid.*
32. Edwards, *Spain of the Catholic Monarchs,* p. 39.
33. Wittlin, *Myself a Goddess,* p. 119.
34. Edwards, *Spain of the Catholic Monarchs,* p. 141.
35. Jaime Vicens Vives, *An Economic History of Spain,* trans. Frances M. López-Morillas (Princeton: Princeton University Press, 1969), p. 295.
36. Teofilo F. Ruiz, *Spanish Society, 1400–1600* (Essex: Pearson Education, 2001), p. 19.
37. Alison Caplan, "The World of Isabel la Católica," in David A. Boruchoff, ed., *Isabel la Católica, Queen of Castile: Critical Essays* (New York: Palgrave Macmillan, 2003), p. 26.
38. Henry Kamen, *Empire: How Spain Became a World Power 1492–1763* (New York: HarperCollins Publishers, 2003), p. 15.
39. Caplan, "World of Isabel la Católica," p. 27.
40. *Ibid.*
41. Henry Kamen, *Spain 1469–1714: A Society of Conflict* (London: Longman, 1991), p. 17.
42. *Ibid.,* p. 27.
43. *Ibid.,* p. 17.
44. Kamen, *Empire,* p. 8.

3. The Conqueror of Granada

1. Paul Johnson, *A History of Christianity* (New York: Simon & Schuster, 1976), p. 191.
2. *Ibid.,* p. 258.
3. *Ibid.,* pp. 191–192.
4. Paul Johnson, *A History of the Jews* (New York: Harper & Row, 1987), p. 224.
5. Henry Kamen, *The Spanish Inquisition: A Historical Revision* (New Haven: Yale University Press, 1997), p. 12.
6. Prescott, *Ferdinand and Isabella,* vol. I, p. 342.
7. *Ibid.*
8. Liss, *Isabel the Queen,* p. 122.
9. Benzion Netanyahu, *The Origins of the Inquisition* (New York: Random House, 1995), p. 1047.
10. Townsend Miller, *The Castles and the Crown, Spain: 1451–1555* (New York: Coward-McCann, 1963), p. 110.
11. Roger Crowley, *1453: The Holy War for Constantinople and the Clash of Islam and the West* (New York: Hyperion, 2005), p. 72.
12. *Ibid.*
13. *Ibid.,* p. 233.
14. *Ibid.,* p. 72.
15. Rubin, *Isabella of Castile,* p. 163.
16. *Ibid.,* p. 187.
17. Edward Peters, "The Origins of the Spanish Inquisition," in Brenda Stalcup, ed., *The Inquisition* (San Diego: Greenhaven Press, 2001), p. 118.
18. Peggy K. Liss, "Isabel, Myth and History," in Boruchoff, ed., *Isabel la Católica,* p. 59.
19. Peters, "Origins of the Spanish Inquisition," p. 119.
20. Fernández-Armesto, *Ferdinand and Isabella,* p. 171.
21. Peter Pierson, *The History of Spain* (Westport, Conn.: Greenwood Press, 1999), p. 51.
22. Fernández-Armesto, *Ferdinand and Isabella,* pp. 173–174.
23. McKendrick, *Ferdinand and Isabella,* p. 127.
24. Rubin, *Isabella of Castile,* p. 338.

25. Vidal González Sánchez, *Isabel la Católica y Su Fama de Santidad, Mito o Realidad?* (Madrid: Ediciones Internacionales Universitarias, 1999), p. 37.

26. Fernández-Armesto, *Ferdinand and Isabella,* p. 183.

27. Miller, *Castles and the Crown,* pp. 84–85.

28. Robert Irwin, *The Alhambra* (Cambridge, Mass.: Harvard University Press, 2004), p. 16.

29. John Ramsey, *Spain: The Rise of the First World Power* (Tuscaloosa: University of Alabama Press, 1973), p. 212.

30. Hare, *Queen of Queens,* p. 114.

31. Caplan, "World of Isabel la Católica," p. 30.

32. Liss, "Isabel, Myth and History," p. 58.

33. Washington Irving, *Chronicle of the Conquest of Granada: From the MSS. of Fray Antonio Agapida* (New York: G. P. Putnam's Sons, 1869), p. 39.

34. Rubin, *Isabella of Castile,* p. 197.

35. Anna Jameson, *Lives of Celebrated Female Sovereigns and Illustrious Women,* ed. Mary E. Hewitt (Philadelphia: Henry T. Coates & Co., 1870), p. 114.

36. Kamen, *Spain 1469–1714,* p. 33.

37. *Quarterly Review,* vol. 64, no. 127.

38. Liss, *Isabel the Queen,* p. 207.

39. Irving, *Conquest of Granada,* p. 239.

40. Rubin, *Isabella of Castile,* p. 238.

4. The Wonder of Europe

1. Kamen, *Empire,* p. 8.

2. Rubin, *Isabella of Castile,* p. 241.

3. Liss, *Isabel the Queen,* p. 211.

4. Walsh, *Isabella the Crusader,* p. 154.

5. Rubin, *Isabella of Castile,* p. 242.

6. Irving, *Conquest of Granada,* p. 418.

7. *Ibid.*

8. Miller, *Castles and the Crown,* p. 131.

9. Irving, *Conquest of Granada,* p. 611

10. Hernando del Pulgar, "The Christian Conquest of Granada (1492)," in *Crónicas de los Reyes de Castilla,* trans. Teofilo Ruiz, in Olivia Remie Constable, ed., *Medieval Iberia: Reading from Christian, Muslim, and Jewish Sources* (Philadelphia: University of Pennsylvania Press, 1997), p. 344.

11. Irving, *Conquest of Granada,* p. 615.

12. Miller, *Castles and the Crown,* pp. 135–136.

13. Rubin, *Isabella of Castile,* p. 289.

14. William H. Prescott, *History of the Reign of Ferdinand and Isabella the Catholic,* vol. II (Philadelphia: J. B. Lippincott Company, 1872), p. 101.

15. Miguel Angel Ladero Quesada, "Isabel and the Moors," in Boruchoff, ed., *Isabel la Católica,* p. 181.

16. Fraser, *Wives of Henry VIII,* p. 9.

17. Walsh, *Isabella the Crusader,* p. 210.

18. Bernard Lewis, *Cultures in Conflict: Christians, Muslims, and Jews in the Age of Discovery* (New York: Oxford University Press, 1995), p. 35.

19. *Ibid.,* pp. 33–34.

20. *Ibid.*

21. Edwards, *Ferdinand and Isabella,* p. 81.
22. Lewis, *Cultures in Conflict,* p. 35.
23. Kamen, *Spain 1469–1714,* p. 42.
24. Fernández-Armesto, *Ferdinand and Isabella,* p. 177.
25. *Ibid.*
26. *Ibid.*
27. Caplan, "World of Isabel la Católica," p. 29.
28. William H. Prescott, *History of the Reign of Ferdinand and Isabella the Catholic,* vol. III (Philadelphia: J. B. Lippincott Company, 1872), p. 206.

5. Destined for England

1. Liss, *Isabel the Queen,* p. 310.
2. Hugh Thomas, *Rivers of Gold: The Rise of the Spanish Empire, from Columbus to Magellan* (New York: Random House, 2003), p. 103.
3. Liss, *Isabel the Queen,* p. 309.
4. Plunket, *Isabel of Castile,* p. 323
5. Francesca Claremont, *Catherine of Aragon* (London: Robert Hale, 1939), p. 55.
6. Fraser, *Wives of Henry VIII,* p. 10.
7. *Ibid.*
8. Mattingly, *Catherine of Aragon,* p. 9.
9. Plunket, *Isabel of Castile,* p. 334.
10. Liss, *Isabel the Queen,* p. 253.
11. Mattingly, *Catherine of Aragon,* p. 9.
12. Miller, *Castles and the Crown,* p. 68.
13. *Ibid.*
14. *Ibid.*
15. *Ibid.,* p. 69.
16. *Ibid.,* pp. 69–70.
17. Walsh, *Isabella the Crusader,* p. 274.
18. *Ibid.,* p. 275.
19. *Ibid.*
20. Rubin, *Isabella of Castile,* p. 376.
21. McKendrick, *Ferdinand and Isabella,* p. 91.
22. Pierson, *History of Spain,* p. 53.
23. *Ibid.*
24. Mary M. Luke, *Catherine, the Queen* (New York: Coward-McCann, 1967), p. 11.
25. Rodrigo González de Puebla to King Ferdinand and Queen Isabella, 25 August 1498, in G. A. Bergenroth, ed., *Calendar of Letters, Despatches, and State Papers, Relating to the Negotiations Between England and Spain Preserved in the Archives at Simancas and Elsewhere, Vol. I: Henry VII 1485–1509* (Nendeln, Liechtenstein: Kraus-Thomson Organization, 1969), p. 190.
26. Bergenroth, *Calendar of Letters, Despatches, and State Papers,* vol. I, p. xlix.
27. Luke, *Catherine, the Queen,* p. 25.
28. King Ferdinand and Queen Isabella to Rodrigo González de Puebla, 25 July 1500, in Bergenroth, *Calendar of Letters, Despatches, and State Papers,* vol. I, p. 240.
29. Thomas, Bishop of London, to King Ferdinand and Queen Isabella, 3 June 1500, in *ibid.,* p. 220.
30. Queen Isabella to Rodrigo González de Puebla, 23 March 1501, in *ibid.,* p. 253.

31. Rodrigo González de Puebla to King Ferdinand and Queen Isabella, 16 June 1500, in *ibid.*, p. 222.

6. *This Rough and Weary World*

1. Luke, *Catherine, the Queen,* p. 28.
2. *Ibid.,* p. 29.
3. *Ibid.,* p. 31.
4. Bergenroth, *Calendar of Letters, Despatches, and State Papers,* vol. I, p. xcii.
5. Fraser, *Wives of Henry VIII,* p. 19.
6. Elizabeth of York, Queen of Henry VII, to Queen Isabella of Castile, 3 December 1497, from Egerton MS 616, fol. 7, in Mary Anne Everett Green, *Letters of Royal & Illustrious Ladies of Great Britain, From the Commencement of the Twelfth Century to the Close of the Reign of Queen Mary* (London: H. Colburn, 1846), p. 115.
7. King Henry VII to King Ferdinand and Queen Isabella, 28 November 1501, in Bergenroth, *Calendar of Letters, Despatches, and State Papers,* vol. I, p. 264.
8. *Ibid.*
9. *Ibid.,* p. 265.
10. Arthur, Prince of Wales, to King Ferdinand and Queen Isabella, 30 November 1501, in *ibid.*
11. Fraser, *Wives of Henry VIII,* p. 30.
12. Liss, *Isabel the Queen,* p. 339.
13. Michael Prawdin, *The Mad Queen of Spain,* trans. Eden and Cedar Paul (London: George Allen and Unwin, 1938), p. 72.
14. Rubin, *Isabella of Castile,* pp. 402–403.
15. Prawdin, *Mad Queen of Spain,* p. 74.
16. *Ibid.,* p. 75.
17. *Ibid.*
18. King Ferdinand and Queen Isabella to Rodrigo González de Puebla, 14 June 1502, in Bergenroth, *Calendar of Letters, Despatches, and State Papers,* vol. I, p. 270.
19. King Ferdinand and Queen Isabella to Rodrigo González de Puebla, 29 May 1502, in *ibid.*, p. 269.
20. *Ibid.,* p. 268.
21. Queen Isabella to the Duke of Estrada, 10 August 1502, in *ibid.,* p. 278.
22. *Ibid.*
23. *Ibid.*
24. *Ibid.,* p. 279.
25. *Ibid.,* p. 282.
26. *Ibid.,* p. 283.
27. Queen Isabella to the Duke of Estrada, 11 April 1503, in *ibid.,* pp. 294–295.
28. Queen Isabella to the Duke of Estrada, 12 April 1503, in *ibid.,* p. 295.
29. Alison Weir, *The Six Wives of Henry VIII* (New York: Ballantine Books, 1991), p. 42.
30. Queen Isabella to the Duke of Estrada, 12 April 1503, in Bergenroth, *Calendar of Letters, Despatches, and State Papers,* vol. I, p. 300.
31. *Ibid.,* p. 301.
32. *Ibid.,* p. 302.
33. King Ferdinand to F. De Rojas, 23 August 1503, in Bergenroth, *Calendar of Letters, Despatches, and State Papers,* vol. I, p. 309.
34. Prescott, *Ferdinand and Isabella,* vol. III, p. 174.

35. *Ibid.,* p. 183.

36. *Ibid.,* p. 175.

37. Plunket, *Isabel of Castile,* pp. 329–330.

38. Arnold H. Mathew, *The Life and Times of Rodrigo Borgia—Pope Alexander VI* (New York: Brentano's, 1912), p. 59.

39. *Ibid.*

40. Ramsey, *Spain,* p. 213.

41. Liss, *Isabel the Queen,* p. 350.

42. Plunket, *Isabel of Castile,* p. 385.

43. Rubin, *Isabella of Castile,* p. 416.

7. The Golden Couple

1. William Thomas Walsh, *Isabella of Spain* (New York: Robert M. McBride & Company, 1930), p. 484.

2. Weir, *Six Wives,* p. 45.

3. Barnet Litvinoff, *1492: The Decline of Medievalism and the Rise of the Modern Age* (New York: Charles Scribner's Sons, 1991), p. 184.

4. John E. Paul, *Catherine of Aragon and Her Friends* (New York: Fordham University Press, 1966), p. 138.

5. Catherine, Princess of Wales, to King Ferdinand, 22 April 1506, in Egerton MS, no. 61, art. 55, fol. 17, in Green, *Letters of Royal & Illustrious Ladies,* pp. 138–140.

6. Luke, *Catherine, the Queen,* p. 71.

7. *Ibid.*

8. Weir, *Six Wives,* p. 57.

9. Luke, *Catherine, the Queen,* p. 84.

10. Mattingly, *Catherine of Aragon,* pp. 92–93.

11. Fraser, *Wives of Henry VIII,* p. 48.

12. King Henry VIII and Katharine, Princess of Wales, in G. A. Bergenroth, ed., *Calendar of Letters, Despatches, and State Papers, Relating to the Negotiations Between England and Spain Preserved in the Archives at Simancas and Elsewhere, Volume II: Henry VIII 1509–1525* (Nendeln, Liechtenstein: Kraus-Thomson Organization, 1969), p. 19.

13. Catherine of Aragon, Queen of Henry VIII, to King Ferdinand II, undated, from Egerton MS 616, art. 56, fol. 25, in Green, *Letters of Royal & Illustrious Ladies,* p. 159.

14. King Ferdinand the Catholic to Katharine, Princess of Wales, undated 1509 in Bergenroth, *Calendar of Letters, Despatches, and State Papers,* vol. II, p. 18.

15. King Ferdinand the Catholic to Katharine, Princess of Wales, 13 September 1509, in *ibid.,* p. 21.

16. Green, *Letters of Royal & Illustrious Ladies,* p. 157.

17. King Henry VIII to King Ferdinand the Catholic, 27 May 1510, in Bergenroth, *Calendar of Letters, Despatches, and State Papers,* vol. II, p. 38.

18. Liss, *Isabel the Queen,* p. 356.

19. Weir, *Six Wives,* p. 96.

20. *Ibid.*

21. H. F. M. Prescott, *Mary Tudor* (New York: Macmillan Company, 1962), pp. 20–21.

22. Josephine Ross, *The Tudors: England's Golden Age* (London: Artus Publishing, 1979), p. 40.

23. Luke, *Catherine, the Queen,* p. 107.

24. Neville Williams, *Henry VIII and His Court* (New York: Macmillan Company, 1971), p. 29.

25. Agnes Strickland, *Lives of the Queens of England from the Norman Conquest,* vol. II (London: G. Bell and Sons, 1912), p. 142.

26. Claremont, *Catherine of Aragon,* p. 144.

8. The Struggle for the Truth

1. Luke, *Catherine, the Queen,* p. 120.

2. Queen Katharine to King Ferdinand the Catholic, 27 May 1510, in Bergenroth, *Calendar of Letters, Despatches, and State Papers,* vol. II, p. 38.

3. Luke, *Catherine, the Queen,* p. 107.

4. Mattingly, *Catherine of Aragon,* p. 164.

5. Luke, *Catherine, the Queen,* pp. 141–142.

6. Claremont, *Catherine of Aragon,* pp. 149–150.

7. *Ibid.,* p. 149.

8. Strickland, *Lives of the Queens of England,* p. 131.

9. Luke, *Catherine, the Queen,* p. 158.

10. Richard Britnell, *The Closing of the Middle Ages? England, 1471–1529* (Oxford: Blackwell Publishers, 1997), p. 156.

11. Eamon Duffy, *The Stripping of the Altars: Traditional Religion in England, c. 1400–c. 1580* (New Haven: Yale University Press, 1992), p. 155.

12. Jasper Ridley, *Henry VIII* (London: Guild Publishing, 1985), pp. 26–27.

13. Duffy, *Stripping of the Altars,* p. 256.

14. *Ibid.,* p. 238.

15. *Ibid.,* p. 239.

16. *Ibid.,* p. 324.

17. Maria Dowling, "A Woman's Place? Learning and the Wives of Henry VIII," in *History Today,* June 1991, p. 38.

18. Strickland, *Lives of the Queens of England,* p. 99.

19. Fraser, *Wives of Henry VIII,* p. 75.

20. Ridley, *Henry VIII,* p. 128.

21. Mattingly, *Catherine of Aragon,* p. 175.

22. *Ibid.,* p. 176.

23. Prescott, *Mary Tudor,* p. 22.

24. J. J. Scarisbrick, *Henry VIII* (Berkeley: University of California Press, 1968), p. 17.

25. Strickland, *Lives of the Queens of England,* p. 145.

26. Ross, *The Tudors,* p. 40.

27. Strickland, *Lives of the Queens of England,* p. 146.

9. The Final Break

1. Fraser, *Wives of Henry VIII,* p. 98.

2. Juan Luis Vives, *The Education of a Christian Woman: A Sixteenth-Century Manual,* ed. and trans. Charles Fantazzi (Chicago: University of Chicago Press, 2000), p. 45.

3. *Ibid.,* p. 50.

4. *Ibid.,* p. 58.

5. *Ibid.,* p. 78.

6. *Ibid.,* p. 63.

7. *Ibid.*

8. *Ibid.,* p. 110.

9. *Ibid.,* p. 118.

10. Mattingly, *Catherine of Aragon,* p. 231.
11. Milton Waldman, *The Lady Mary: A Biography of Mary Tudor 1516–1558* (New York: Charles Scribner's Sons, 1972), p. 32.
12. *Ibid.,* p. 19
13. Williams, *Henry VIII and His Court,* p. 107.
14. *Ibid.,* p. 100.
15. Vives, *Education of a Christian Woman,* p. 263.
16. Strickland, *Lives of the Queens of England,* pp. 148–149.
17. Mattingly, *Catherine of Aragon,* p. 109.
18. E. W. Ives, *Anne Boleyn* (Oxford: Basil Blackwell, 1986), p. 197.
19. Strickland, *Lives of the Queens of England,* pp. 149–150.
20. Mattingly, *Catherine of Aragon,* p. 285.
21. *Ibid.*
22. *Ibid.,* p. 286.
23. *Ibid.*
24. Fraser, *Wives of Henry VIII,* p. 161.
25. Francis Gasquet, ed., *The First Divorce of Henry VIII as Told in the State Papers,* by Mrs. Hope (London: Kegan Paul, Trench, Trubner, & Co., 1894), p. 125.
26. *Ibid.,* p. 95.
27. Fraser, *Wives of Henry VIII,* p. 150.
28. *Ibid.*
29. Katharine of Arragon to Charles V, 6 November 1531, in James Gairdner, *Letters and Papers, Foreign and Domestic, of the Reign of Henry VIII,* vol. V (Vaduz, Liechtenstein: Kraus Reprint, 1965), p. 239.
30. J. A. Froude, *The Divorce of Catherine of Aragon: The Story as Told by the Imperial Ambassadors Resident at the Court of Henry VIII* (New York: AMS Press, 1970), p. 32.
31. Fraser, *Wives of Henry VIII,* p. 148.
32. Luke, *Catherine, the Queen,* p. 321.
33. *Ibid.*
34. Martin Hume, *The Wives of Henry the Eighth and the Parts They Played in History* (London: Eveleigh Nash, 1905), p. 160.
35. Gasquet, *First Divorce of Henry VIII,* p. 88.
36. *Ibid.,* p. 89.
37. John F. Thornton and Susan B. Varenne, eds., *Saint Thomas More: Selected Writings* (New York: Vintage Books, 2003), pp. 245–246.
38. Scarisbrick, *Henry VIII,* p. 167.
39. Richard Rex, *The Tudors* (Stroud, U.K.: Tempus, 2002), p. 60.
40. Scarisbrick, *Henry VIII,* p. 256.
41. *Ibid.,* p. 257.
42. *Ibid.,* p. 164.
43. *Ibid.,* p. 214.
44. Vives, *Education of a Christian Woman,* p. 157.
45. *Ibid.,* p. 175.
46. *Ibid.*
47. *Ibid.,* p. 177. Italics added for emphasis.
48. *Ibid.,* p. 186. Italics added for emphasis.
49. Luke, *Catherine, the Queen,* p. 193.
50. Ives, *Anne Boleyn,* p. 153.

51. Mattingly, *Catherine of Aragon,* p. 270.

52. Luke, *Catherine, the Queen,* p. 107.

53. William Bradford, ed., *Correspondence of the Emperor Charles V and His Ambassadors at the Courts of England and France* (London: Richard Bentley, 1850), pp. 300–301.

54. Froude, *Divorce of Catherine of Aragon,* p. 168.

55. Mattingly, *Catherine of Aragon,* p. 305.

56. *Ibid.,* p. 306.

57. *Ibid.*

58. Weir, *Six Wives,* p. 219.

59. *Ibid.*

60. Mattingly, *Catherine of Aragon,* pp. 332–333.

61. *Ibid.,* p. 333.

62. Froude, *Divorce of Catherine of Aragon,* p. 179.

63. *Ibid.,* p. 162.

64. Hume, *Wives of Henry the Eighth,* p. 205, n. 1.

65. *Ibid.*

66. *Ibid.,* p. 206.

67. Geoffrey de C. Parmiter, *The King's Great Matter: A Study of Anglo-Papal Relations 1527–1534* (London: Longmans, 1967), p. 242.

68. Prescott, *Mary Tudor,* p. 41.

69. *Ibid.*

70. *Ibid.*

71. *Ibid.*

72. Luke, *Catherine, the Queen,* p. 440.

73. *Ibid.,* p. 441.

74. Froude, *Divorce of Catherine of Aragon,* p. 305.

75. Luke, *Catherine, the Queen,* p. 442.

76. Mattingly, *Catherine of Aragon,* p. 291.

77. *Ibid.,* p. 272.

78. Luke, *Catherine, the Queen,* p. 441.

79. Susan Brigden, *New Worlds, Lost Worlds: The Rule of the Tudors, 1485–1603* (New York: Viking Press, 2000), p. 120.

80. Parmiter, *The King's Great Matter,* p. 258.

81. Waldman, *The Lady Mary,* pp. 63–64.

82. Mattingly, *Catherine of Aragon,* p. 389.

83. *Ibid.,* p. 376.

84. Richard Marius, *Thomas More* (New York: Alfred A. Knopf, 1984), pp. 45–46.

85. Ridley, *Henry VIII,* p. 247.

86. Paul, *Catherine of Aragon and Her Friends,* p. 190.

87. Ross, *The Tudors,* p. 67.

88. Ridley, *Henry VIII,* p. 245.

89. Paul, *Catherine of Aragon and Her Friends,* p. 199.

90. Claremont, *Catherine of Aragon,* p. 243.

91. Fraser, *Wives of Henry VIII,* p. 222.

92. Froude, *Divorce of Catherine of Aragon,* p. 213.

93. *Ibid.,* p. 277.

94. Williams, *Henry VIII and His Court,* p. 138.

95. Strickland, *Lives of the Queens of England,* pp. 160–161.

96. Waldman, *The Lady Mary,* p. 85.
97. *Ibid.,* p. 8.
98. Strickland, *Lives of the Queens of England,* p. 168.
99. Luke, *Catherine, the Queen,* p. 486.
100. Hume, *Wives of Henry the Eighth,* p. 255.
101. Miller, *Castles and the Crown,* p. 113.
102. Walsh, *Isabella the Crusader,* p. 471.

10. The Pragmatic Sanction

1. Margaret Goldsmith, *Maria Theresa of Austria* (London: Arthur Barker, 1936), p. 4.
2. Andrew Wheatcroft, *The Habsburgs: Embodying Empire* (London: Viking Press, 1995), p. 210.
3. *Ibid.*
4. *Ibid.*
5. William J. McGill, Jr., *Maria Theresa* (New York: Twayne Publishers, 1972), p. 19.
6. Robert Pick, *Empress Maria Theresa: The Earlier Years, 1717–1757* (New York: Harper & Row, 1966), p. 17.
7. *Ibid.*
8. Goldsmith, *Maria Theresa,* pp. 29–30.
9. Pick, *Empress Maria Theresa,* p. 12.
10. Wheatcroft, *The Habsburgs,* p. 212.
11. *Ibid.*
12. Mary Maxwell Moffat, *Maria Theresa* (New York: E. F. Dutton and Company, 1911), p. 16.
13. Goldsmith, *Maria Theresa,* p. 32.

11. Archduchess and Queen

1. Goldsmith, *Maria Theresa,* p. 40.
2. *Ibid.,* p. 42.
3. *Ibid.,* p. 43.
4. Moffat, *Maria Theresa,* p. 53.
5. *Ibid.,* p. 54.
6. Crankshaw, *Maria Theresa,* p. 25.
7. *Ibid.*
8. Pick, *Empress Maria Theresa,* p. 38.
9. Goldsmith, *Maria Theresa,* p. 57.
10. McGill, *Maria Theresa,* p. 29.
11. J. Alexander Mahan, *Maria Theresa of Austria* (New York: Thomas Y. Crowell Company, 1932), pp. 52–53.
12. *Ibid.,* p. 53.
13. Pick, *Empress Maria Theresa,* p. 52.
14. Crankshaw, *Maria Theresa,* p. 6.
15. Mahan, *Maria Theresa of Austria,* pp. 55–56.
16. *Ibid.,* p. 56.
17. McGill, *Maria Theresa,* p. 20.

12. Forsaken by the Whole World

1. Constance Lily Morris, *Maria Theresa: The Last Conservative* (New York: Alfred A. Knopf, 1937), p. 46.

2. Pick, *Empress Maria Theresa,* p. 62.

3. Morris, *Maria Theresa,* p. 47.

4. Frank A. J. Szabo, *Kaunitz and Enlightened Absolutism 1753–1780* (Cambridge: Cambridge University Press, 1994), p. 41.

5. Crankshaw, *Maria Theresa,* p. 32.

6. C. A. Macartney, *Maria Theresa and the House of Austria* (Mystic, Conn.: Lawrence Verry, 1969), p. 21.

7. Crankshaw, *Maria Theresa,* p. 30.

8. Maria Theresa's Political Testament, in C. A. Macartney, ed., *The Habsburg and Hohenzollern Dynasties in the Seventeenth and Eighteenth Centuries* (New York: Walker & Company, 1970), p. 96.

9. *Ibid.,* p. 98.

10. *Ibid.,* p. 99.

11. Goldsmith, *Maria Theresa,* p. 67.

12. Szabo, *Kaunitz,* p. 4.

13. Macartney, *Maria Theresa and the House of Austria,* p. 34.

14. Henri de Catt, *Frederick the Great: The Memoirs of His Reader Henri de Catt (1758–1760),* vol. I, trans. F. S. Flint (Boston: Houghton Mifflin Company, 1917), p. 60.

15. *Ibid.,* pp. 60–61.

16. Moffat, *Maria Theresa,* p. 82.

17. Goldsmith, *Maria Theresa,* p. 88.

18. Mahan, *Maria Theresa of Austria,* p. 112.

19. Moffat, *Maria Theresa,* pp. 85–86.

20. Dorothy Gies McGuigan, *The Habsburgs* (Garden City, N.Y.: Doubleday & Company, 1966), p. 228.

21. Macartney, *Maria Theresa and the House of Austria,* p. 37.

22. William Coxe, *History of the House of Austria,* vol. III (London: Henry G. Bohn, 1854), p. 269.

23. *Ibid.,* p. 270.

24. *Ibid.,* p. 271.

25. Crankshaw, *Maria Theresa,* p. 92.

26. *Ibid.,* pp. 93–94.

27. Morris, *Maria Theresa,* pp. 82–83.

28. Macartney, *Maria Theresa and the House of Austria,* p. 42.

29. Charles Ingrao, *The Habsburg Monarchy 1618–1815* (Cambridge: Cambridge University Press, 1994), p. 159.

30. Karl A. Roider, *Maria Theresa* (Englewood Cliffs, N.J.: Prentice-Hall, 1973), p. 28.

13. The Joan of Arc of the Danube

1. McGill, *Maria Theresa,* p. 43.

2. Moffat, *Maria Theresa,* p. 123.

3. Maria Theresa's Political Testament, p. 118.

4. Moffat, *Maria Theresa,* p. 152.

5. Coxe, *House of Austria,* vol. III, p. 322.

6. Morris, *Maria Theresa,* p. 146.

7. Coxe, *House of Austria,* vol. III, p. 283.

8. *Ibid.*

9. Mahan, *Maria Theresa of Austria,* p. 131.

10. McGuigan, *The Habsburgs,* p. 231.

11. Morris, *Maria Theresa,* pp. 144–145.

12. Macartney, *Maria Theresa and the House of Austria,* p. 47.

13. Mahan, *Maria Theresa of Austria,* p. 168.

14. Maria Theresa's Political Testament, p. 115.

15. Count Otto Christopher Podewils to Frederick II, King of Prussia, January 1747, in Roider, *Maria Theresa,* pp. 99–100.

16. Maria Theresa's Political Testament, p. 115.

17. Crankshaw, *Maria Theresa,* p. 157.

18. *Ibid.,* p. 167.

19. Maria Theresa's Political Testament, p. 129.

20. Coxe, *House of Austria,* vol. III, p. 346.

21. J. Franck Bright, *Maria Theresa* (London: Macmillan and Co. Ltd., 1930), p. 67.

22. *Ibid.,* p. 64.

23. *Ibid.,* p. 75.

24. Empress Maria Theresa to Archduke Maximilian, April 1774, in Roider, *Maria Theresa,* p. 79.

25. McGill, *Maria Theresa,* p. 77.

26. Ingrao, *Habsburg Monarchy,* p. 169.

27. *Ibid.,* p. 168.

28. Mahan, *Maria Theresa of Austria*, p. 179.

14. Magna Mater Austriae

1. Maria Theresa's Political Testament, pp. 99–100.

2. Morris, *Maria Theresa,* p. 155.

3. McGill, *Maria Theresa,* p. 74.

4. Mahan, *Maria Theresa of Austria,* p. 239.

5. Empress Maria Theresa to Archduke Maximilian, April 1774, in Roider, *Maria Theresa,* pp. 76–77.

6. *Ibid.,* pp. 78–79.

7. *Ibid.,* p. 80.

8. *Ibid.,* p. 81.

9. Antonia Fraser, *Marie Antoinette: The Journey* (New York: Nan A. Talese, 2001), p. 9.

10. *Ibid.,* p. 10.

11. Coxe, *House of Austria,* vol. III, p. 364.

12. *Ibid.,* p. 362.

13. Goldsmith, *Maria Theresa,* p. 182.

14. Pick, *Empress Maria Theresa,* p. 251.

15. Evelyne Lever, *Madame de Pompadour: A Life,* trans. Catherine Temerson (New York: Farrar, Straus & Giroux, 2002), p. 199.

16. Pick, *Empress Maria Theresa,* p. 254.

17. *Ibid.,* p. 217.

18. McGuigan, *The Habsburgs,* p. 240.

19. Hilaire Belloc, *Marie Antoinette* (New York: Tess Press, n.d.; originally published 1909), p. 13.

20. Saul K. Padover, *The Revolutionary Emperor: Joseph II of Austria* (Hamden, Conn.: Archon Books, 1967), p. 39.

21. Pick, *Empress Maria Theresa,* p. 219.
22. *Ibid.,* p. 221.
23. Jeanne Louise Henriette Campan, *Memoirs of the Private Life of Marie Antoinette,* vol. I (New York: Tudor Publishing Co., 1934), p. 33.
24. McGuigan, *The Habsburgs,* p. 240.
25. Pick, *Empress Maria Theresa,* p. 221.
26. Morris, *Maria Theresa,* p. 255.
27. Lady Younghusband, *Marie-Antoinette: Her Early Youth (1770–1774)* (London: Macmillan and Co., 1912), p. 4.
28. Crankshaw, *Maria Theresa,* p. 267.
29. Jameson, *Lives of Celebrated Female Sovereigns,* p. 298.
30. G. P. Gooch, *Maria Theresa and Other Studies* (London: Longmans, Green and Co., 1951), p. 18.
31. Maria Theresa to Countess Sophia Amalia Enzenberg, February 12, 1766, in Roider, *Maria Theresa,* p. 74.
32. Roider, *Maria Theresa,* p. 75.
33. Crankshaw, *Maria Theresa,* pp. 267–268.
34. *Ibid.,* p. 268.
35. McGuigan, *The Habsburgs,* p. 241.
36. Maria Theresa to Joseph, 5 July 1777, in Macartney, *Habsburg and Hohenzollern Dynasties,* p. 150.
37. Szabo, *Kaunitz,* p. 248.
38. Victor L. Tapié, *The Rise and Fall of the Habsburg Monarchy,* trans. Stephen Hardman (New York: Praeger Publishers, 1969), p. 187.
39. Szabo, *Kaunitz,* p. 247.
40. Maria Theresa to Ferdinand, 30 January and 13 February 1777, in Roider, *Maria Theresa,* p. 61.
41. Ingrao, *Habsburg Monarchy,* p. 187.

15. Marriage to the Dauphin

1. Desmond Seward, *Marie Antoinette* (New York: St. Martin's Press, 1981), p. 17.
2. Padover, *Revolutionary Emperor,* p. 39.
3. Crankshaw, *Maria Theresa,* p. 197.
4. Padover, *Revolutionary Emperor,* p. 45.
5. Maria Theresa to Joseph, July 1777, in Macartney, *Habsburg and Hohenzollern Dynasties,* p. 153.
6. Padover, *Revolutionary Emperor,* p. 49.
7. *Ibid.,* p. 55.
8. Crankshaw, *Maria Theresa,* p. 115.
9. *Ibid.,* pp. 115–116.
10. Fraser, *Marie Antoinette,* p. 36.
11. Younghusband, *Marie-Antoinette,* p. 130.
12. *Ibid.,* p. 131.
13. Seward, *Marie Antoinette,* p. 26.
14. Fraser, *Marie Antoinette,* p. 53.
15. *Ibid.*
16. André Castelot, *Queen of France: A Biography of Marie Antoinette,* trans. Denise Folliot (New York: Harper & Brothers, 1957), p. 17.

17. Carolly Erickson, *To the Scaffold: The Life of Marie Antoinette* (New York: William Morrow and Company, 1991), p. 49.

18. Belloc, *Marie Antoinette,* p. 37.

19. Castelot, *Queen of France,* p. 22.

20. Joan Haslip, *Marie Antoinette* (New York: Weidenfeld & Nicolson, 1987), p. 16.

21. Castelot, *Queen of France,* p. 40.

22. Maria Theresa's Political Testament, p. 115.

23. Stefan Zweig, *Marie Antoinette: The Portrait of an Average Woman,* trans. Eden and Cedar Paul (Garden City, N.Y.: Garden City, Publishing Co., 1933), p. 53.

24. Moffat, *Maria Theresa,* pp. 316–317.

25. *Ibid.,* p. 318.

26. Morris, *Maria Theresa,* p. 287.

27. Marie Antoinette to Maria Theresa, 12 July 1770, in Lillian C. Smythe, *The Guardian of Marie Antoinette: Letters from the Comte de Mercy-Argenteau, Austrian Ambassador to the Court of Versailles, to Marie Thérèse, Empress of Austria 1770–1780,* vol. I (New York: Dodd Mead and Company, 1902), p. 21.

28. Haslip, *Marie Antoinette,* p. 29.

29. Younghusband, *Marie-Antoinette,* p. 173.

30. Castelot, *Queen of France,* p. 45.

31. *Ibid.,* p. 46.

32. Mercy-Argenteau to Maria Theresa, 20 August 1770, in Smythe, *Guardian of Marie Antoinette,* vol. I, p. 37.

33. Mercy-Argenteau to Maria Theresa, 23 January 1771, in *ibid.,* p. 78.

34. Maria Theresa to Mercy-Argenteau, 2 October 1770, in *ibid.,* p. 37.

35. Philip Mansel, *Louis XVIII* (Stroud, U.K.: Sutton Publishing, 1999), p. 15.

36. Younghusband, *Marie-Antoinette,* p. 253.

37. Mercy-Argenteau to Maria Theresa, 16 November 1771, in Olivier Bernier, *Imperial Mother, Royal Daughter: The Correspondence of Marie Antoinette and Maria Theresa* (London: Sidgwick & Jackson, 1986), p. 84.

38. Evelyne Lever, *Marie Antoinette: The Last Queen of France,* trans. Catherine Temerson (New York: Farrar, Straus & Giroux, 2000), p. 38.

39. Younghusband, *Marie-Antoinette,* p. 380.

40. Belloc, *Marie Antoinette,* p. 17.

41. *Ibid.*

42. Mercy-Argenteau to Maria Theresa, 10 April 1771, in Smythe, *Guardian of Marie Antoinette,* vol. I, p. 96.

43. Lever, *Marie Antoinette,* p. 46.

44. Maria Theresa to Marie Antoinette, 4 May 1770, in Bernier, *Imperial Mother, Royal Daughter,* p. 35.

45. Maria Theresa to Marie Antoinette, 10 February 1771, in Smythe, *Guardian of Marie Antoinette,* vol. I, p. 83.

46. Maria Theresa to Marie Antoinette, 1 November 1770, in *ibid.,* p. 54.

47. Maria Theresa to Mercy-Argenteau, 15 March 1771, in *ibid.,* p. 87.

48. Marie Antoinette to Maria Theresa, 12 July 1770, in Bernier, *Imperial Mother, Royal Daughter,* p. 39.

16. Motherly Advice

1. Younghusband, *Marie-Antoinette,* p. 475.
2. Maria Theresa to Marie Antoinette, 8 May 1771, in Smythe, *Guardian of Marie Antoinette,* vol. I, p. 101.
3. Marie Antoinette to Maria Theresa, 2 September 1771, in *ibid.,* p. 148.
4. Maria Theresa to Marie Antoinette, 17 August 1771, in *ibid.,* p. 130.
5. Maria Theresa to Marie Antoinette, 31 October 1771, in Bernier, *Imperial Mother, Royal Daughter,* p. 81.
6. Maria Theresa to Count Mercy-Argenteau, 30 September 1771, in Smythe, *Guardian of Marie Antoinette,* vol. I, p. 149.
7. Maria Theresa to Marie Antoinette, 30 September 1771, in *ibid.,* pp. 150–151.
8. Marie Antoinette to Maria Theresa, 15 November 1771, in Bernier, *Imperial Mother, Royal Daughter,* p. 83.
9. Moffat, *Maria Theresa,* p. 257.
10. Maria Theresa to Maria Christina, April 1766, in Roider, *Maria Theresa,* pp. 82–85.
11. Maria Theresa to Marie Antoinette, August 17, 1771, in *ibid.,* p. 89.
12. Marie Antoinette to Maria Theresa, 19 December 1771, in Smythe, *Guardian of Marie Antoinette,* vol. I, p. 167.
13. Younghusband, *Marie-Antoinette,* p. 521.
14. Maria Theresa to Mercy-Argenteau, 4 January 1772, in Smythe, *Guardian of Marie Antoinette,* vol. I, p. 177.
15. Lever, *Marie Antoinette,* p. 45.
16. Mercy-Argenteau to Maria Theresa, 16 June 1773, in Smythe, *Guardian of Marie Antoinette,* vol. I, pp. 264–265.
17. Younghusband, *Marie-Antoinette,* p. 543.
18. Marie Antoinette to Maria Theresa, 14 June 1773, in Smythe, *Guardian of Marie Antoinette,* vol. I, p. 263.
19. Younghusband, *Marie-Antoinette,* p. 544.
20. Fraser, *Marie Antoinette,* p. 105.
21. *Ibid.,* p. 106.
22. *Ibid.*
23. Marie Antoinette to Maria Theresa, 14 July 1772, in Smythe, *Guardian of Marie Antoinette,* vol. I, p. 204.
24. Maria Theresa to Mercy-Argenteau, 31 August 1773, in *ibid.,* pp. 284–285.
25. Marie Antoinette to Maria Theresa, 13 October 1771, in *ibid.,* p. 153.
26. Marie Antoinette to Maria Theresa, 13 January 1773, in *ibid.,* p. 227.
27. Campan, *Private Life,* vol. I, p. 71.
28. Younghusband, *Marie-Antoinette,* p. 568.
29. *Ibid.,* p. 569.
30. Zweig, *Marie Antoinette,* p. 73.
31. *Ibid.,* p. 81.
32. Marie Antoinette to Maria Theresa, 22 June 1775, in Smythe, *Guardian of Marie Antoinette,* vol. II, p. 418.
33. Gooch, *Maria Theresa and Other Studies,* p. 150.
34. *Ibid.*
35. *Ibid.,* p. 152.
36. *Ibid.*

37. Nesta H. Webster, *Louis XVI and Marie Antoinette: Before the Revolution* (New York: G. P. Putnam's Sons, 1937), p. 42.

38. Henriette Lucie Dillon, Marquise de La Tour du Pin, *Memoirs of Madame de La Tour du Pin,* ed. and trans. Felice Harcourt (New York: McCall Publishing Company, 1971), p. 27.

39. *Ibid.,* p. 26.

40. Smythe, *Guardian of Marie Antoinette,* vol. I, p. 160.

41. N. W. Wraxall, *Historical Memoirs of My Own Time* (Philadelphia: Lea and Blanchard, 1845), p. 59.

42. Haslip, *Marie Antoinette,* p. 58.

43. Webster, *Louis XVI and Marie Antoinette: Before the Revolution,* p. 30.

44. Erickson, *To the Scaffold,* p. 99.

45. Mercy-Argenteau to Maria Theresa, 18 March 1775, in Smythe, *Guardian of Marie Antoinette,* vol II, p. 413.

46. Haslip, *Marie Antoinette,* p. 64.

47. Amanda Foreman, *Georgiana, Duchess of Devonshire* (New York: Random House, 1998), p. 38.

48. Haslip, *Marie Antoinette,* p. 49.

49. Caroline Weber, *Queen of Fashion: What Marie Antoinette Wore to the Revolution* (New York: Henry Holt and Company, 2006), p. 104.

50. *Ibid.,* p. 105.

51. Marie Antoinette to Maria Theresa, undated 1775, in Smythe, *Guardian of Marie Antoinette,* vol. II, p. 412.

52. Maria Theresa to Mercy-Argenteau, 31 July 1775, in *ibid.,* pp. 426–427.

53. Maria Theresa to Marie Antoinette, 30 July 1775, in Bernier, *Imperial Mother, Royal Daughter,* pp. 171–172.

17. L'Autrichienne

1. Campan, *Private Life,* vol. I, p. 95.

2. John Hardman, *French Politics 1774–1789: From the Accession of Louis XVI to the Fall of the Bastille* (London: Longman, 1995), pp. 198–199.

3. Mercy-Argenteau to Maria Theresa, 16 August 1775, in Smythe, *Guardian of Marie Antoinette,* vol. II, p. 428.

4. Mercy-Argenteau to Maria Theresa, 17 September 1776, in *ibid.,* p. 445.

5. Maria Theresa to Mercy-Argenteau, 28 August 1774, in *ibid.,* pp. 393–394.

6. Younghusband, *Marie-Antoinette,* p. 140.

7. Goldsmith, *Maria Theresa,* p. 240.

8. *Ibid.,* p. 231.

9. Roider, *Maria Theresa,* p. 129.

10. Goldsmith, *Maria Theresa,* p. 236.

11. Joseph II to Maria Theresa, 3 July 1777, in Smythe, *Guardian of Marie Antoinette,* vol. II, p. 513.

12. Morris, *Maria Theresa,* p. 293.

13. *Ibid.,* pp. 293–294.

14. Mercy-Argenteau to Maria Theresa, 16 April 1777, in Smythe, *Guardian of Marie Antoinette,* vol. II, pp. 491–492.

15. Marie Antoinette to Maria Theresa, 15 July 1778, in *ibid.,* p. 592.

16. Goldsmith, *Maria Theresa,* p. 265.

17. *Ibid.,* p. 267.
18. Smythe, *Guardian of Marie Antoinette,* vol. II, p. 615.
19. Campan, *Private Life,* vol. I, p. 33.
20. Maria Theresa to Marie Antoinette, 13 January 1779, in Smythe, *Guardian of Marie Antoinette,* vol. II, pp. 622–623.
21. Fraser, *Marie Antoinette,* p. 63.
22. Pick, *Empress Maria Theresa,* p. 262.
23. Castelot, *Queen of France,* p. 148.
24. Roider, *Maria Theresa,* p. 138.
25. *Ibid.,* p. 140.
26. Gooch, *Maria Theresa and Other Studies,* p. 115.
27. *Ibid.,* p. 116.
28. McGill, *Maria Theresa,* p. 143.
29. Macartney, *Maria Theresa and the House of Austria,* p. 154.
30. McGill, *Maria Theresa,* p. 143.
31. Mahan, *Maria Theresa of Austria,* p. 339.
32. Marie Antoinette to Joseph II, 10 December 1780, in Bernier, *Imperial Mother, Royal Daughter,* p. 307.

18. The Guillotine Awaits

1. Fraser, *Marie Antoinette,* p. 191.
2. Weber, *Queen of Fashion,* p. 161.
3. Philip Mansel, *Prince of Europe: The Life of Charles-Joseph de Ligne 1735–1814* (London: Weidenfeld & Nicolson, 2003), p. 71.
4. Haslip, *Marie Antoinette,* p. 150.
5. Webster, *Louis XVI and Marie Antoinette: Before the Revolution,* p. 294.
6. Desmond Seward, *The Bourbon Kings of France* (New York: Harper & Row, 1976), p. 197.
7. William Hague, *William Pitt the Younger* (New York: Alfred A. Knopf, 2004), p. 320.
8. Campan, *Private Life,* vol. II, p. 36.
9. Webster, *Louis XVI and Marie Antoinette: Before the Revolution,* p. 290.
10. Munro Price, *The Road from Versailles: Louis XVI, Marie Antoinette, and the Fall of the French Monarchy* (New York: St. Martin's Griffin, 2002), p. 26.
11. Lever, *Marie Antoinette,* p. 191.
12. Elisabeth de Feydeau, *A Scented Palace: The Secret History of Marie Antoinette's Perfumer,* trans. Jane Lizop (London: I. B. Tauris, 2006), p. 83.
13. Price, *Road from Versailles*, p. 30.
14. *Ibid.,* p. 31.
15. Haslip, *Marie Antoinette,* p. 186.
16. Dorothy Moulton Mayer, *Marie Antoinette: The Tragic Queen* (New York: Coward-McCann, 1969), p. 179.
17. *Ibid.,* p. 195.
18. Will and Ariel Durant, *Rousseau and the Revolution: A History of Civilization in France, England, and Germany from 1756, and in the Remainder of Europe from 1715, to 1789* (New York: Simon & Schuster, 1967), p. 962.
19. Seward, *Bourbon Kings,* p. 205.
20. Haslip, *Marie Antoinette,* p. 199.
21. Simon Schama, *Citizens: A Chronicle of the French Revolution* (New York: Alfred A. Knopf, 1989), p. 445.

22. Louis-Philippe, King of the French, *Louis-Philippe Memoirs 1773–1793*, trans. John Hardman (New York: Harcourt Brace Jovanovich, 1977), p. 56.

23. Seward, *Bourbon Kings*, p. 206.

24. Nesta H. Webster, *Louis XVI and Marie Antoinette: During the Revolution* (New York: G. P. Putnam's Sons, 1938), p. 64.

25. *Ibid.,* p. 66.

26. Angelica Goodden, *The Sweetness of Life: A Biography of Elisabeth Louise Vigée Le Brun* (London: André Deutsch, 1997), p. 85.

27. Deborah Cadbury, *The Last King of France: A True Story of Revolution, Revenge, and DNA* (New York: St. Martin's Press, 2002), p. 45.

28. Philippe Huisman and Marguerite Jallut, *Marie Antoinette* (New York: Viking Press, 1971), p. 202.

29. Seward, *Bourbon Kings*, p. 207.

30. Haslip, *Marie Antoinette*, p. 223.

31. Fraser, *Marie Antoinette*, pp. 358–359.

32. Timothy Tackett, *When the King Took Flight* (Cambridge, Mass.: Harvard University Press, 2003), p. 56.

33. Webster, *Louis XVI and Marie Antoinette: During the Revolution*, p. 155.

34. Olivier Bernier, *Words of Fire, Deeds of Blood: The Mob, the Monarchy, and the French Revolution* (Boston: Little, Brown, 1989), p. 280.

35. *Ibid.,* p. 283.

36. Haslip, *Marie Antoinette*, p. 259.

37. Bernier, *Words of Fire, Deeds of Blood*, p. 350.

38. Mayer, *Marie Antoinette*, p. 295.

39. Marie-Thérèse Charlotte, Duchesse d'Angoulême, *The Ruin of a Princess: As Told by Marie-Thérèse Charlotte, the Duchesse d'Angoulême; Madame Elizabeth, Sister of Louis XVI, and Cléry, the King's Valet de Chambre,* trans. Katharine Prescott Wormeley (New York: Lamb Publishing Co., 1912), p. 147.

40. *Ibid.,* p. 170.

41. Fraser, *Marie Antoinette*, p. 394.

42. d'Angoulême, *Ruin of a Princess*, p. 182.

43. *Ibid.,* p. 199.

44. *Ibid.,* p. 203.

45. Webster, *Louis XVI and Marie Antoinette: During the Revolution,* pp. 317 and 368.

46. Elizabeth Wormeley Latimer, *My Scrap-Book of the French Revolution* (Chicago: A. C. McClurg and Company, 1898), p. 217.

47. Webster, *Louis XVI and Marie Antoinette: During the Revolution,* p. 321.

48. Fraser, *Marie Antoinette*, p. 417.

49. Erickson, *To the Scaffold*, p. 343.

50. Haslip, *Marie Antoinette*, p. 207.

51. Ronald Gower, *Last Days of Marie Antoinette: An Historical Sketch* (London: Kegan Paul, Trench & Co., 1885), pp. 134–135.

52. Fraser, *Marie Antoinette*, p. 440.

19. Destined to Reign

1. Lynn Vallone, *Becoming Victoria* (New Haven: Yale University Press, 2001), p. 27.

2. Stanley Weintraub, *Victoria: An Intimate Biography* (New York: E. P. Dutton, 1987), p. 61.

3. Longford, *Queen Victoria*, p. 32.

4. Monica Charlot, *Victoria: The Young Queen* (Oxford: Basil Blackwell, 1991), p. 52.

5. *Ibid.*

6. Vallone, *Becoming Victoria,* p. 68.

7. *Ibid.,* p. 67.

8. King Leopold of the Belgians to Princess Victoria, 22 May 1832, in John Raymond, ed., *Queen Victoria's Early Letters* (New York: Macmillan Company, 1963), p. 8.

9. Princess Victoria to King Leopold of the Belgians, 22 October 1834, in *ibid.,* p. 9.

10. Vallone, *Becoming Victoria,* p. 108.

11. Sidney Lee, *Queen Victoria: A Biography* (London: Smith, Elder & Co., 1908), pp. 45–46.

12. Walter Walsh, *The Religious Life and Influence of Queen Victoria* (London: Swan Sonnenschein & Co., 1902), p. 257.

13. *Ibid.*

14. Extract from Queen Victoria's Journal, 20 June 1837, in Raymond, *Queen Victoria's Early Letters,* p. 21.

15. Weintraub, *Victoria,* p. 99.

16. Theo Aronson, *Heart of a Queen: Queen Victoria's Romantic Attachments* (London: John Murray, 1991), p. 19.

17. *Ibid.,* p. 20.

18. Longford, *Queen Victoria,* p. 53.

19. Robert Rhodes James, *Prince Albert: A Biography* (New York: Alfred A. Knopf, 1984), pp. 82–83.

20. *Ibid.,* p. 83.

21. Prince Albert to Queen Victoria, 7 February 1840, in Kurt Jagow, ed., *Letters of the Prince Consort 1831–1861* (New York: E. P. Dutton & Company, 1938), p. 60.

22. James, *Prince Albert,* p. 83.

23. Queen Victoria to King Leopold of the Belgians, 11 February 1840, in Raymond, *Queen Victoria's Early Letters,* p. 42.

24. Deborah Jaffé, *Victoria: A Celebration* (London: Carlton Books, 2000), p. 54.

25. Longford, *Queen Victoria,* p. 153.

26. Richard Hough, *Victoria and Albert: Their Love and Their Tragedies* (London: Richard Cohen Books, 1996), pp. 80–81.

27. Charlot, *Victoria,* p. 195.

28. Prince Albert to Duchess Caroline of Saxe-Gotha-Altenburg, 12 February 1841, in Jagow, *Letters of the Prince Consort,* p. 72.

29. Queen Victoria to King Leopold of the Belgians, 5 January 1841, in Raymond, *Queen Victoria's Early Letters,* p. 45.

30. Weintraub, *Victoria,* p. 159.

20. Victoria Regina

1. Charlot, *Victoria,* p. 262. -

2. Weintraub, *Victoria,* p. 170.

3. Aronson, *Heart of a Queen,* p. 66.

4. Prince Albert to Baron von Stockmar, 6 January 1846, in Jagow, *Letters of the Prince Consort,* p. 99.

5. Anonymous, *The Private Life of the Queen by a Member of the Royal Household* (New York: D. Appleton and Company, 1901), p. 154.

6. *Ibid.,* p. 164.

7. Queen Victoria to Major-General Sir Howard Elphinstone, 18 October 1859, in Mary

Howard McClintock, *The Queen Thanks Sir Howard: The Life of Major-General Sir Howard Elphinstone, V.C., K.C.B., C.M.G.* (London: John Murray, 1945), p. 33.

8. Longford, *Queen Victoria,* p. 190.

9. Walter Arnstein, *Queen Victoria* (New York: Palgrave Macmillan, 2003), p. 80.

10. Longford, *Queen Victoria,* p. 280.

11. Queen Victoria to King Leopold of the Belgians, 3 May 1851, in Arthur Christopher Benson and Viscount Esher, eds., *The Letters of Queen Victoria: A Selection from Her Majesty's Correspondence Between the Years 1837 and 1861* (London: John Murray, 1908), vol. II, p. 317.

12. Jerrold M. Packard, *Victoria's Daughters* (New York: St. Martin's Press, 1998), p. 24.

13. Prince Albert to Baron von Stockmar, 17 December 1843, in Jagow, *Letters of the Prince Consort,* p. 86.

14. Alan Palmer, *The Kaiser: Warlord of the Second Reich* (London: Weidenfeld & Nicolson, 1978), p. 8.

15. Richard Barkeley, *The Empress Frederick: Daughter of Queen Victoria* (London: Macmillan & Co., 1956), p. 20.

16. Cecil Woodham-Smith, *Queen Victoria: From Her Birth to the Death of the Prince Consort* (New York: Alfred A. Knopf, 1972), p. 272.

17. Daphne Bennett, *Vicky: Princess Royal of England and German Empress* (New York: St. Martin's Press, 1971), p. 23.

18. Hannah Pakula, *An Uncommon Woman: The Empress Frederick, Daughter of Queen Victoria, Wife of the Crown Prince of Prussia, Mother of Kaiser Wilhelm* (New York: Touchstone Books, 1997), p. 50.

21. The Warrior Queen and the Princess Bride

1. Pakula, *Uncommon Woman,* p. 53.

2. Arnstein, *Queen Victoria,* p. 98.

3. E. F. Benson, *Queen Victoria* (London: Longmans, Green and Co., 1935), p. 171.

4. Arnstein, *Queen Victoria,* p. 98.

5. Lee, *Queen Victoria,* p. 243.

6. Arnstein, *Queen Victoria,* p. 99.

7. *Ibid.,* p. 98.

8. Queen Victoria to King Leopold of the Belgians, 6 February 1855, in Benson and Esher, eds., *Letters of Queen Victoria* (London: John Murray, 1908), vol. III, p. 101.

9. Dowager Duchess of Argyll, ed., *George Douglas, Eighth Duke of Argyll: Autobiography and Memoirs* (New York: E. P. Dutton and Company, 1906), vol. I, pp. 500–501.

10. Queen Victoria to King Leopold of the Belgians, 27 February 1855, in Raymond, *Queen Victoria's Early Letters,* pp. 208–209.

11. Queen Victoria to King Leopold of the Belgians, 2 May 1855, in *ibid.,* p. 210.

12. Packard, *Victoria's Daughters,* p. 45.

13. Longford, *Queen Victoria,* p. 260.

14. Pakula, *Uncommon Woman,* p. 68.

15. Prince Albert to Baron von Stockmar, 29 September 1855, in Jagow, *Letters of the Prince Consort,* p. 238.

16. Queen Victoria to King Leopold of the Belgians, 22 September 1855, in Raymond, *Queen Victoria's Early Letters,* p. 215.

17. Prince Albert to Baron von Stockmar, 2 October 1855, in Jagow, *Letters of the Prince Consort,* p. 239.

18. Pakula, *Uncommon Woman,* p. 68.
19. Queen Victoria to Princess Augusta of Prussia, 9 June 1856, in Hector Bolitho, ed., *Further Letters of Queen Victoria: From the Archives of the House of Brandenburg-Prussia* (London: Thornton Butterworth, 1939), p. 67.
20. Queen Victoria to Princess Augusta of Prussia, 28 January 1858, in *ibid.,* p. 98.
21. Prince Albert to Prince Frederick Wilhelm of Prussia, 6 November 1855, in Jagow, *Letters of the Prince Consort,* p. 244.
22. Bolitho, *Further Letters of Queen Victoria,* p. 58.
23. Pakula, *Uncommon Woman,* p. 74.
24. Queen Victoria to the Earl of Clarendon, 25 October 1857, in Benson and Esher, *Letters of Queen Victoria,* vol. III, p. 253.
25. Pakula, *Uncommon Woman,* p. 81.
26. Queen Victoria to Princess Victoria, 25 January 1858, in Roger Fulford, ed., *Dearest Child: Letters Between Queen Victoria and the Princess Royal 1858–1861* (New York: Holt, Rinehart and Winston, 1964), p. 27.
27. Pakula, *Uncommon Woman,* p. 82.
28. The Princess Royal to Prince Albert, undated in Fulford, *Dearest Child,* p. 31.
29. Queen Victoria to the Princess Royal, 2 February 1858, in *ibid.,* pp. 28–29.
30. Queen Victoria to King Leopold of the Belgians, 9 February 1858, in Benson and Esher, *Letters of Queen Victoria,* vol. III, p. 264.
31. Queen Victoria to the Princess Royal, 9 February 1858, in Fulford, *Dearest Child,* pp. 36–37.
32. Queen Victoria to the Princess Royal, 15 February 1858, in *ibid.,* p. 44.
33. Pakula, *Uncommon Woman,* p. 78.
34. Hough, *Victoria and Albert,* p. 122.

22. England's Daughter

1. Pakula, *Uncommon Woman,* pp. 69–70.
2. The Princess Royal to Prince Albert, 27 February 1858, in Fulford, *Dearest Child,* p. 64.
3. Queen Victoria to King Leopold of the Belgians, 12 January 1858, in Benson and Esher, *Letters of Queen Victoria,* vol. III, p. 263.
4. Meriel Buchanan, *Queen Victoria's Relations* (London: Cassell & Co., 1954), p. 7.
5. The Princess Royal to Prince Albert, 27 February 1858, in Fulford, *Dearest Child,* p. 64.
6. Barkeley, *Empress Frederick,* p. 25.
7. Pakula, *Uncommon Woman,* pp. 121–122.
8. Queen Victoria to the Princess Royal, 14 April 1858, in Fulford, *Dearest Child,* p. 89.
9. The Princess Royal to Queen Victoria, undated, in *ibid.,* n. 1.
10. John C. G. Röhl, *Young Wilhelm: The Kaiser's Early Life, 1859–1888* (Cambridge: Cambridge University Press, 1993), pp. 8–9.
11. Charles Lowe, *The German Emperor William II* (New York: Frederick Warne & Co., n.d.), p. 13.
12. Queen Victoria to Princess Augusta, 30 January 1859, in Bolitho, *Further Letters of Queen Victoria,* p. 105.
13. Queen Victoria to King Leopold of the Belgians, 1 March 1859, in Benson and Esher, *Letters of Queen Victoria,* vol. III, p. 324.
14. Charlot, *Victoria,* p. 402.
15. Röhl, *Young Wilhelm,* p. 83.
16. The Crown Princess of Prussia to Queen Victoria, 28 April 1863, in Roger Fulford, ed.,

Dearest Mama: Letters Between Queen Victoria and the Crown Princess of Prussia 1861–1864 (London: Evans Brothers, 1968), p. 203.

17. Röhl, *Young Wilhelm,* p. 97.

18. James Pope-Hennessy, *Queen Mary 1867–1953* (New York: Alfred A. Knopf, 1960), p. 249.

19. Röhl, *Young Wilhelm,* p. 84.

20. *Ibid.*

21. The Princess Royal to Queen Victoria, 4 June 1861, in Fulford, *Dearest Child,* pp. 337–338.

22. Philip Magnus, *King Edward the Seventh* (London: John Murray, 1964), p. 46.

23. Queen Victoria to King Leopold of the Belgians, 16 March 1861, in Benson and Esher, *Letters of Queen Victoria,* vol. III, p. 435.

24. Hector Bolitho, *The Reign of Queen Victoria* (New York: Macmillan Company, 1948), p. 185.

25. Prince Albert to Baron von Stockmar, 5 April 1861, in Jagow, *Letters of the Prince Consort,* p. 360.

26. Dean of Windsor and Hector Bolitho, eds., *Letters of Lady Augusta Stanley: A Young Lady at Court 1849–1863* (New York: George H. Doran Company, 1927), p. 245.

27. *Ibid.*

28. *Ibid.,* p. 247.

29. The Princess Royal to Queen Victoria and Queen Victoria to Princess Victoria, 16 December 1861, in Fulford, *Dearest Child,* p. 375.

30. The Crown Princess of Prussia to Queen Victoria, 21 December 1861, in Fulford, *Dearest Mama,* pp. 25–26.

31. Egon Caesar Conte Corti, *The English Empress: A Study in the Relations Between Queen Victoria and Her Eldest Daughter, Empress Frederick of Germany* (London: Cassell and Company, 1957), p. 76.

32. *Ibid.*

33. Magdalen Ponsonby to her mother, December 1861, in Magdalen Ponsonby, ed., *A Lady in Waiting to Queen Victoria: Being Some Letters, and a Journal of Lady Ponsonby* (New York: J. H. Sears & Company, 1927), p. 47.

34. Queen Victoria to King Leopold of the Belgians, 20 December 1861, in Benson and Esher, *Letters of Queen Victoria,* vol. III, pp. 473–474.

35. Queen Victoria to King Leopold of the Belgians, 24 December 1861, in *ibid.,* p. 476.

36. Corti, *English Empress,* p. 80.

37. *Ibid.,* p. 81.

38. *Ibid.,* p. 82.

39. *Ibid.,* p. 87.

40. E. F. Benson, *Queen Victoria's Daughters* (New York: D. Appleton-Century Company, 1938), p. 84.

41. Queen Victoria to the Crown Princess of Prussia, 2 July 1862, in Fulford, *Dearest Mama,* p. 85.

42. Queen Victoria to the Crown Princess of Prussia, 27 December 1861, in *ibid.,* pp. 30–31.

43. Queen Victoria to the Crown Princess of Prussia, 29 July 1862, in *ibid.,* p. 98.

44. The Crown Princess of Prussia to Queen Victoria, 29 December 1861, in *ibid.,* p. 32.

45. Queen Victoria to the Crown Princess of Prussia, 25 March 1869, in *ibid.,* p. 186.

46. Queen Victoria to the Crown Princess of Prussia, 2 May 1868, in Roger Fulford, ed., *Your Dear Letter: Private Correspondence of Queen Victoria and the Crown Princess of Prussia 1865–1871* (New York: Charles Scribner's Sons, 1971), p. 186.

47. Queen Victoria to the Crown Princess of Prussia, 8 June 1863, in Fulford, *Dearest Mama,* p. 226.

48. Aronson, *Heart of a Queen,* p. 135.
49. Queen Victoria to the Crown Princess of Prussia, 5 June 1865, in Fulford, *Your Dear Letter,* p. 29.
50. Longford, *Queen Victoria,* p. 325.
51. Prince Nicholas of Greece, *My Fifty Years* (London: Hutchinson & Co., n.d.), p. 136.
52. *Ibid.*, pp. 135–136.
53. Andreas Dorpalen, "Emperor Frederick III and the German Liberal Movement," *American Historical Review,* vol. 54, no. 1 (October 1948), p. 8.
54. Edward Crankshaw, *Bismarck* (Harmondsworth, U.K.: Penguin Books, 1981), p. 127.
55. The Crown Princess of Prussia to Queen Victoria, 5 June 1863, in Fulford, *Dearest Mama,* p. 224.
56. *Ibid.*
57. *Ibid.,* p. 225.
58. Dorpalen, "Emperor Frederick III," p. 12.
59. Queen Victoria to the Crown Princess of Prussia, 8 June 1863, in Fulford, *Dearest Mama,* p. 225.
60. *Ibid.,* p. 226.
61. The Crown Princess of Prussia to Queen Victoria, 8 June 1863, in *ibid.,* p. 228.
62. The Crown Princess of Prussia to Queen Victoria, 21 June 1863, in *ibid.,* p. 230.
63. Queen Victoria to the Crown Princess of Prussia, 13 June 1863, in *ibid.,* p. 231.
64. Röhl, *Young Wilhelm,* p. 94.
65. *Ibid.*
66. Pakula, *Uncommon Woman,* p. 178.
67. The Crown Princess of Prussia to Queen Victoria, 8 July 1862, in Fulford, *Dearest Mama,* pp. 89–90.
68. The Crown Princess of Prussia to Queen Victoria, 15 January 1864, in *ibid.,* p. 291.
69. Queen Victoria to the Crown Princess of Prussia, 22 June 1864, in *ibid.,* p. 349.
70. Introduction by Fulford in *ibid.,* pp. 17–18.
71. Frederick Ponsonby, ed., *Letters of the Empress Frederick* (London: Macmillan and Co., 1929), p. 39.
72. Corti, *English Empress,* p. 85.
73. The Crown Princess of Prussia to Queen Victoria, 3 July 1863, in Fulford, *Dearest Mama,* pp. 241–242.
74. *Ibid.,* p. 243.
75. Queen Victoria to the Crown Princess of Prussia, 8 July 1863, in *ibid.,* p. 244.
76. Corti, *English Empress,* p. 161.
77. Buchanan, *Queen Victoria's Relations,* p. 12.
78. The Crown Princess of Prussia to Queen Victoria, 3 July 1863, in Fulford, *Dearest Mama,* pp. 242–243.

23. The British and German Empires

1. Windsor and Bolitho, *Lady Augusta Stanley,* p. 260.
2. Queen Victoria to the Crown Princess of Prussia, 25 March 1864, in Fulford, *Dearest Mama,* p. 311.
3. Packard, *Victoria's Daughters,* p. 89.
4. Röhl, *Young Wilhelm,* p. 89.
5. Pakula, *Uncommon Woman,* p. 149.
6. Corti, *English Empress,* p. 70.

7. *Ibid.,* pp. 70–71.

8. Packard, *Victoria's Daughters,* p. 164.

9. Röhl, *Young Wilhelm,* p. 84.

10. *Ibid.*

11. Queen Victoria to the Crown Princess of Prussia, 1 June 1863, in Fulford, *Dearest Mama,* p. 222.

12. The Crown Princess of Prussia to Queen Victoria, 8 June 1863, in *ibid.,* n. 1.

13. Barkeley, *Empress Frederick,* p. 116.

14. Princess Alice to Queen Victoria, 13 June 1869, in Alice, Grand Duchess of Hesse, *Letters to Her Majesty, the Queen,* vol. II (Leipzig: Bernhard Tauchnitz, 1885), p. 53.

15. The Crown Princess of Prussia to Queen Victoria, 19 June 1866, in Fulford, *Your Dear Letter,* p. 77.

16. Lamar Cecil, *Wilhelm II: Prince and Emperor, 1859–1900* (Chapel Hill: University of North Carolina Press, 1989), p. 6.

17. *Ibid.*

18. Dorpalen, "Emperor Frederick III," p. 4.

19. Queen Victoria to the Crown Princess of Prussia, 31 May 1879, in Fulford, *Your Dear Letter,* p. 280.

20. Pope-Hennessy, *Queen Mary,* p. 305.

21. William M. Kuhn, *Henry and Mary Ponsonby: Life at the Court of Queen Victoria* (London: Duckworth, 2002), p. 205.

22. Queen Victoria to the Crown Princess of Prussia, 24 February 1874, in Roger Fulford, ed., *Darling Child: Private Correspondence of Queen Victoria and the Crown Princess of Prussia 1871–1878* (London: Evans Brothers, 1976), p. 130.

23. Kuhn, *Henry and Mary Ponsonby,* pp. 205–206.

24. Frank Hardie, *The Political Influence of the British Monarchy 1868–1952* (New York: Harper & Row, 1970), p. 11.

25. Theo Aronson, *Victoria and Disraeli: The Making of a Romantic Partnership* (New York: Macmillan Publishing Co., 1977), p. 149.

26. Aronson, *Heart of a Queen,* p. 176.

27. *Ibid.*

28. Queen Victoria to the Crown Princess of Prussia, 26 September 1882, in Roger Fulford, ed., *Beloved Mama: Private Correspondence of Queen Victoria and the German Crown Princess 1878–1885* (London: Evans Brothers, 1981), p. 126.

29. Aronson, *Heart of a Queen,* p. 181.

30. *Ibid.,* p. 182.

31. Aronson, *Victoria and Disraeli,* p. 194.

32. The Crown Princess of Prussia to Lady Ponsonby, 17 October 1884, in Ponsonby, *Lady in Waiting,* p. 244.

33. The Crown Princess of Prussia to Lady Ponsonby, 23 May 1885, in *ibid.,* p. 248.

34. The Crown Princess of Prussia to Queen Victoria, 5 August 1866, in Fulford, *Your Dear Letter,* p. 86.

35. The Crown Princess of Prussia to Queen Victoria, 20 May 1868, in *ibid.,* p. 190.

36. Queen Victoria to Major-General Sir Howard Elphinstone, 27 December 1884, in McClintock, *Queen Thanks Sir Howard,* p. 231.

37. Pakula, *Uncommon Woman,* p. 294.

38. The Crown Princess of Prussia to Lady Ponsonby, undated 1871, in Ponsonby, *Lady in Waiting,* pp. 241–242.

39. The Crown Princess of Prussia to Queen Victoria, 10 December 1866, in Fulford, *Your Dear Letter,* p. 112.

40. The Crown Princess of Prussia to Prince Arthur, undated, in McClintock, *Queen Thanks Sir Howard,* p. 94.

41. Bennett, *Vicky,* p. 226.

42. Queen Victoria to the Crown Princess of Prussia, 20 July 1870, in Ponsonby, *Letters of the Empress Frederick,* p. 77.

43. Jerrold M. Packard, *Farewell in Splendor: The Passing of Queen Victoria and Her Age* (New York: E. P. Dutton, 1995), p. 49.

44. *Ibid.,* p. 51.

45. Queen Victoria to Queen Augusta of Prussia, 6 September 1870, in Bolitho, *Further Letters of Queen Victoria,* p. 176.

46. Queen Victoria to Queen Augusta of Prussia, 7 December 1870, in *ibid.,* p. 180.

47. Theo Aronson, *The Kaisers* (Indianapolis: Bobbs-Merrill Company, 1971), p. 118.

48. Queen Victoria to Princess Victoria of Hesse, 22 August 1883, in Richard Hough, *Advice to a Grand-daughter: Letters from Queen Victoria to Princess Victoria of Hesse* (New York: Simon & Schuster, 1975), p. 51.

49. Queen Victoria to the Crown Princess of Prussia, 11 October 1874, in Fulford, *Darling Child,* p. 157.

50. *Ibid.*

51. Queen Victoria to the Crown Princess of Prussia, 26 July 1873, in Christopher Hibbert, ed., *Queen Victoria in Her Letters and Journals* (Stroud, U.K.: Stroud Publishing, 2000), p. 233.

52. Longford, *Queen Victoria,* p. 204.

53. Queen Victoria to the Crown Princess of Prussia, 26 July 1873, in Hibbert, *Queen Victoria,* p. 233.

54. *Ibid.*

55. Longford, *Queen Victoria,* p. 402.

56. *Alice, Grand Duchess of Hesse, Princess of Great Britain and Ireland: Biographical Sketch and Letters* (New York: G. P. Putnam's Sons, 1885), p. 377.

57. Fulford, *Beloved Mama,* p. 1.

58. Queen Victoria to the Crown Princess of Prussia, 17 June 1878, in Fulford, *Darling Child,* p. 293.

24. Mourning and Jubilation

1. F. A. Wellesley, ed., *The Paris Embassy During the Second Empire: Selections from the Papers of Henry Richard Charles Wellesley, 1st Earl Cowley* (London: Thornton Butterworth, 1928), p. 241.

2. McClintock, *Queen Thanks Sir Howard,* p. 5.

3. Queen Victoria to the Crown Princess of Prussia, 24 June 1863, in Fulford, *Dearest Mama,* pp. 234–235.

4. Sir Howard Elphinstone, Diary entry of 20 January 1860, in McClintock, *Queen Thanks Sir Howard,* p. 39.

5. Queen Victoria to Queen Augusta of Prussia, 20 November 1873, in Bolitho, *Further Letters of Queen Victoria,* p. 199.

6. Charlotte Zeepvat, *Prince Leopold: The Untold Story of Queen Victoria's Youngest Son* (Stroud, U.K.: Sutton Publishing, 1998), p. 19.

7. Queen Victoria to the Crown Princess of Prussia, 11 April 1868, in Fulford, *Your Dear Letter*, p. 184.

8. Zeepvat, *Prince Leopold*, p. 144.

9. Queen Victoria's Journal, 28 March 1884, in Hibbert, *Queen Victoria*, p. 285.

10. Queen Victoria to the Dean of Windsor, 9 April 1884, in G. K. A. Bell, *Randall Davidson: Archbishop of Canterbury* (London: Oxford University Press, Humphrey Milford, 1935), p. 81.

11. Queen Victoria to the Crown Princess of Prussia, 5 February 1873, in Fulford, *Darling Child*, p. 76.

12. Poultney Bigelow, *Prussian Memories 1864–1914* (New York: G. P. Putnam's Sons, 1915), p. 44.

13. *Ibid.*, p. 45.

14. *Ibid.*, pp. 45–46.

15. Anne Topham, *Memories of the Kaiser's Court* (New York: Dodd, Mead and Company, 1914), p. 289.

16. Olivier Bernier, "The Royal Retreat at Potsdam" in the *New York Times*, June 9, 1991.

17. Bigelow, *Prussian Memories*, p. 46.

18. Topham, *Memories of the Kaiser's Court*, pp. 289–290.

19. Aronson, *The Kaisers*, p. 120.

20. Sir Howard Elphinstone, 24 January 1879, in McClintock, *Queen Thanks Sir Howard*, p. 201.

21. Pakula, *Uncommon Woman*, p. 358.

22. The Crown Princess of Prussia to Queen Victoria, 29 January 1880, in Fulford, *Beloved Mama*, p. 63.

23. Sir Howard Elphinstone, 24 January 1879, in McClintock, *Queen Thanks Sir Howard*, p. 201.

24. The Crown Princess of Prussia to Queen Victoria, 24 May 1880, in Fulford, *Beloved Mama*, p. 79.

25. Bennett, *Vicky*, p. 223.

26. Aronson, *The Kaisers*, p. 118.

27. *Ibid.*, p. 119.

28. McClintock, *Queen Thanks Sir Howard*, p. 41.

29. Queen Victoria to the Prince of Wales, 2 June 1861, in *ibid.*, p. 42.

30. Bennett, *Vicky*, p. 235.

31. Packard, *Victoria's Daughters*, p. 236.

32. Cecil, *Wilhelm II*, p. 84.

33. Queen Victoria to the Crown Princess of Prussia, 3 January 1885, in Fulford, *Beloved Mama*, p. 177.

34. Queen Victoria to the Crown Princess of Prussia, 30 October 1877, in Fulford, *Darling Child*, p. 269.

35. Queen Victoria to the Crown Princess of Prussia, 30 December 1884, in Fulford, *Beloved Mama*, p. 176.

36. Queen Victoria to the Crown Princess of Prussia, 10 January 1885, in *ibid.*, p. 178.

37. Princess Alice of Albany, *For My Grandchildren: Some Reminiscences of Her Royal Highness Princess Alice, Countess of Athlone* (London: Evans Brothers, 1966), pp. 68–69.

38. *Ibid.*, p. 71.

39. Viscount Palmerston to Queen Victoria, 23 August 1859, in Raymond, *Queen Victoria's Early Letters*, p. 257.

40. Queen Victoria's Journal entry, 21 June 1887, in Hibbert, *Queen Victoria,* p. 305.

41. *Ibid.,* p. 306.

42. Queen Victoria to the Crown Princess of Prussia, 24 August 1887, in Agatha Ramm, ed., *Beloved and Darling Child: Last Letters Between Queen Victoria and Her Eldest Daughter 1886–1901* (Stroud, U.K.: Alan Sutton, 1990), pp. 53–54.

43. The Crown Princess of Prussia to Lady Ponsonby, 5 October 1887, in Ponsonby, *Lady in Waiting,* p. 258.

44. *Ibid.,* p. 259.

45. *Ibid.*

46. The Crown Princess of Prussia to Queen Victoria, 11 December 1880, in Fulford, *Beloved Mama,* pp. 93–94.

47. Arthur Ponsonby, *Henry Ponsonby: Queen Victoria's Private Secretary, His Life from His Letters* (New York: Macmillan Company, 1944), p. 175.

48. *Ibid.,* p. 197.

49. *Ibid.,* p. 70.

50. Lowe, *German Emperor William II,* p. 42.

25. The Ninety-nine-Day Empress

1. Ponsonby, *Lady in Waiting,* p. 243.

2. Princess Catherine Radziwill, *Memories of Forty Years* (New York: Funk & Wagnalls Company, 1915), pp. 7–8.

3. Greg King, *Twilight of Splendor: The Court of Queen Victoria During Her Diamond Jubilee Year* (Hoboken, N.J.: John Wiley & Sons, 2007), p. 7.

4. Packard, *Farewell in Splendor,* p. 51.

5. Vincent Corbett, *Reminiscences: Autobiographical and Diplomatic of Sir Vincent Corbett, K.C.V.O., Late a Minister in H.M. Diplomatic Service* (London: Hodder & Stoughton, n.d.), p. 67.

6. Röhl, *Young Wilhelm,* p. 86.

7. Pakula, *Uncommon Woman,* p. 398.

8. Cecil, *Wilhelm II,* p. 8.

9. Pakula, *Uncommon Woman,* p. 398.

10. Cecil, *Wilhelm II,* p. 8.

11. Packard, *Farewell in Splendor,* p. 52.

12. Lady Ponsonby to Sir Henry Ponsonby, December 1887, in Ponsonby, *Lady in Waiting,* p. 265.

13. John van der Kiste, *Kaiser Wilhelm II: Germany's Last Emperor* (Stroud, U.K.: Sutton Publishing, 1999), p. 44.

14. Packard, *Farewell in Splendor,* p. 55.

15. Cecil, *Wilhelm II,* p. 109.

16. Packard, *Farewell in Splendor,* p. 56.

17. Cecil, *Wilhelm II,* p. 112.

18. McClintock, *Queen Thanks Sir Howard,* pp. 241–242.

19. Radziwill, *Memories of Forty Years,* p. 213.

20. Queen Victoria to Empress Victoria, 10 March 1888, in Ramm, *Beloved and Darling Child,* pp. 62–63.

21. Walburga Paget, *Embassies of Other Days: And Further Recollections of Walburga, Lady Paget,* vol. II (New York: George H. Doran Company, 1923), p. 440.

22. Cecil, *Wilhelm II,* p. 44.

23. *Ibid.,* p. 110.

24. Christopher Clark, *Iron Kingdom: The Rise and Downfall of Prussia, 1600–1947* (Cambridge, Mass.: Belknap Press, Harvard University Press, 2006), p. 520.

25. *Ibid.,* p. 588.

26. Cecil, *Wilhelm II,* p. 110.

27. Pakula, *Uncommon Woman,* p. 398.

28. Röhl, *Young Wilhelm,* p. 806.

29. *Ibid.,* p. 804.

30. *Ibid.,* p. 805.

31. Cecil, *Wilhelm II,* p. 113.

32. Paget, *Embassies of Other Days,* vol. II, p. 447.

33. *Ibid.,* pp. 447–448.

34. Longford, *Queen Victoria,* p. 506.

35. Empress Victoria to Lady Ponsonby, 26 April 1888, in Ponsonby, *Lady in Waiting,* p. 269.

36. Queen Victoria's Journal entry, 24 April 1888, in Hibbert, *Queen Victoria,* p. 311.

37. Queen Victoria's Journal entry, 26 April 1888, in *ibid.*

38. Queen Victoria to Empress Victoria, 27 April 1888, in Ramm, *Beloved and Darling Child,* p. 67.

39. Ponsonby, *Letters of the Empress Frederick,* p. 306.

40. Corti, *English Empress,* p. 290.

41. *Ibid.,* p. 297.

42. Pakula, *Uncommon Woman,* p. 488.

43. Corti, *English Empress,* p. 298.

44. *Ibid.,* p. 301.

45. Radziwill, *Memories of Forty Years,* p. 193.

46. Edward Legge, *The Public and Private Life of Kaiser William II* (London: Eveleigh Nash, 1915), p. 63.

47. Queen Victoria to Empress Augusta, 22 June 1888, in Bolitho, *Further Letters of Queen Victoria,* p. 270.

48. Queen Victoria's Journal entry, 15 June 1888, in Hibbert, *Queen Victoria,* p. 312.

49. Corti, *English Empress,* p. 281.

50. Ponsonby, *Letters of the Empress Frederick,* p. 319.

51. Queen Victoria to Empress Victoria, 15 June 1888, in Ramm, *Beloved and Darling Child,* p. 72.

52. Queen Victoria to Emperor Wilhelm II, 15 June 1888, in Hibbert, *Queen Victoria,* p. 312.

53. Palmer, *The Kaiser,* p. 34.

54. Radziwill, *Memories of Forty Years,* pp. 214–215.

55. Pakula, *Uncommon Woman,* p. 120.

26. Apotheosis and Anguish

1. Princess Alice, *For My Grandchildren,* p. 70.

2. Paget, *Embassies of Other Days,* vol. II, p. 469.

3. Queen Victoria's Journal, 19 November 1888, in Hibbert, *Queen Victoria,* p. 314.

4. Corti, *English Empress,* p. 319.

5. John Röhl, *Wilhelm II: The Kaiser's Personal Monarchy 1888–1900* (Cambridge: Cambridge University Press, 2004), pp. 52–53.

6. *Ibid.,* p. 56.

7. *Ibid.*

8. Ponsonby, *Letters of the Empress Frederick,* p. 369.

9. Paget, *Embassies of Other Days,* vol. II, pp. 530–531.

10. Buchanan, *Queen Victoria's Relations,* pp. 17–18.

11. *Ibid.,* p. 18.

12. Cecil, *Wilhelm II,* p. 114.

13. Röhl, *Wilhelm II,* p. 34.

14. *Ibid.,* p. 22

15. *Ibid.,* p. 68.

16. *Ibid.*

17. John C. G. Röhl, *The Kaiser and His Court: Wilhelm II and the Government of Germany* (Cambridge: Cambridge University Press, 1987), p. 15.

18. *Ibid.*

19. Röhl, *Wilhelm II,* p. 67.

20. *Ibid.*

21. Queen Victoria to Princess Victoria of Hesse, 2 October 1888, in Hough, *Advice to a Grand-daughter,* pp. 96–97.

22. Paget, *Embassies of Other Days,* vol. IV, p. 461.

23. Röhl, *Wilhelm II,* p. 67.

24. *Ibid.,* pp. 67–68.

25. Corti, *English Empress,* p. 318.

26. *Ibid.,* pp. 318–319.

27. Ponsonby, *Letters of the Empress Frederick,* p. 328.

28. Buchanan, *Queen Victoria's Relations*, p. 17.

29. Marie de Bunsen, *Lost Courts of Europe: The World I Used to Know 1860–1912* (New York: Harper & Brothers, 1930), p. 190.

30. Princess Victoria of Prussia to the Empress Frederick, 5 June 1889, in James Pope-Hennessy, ed., *Queen Victoria at Windsor and Balmoral: Letters from Her Granddaughter, Princess Victoria of Prussia, 1889* (London: George Allen and Unwin, 1959), pp. 44–45.

31. Cecil, *Wilhelm II,* p. 74.

32. Corti, *English Empress,* p. 213.

33. Queen Victoria to the Empress Frederick, 7 July 1888, in Ramm, *Beloved and Darling Child,* p. 73.

34. Arthur Gould Lee, ed., *The Empress Frederick Writes to Sophie: Her Daughter, Crown Princess and Later Queen of the Hellenes, Letters 1889–1901* (London: Faber & Faber, 1955), p. 15.

35. *Ibid.,* p. 118.

36. *Ibid.,* p. 73.

37. *Ibid.,* p. 86.

38. Pakula, *Uncommon Woman,* p. 555.

39. Queen Victoria to the Crown Princess of Prussia, 21 May 1878, in Fulford, *Darling Child,* p. 290.

40. Queen Victoria to Lord Salisbury, 15 October 1888, in Hibbert, *Queen Victoria,* p. 313.

41. *Ibid.*

42. Cecil, *Wilhelm II,* p. 120.

43. Aronson, *The Kaisers,* p. 203.

44. Bell, *Randall Davidson,* p. 151.

45. Desmond Chapman-Huston, ed., and Daisy, Princess of Pless, *What I Left Unsaid* (London: Cassell and Company, 1936), p. 253.

46. Aronson, *The Kaisers*, p. 223.

47. Ponsonby, *Letters of the Empress Frederick*, p. 413.

48. Cecil, *Wilhelm II*, p. 72.

49. *Ibid.*, pp. 72–73.

50. Packard, *Victoria's Daughters*, p. 95.

51. King Leopold to Queen Victoria, 16 January 1838, in Benson and Esher, *Letters of Queen Victoria*, vol. I (London: John Murray, 1908), p. 105.

52. Hibbert, *Queen Victoria*, p. 2.

53. Queen Victoria to Earl Russell, 15 February 1864, in George Earl Buckle, *The Letters of Queen Victoria, Second Series, A Selection from Her Majesty's Correspondence and Journal Between the Years 1862 and 1878, Volume I, 1862–1869* (London: John Murray, 1926), p. 158.

54. Edward, Duke of Windsor, *A King's Story: The Memoirs of H.R.H. the Duke of Windsor* (London: Prion Books, 1998), pp. 2–3.

55. James Morris, *Pax Britannica: The Climax of an Empire* (London: Folio Society, 1992), p. 1.

56. Queen Victoria's Journal entry, 22 June 1897, in Hibbert, *Queen Victoria*, p. 335.

57. Morris, *Pax Britannica*, p. 1.

58. *Ibid.*, p. 6.

59. *Ibid.*, p. 2.

60. *Ibid.*, p. 11.

61. Queen Victoria's Journal entry, 21 June 1897, in Hibbert, *Queen Victoria*, p. 335.

62. Queen Victoria's Journal entry, 22 June 1897, in *ibid.*

63. *Ibid.*

64. The Empress Frederick to Queen Victoria, 3 July 1897, in Ramm, *Beloved and Darling Child*, pp. 204–205.

65. Arnstein, *Queen Victoria*, pp. 165–166.

66. Pakula, *Uncommon Woman*, p. 579.

67. Lee, *Empress Frederick Writes to Sophie*, p. 277.

68. The Empress Frederick to Queen Victoria, 19 December 1890, in Ramm, *Beloved and Darling Child*, p. 118.

27. To Face Life with Courage

1. Lee, *Empress Frederick Writes to Sophie*, p. 167.

2. Pakula, *Uncommon Woman*, p. 569.

3. Queen Victoria's Journal entry, 24 May 1897, in Hibbert, *Queen Victoria*, p. 334.

4. Fulford, *Beloved Mama*, p. 12.

5. Queen Victoria to the King of Prussia, 4 April 1856, in Bolitho, *Further Letters of Queen Victoria*, p. 62.

6. Queen Victoria to the Crown Princess of Prussia, 25 May 1881, in Fulford, *Beloved Mama*, p. 104.

7. Edward, Duke of Windsor, *King's Story*, p. 9.

8. Hannah Pakula, *The Last Romantic: A Biography of Queen Marie of Romania* (New York: Touchstone Books, 1986), p. 127.

9. Pope-Hennessy, *Queen Mary*, p. 195.

10. Queen Victoria's Journal entry, 31 July 1900, in Hibbert, *Queen Victoria*, p. 346.

11. Queen Victoria to Queen Augusta of Prussia, 17 October 1872, in *ibid.*, p. 191.

12. Queen Victoria to King Leopold I of the Belgians, autumn 1865, in *ibid.*, p. 158.

13. Lee, *Empress Frederick Writes to Sophie*, pp. 326–327.

14. Hough, *Advice to a Grand-daughter,* p. 145.
15. Weintraub, *Victoria,* p. 620.
16. Longford, *Queen Victoria,* p. 554.
17. Queen Victoria to the Empress Frederick, 21 May 1900, in Ramm, *Beloved and Darling Child,* p. 251.
18. Ponsonby, *Letters of the Empress Frederick,* p. 464.
19. de Bunsen, *Lost Courts of Europe,* p. 192.
20. *Ibid.,* p. 197.
21. *Ibid.*
22. Aronson, *The Kaisers,* p. 209.
23. de Bunsen, *Lost Courts of Europe,* p. 211.
24. Queen Victoria to the Empress Frederick, 12 January 1899, in Ramm, *Beloved and Darling Child,* p. 223.
25. The Empress Frederick to Queen Victoria, 10 February 1900, in *ibid.,* p. 246.
26. Lee, *Empress Frederick Writes to Sophie,* p. 337.
27. *Ibid.*
28. *Ibid.,* p. 341.
29. de Bunsen, *Lost Courts of Europe,* p. 222.
30. Queen Victoria to the Empress Frederick, 6 April 1900, in Ramm, *Beloved and Darling Child,* p. 248.
31. Packard, *Victoria's Daughters,* p. 305.
32. *Ibid.*
33. Queen Victoria to the Empress Frederick, 6 January 1901, in Ramm, *Beloved and Darling Child,* pp. 258–259.
34. Michaela Reid, *Ask Sir James: Sir James Reid, Personal Physician to Queen Victoria and Physician-in-Ordinary to Three Monarchs* (New York: Viking Press, 1987), p. 212.
35. Pope-Hennessy, *Queen Mary,* p. 347.
36. Lee, *Empress Frederick Writes to Sophie,* p. 343.
37. Pakula, *Uncommon Woman,* p. 592.
38. Ponsonby, *Letters of the Empress Frederick,* pp. ix–x.
39. *Ibid.,* p. x.
40. Barkeley, *Empress Frederick,* p. 308.
41. *Ibid.*
42. *Ibid.,* p. 309.
43. Lee, *Empress Frederick Writes to Sophie,* p. 347.
44. Aronson, *The Kaisers,* pp. 242–243.

Epilogue

1. Rennell Rodd, *Frederick Crown Prince and Emperor: A Biographical Sketch Dedicated to His Memory* (London: David Stott, 1888), p. x.
2. Diana Fotescue, ed., *Americans and Queen Marie of Roumania: A Selection of Documents* (Iasi: Center for Romanian Studies, 1998), p. 137.
3. James, *Prince Albert,* pp. 94–95.

Bibliography

Albany, Princess Alice of. *For My Grandchildren: Some Reminiscences of Her Royal Highness Princess Alice, Countess of Athlone.* London: Evans Brothers, 1966.

Alice, Grand Duchess of Hesse. *Alice, Grand Duchess of Hesse, Princess of Great Britain and Ireland: Biographical Sketch and Letters.* New York: G. P. Putnam's Sons, 1885.

———. *Letters to Her Majesty, the Queen.* Vol. II. Leipzig: Bernhard Tauchnitz, 1885.

d'Angoulême, Marie-Thérèse Charlotte, Duchesse. *The Ruin of a Princess: As Told by Marie-Thérèse Charlotte, the Duchesse d'Angoulême; Madame Elizabeth, Sister of Louis XVI, and Cléry, the King's Valet de Chambre.* Translated by Katharine Prescott Wormeley. New York: Lamb Publishing Co., 1912.

Anonymous. *The Private Life of the Queen by a Member of the Royal Household.* New York: D. Appleton and Company, 1901.

Argyll, Dowager Duchess of, ed. *George Douglas, Eighth Duke of Argyll: Autobiography and Memoirs.* Vol. I. New York: E. P. Dutton and Company, 1906.

Arnstein, Walter. *Queen Victoria.* New York: Palgrave Macmillan, 2003.

Aronson, Theo. *Heart of a Queen: Queen Victoria's Romantic Attachments.* London: John Murray, 1991.

———. *The Kaisers.* Indianapolis: Bobbs-Merrill Company, 1971.

———. *Victoria and Disraeli: The Making of a Romantic Partnership.* New York: Macmillan Publishing Co., 1977.

Barkeley, Richard. *The Empress Frederick: Daughter of Queen Victoria.* London: Macmillan & Co., 1956.

Bell, G. K. A. *Randall Davidson: Archbishop of Canterbury.* Vol. I. London: Oxford University Press, Humphrey Milford, 1935.

Belloc, Hilaire. *Marie Antoinette.* New York: Tess Press, n.d.; originally published 1909.

Bennett, Daphne. *Vicky: Princess Royal of England and German Empress.* New York: St. Martin's Press, 1971.

Benson, Arthur Christopher, and Viscount Esher, eds. *The Letters of Queen Victoria: A Selection from Her Majesty's Correspondence Between the Years 1837 and 1861.* Vols. I, II, III. London: John Murray, 1908.

Benson, E. F. *Queen Victoria.* London: Longmans, Green and Co., 1935.

———. *Queen Victoria's Daughters.* New York: D. Appleton-Century Company, 1938.

Bergenroth, G. A., ed. *Calendar of Letters, Despatches, and State Papers, Relating to the Negotiations Between England and Spain Preserved in the Archives at Simancas and Elsewhere. Volume I: Henry VII 1485–1509.* Nendeln, Liechtenstein: Kraus-Thomson Organization, 1969.

———. *Calendar of Letters, Despatches, and State Papers, Relating to the Negotiations Between England and Spain Preserved in the Archives at Simancas and Elsewhere. Volume II: Henry VIII 1509–1525.* Nendeln, Liechtenstein: Kraus-Thomson Organization, 1969.

Bernier, Olivier. *Imperial Mother, Royal Daughter: The Correspondence of Marie Antoinette and Maria Theresa.* London: Sidgwick & Jackson, 1986.

———. "The Royal Retreat at Potsdam." *The New York Times,* June 9, 1991.

———. *Words of Fire, Deeds of Blood: The Mob, the Monarchy, and the French Revolution.* Boston: Little, Brown, 1989.

Bigelow, Poultney. *Prussian Memories 1864–1914.* New York: G. P. Putnam's Sons, 1915.

Bolitho, Hector, ed. *Further Letters of Queen Victoria: From the Archives of the House of Brandenburg-Prussia.* London: Thornton Butterworth, 1939.

———. *The Reign of Queen Victoria.* New York: Macmillan Company, 1948.

Bradford, William, ed. *Correspondence of the Emperor Charles V and His Ambassadors at the Courts of England and France.* London: Richard Bentley, 1850.

Brigden, Susan. *New Worlds, Lost Worlds: The Rule of the Tudors, 1485–1603.* New York: Viking Press, 2000.

Bright, J. Franck. *Maria Theresa.* London: Macmillan and Co. Ltd., 1930.

Britnell, Richard. *The Closing of the Middle Ages? England, 1471–1529.* Oxford: Blackwell Publishers, 1997.

Buchanan, Meriel. *Queen Victoria's Relations.* London: Cassell & Co., 1954.

Buckle, George Earl, ed. *The Letters of Queen Victoria, Second Series, A Selection from Her Majesty's Correspondence and Journal Between the Years 1862 and 1878. Vol. I: 1862–1869.* London: John Murray, 1926.

Bunsen, Marie de. *Lost Courts of Europe: The World I Used to Know 1860–1912.* New York: Harper & Brothers, 1930.

Cadbury, Deborah. *The Last King of France: A True Story of Revolution, Revenge, and DNA.* New York: St. Martin's Press, 2002.

Campan, Jeanne Louise Henriette. *Memoirs of the Private Life of Marie Antoinette.* Vols. I, II. New York: Tudor Publishing Co., 1934.

Caplan, Alison. "The World of Isabel la Católica." In David A. Boruchoff, ed., *Isabel la Católica, Queen of Castile: Critical Essays.* New York: Palgrave Macmillan, 2003.

Castelot, André. *Queen of France: A Biography of Marie Antoinette.* Translated by Denise Folliot. New York: Harper & Brothers, 1957.

Catt, Henri de. *Frederick the Great: The Memoirs of His Reader Henri de Catt (1758–1760).* Vol. I. Translated by F. S. Flint. Boston: Houghton Mifflin Company, 1917.

Cecil, Lamar. *Wilhelm II: Prince and Emperor, 1859–1900.* Chapel Hill: University of North Carolina Press, 1989.

Chapman-Huston, Desmond, ed., and Daisy, Princess of Pless. *What I Left Unsaid.* London: Cassell and Company, 1936.

Charlot, Monica. *Victoria: The Young Queen.* Oxford: Basil Blackwell, 1991.

Claremont, Francesca. *Catherine of Aragon.* London: Robert Hale, 1939.

Clark, Christopher. *Iron Kingdom: The Rise and Downfall of Prussia, 1600–1947.* Cambridge, Mass.: Belknap Press, Harvard University Press, 2006.

Constable, Olivia Remie, ed. *Medieval Iberia: Readings from Christian, Muslim, and Jewish Sources*. Philadelphia: University of Pennsylvania Press, 1997.

Corbett, Vincent. *Reminiscences: Autobiographical and Diplomatic of Sir Vincent Corbett, K.C.V.O., Late a Minister in H.M. Diplomatic Service*. London: Hodder & Stoughton, n.d.

Corti, Egon Caesar Conte. *The English Empress: A Study in the Relations Between Queen Victoria and Her Eldest Daughter, Empress Frederick of Germany*. London: Cassell and Company, 1957.

Coxe, William. *History of the House of Austria*. Vol. III. London: Henry G. Bohn, 1854.

Crankshaw, Edward. *Bismarck*. Harmondsworth, U.K.: Penguin Books, 1981.

———. *Maria Theresa: A Biography*. New York: Viking Press, 1969.

Crowley, Roger. *1453: The Holy War for Constantinople and the Clash of Islam and the West*. New York: Hyperion, 2005.

Dillon, Henriette Lucie, Marquise de La Tour du Pin. *Memoirs of Madame de La Tour du Pin*. Edited and translated by Felice Harcourt. New York: McCall Publishing Company, 1971.

Dorpalen, Andreas. "Emperor Frederick III and the German Liberal Movement," *American Historical Review*, vol. 54, no. 1 (October 1948).

Dowling, Maria. "A Woman's Place? Learning and the Wives of Henry VIII," *History Today*, June 1991.

Duffy, Eamon. *The Stripping of the Altars: Traditional Religion in England, c. 1400–c. 1580*. New Haven: Yale University Press, 1992.

Durant, Will, and Ariel Durant. *Rousseau and the Revolution: A History of Civilization in France, England, and Germany from 1756, and in the Remainder of Europe from 1715, to 1789*. New York: Simon & Schuster, 1967.

Edward, Duke of Windsor. *A King's Story: The Memoirs of H.R.H. the Duke of Windsor*. London: Prion Books, 1998.

Edwards, John. *Ferdinand and Isabella: Profiles in Power*. Harlow, U.K.: Pearson Education, 2005.

———. *The Monarchies of Ferdinand and Isabella*. London: Historical Association, 1996.

———. *The Spain of the Catholic Monarchs 1474–1520*. Oxford: Blackwell Publishers, 2000.

Erickson, Carolly. *To the Scaffold: The Life of Marie Antoinette*. New York: William Morrow and Company, 1991.

Ezquerra, Alfredo Alvar. *Isabel la Católica: Una Reina Vencedora, una Mujer Derrotada*. Madrid: Ediciones Temas de Hoy, 2002.

Fernández, Luis Suárez. *Isabel, Mujer y Reina*. Madrid: Ediciones Rialp, 1992.

Fernández-Armesto, Felipe. *Ferdinand and Isabella*. New York: Dorset Press, 1975.

Feydeau, Elisabeth de. *A Scented Palace: The Secret History of Marie Antoinette's Perfumer*. Translated by Jane Lizop. London: I. B. Tauris, 2006.

Foreman, Amanda. *Georgiana, Duchess of Devonshire*. New York: Random House, 1998.

Fotescue, Diana, ed. *Americans and Queen Marie of Roumania: A Selection of Documents*. Iasi: Center for Romanian Studies, 1998.

Fraser, Antonia. *Marie Antoinette: The Journey*. New York: Nan A. Talese, 2001.

———. *The Warrior Queens*. New York: Alfred A. Knopf, 1989.

———. *The Wives of Henry VIII*. New York: Alfred A. Knopf, 1993.

Froude, J. A. *The Divorce of Catherine of Aragon: The Story as Told by the Imperial Ambassadors Resident at the Court of Henry VIII*. New York: AMS Press, 1970.

Fulford, Roger, ed. *Beloved Mama: Private Correspondence of Queen Victoria and the German Crown Princess 1878–1885*. London: Evans Brothers, 1981.

———. *Darling Child: Private Correspondence of Queen Victoria and the Crown Princess of Prussia 1871–1878*. London: Evans Brothers, 1976.

———. *Dearest Child: Letters Between Queen Victoria and the Princess Royal 1858–1861.* New York: Holt, Rinehart and Winston, 1964.

———. *Dearest Mama: Letters Between Queen Victoria and the Crown Princess of Prussia 1861–1864.* London: Evans Brothers, 1968.

———. *Your Dear Letter: Private Correspondence of Queen Victoria and the Crown Princess of Prussia 1865–1871.* New York: Charles Scribner's Sons, 1971.

Gairdner, James. *Letters and Papers, Foreign and Domestic, of the Reign of Henry VIII.* Vol. V. Vaduz, Liechtenstein: Kraus Reprint, 1965.

Gasquet, Francis, ed. *The First Divorce of Henry VIII as Told in the State Papers,* by Mrs. Hope. London: Kegan Paul, Trench, Trubner, & Co., 1894.

Goldsmith, Margaret. *Maria Theresa of Austria.* London: Arthur Barker, 1936.

Gooch, G. P. *Maria Theresa and Other Studies.* London: Longmans, Green and Co., 1951.

Goodden, Angelica. *The Sweetness of Life: A Biography of Elisabeth Louise Vigée Le Brun.* London: André Deutsch, 1997.

Gower, Ronald. *Last Days of Marie Antoinette: An Historical Sketch.* London: Kegan Paul, Trench & Co., 1885.

Greece, Prince Nicholas of. *My Fifty Years.* London: Hutchinson & Co., n.d.

Green, Mary Anne Everett. *Letters of Royal & Illustrious Ladies of Great Britain, From the Commencement of the Twelfth Century to the Close of the Reign of Queen Mary.* London: H. Colburn, 1846.

Hague, William. *William Pitt the Younger.* New York: Alfred A. Knopf, 2004.

Hardie, Frank. *The Political Influence of the British Monarchy 1868–1952.* New York: Harper & Row, 1970.

Hardman, John. *French Politics 1774–1789: From the Accession of Louis XVI to the Fall of the Bastille.* London: Longman, 1995.

Hare, Christopher. *A Queen of Queens & the Making of Spain.* London: Harper & Brothers, 1906.

Haslip, Joan. *Marie Antoinette.* New York: Weidenfeld & Nicolson, 1987.

Hibbert, Christopher, ed. *Queen Victoria in Her Letters and Journals.* Stroud, U.K.: Stroud Publishing, 2000.

Hough, Richard. *Advice to a Grand-daughter: Letters from Queen Victoria to Princess Victoria of Hesse.* New York: Simon & Schuster, 1975.

———. *Victoria and Albert: Their Love and Their Tragedies.* London: Richard Cohen Books, 1996.

Huisman, Philippe, and Marguerite Jallut. *Marie Antoinette.* New York: Viking Press, 1971.

Hume, Martin. *The Wives of Henry the Eighth and the Parts They Played in History.* London: Eveleigh Nash, 1905.

Ingrao, Charles. *The Habsburg Monarchy 1618–1815.* Cambridge: Cambridge University Press, 1994.

Irving, Washington. *Chronicle of the Conquest of Granada: From the MSS. of Fray Antonio Agapida.* New York: G. P. Putnam's Sons, 1869.

Irwin, Robert. *The Alhambra.* Cambridge, Mass.: Harvard University Press, 2004.

Ives, E. W. *Anne Boleyn.* Oxford: Basil Blackwell, 1986.

Jaffé, Deborah. *Victoria: A Celebration.* London: Carlton Books, 2000.

Jagow, Kurt, ed. *Letters of the Prince Consort 1831–1861.* New York: E. P. Dutton & Company, 1938.

James, Robert Rhodes. *Prince Albert: A Biography.* New York: Alfred A. Knopf, 1984.

Jameson, Anna. *Lives of Celebrated Female Sovereigns and Illustrious Women.* Edited by Mary E. Hewitt. Philadelphia: Henry T. Coates & Co., 1870.

Johnson, Paul. *A History of Christianity.* New York: Simon & Schuster, 1976.

———. *A History of the Jews.* New York: Harper & Row, 1987.

Kamen, Henry. *Empire: How Spain Became a World Power 1492–1763.* New York: HarperCollins Publishers, 2003.

———. *Spain 1469–1714: A Society of Conflict.* London: Longman, 1991.

———. *The Spanish Inquisition: A Historical Revision.* New Haven: Yale University Press, 1997.

King, Greg. *Twilight of Splendor: The Court of Queen Victoria During Her Diamond Jubilee Year.* Hoboken, N.J.: John Wiley & Sons, 2007.

Kuhn, William M. *Henry and Mary Ponsonby: Life at the Court of Queen Victoria.* London: Duckworth, 2002.

Latimer, Elizabeth Wormeley. *My Scrap-Book of the French Revolution.* Chicago: A. C. McClurg and Company, 1898.

Lee, Arthur Gould, ed. *The Empress Frederick Writes to Sophie: Her Daughter, Crown Princess and Later Queen of the Hellenes, Letters 1889–1901.* London: Faber & Faber, 1955.

Lee, Sidney. *King Edward VII: A Biography. Volume II: The Reign.* New York: Macmillan Co., 1927.

———. *Queen Victoria: A Biography.* London: Smith, Elder & Co., 1908.

Legge, Edward. *The Public and Private Life of Kaiser William II.* London: Eveleigh Nash, 1915.

Lever, Evelyne. *Madame de Pompadour: A Life.* Translated by Catherine Temerson. New York: Farrar, Straus & Giroux, 2002.

———. *Marie Antoinette: The Last Queen of France.* Translated by Catherine Temerson. New York: Farrar, Straus & Giroux, 2000.

Lewis, Bernard. *Cultures in Conflict: Christians, Muslims, and Jews in the Age of Discovery.* New York: Oxford University Press, 1995.

Liss, Peggy K. "Isabel, Myth and History." In David A. Boruchoff, ed., *Isabel la Católica, Queen of Castile: Critical Essays.* New York: Palgrave Macmillan, 2003.

———. *Isabel the Queen: Life and Times.* New York: Oxford University Press, 1992.

Litvinoff, Barnet. *1492: The Decline of Medievalism and the Rise of the Modern Age.* New York: Charles Scribner's Sons, 1991.

Longford, Elizabeth. *Queen Victoria: Born to Succeed.* New York: Harper & Row, 1964.

Louis-Philippe, King of the French. *Louis-Philippe Memoirs 1773–1793.* Translated by John Hardman. New York: Harcourt Brace Jovanovich, 1977.

Lowe, Charles. *The German Emperor William II.* New York: Frederick Warne & Co., n.d.

Luke, Mary M. *Catherine, the Queen.* New York: Coward-McCann, 1967.

Macartney, C. A., ed. *The Habsburg and Hohenzollern Dynasties in the Seventeenth and Eighteenth Centuries.* New York: Walker & Company, 1970.

———. *Maria Theresa and the House of Austria.* Mystic, Conn.: Lawrence Verry, 1969.

Magnus, Philip. *King Edward the Seventh.* London: John Murray, 1964.

Mahan, J. Alexander. *Maria Theresa of Austria.* New York: Thomas Y. Crowell Company, 1932.

Mansel, Philip. *Louis XVIII.* Stroud, U.K.: Sutton Publishing, 1999.

———. *Prince of Europe: The Life of Charles-Joseph de Ligne 1735–1814.* London: Weidenfeld & Nicolson, 2003.

Marius, Richard. *Thomas More.* New York: Alfred A. Knopf, 1984.

Mathew, Arnold H. *The Life and Times of Rodrigo Borgia—Pope Alexander VI.* New York: Brentano's, 1912.

Mattingly, Garrett. *Catherine of Aragon.* Boston: Little, Brown and Company, 1941.

Mayer, Dorothy Moulton. *Marie Antoinette: The Tragic Queen.* New York: Coward-McCann, 1969.

McGill, William J., Jr., *Maria Theresa.* New York: Twayne Publishers, 1972.

McGuigan, Dorothy Gies. *The Habsburgs.* Garden City, N.Y.: Doubleday & Company, 1966.

McKendrick, Melveena. *Ferdinand and Isabella.* New York: Harper & Row, 1968.

McClintock, Mary Howard. *The Queen Thanks Sir Howard: The Life of Major-General Sir Howard Elphinstone, V.C., K.C.B., C.M.G.* London: John Murray, 1945.

Merriman, Roger Bigelow. *The Rise of the Spanish Empire in the Old World and in the New. Volume I: The Middle Ages.* New York: Macmillan, 1918–1934.

Miller, Townsend. *The Castles and the Crown, Spain: 1451–1555.* New York: Coward-McCann, 1963.

———. *Henry IV of Castile 1425–1474.* Philadelphia: J. B. Lippincott Company, 1972.

Moffat, Mary Maxwell. *Maria Theresa.* New York: E. F. Dutton and Company, 1911.

Morris, Constance Lily. *Maria Theresa: The Last Conservative.* New York: Alfred A. Knopf, 1937.

Morris, James. *Pax Britannica: The Climax of an Empire.* London: Folio Society, 1992.

Netanyahu, Benzion. *The Origins of the Inquisition.* New York: Random House, 1995.

Packard, Jerrold M. *Farewell in Splendor: The Passing of Queen Victoria and Her Age.* New York: E. P. Dutton, 1995.

———. *Victoria's Daughters.* New York: St. Martin's Press, 1998.

Padover, Saul K. *The Revolutionary Emperor: Joseph II of Austria.* Hamden, Conn.: Archon Books, 1967.

Paget, Walburga. *Embassies of Other Days: And Further Recollections of Walburga, Lady Paget.* Vol. II. New York: George H. Doran Company, 1923.

Pakula, Hannah. *The Last Romantic: A Biography of Queen Marie of Romania.* New York: Touchstone Books, 1986.

———. *An Uncommon Woman: The Empress Frederick, Daughter of Queen Victoria, Wife of the Crown Prince of Prussia, Mother of Kaiser Wilhelm.* New York: Touchstone Books, 1997.

Palmer, Alan. *The Kaiser: Warlord of the Second Reich.* London: Weidenfeld & Nicolson, 1978.

Parmiter, Geoffrey de C. *The King's Great Matter: A Study of Anglo-Papal Relations 1527–1534.* London: Longmans, 1967.

Paul, John E. *Catherine of Aragon and Her Friends.* New York: Fordham University Press, 1966.

Peters, Edward. "The Origins of the Spanish Inquisition." In Brenda Stalcup, ed., *The Inquisition.* San Diego: Greenhaven Press, 2001.

Pick, Robert. *Empress Maria Theresa: The Earlier Years, 1717–1757.* New York: Harper & Row, 1966.

Pierson, Peter. *The History of Spain.* Westport, Conn.: Greenwood Press, 1999.

Plunket, Ierne L. *Isabel of Castile and the Making of the Spanish Nation 1451–1502.* New York: G. P. Putnam's Sons, 1915.

Ponsonby, Arthur. *Henry Ponsonby: Queen Victoria's Private Secretary, His Life from His Letters.* New York: Macmillan Company, 1944.

Ponsonby, Frederick, ed. *Letters of the Empress Frederick.* London: Macmillan and Co., 1929.

Ponsonby, Magdalen, ed. *A Lady in Waiting to Queen Victoria: Being Some Letters, and a Journal of Lady Ponsonby.* New York: J. H. Sears & Company, 1927.

Pope-Hennessy, James. *Queen Mary 1867–1953.* New York: Alfred A. Knopf, 1960.

———, ed. *Queen Victoria at Windsor and Balmoral: Letters from Her Granddaughter, Princess Victoria of Prussia, 1889.* London: George Allen and Unwin, 1959.

Prawdin, Michael. *The Mad Queen of Spain.* Translated by Eden and Cedar Paul. London: George Allen and Unwin, 1938.

Prescott, H. F. M. *Mary Tudor.* New York: Macmillan Company, 1962.

Prescott, William H. *History of the Reign of Ferdinand and Isabella the Catholic.* Vol. I. Philadelphia: J. B. Lippincott Company, 1865.

———. *History of the Reign of Ferdinand and Isabella the Catholic.* Vol. II. Philadelphia: J. B. Lippincott Company, 1872.

———. *History of the Reign of Ferdinand and Isabella the Catholic.* Vol. III. Philadelphia: J. B. Lippincott Company, 1872.

Price, Munro. *The Road from Versailles: Louis XVI, Marie Antoinette, and the Fall of the French Monarchy.* New York: St. Martin's Griffin, 2002.

Quarterly Review, vol. 64, no. 127.

Quesada, Miguel Angel Ladero. "Isabel and the Moors." In David A. Boruchoff, ed., *Isabel la Católica: Queen of Castile: Critical Essays.* New York: Palgrave Macmillan, 2003.

Radziwill, Princess Catherine. *Memories of Forty Years.* New York: Funk & Wagnalls Company, 1915.

Ramm, Agatha, ed. *Beloved and Darling Child: Last Letters Between Queen Victoria and Her Eldest Daughter 1886–1901.* Stroud, U.K.: Alan Sutton, 1990.

Ramsey, John. *Spain: The Rise of the First World Power.* Tuscaloosa: University of Alabama Press, 1973.

Raymond, John, ed. *Queen Victoria's Early Letters.* New York: Macmillan Company, 1963.

Reid, Michaela. *Ask Sir James: Sir James Reid, Personal Physician to Queen Victoria and Physician-in-Ordinary to Three Monarchs.* New York: Viking Press, 1987.

Rex, Richard. *The Tudors.* Stroud, U.K.: Tempus, 2002.

Ridley, Jasper. *Henry VIII.* London: Guild Publishing, 1985.

Rodd, Rennell. *Frederick Crown Prince and Emperor: A Biographical Sketch Dedicated to His Memory.* London: David Stott, 1888.

Röhl, John C. G. *Wilhelm II: The Kaiser's Personal Monarchy 1888–1900.* Cambridge: Cambridge University Press, 2004.

———. *The Kaiser and His Court: Wilhelm II and the Government of Germany.* Cambridge: Cambridge University Press, 1987.

———. *Young Wilhelm: The Kaiser's Early Life, 1859–1888.* Cambridge: Cambridge University Press, 1993.

Roider, Karl A. *Maria Theresa.* Englewood Cliffs, N.J.: Prentice-Hall, 1973.

Ross, Josephine. *The Tudors: England's Golden Age.* London: Artus Publishing, 1979.

Rossell, Cayetano, ed. *Cronicas de los Reyes de Castilla, Desde don Alfonso el Sabio, Hasta los Católicos don Fernando y doña Isabel. Coleccion Ordenada por don Cayetano Rosell,* vol. 70. Madrid: M. Rivadeneyra, 1878.

Rubin, Nancy. *Isabella of Castile: The First Renaissance Queen.* New York: St. Martin's Press, 1992.

Ruiz, Teofilo F. *Spanish Society, 1400–1600.* Essex, U.K.: Pearson Education, 2001.

Sánchez, Vidal González. *Isabel la Católica y Su Fama de Santidad, Mito o Realidad?* Madrid: Ediciones Internacionales Universitarias, 1999.

Scarisbrick, J. J. *Henry VIII.* Berkeley: University of California Press, 1968.

Schama, Simon. *Citizens: A Chronicle of the French Revolution.* New York: Alfred A. Knopf, 1989.

Seward, Desmond. *The Bourbon Kings of France.* New York: Harper & Row, 1976.

———. *Marie Antoinette.* New York: St. Martin's Press, 1981.

Smythe, Lillian C. *The Guardian of Marie Antoinette: Letters from the Comte de Mercy-Argenteau,*

Austrian Ambassador to the Court of Versailles, to Marie Thérèse, Empress of Austria 1770–1780. Vols. I, II. New York: Dodd Mead and Company, 1902.

Strickland, Agnes. *Lives of the Queens of England from the Norman Conquest.* Vol. II. London: G. Bell and Sons, 1912.

Szabo, Frank A. J. *Kaunitz and Enlightened Absolutism 1753–1780.* Cambridge: Cambridge University Press, 1994.

Tackett, Timothy. *When the King Took Flight.* Cambridge, Mass.: Harvard University Press, 2003.

Tapié, Victor L. *The Rise and Fall of the Habsburg Monarchy.* Translated by Stephen Hardman. New York: Praeger Publishers, 1969.

Thomas, Hugh. *Rivers of Gold: The Rise of the Spanish Empire, from Columbus to Magellan.* New York: Random House, 2003.

Thornton, John F., and Susan B. Varenne, eds. *Saint Thomas More: Selected Writings.* New York: Vintage Books, 2003.

Topham, Anne. *Memories of the Kaiser's Court.* New York: Dodd, Mead and Company, 1914.

Vallone, Lynn. *Becoming Victoria.* New Haven, Conn.: Yale University Press, 2001.

van der Kiste, John. *Kaiser Wilhelm II: Germany's Last Emperor.* Stroud, U.K.: Sutton Publishing, 1999.

Vives, Jaime Vicens. *An Economic History of Spain.* Translated by Frances M. López-Morillas. Princeton: Princeton University Press, 1969.

Vives, Juan Luis. *The Education of a Christian Woman: A Sixteenth-Century Manual.* Edited and translated by Charles Fantazzi. Chicago: University of Chicago Press, 2000.

Waldman, Milton. *The Lady Mary: A Biography of Mary Tudor 1516–1558.* New York: Charles Scribner's Sons, 1972.

Walsh, Walter. *The Religious Life and Influence of Queen Victoria.* London: Swan Sonnenschein & Co., 1902.

———. *Isabella of Spain: The Last Crusader.* New York: Robert M. McBride & Company, 1930.

Walsh, William Thomas. *Isabella the Crusader.* New York: Sheed & Ward, 1935.

Weber, Caroline. *Queen of Fashion: What Marie Antoinette Wore to the Revolution.* New York: Henry Holt and Company, 2006.

Webster, Nesta H. *Louis XVI and Marie Antoinette: Before the Revolution.* New York: G. P. Putnam's Sons, 1937.

———. *Louis XVI and Marie Antoinette: During the Revolution.* New York: G. P. Putnam's Sons, 1938.

Weintraub, Stanley. *Victoria: An Intimate Biography.* New York: E. P. Dutton, 1987.

Weir, Alison. *The Six Wives of Henry VIII.* New York: Ballantine Books, 1991.

Wellesley, F. A., ed. *The Paris Embassy During the Second Empire: Selections from the Papers of Henry Richard Charles Wellesley, 1st Earl Cowley.* London: Thornton Butterworth, 1928.

Wheatcroft, Andrew. *The Habsburgs: Embodying Empire.* London: Viking Press, 1995.

Williams, Neville. *Henry VIII and His Court.* New York: Macmillan Company, 1971.

Windsor, Dean of, and Hector Bolitho, eds. *Letters of Lady Augusta Stanley: A Young Lady at Court 1849–1863.* New York: George H. Doran Company, 1927.

Wittlin, Alma. *Myself a Goddess: A New Biography of Isabella of Spain.* London: Ivor Nicholson and Watson, 1936.

Woodham-Smith, Cecil. *Queen Victoria: From Her Birth to the Death of the Prince Consort.* New York: Alfred A. Knopf, 1972.

Wraxall, N. W. *Historical Memoirs of My Own Time.* Philadelphia: Lea and Blanchard, 1845.

Yalom, Marilyn. *Birth of the Chess Queen: A History.* New York: HarperCollins Publishers, 2004.

Younghusband, Lady. *Marie-Antoinette: Her Early Youth (1770–1774)*. London: Macmillan and Co., 1912.

Zeepvat, Charlotte. *Prince Leopold: The Untold Story of Queen Victoria's Youngest Son*. Stroud, U.K.: Sutton Publishing, 1998.

Zweig, Stefan. *Marie Antoinette: The Portrait of an Average Woman*. Translated by Eden and Cedar Paul. Garden City, N.Y.: Garden City Publishing Co., 1933.

Acknowledgments

A word of heartfelt thanks goes to the many individuals who have helped me with this book, beginning with the numerous historians and biographers who have written previously on the protagonists. I have based my work on their research and writing and am grateful that so many have brought to light the fascinating lives of Queen Isabella, Catherine of Aragon, Empress Maria Theresa, Queen Marie Antoinette, Queen Victoria, and the Empress Frederick.

I owe a debt of gratitude to my editor, Tershia d'Elgin, who helped iron out the infelicities in the text. Many thanks go out to my literary agent, Julie Castiglia, of the Castiglia Literary Agency, and to Charles Spicer, executive editor at St. Martin's Press, for all their help and support for the project. Thanks as well go to Michael Homler, Allison Caplin, and the staff at St. Martin's Press for their help.

I am also grateful to all my friends for their support, and my family especially, who have been patient and understanding as I delved into researching and writing on another set of royal women. Special thanks also go to my husband, who made many useful critical suggestions, gave computer expertise, and provided invaluable advice and support.

Index

America
  discovery of, 52
  European territories in, 164, 176, 215, 219
  Spain in, 67, 81, 134
American Revolution, France and, 215, 219,
  221
Ancien Régime, death of, 230
Anglo-French alliance (1500s), 98–99
Anglo-German relations, 321, 324, 328–29
Anglo-Prussian alliance, 256
Anglo-Russian relations, 329
Anglo-Spanish alliance, 78, 98
Anna of Russia, Empress, 143
annus mirabilis, 52
anti-Semitism, 29–30
anusim, 30
Aquinas, Saint Thomas, 7, 28, 33
Aquitaine, 59
Aragon, 11, 13, 15, 20, 27, 38
Arama, Rabbi Yitzhak, 30
Arévalo, 5
Argentina, 326–27
Argyll, Duke of (Marquess of Lorne), 259,
  281
Arianism, 28
aristocracy
  of Habsburg domains, 168–70
  of Spain, 22–23
Aristotle, 7
army, reforms of Maria Theresa, 170
Arthur, Prince of Wales (son of Henry VII),
  58–59, 68–69, 71, 74, 106
  death of, 74
Arthur (son of Queen Victoria), 252, 282
Ashanti War in 1896, 331
Asia, 254
Assembly of Notables at Versailles (1787),
  227–28
Auersperg, Countess, 181–82
Augusta of Saxe-Weimar, Princess (mother of
  Fritz), 255, 256, 258, 262, 288, 289, 315
Augusta Viktoria (Dona) of Schleswig-
  Holstein-Sonderburg-Augustenburg
  (wife of Wilhelm II), 298, 323
Augustine, Saint, 6, 61
Augustine Friars, 191
Augustinerkirche, 142
Australia, 254, 302

Austria, 133, 134, 135–36, 139, 143–45, 164,
  165, 166–67, 168, 176–78, 183, 184, 189,
  219, 233, 279, 284
  alliance with France, 135–36, 176–78, 183,
    189
  defeats by Turks, 143–45
  war against, declared by Revolutionary
    France, 233
Austrian Enlightenment, 171–72
Austrian Netherlands, 146
Austro-Prussian War of 1866, 284
l'Autrichienne, 214
Ayesha, 42

Bahamas, 56
Balfour, Arthur, 333
Balmoral, 253, 261, 275
Barrientos, Fray Lope, 5
Bartenstein, Baron Johann, 142–43, 150, 156,
  169
Bastille, fall of, 230
Battle of Bosworth Field, 58
Battle of Flodden Field, 96
Battle of Gross-Jägersdorf, 178
Battle of Kolin, 177–78
Battle of Kunersdorf, 178
Battle of Mollwitz, 156–57
Battle of Rossbach, 178
Battle of the Spurs, 96
Bavaria, 140, 153–54, 157, 159, 164
Bay of Biscay, 71
Baza, 48–49
Beatrice (daughter of Queen Victoria), 295,
  299, 331
Beaufort, Margaret, 86
Beaumarchais, Pierre de, 209
Becket, Thomas, 99
Bedchamber Crisis, 250
Belle-Isle, Marshal, 157, 164–65
Bellevue, 206
Bellini, Giovanni, 62
Benedictine Abbey at Melk, 192
benevolent despotism, 169
Berlin, 148, 282
Berlin Schloss, 265
Bertie. *See* Edward VII
Bertin, Madame Rose, 211
Bigelow, Poultney, 295, 296

Philip of Austria, Archduke of Austria, 64,
72–73, 81, 85, 86
Philippines, 134
Piacenza, 146, 166
Pico della Mirandola, Giovanni, 62
Plantagenet Royal House, 44, 58
Plato, 109
Plutarch, 109
Podewils, Count Otto, 167
pogroms, 29
Poland, 40, 140, 155, 157, 194–95, 219
partition of, 194–95, 219
Pole, Margaret, 116
Pole, Reginald, 116
Polignac, Cardinal, 136
Polignac, comte Jules de, 210, 221, 230
Polignac, comtesse Yolande de, 210–11, 212,
216, 221, 230
Polish Succession, 142
Political Testament (Maria Theresa), 174
Pompadour, Madame de, 176, 177, 198, 206,
295
Ponsonby, Frederick, 337
Ponsonby, Henry, 285, 305
Ponsonby, Lady, 303, 306, 308–9, 314
Poppelau, Nicolaus von, 38
Portugal, 18–20, 22, 59–60, 140
Royal House of, 59–60
war with, 18–20
Potsdam, 178
poufs, 211–12
"Pragmatic Army," 164
Pragmatic Sanction, 135, 139, 142, 143, 147,
149, 152, 153, 157, 164
Prague, 159, 164
Prince Imperial (Eugénie's son), 300
Protestantism, 102, 128, 130, 291
Prudentius, 61
Prussia, 139, 140, 148, 154–55, 157, 164–66,
176–78, 181, 219, 220, 255–56, 261, 262,
267–68, 276–80, 284–85, 288, 290,
303–4, 307–8, 325–26
Bismarck and, 278–79
conservatives vs. liberals in, 267–68, 277,
279–80, 284–85, 303–4, 307–8
dislike of Vicky's British ways, 267-68,
278–80, 284–85, 303-4, 306–8,
318–19

Habsburg conflicts with, 154–55, 165–66
hegemonic dreams of, 284
militaristic nature of, 255–56, 267
patriarchal attitude in, 307–8
Royal House, 295
Vicky's dislike of, 288, 325–26
Prussian-Danish War, 284
Puerto Rico, 66
Pulgar, Fernando del, 51

Queen's Hamlet, 225
Queen's Hospitals, 41

Radolinski, Count Hugo von, 315
Radziwill, Princess Catherine, 306
Ramillies, 135
Raphael, 62, 103
Rasputin, 294–95
Reconquista, 7–8, 36–45, 47–51
Reform Acts of 1867 and 1884, 302
Reformation, 35, 102, 130
Reichstag, 290
religion
fusion with monarchy under Isabella,
20–22, 24, 53–56
Maria Theresa's desire for unity of,
186–88
role of, in lives of royalty, 291
Renaissance humanism, 62
Renan, Ernest, 291
Rheims, Archbishop of, 193
Rheims, Cathedral at, 205
Richard, Duke of York, 72
Richard III, King of England, 58
Richelieu, Duc de, 136
Robespierre, Maximilien, 237
Robinson, Sir Thomas, 145, 146
Robot Patent, 184
Rochefoucauld-Liancourt, Duc de, 230
Rohan, Prince Louis de, Bishop of
Strasbourg, 193, 221, 226–27
Roman Catholic Church, 5, 7, 21, 99–100,
169–70, 233, 290–91
Bismarck's assault on, 290–91
in England, 99–100
in French Revolution, 233
in Habsburg domains, 169–70
Romania, 331